PHOTOGRAPHS BY FLIP SCHULKE

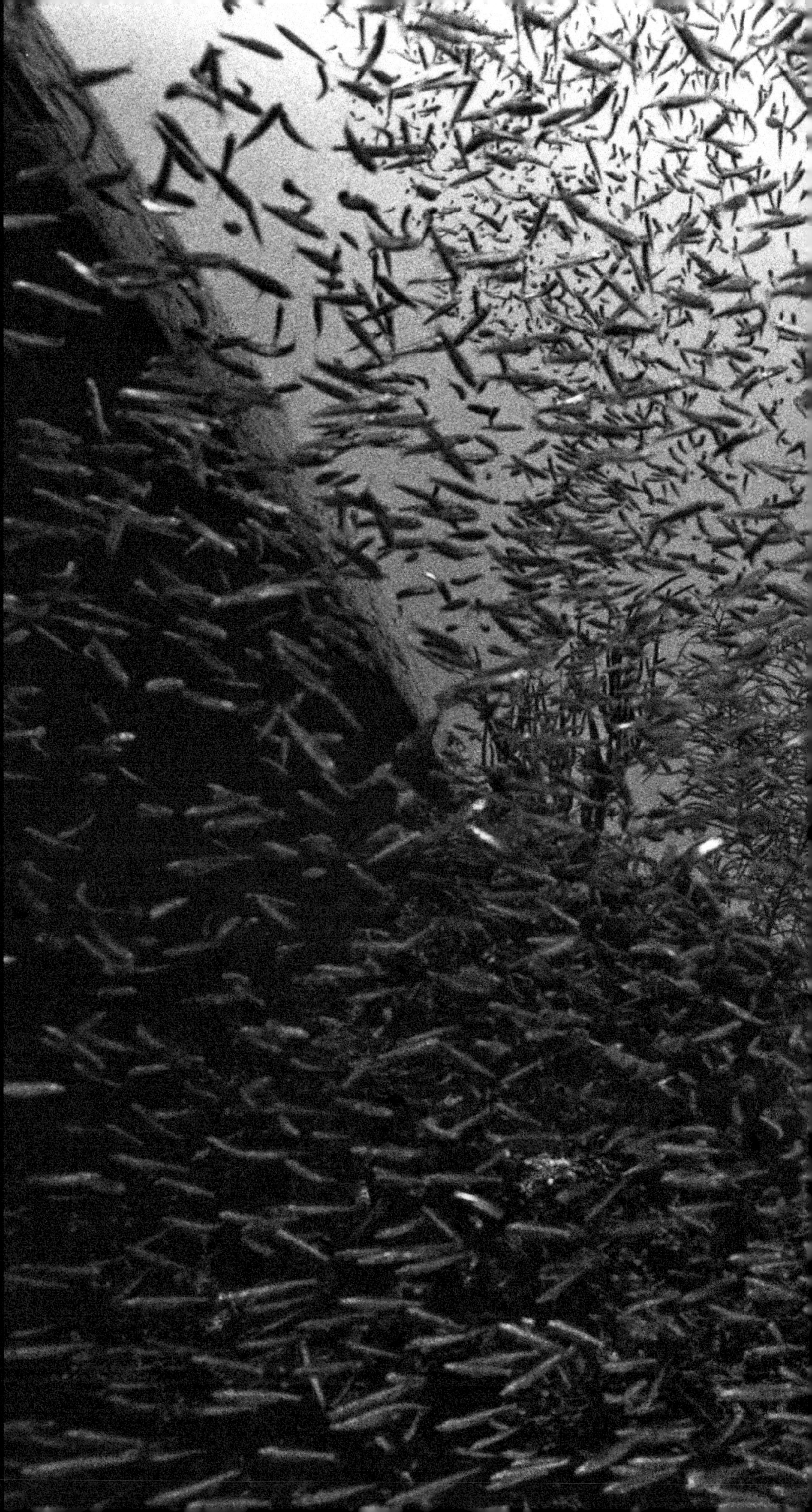

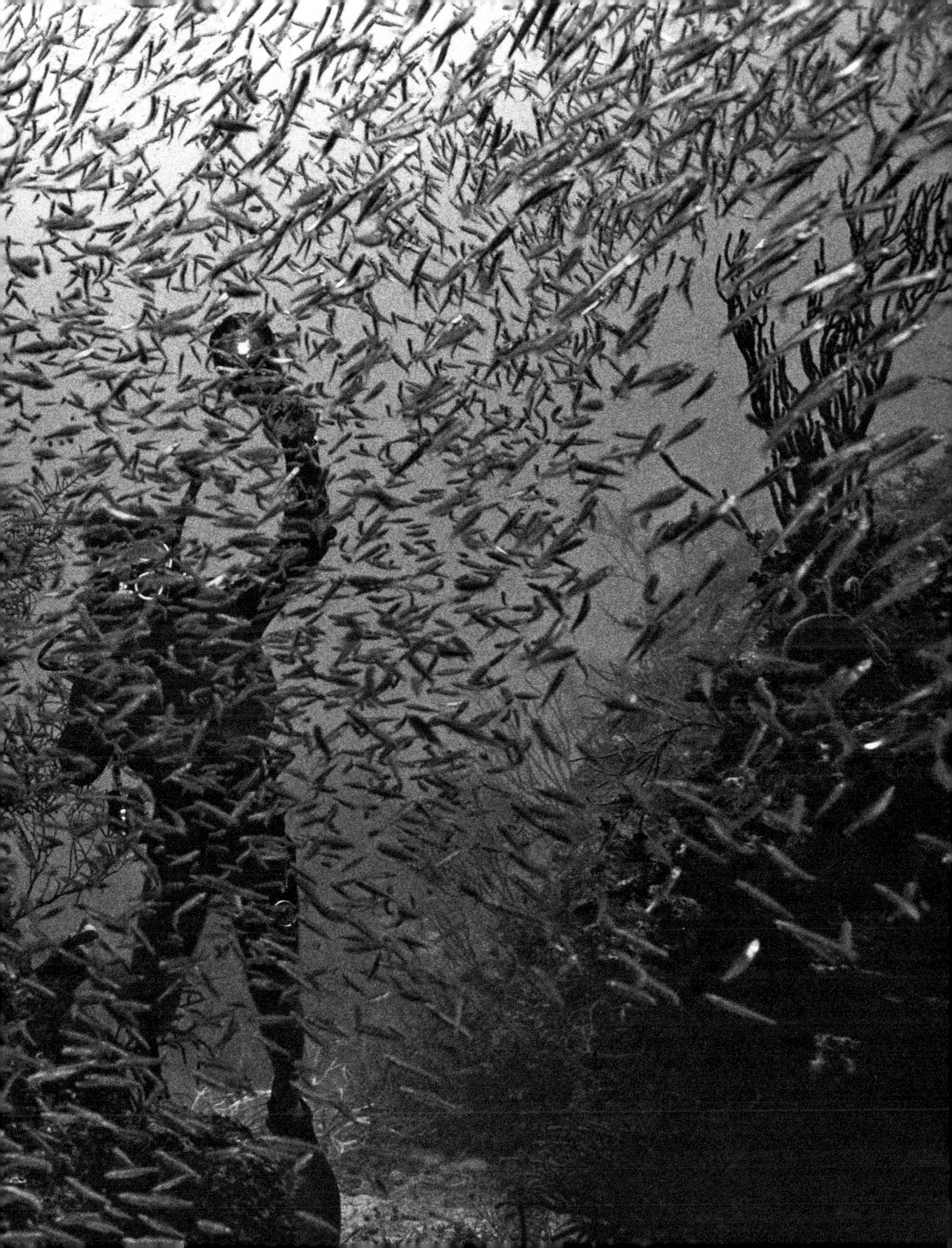

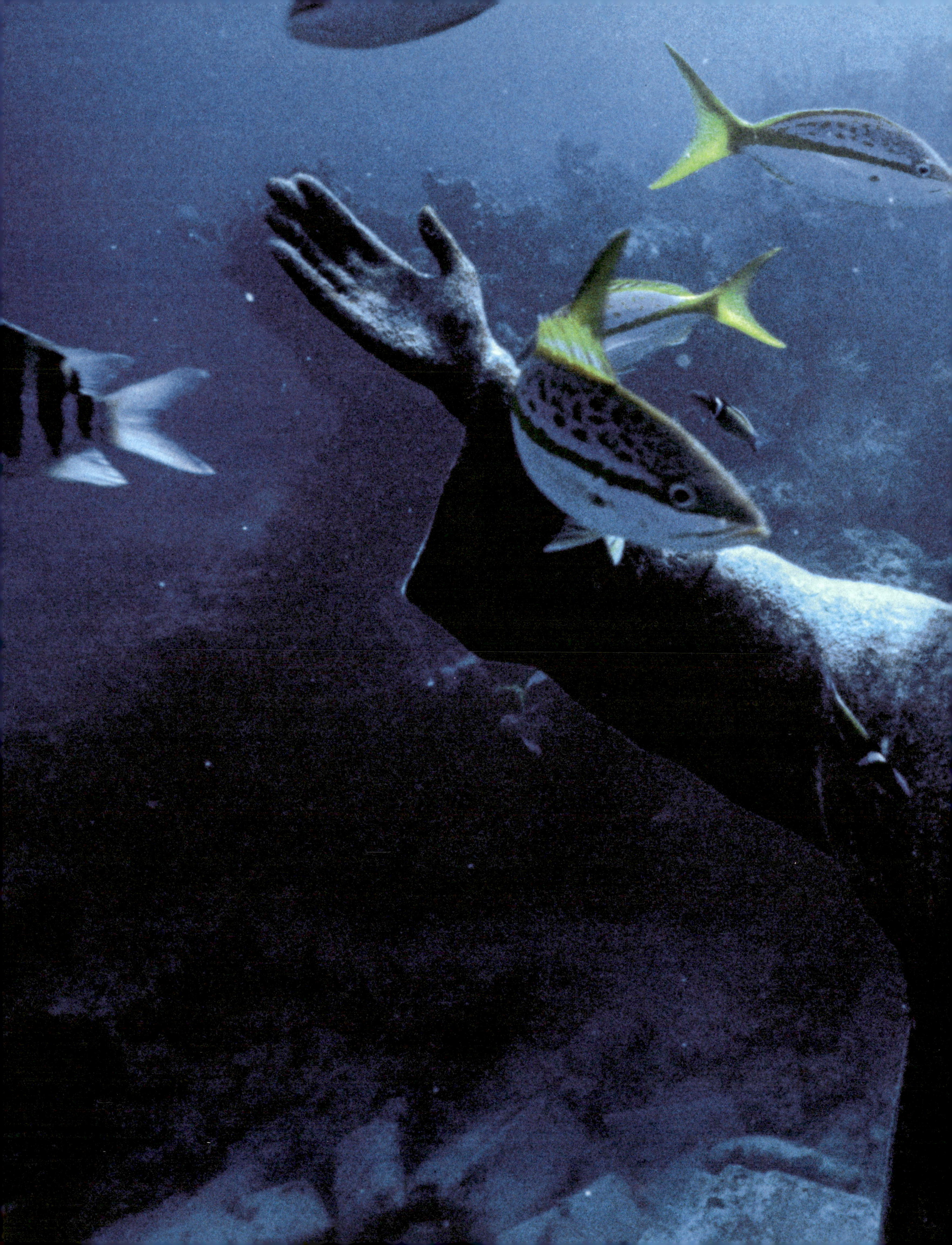

ALL–AMERICAN XIV

AFFAIRS OF THE HEART

BRUCE WEBER

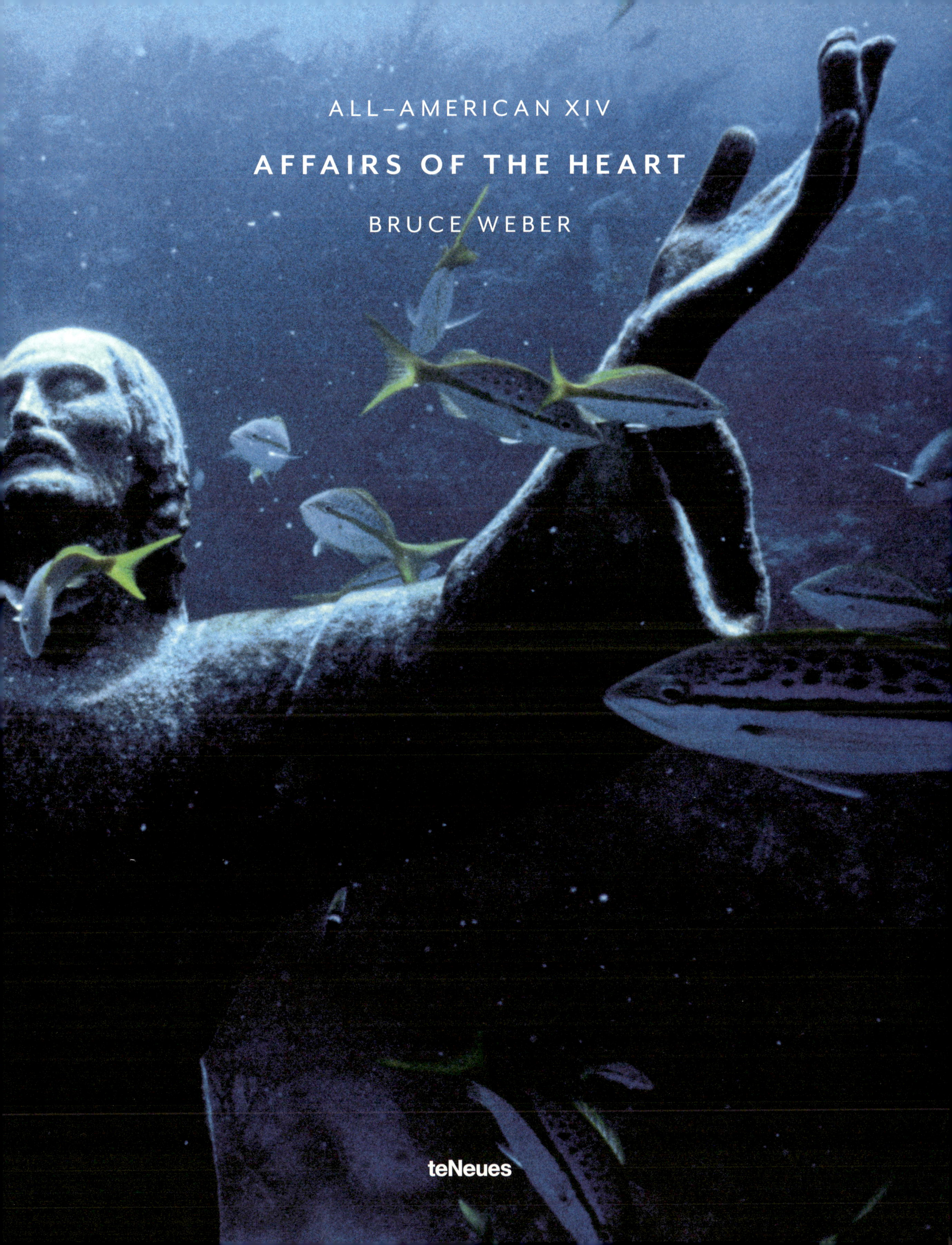

teNeues

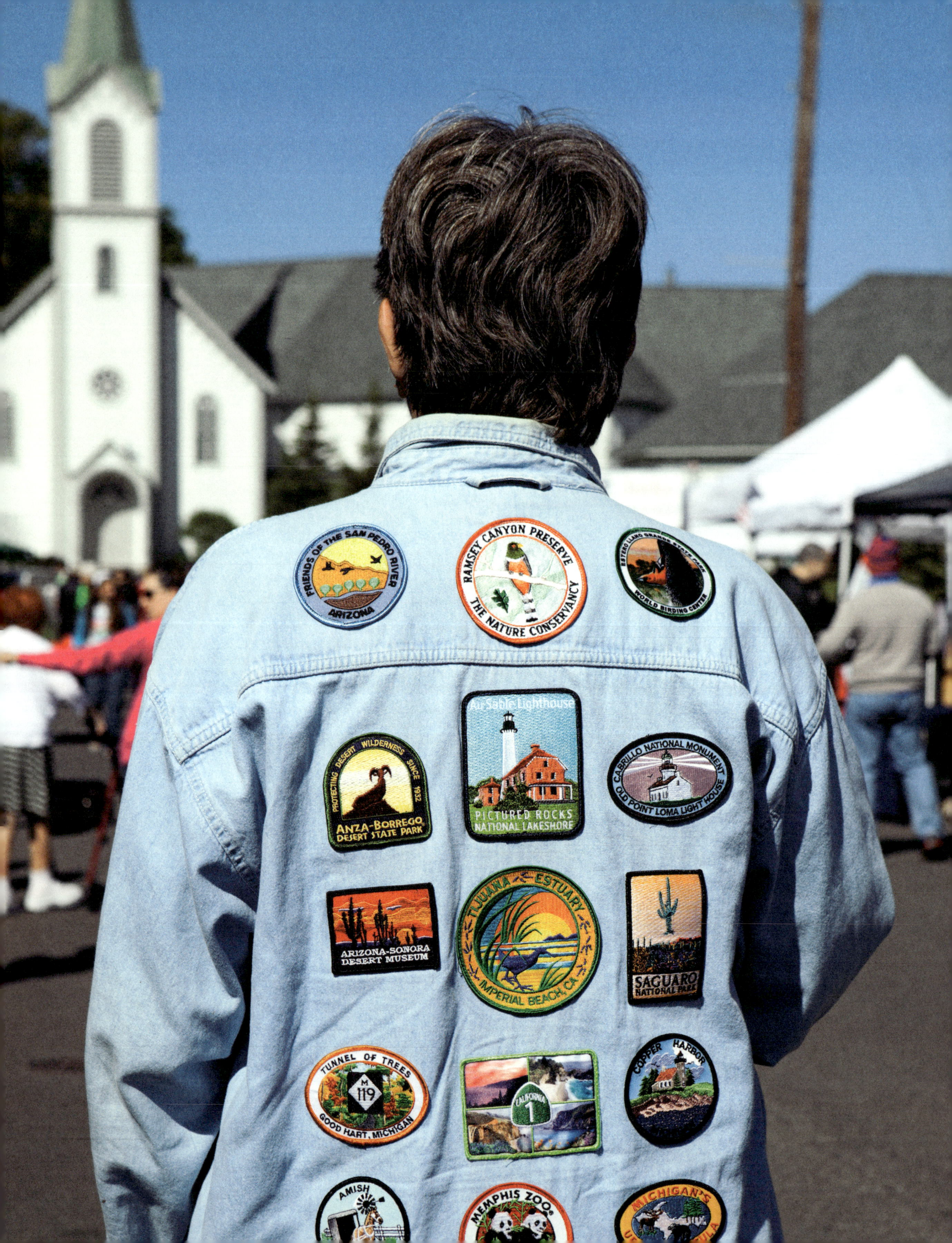

FRIENDS OF THE SAN PEDRO RIVER
ARIZONA
RAMSEY CANYON PRESERVE
THE NATURE CONSERVANCY
WORLD BIRDING CENTER
PROTECTING DESERT WILDERNESS SINCE 1932
ANZA-BORREGO DESERT STATE PARK
Au Sable Lighthouse
PICTURED ROCKS NATIONAL LAKESHORE
CABRILLO NATIONAL MONUMENT
OLD POINT LOMA LIGHT HOUSE
ARIZONA-SONORA DESERT MUSEUM
TIJUANA ESTUARY
IMPERIAL BEACH, CA
SAGUARO NATIONAL PARK
TUNNEL OF TREES
M 119
GOOD HART, MICHIGAN
CALIFORNIA 1
COPPER HARBOR
AMISH
MEMPHIS ZOO
MICHIGAN'S

WHAT *AMERICA* LOOKED LIKE *TO ME*

THE STORY OF A
SMALL TOWN IN MICHIGAN NAMED
Harbor Springs
AS REMEMBERED & PHOTOGRAPHED BY
Poppy de Villeneuve

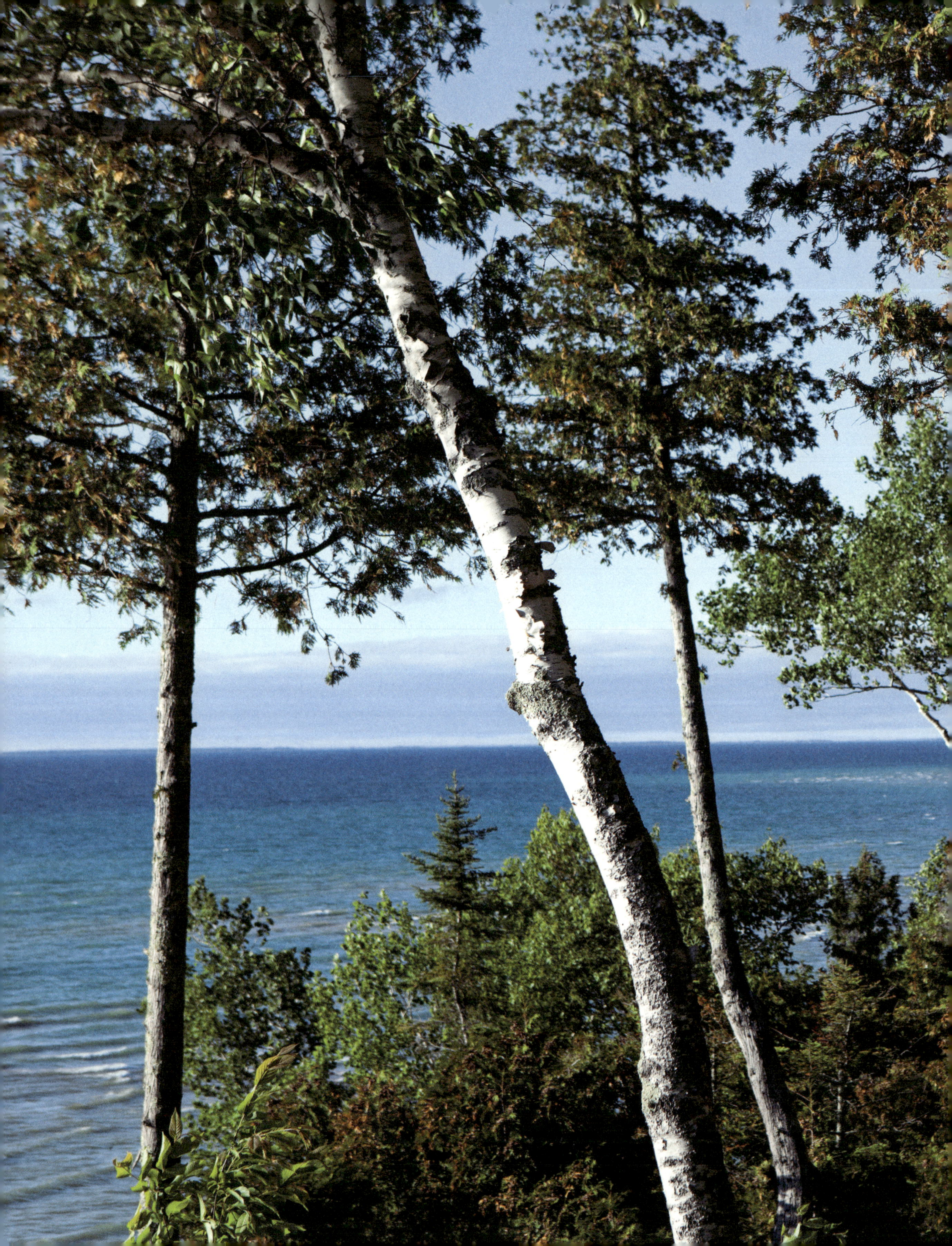

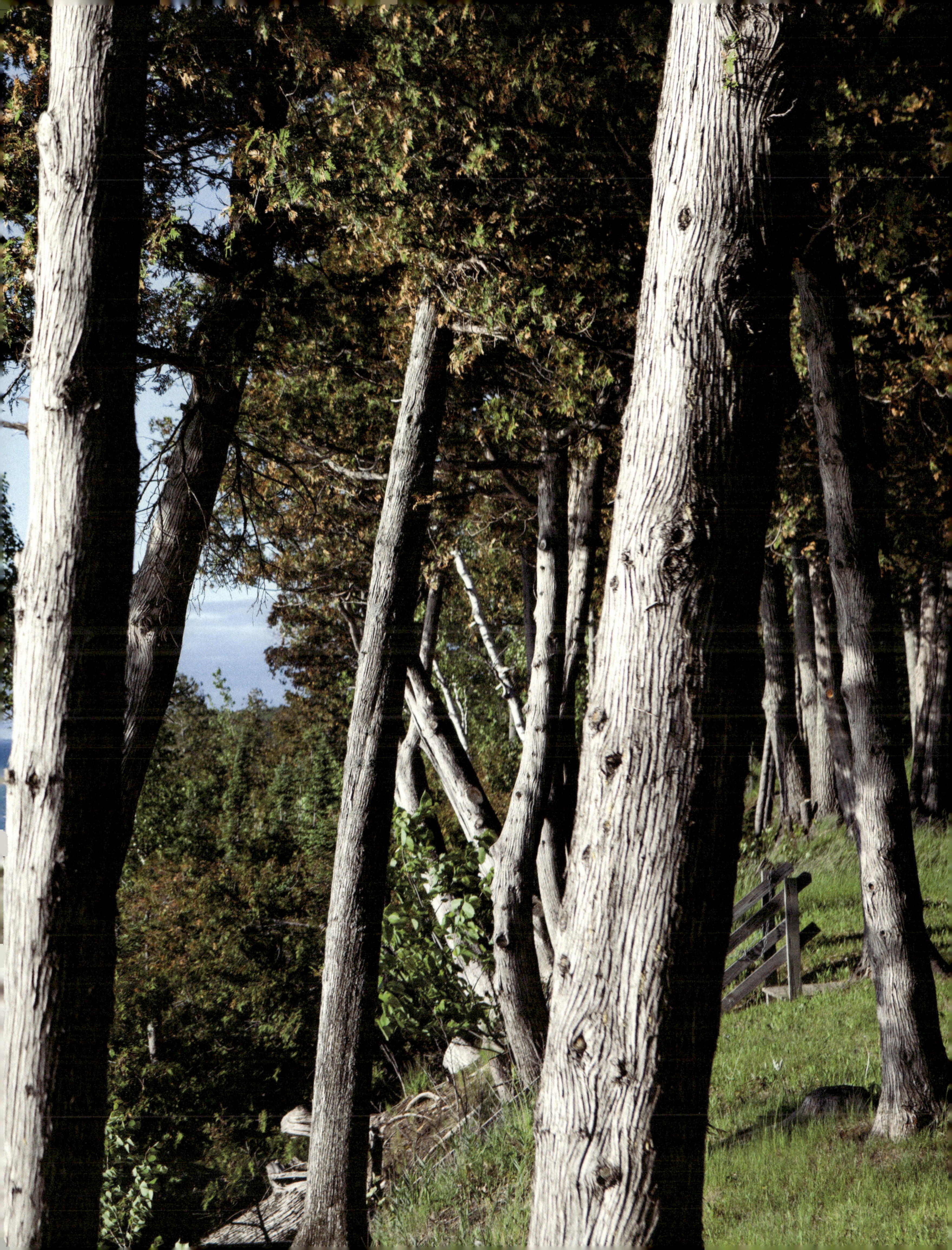

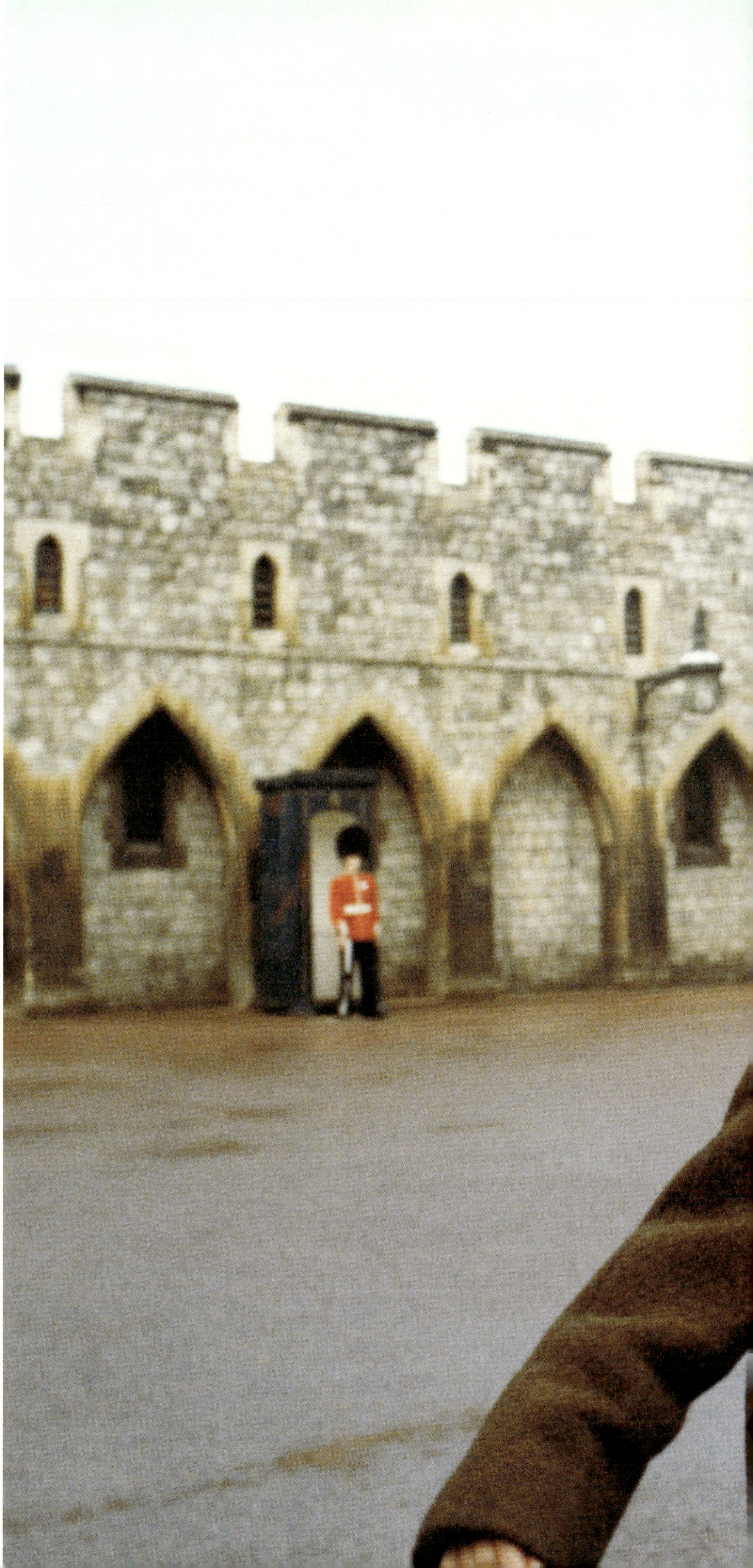

I grew up in West Sussex in the English countryside with my mom and my sister, Daisy—that's her on the right. This picture was taken at Windsor Castle during the changing of the guard. My mom's parents had just flown in from Shaker Heights, Ohio, the town where she grew up. Whenever my grand parents visited, my mom would arrange for us to do all sorts of really touristy English things.

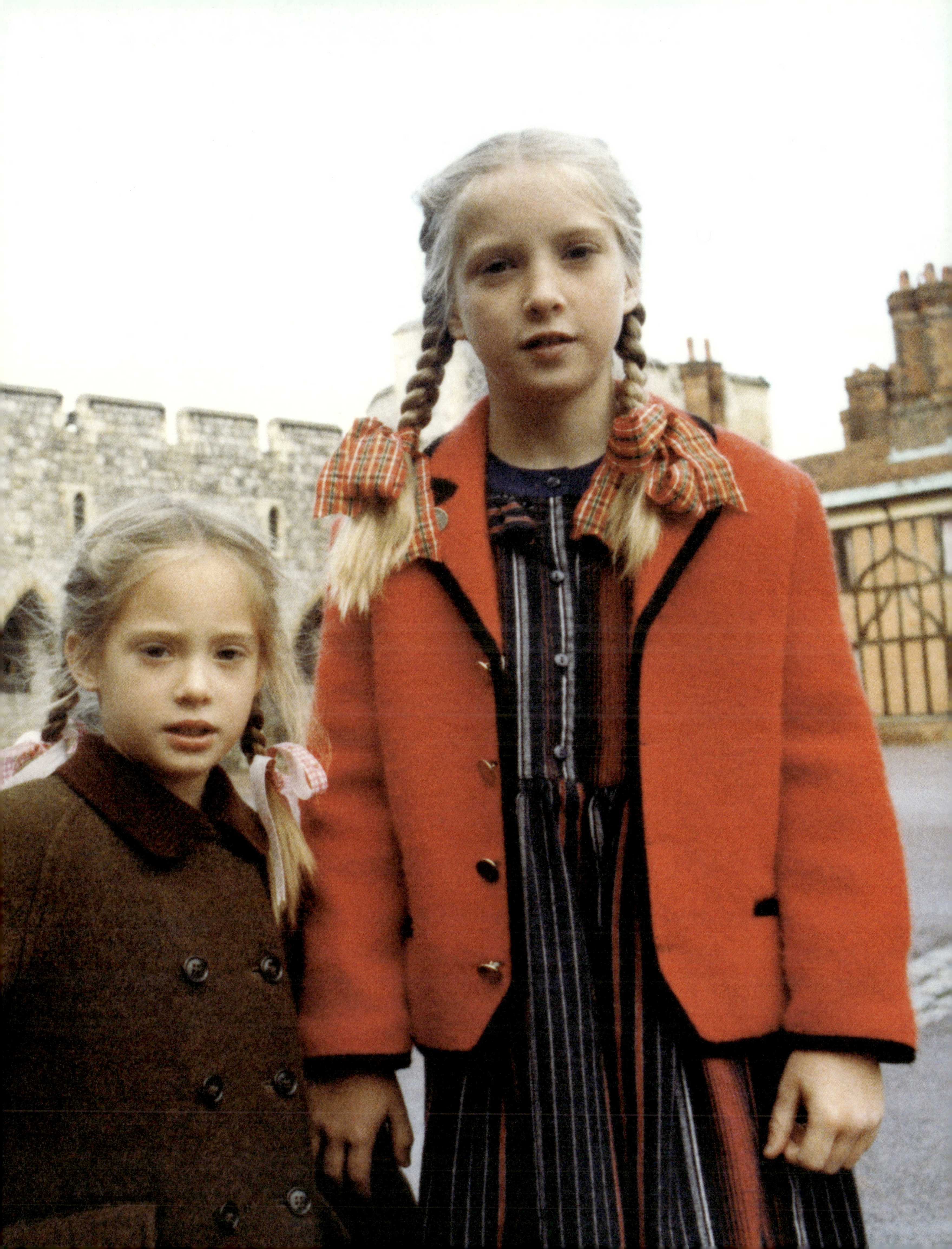

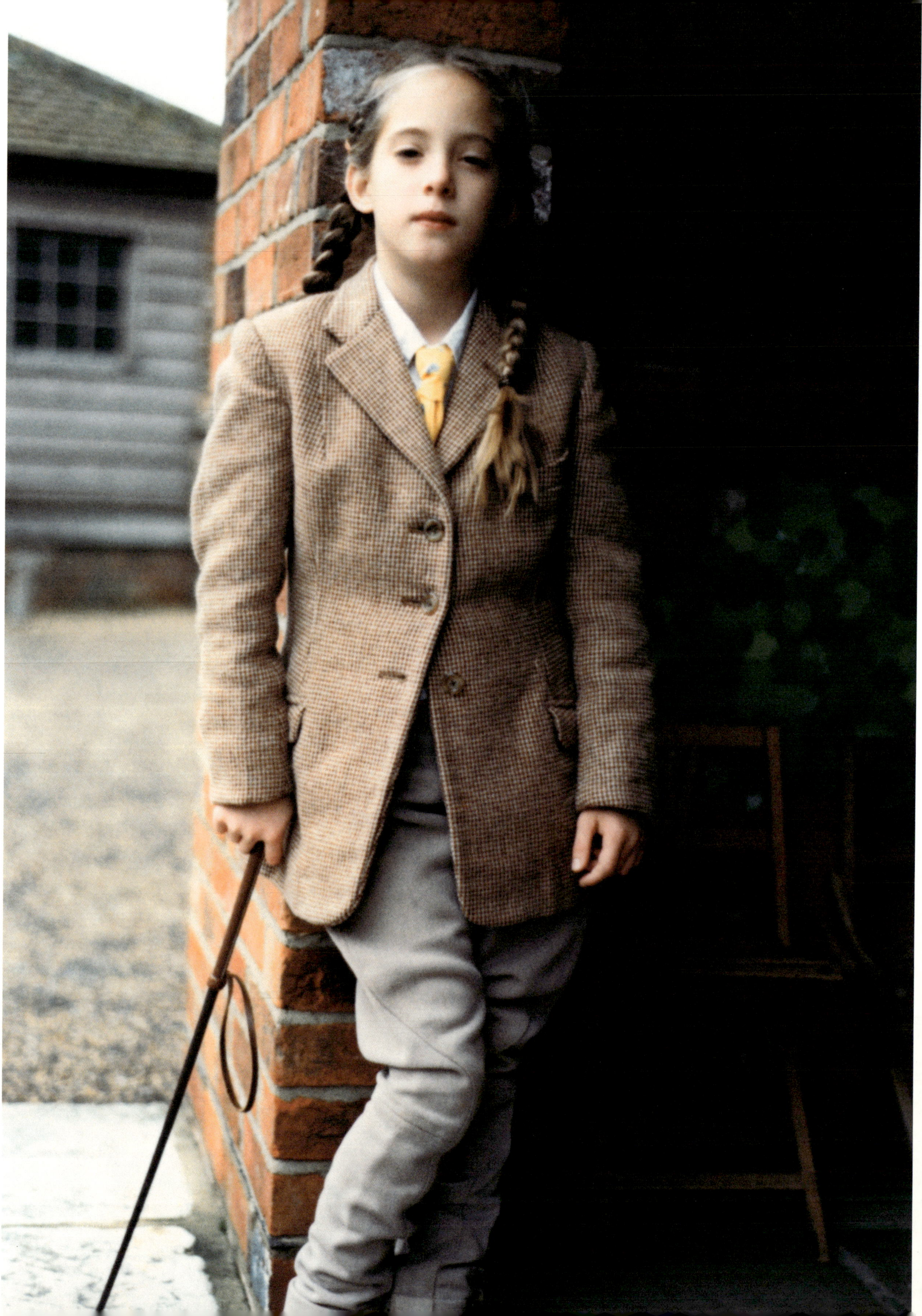

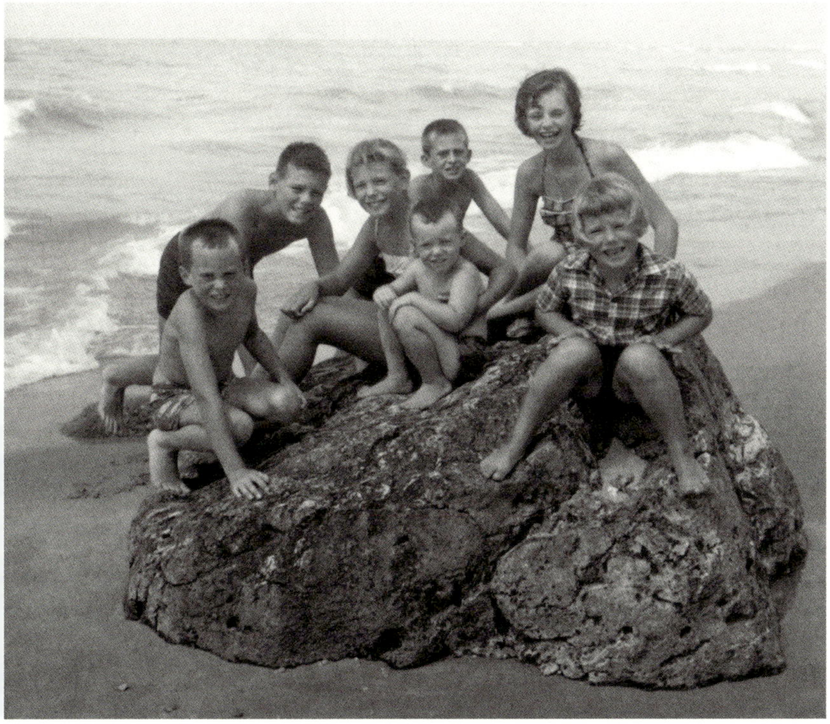

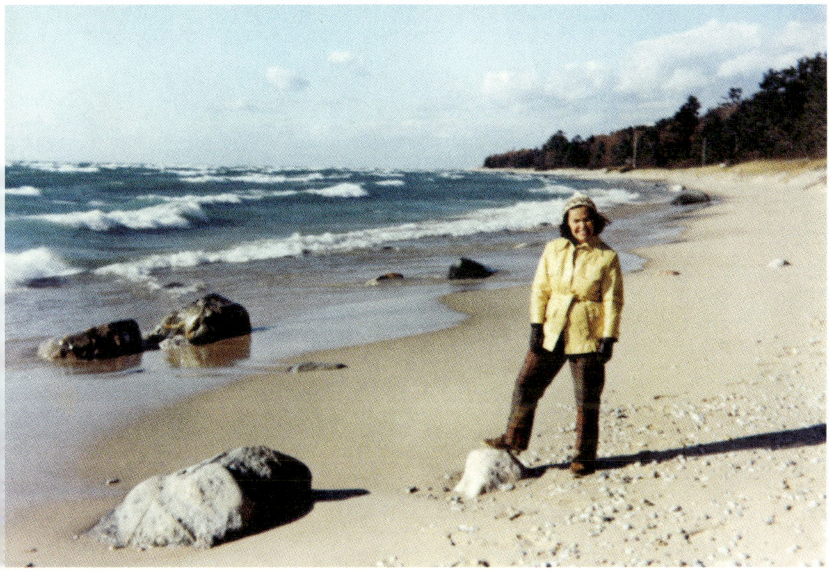

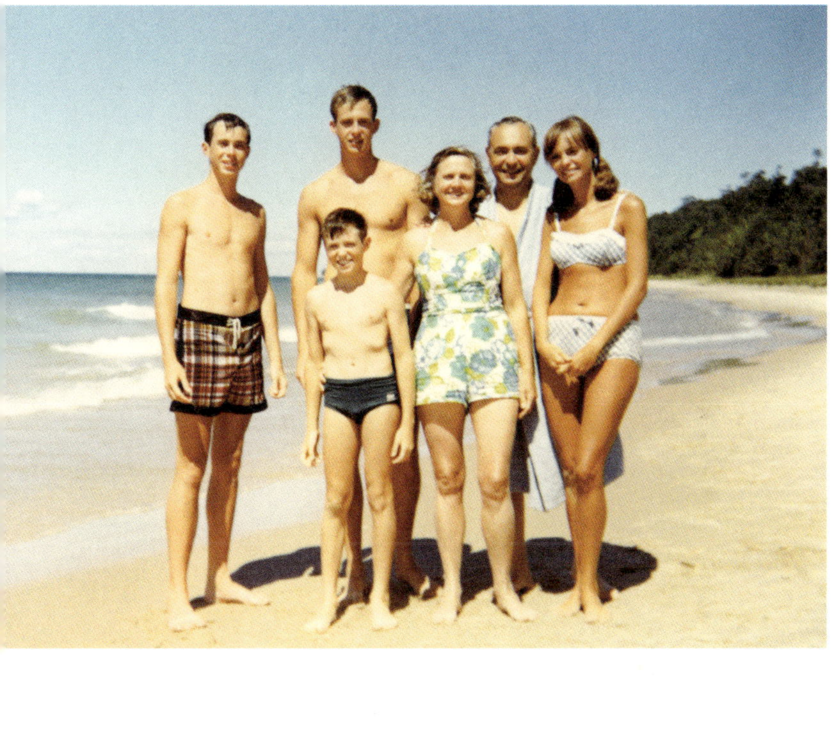

My family started coming to Harbor Springs, Michigan, in 1954. My grandfather's sister, Florence ("Flossie"), became good friends with a man named Tru Cummings, who owned a stretch of land along Lake Michigan. Tru helped Flossie build a little cottage on Lower Shore Drive, which runs along the waterfront. She invited my grandparents to bring their kids up to visit from Ohio. There was my mom, Jan, who was about 10 years old, and her 3 younger brothers—Jim, John, and Tom. I think in the 1950s Harbor Springs was an ideal little American town—a perfect getaway for my grandfather, who worked all year in a big law firm.

When I was a kid, Harbor Springs was this magical experience of America, a place where I could see all my relatives in an almost fantasy version of what family life could be. I grew up in England together with my mother and sister—my father wasn't present after a certain point—so our family unit was different from many others I saw. We didn't have lots of cousins or aunts or uncles living nearby, so those two weeks we spent in Michigan each summer were really important for my connection to that part of life.

Harbor Springs will be forever associated in my mind with my grandparents—it's where I really got to know them. I would sit for hours on the swivel stools in the kitchen and watch my nanny baking cinammon rolls and blueberry pie. My grandfather really indulged us kids—he'd let me do things like dress him up as Orphan Annie, complete with freckles and a wig. Because he had polio and was confined to a wheelchair, he couldn't go down to the water, so we'd come back to the porch after a day of playing with lots of stories to tell him. My grandfather always wanted to hear what we had gotten in to. That visual of his wheelchair has stayed with me to this day. I think those kinds of objects form the foundation of how you see the world when you're a child.

Those summer days all flowed into one another. All the cousins shared a big room upstairs, so I would wake up early in my Mickey Mouse tent and have breakfast and then run down to the beach to search for Petoskey stones—small coral fossils you find only on Lake Michigan—or just roam around

Opposite: Me in my riding kit, on my way to riding school in Midhurst, England. It's a polo town, so there's lots of equestrian activity there. I was an awful rider, but looked pretty capable in this outfit. *This page—top*: My mom (in the back on the right), together with her brothers, Jim, John and Tom, with the Sedar kids on "Jimmy's Rock" in front of the house on Lower Shore Drive; *Center*: My great-aunt Florence ("Flossie"), who built the house we would visit each summer. This was taken in 1981, when there used to be a really substantial sandy beach—now the shoreline has receded and become very rocky. *Bottom*: This is the kind of family portrait my grandparents would do for their annual Christmas card—this one was taken in 1965. My grandfather contracted polio, so this is one of the few photographs of him on the beach where he's not in his wheelchair.

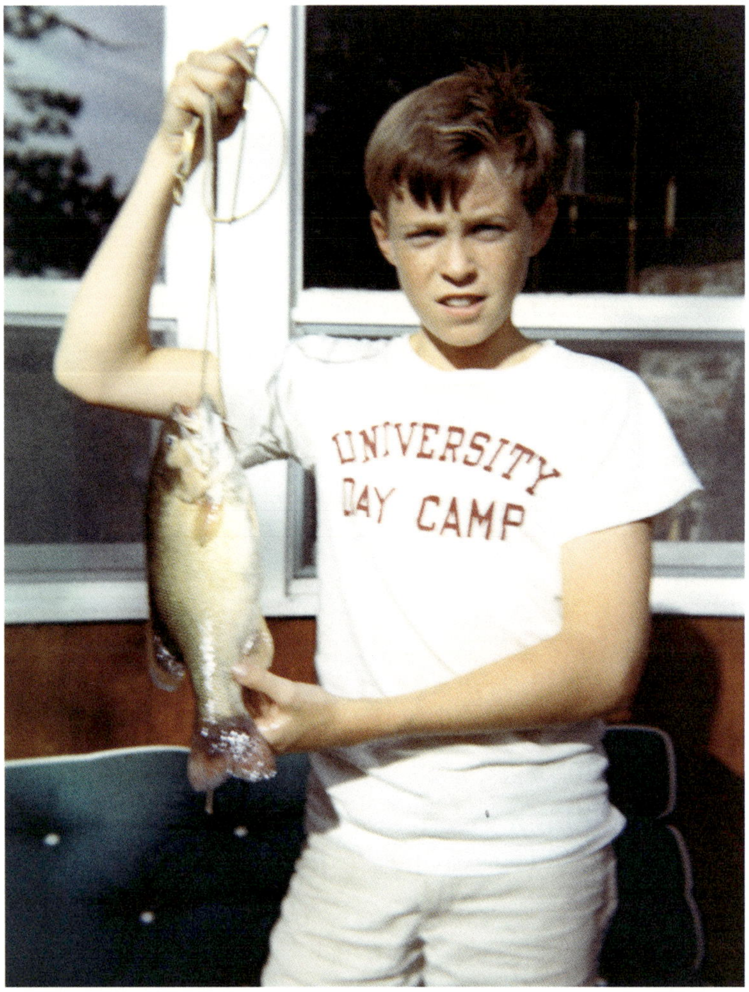

the forest, creating little huts and forts and making up adventures. Sometimes we'd take the sailboat out, or go into town for fudge or ice cream. There was a silkscreening shop in Harbor Springs that I loved, where we could get creative and design our own T-shirts. Other times we'd drive to Petoskey to make friendship bracelets with the cousins at a bead place called Indian Hills, which is run by members of the Little Traverse Bay Bands of Odawa Indians. We'd all eventually end up at home for dinner, and I'd always have to shuck the corn. That's a terribly boring job.

There's something very specific about the way Northern Michigan looks and smells. It's a beach town, but the freshness of the air from the lake and pines is so unique. It feels a little heavier, in the same way Maine or Vermont does—that cozy, woodsy, honey-bear kind of feeling. And coming from England, I felt everything there was so abundant—the scale of the lake and forest seemed to dwarf everything else. The dinghies we'd sail felt *tiny* in the lake; the wild turkeys were *enormous*. Back home in Sussex, a sandwich meant some cucumber with a slice of cheese—at Gurney's in Harbor

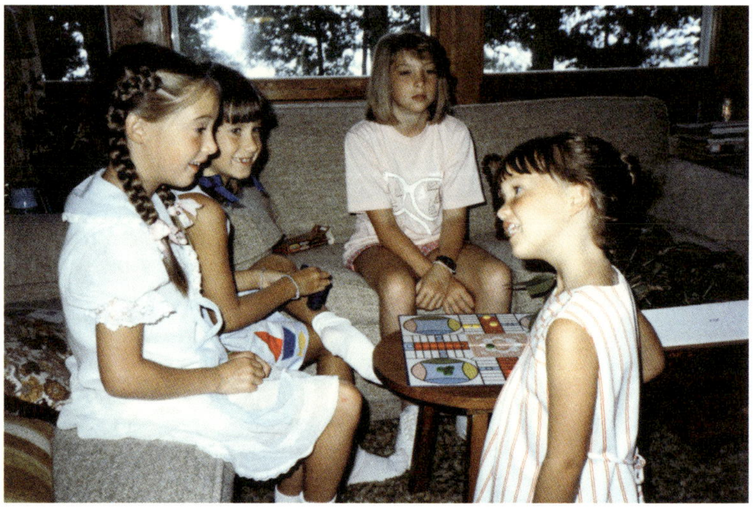

Springs, you got a giant pickle and four layers of turkey on this pillowy white bread. No rationing, whatsoever.

When school ended in England, we would shed our uniforms and travel to Michigan, where a distinct feeling of freedom and playfulness would take over. As time passed, my sister and I developed "summer friendships" with local kids who lived nearby. Some of them had cool boats that I was a little envious of; one family had a huge yellow raft we would spend hours diving off. When I got a bit older, my friend Lauren and I would go into town by ourselves sometimes. The summer I was 13, I met Kevin, a sweet local boy with floppy blonde hair who delivered pizzas and was a pro snowboarder. We both lied about our age—I said I was 16, which was a bit of a jump; he said he was 17. When I had to stay home and babysit my cousins, Kevin would come over and bring me pizza and we

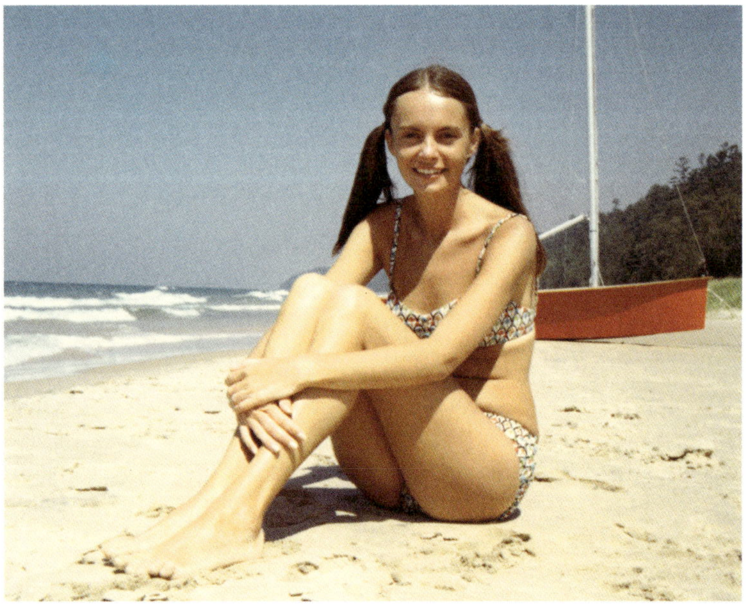

Top: Uncle Tom with his catch, outside Flossie's house. He attended University School in Shaker Heights, Ohio. *Right*: There I am in my Little Bo Peep outfit, playing Parcheesi with my cousins Alyssa and Sarah and my sister, Daisy. I can't help but notice that everyone else is dressed normally. *Bottom*: My mom in Harbor Springs in 1968. After high school, she studied architecture and design at the University of Michigan, following in her mother's footsteps. After graduation, she was discovered by a casting scout while working as an art teacher in Flint, Michigan. Her modeling career took her to New York, then Milan and Paris, where she worked with Guy Bourdin, Norman Parkinson, and Helmut Newton. She eventually settled in London where she met and married my father, the photographer Justin de Villeneuve.

would make out in the back of his car. Then we'd pick up Lauren and go to Five Mile Creek and chill cans of beer in the water. That was a great summer.

There was a stretch of years when I was in boarding school that we didn't visit Harbor Springs. Life in England took over for a while. When I moved to New York we started visiting again, because it continues to be the best way for Daisy and my mom and me to connect with all of the family. It's also become an important place for me to share with friends.

When you revisit a familiar place, sometimes it's hard to tell whether it has changed or whether you've just changed. The truth must lie between the two. Our family has grown and evolved—all the kids in these snapshots are adults now; my cousins have children of their own. I think as a result, the time we share isn't as simple as it used to be. I still feel close to everyone of course, but in a different way. My grandmother also passed away this past April, a deep loss we're all adjusting to.

I think all these things affect how I understand the town and my experiences there. I notice there are more touristy boutiques, but strangely they make the town feel less fancy and a little more generic. I think there's something to what Chris Howse from the fudge shop told me—these days, children have fewer unique environments to explore, places that become those indelible touchstones of memory. There's a certain standardization of small towns in America, and I don't think Harbor Springs is immune to those trends. We have our photographs. We have mementos. But that sense of getting completely lost in a very different kind of place—like I felt when I visited Michigan as a child—is becoming a little more rare. At the same time, I met lots of young people on this trip who are starting new businesses like Pond Hill Farm and Cool House Labs—their work is helping to shape the town's future in a very positive way.

We all experience change in our lives, so there's something very reassuring about those things that endure, places we can mark ourselves against. Though it's different in many ways from the town I remember, visiting Harbor Springs this year as a photographer revealed something about who I have become. It was quite nice to be working there, to be seen by my family and people I know as an artist—not that my creative life seems just like some strange school project. There's something important about being able to show people what I do, particularly in a small American town where people have more conventional jobs. At the same time, it was really nice to be reminded of who I was as a kid, to think that I still have that person within me. It's important to protect that part of myself. I think that's why we all keep going back to our summer places—we need to let ourselves breathe, to remind that childlike side of ourselves to play and explore.

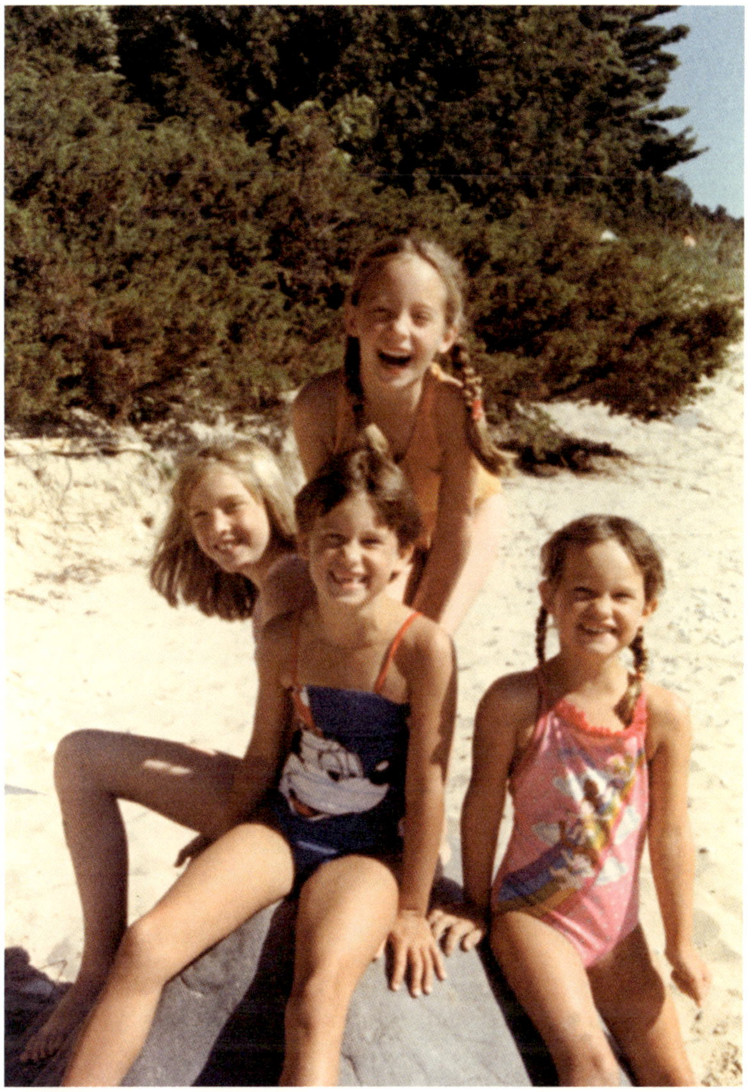

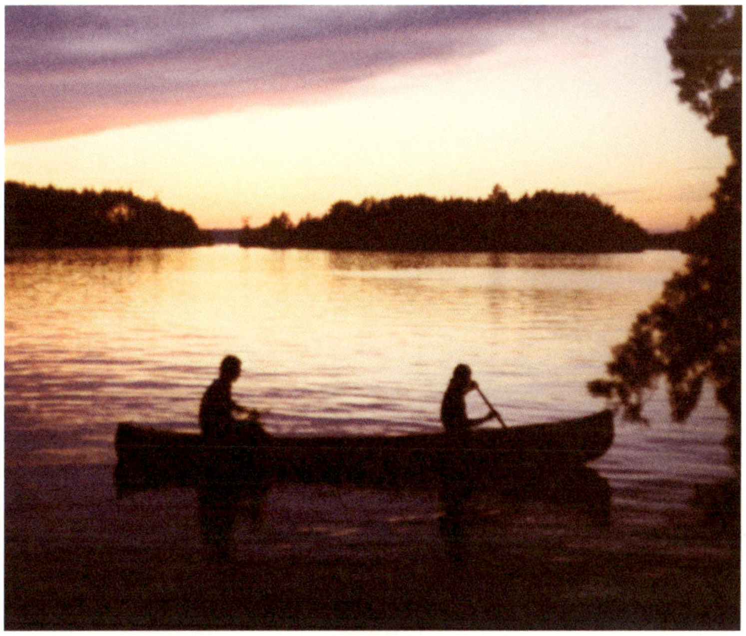

Top: The summer of 1986, again with Daisy, Alyssa, and Sarah. Daisy is an illustrator who is now living in Paris. Alyssa works as a copywriter in Knoxville, Tennessee, and Sarah is a counselor living in Jacksonville, Florida. Both Alyssa and Sarah travel with their children to Harbor Springs each summer, continuing the tradition. *Bottom*: A typical Lake Michigan scene from 1972 *Following spread*: Peter and Joe Crittenden, two young guys I met at the farmer's market.

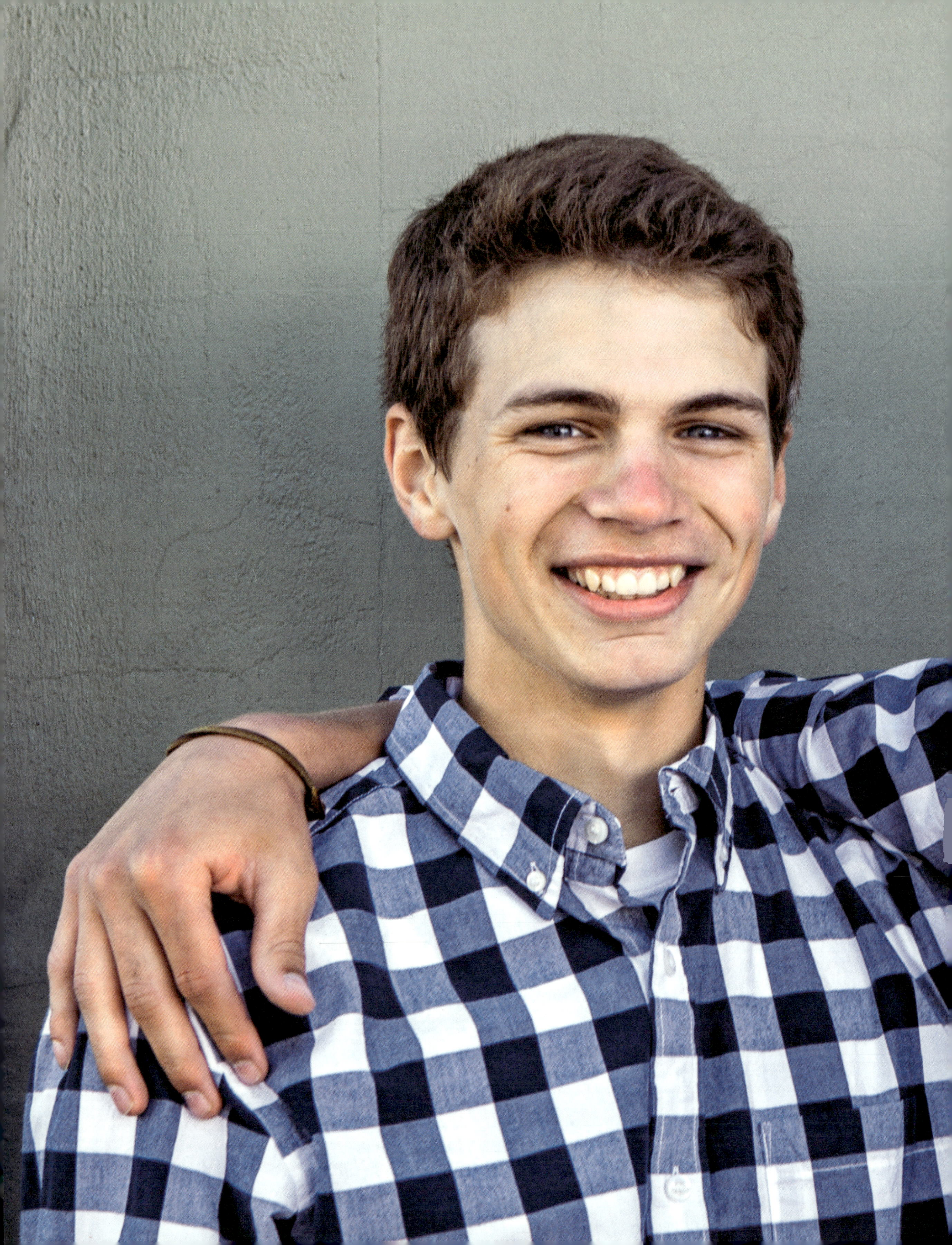

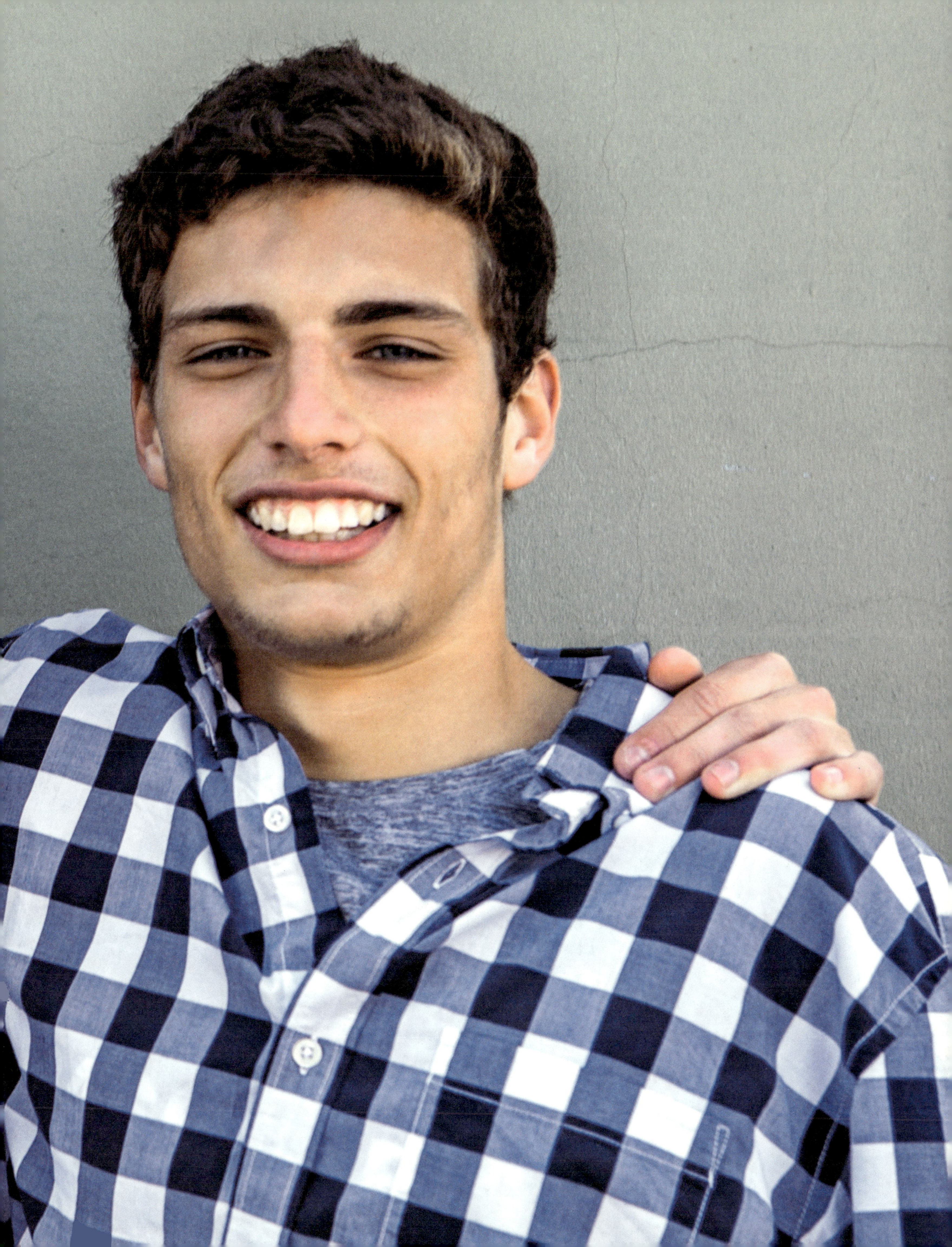

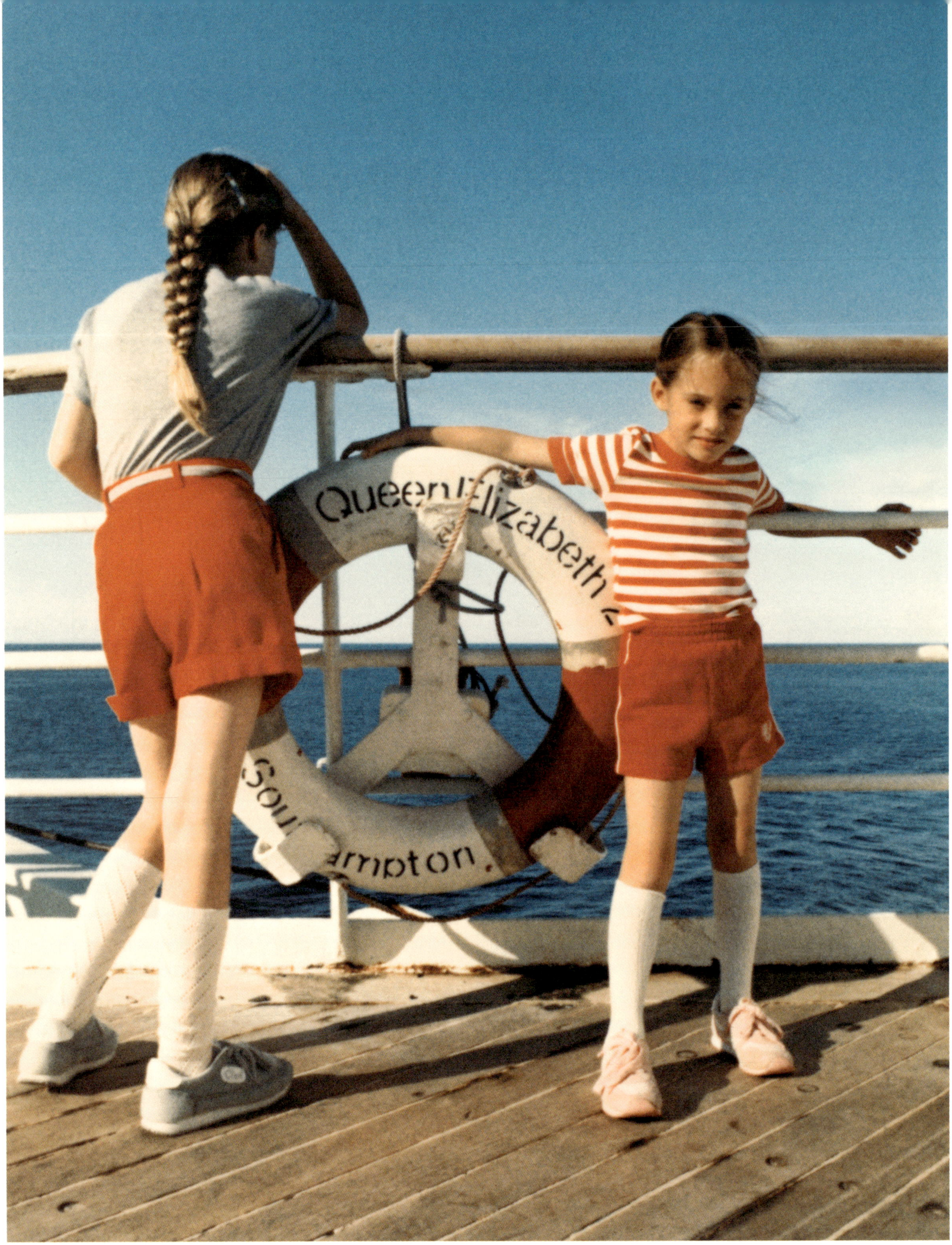

This page: Daisy and me aboard the QE2 en route to New York from Southampton with our grandparents in 1985. The boat had a dance floor that lit up square by square when you stepped on it, and Michael Jackson's *Thriller* video played constantly on screens in the discotheque. *Opposite*: Drew Dunkel and Cade Trudeau after their Little League game against Harbor Springs. The Petoskey team lost that day, and Drew—their pitcher—took it especially hard.

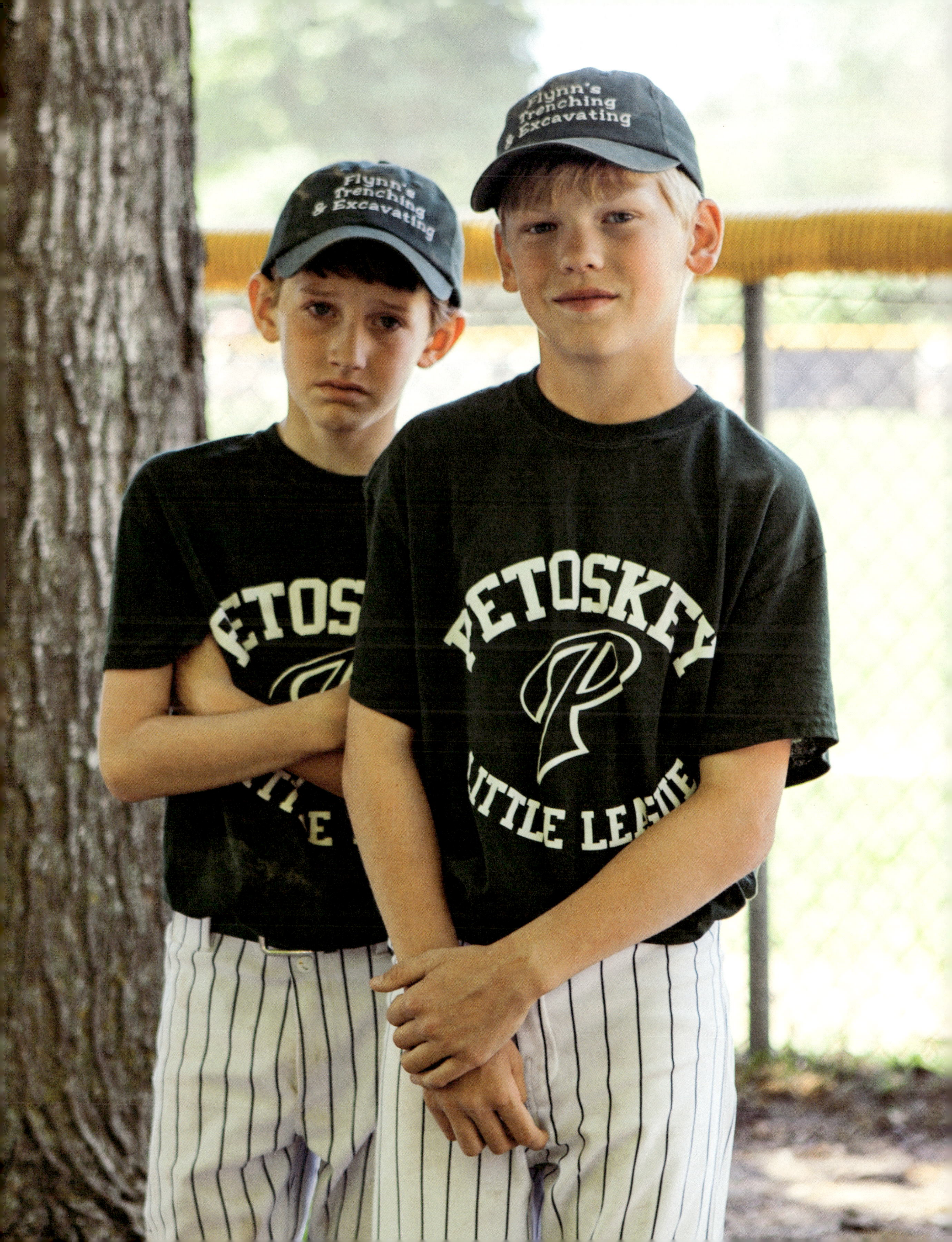
Flynn's
Trenching
& Excavating
PETOSKEY
LITTLE LEAGUE

I visited Tom Graham at his house on the bluff in Harbor Springs. He's a prominent local real estate broker and an avid collector of historic postcards. As Tom pulled away in his Suburban, he called out, "This is just the prettiest little town in America!"

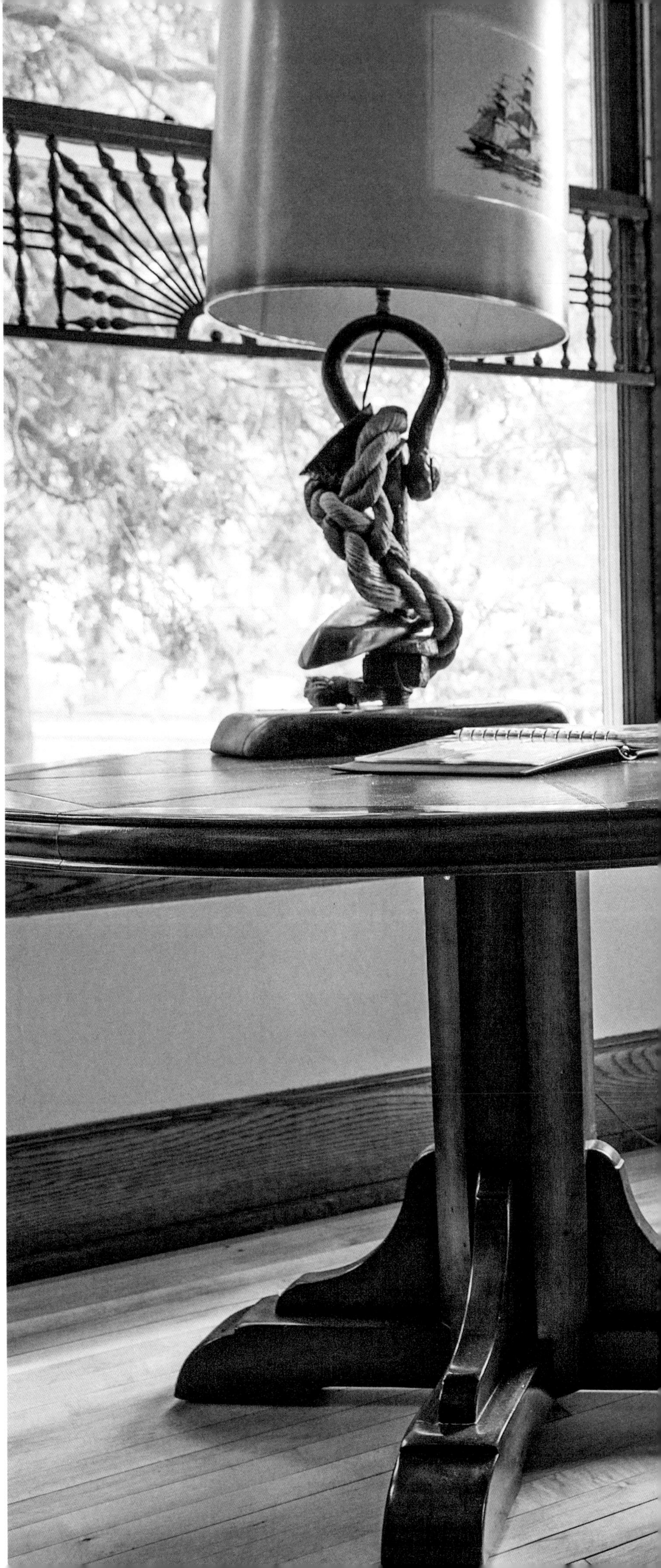

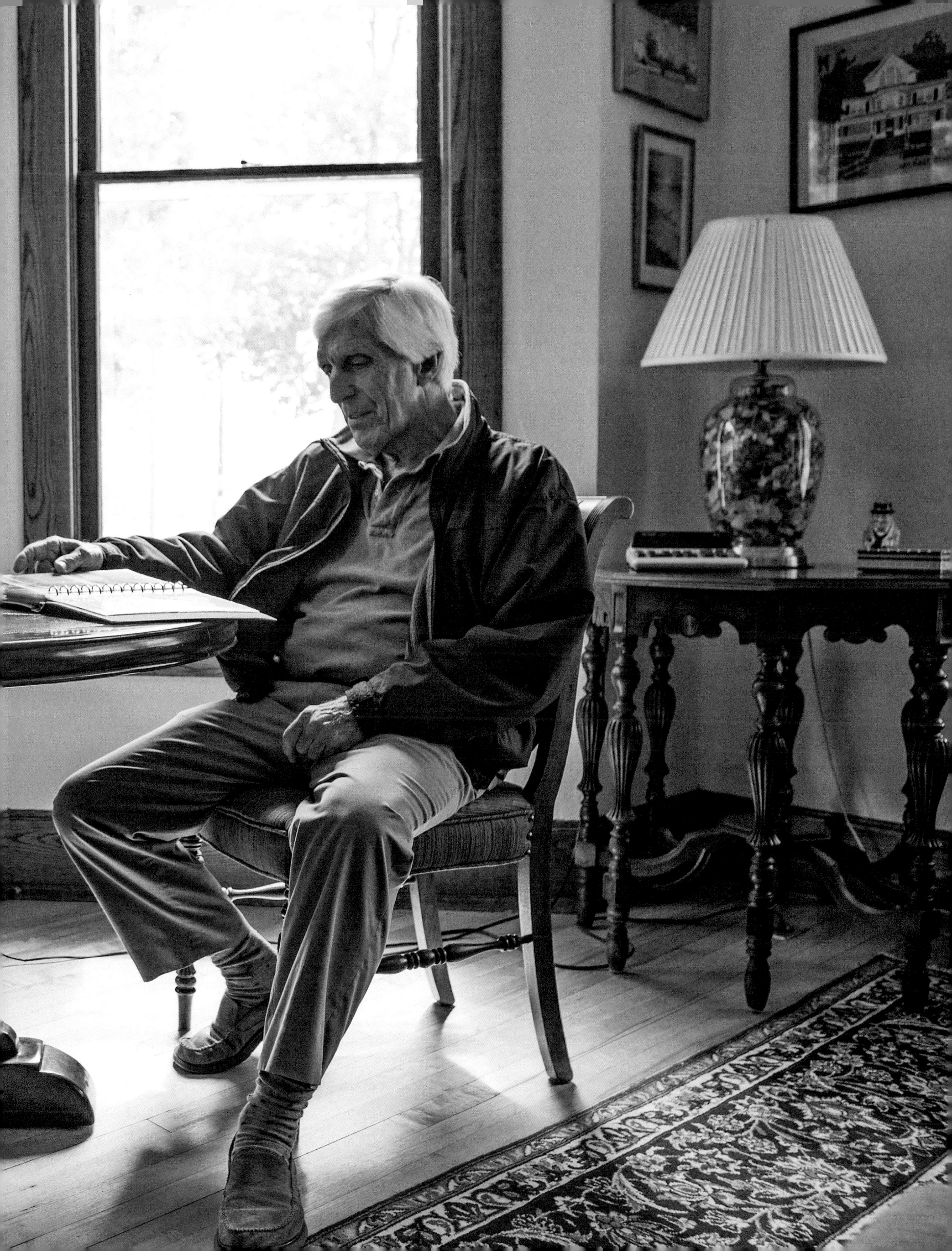

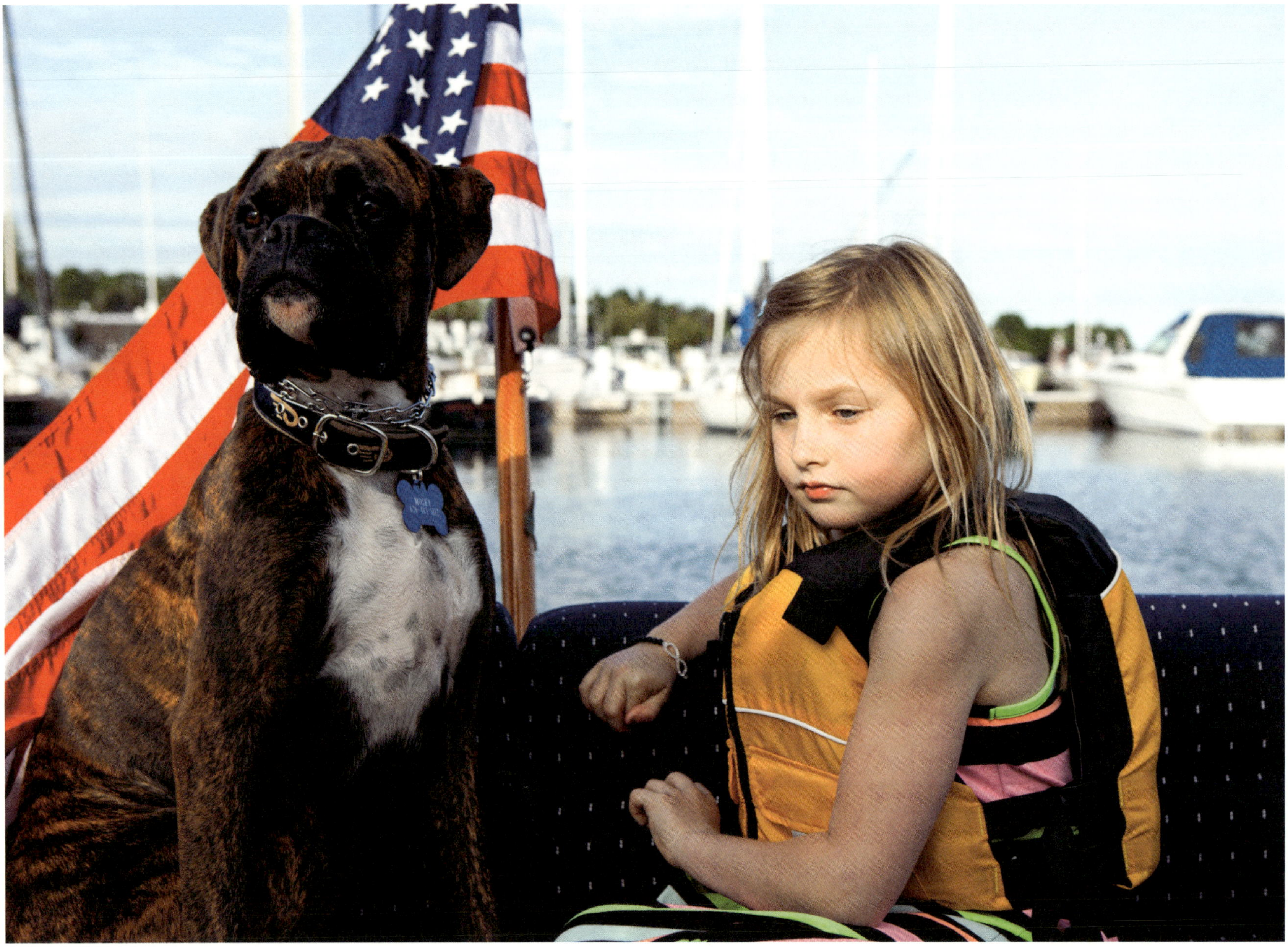

Beatrice is the daughter of my childhood friend Lauren Lapham. Lauren lived two houses down from us on Lower Shore Drive, and we would take canoes out on the lake and eat s'mores at night on her beach. She owns her own house now on Lower Shore Drive with her husband and three children, traveling there each summer from Los Angeles.

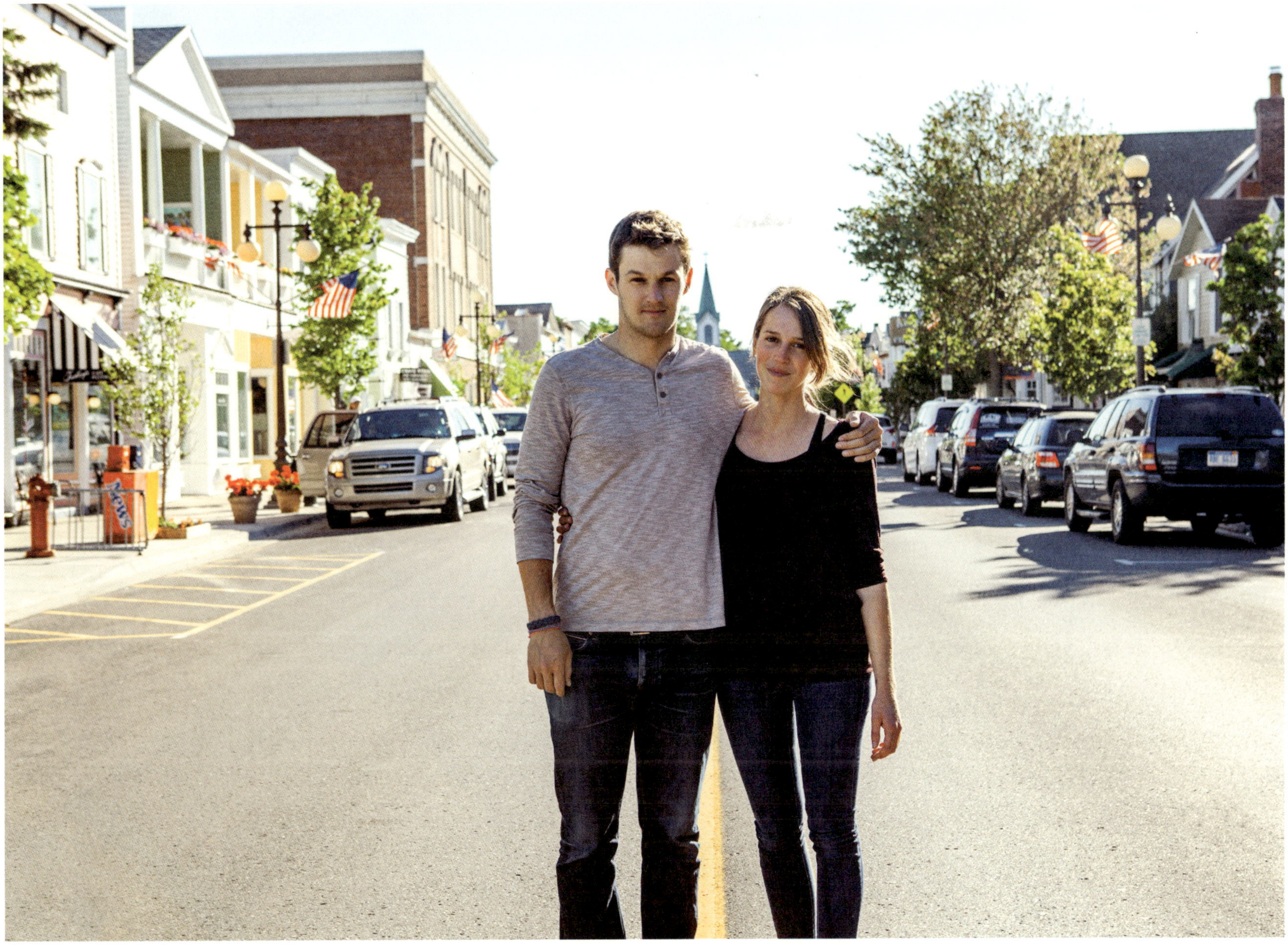

Jordan Breighner, the founder of Cool House Labs—a tech incubator based in Harbor Springs—with his girlfriend, Katherine Brines, an abstract painter. Jordan and Katherine are part of a new generation of entrepeneurs and artists who are imagining the town's future in new and exciting ways. Over the years, the economy of Harbor Springs seemed to falter—businesses like the silkscreening shop and Juilleret's Diner that I loved as a kid closed down. But recently, the town is experiencing a bit of a comeback. Like its ever-shifting shoreline, Harbor Springs looks different today.

This page: From the left—Flossie and Jim Ward (my mother's first husband), together with Uncle Jim and Uncle Tom in 1965. My grandmother was a gym teacher, so she may have orchestrated this contest. *Opposite*: Turkey's, the neighborhood lunch spot owned by Jeff Graham, whose family has been in Harbor Springs since 1903. The restaurant takes its name from an ill-fated moment in Jeff's high-school football career, when two sprained ankles had him hobbling around the field like a turkey.

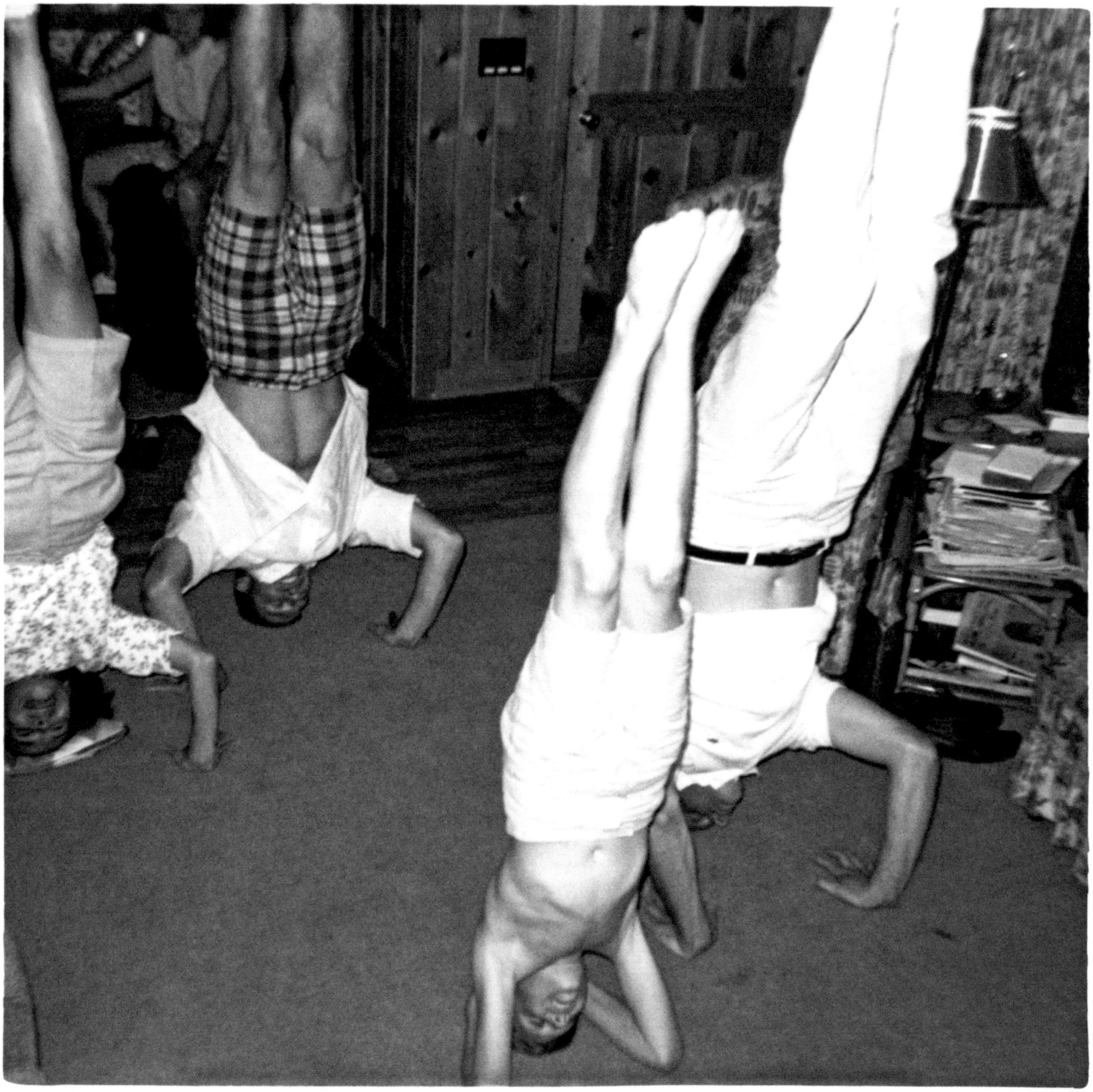

AUG • 65 •

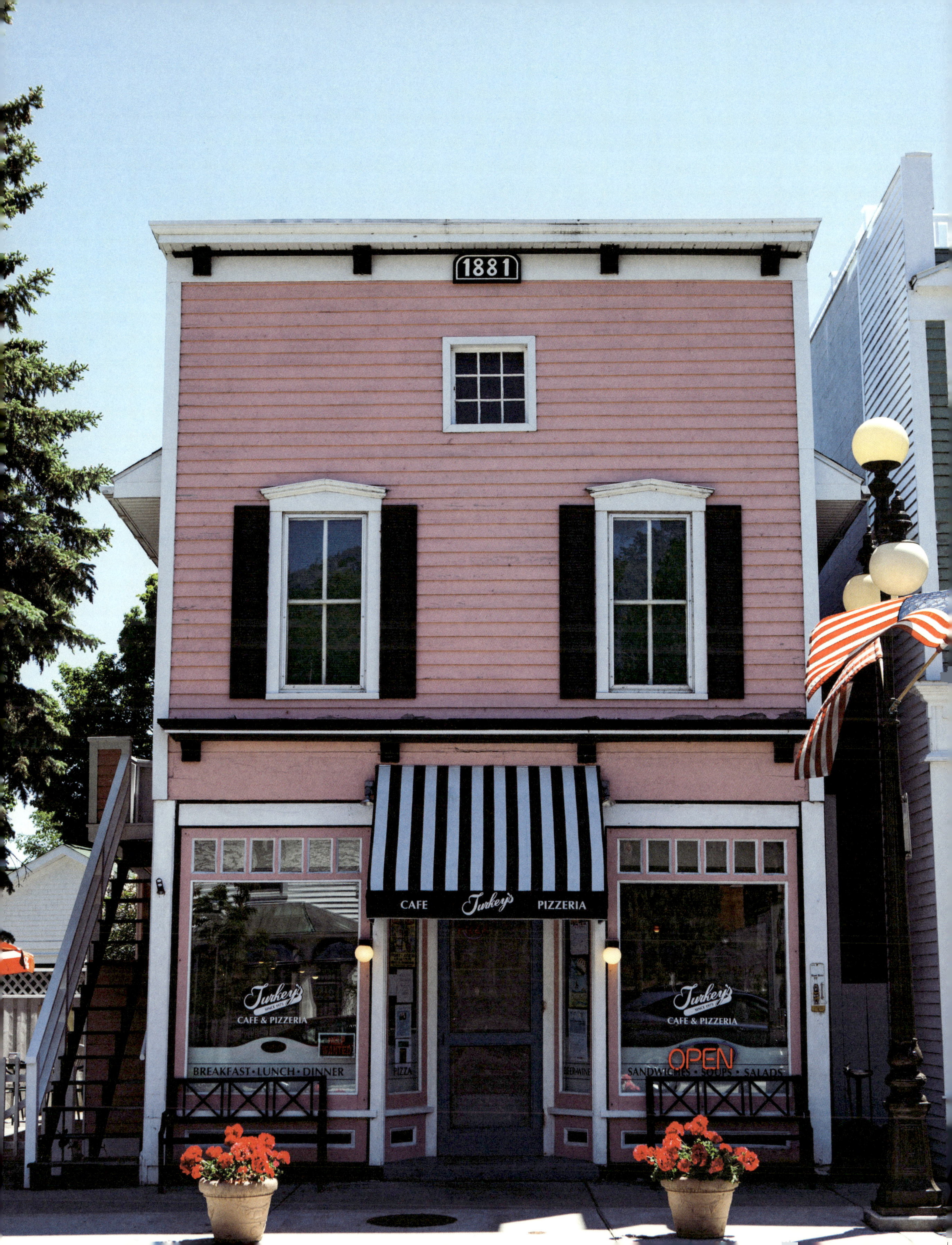
1881
CAFE
Turkey's
PIZZERIA
Turkey's
CAFE & PIZZERIA
BREAKFAST • LUNCH • DINNER
OPEN

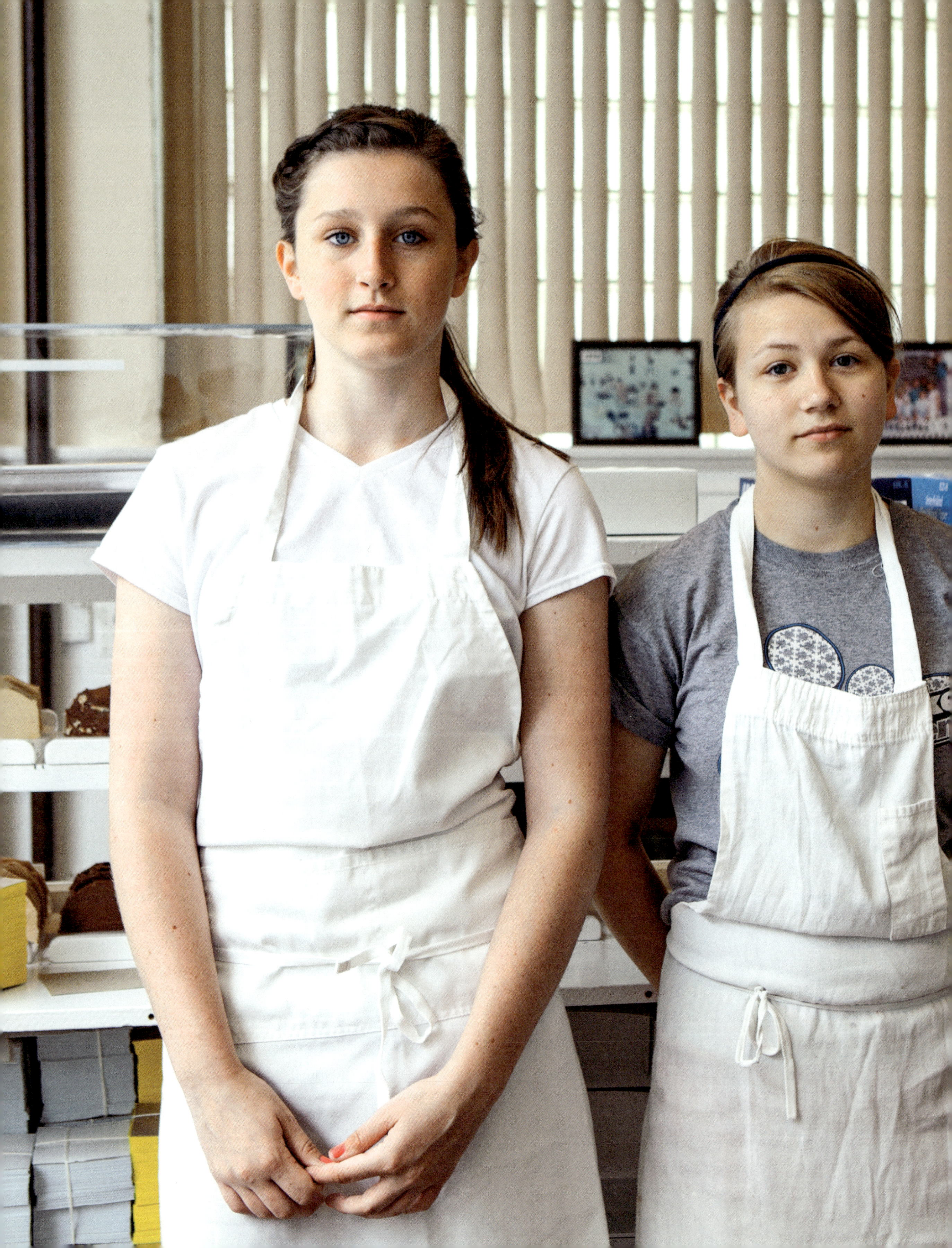

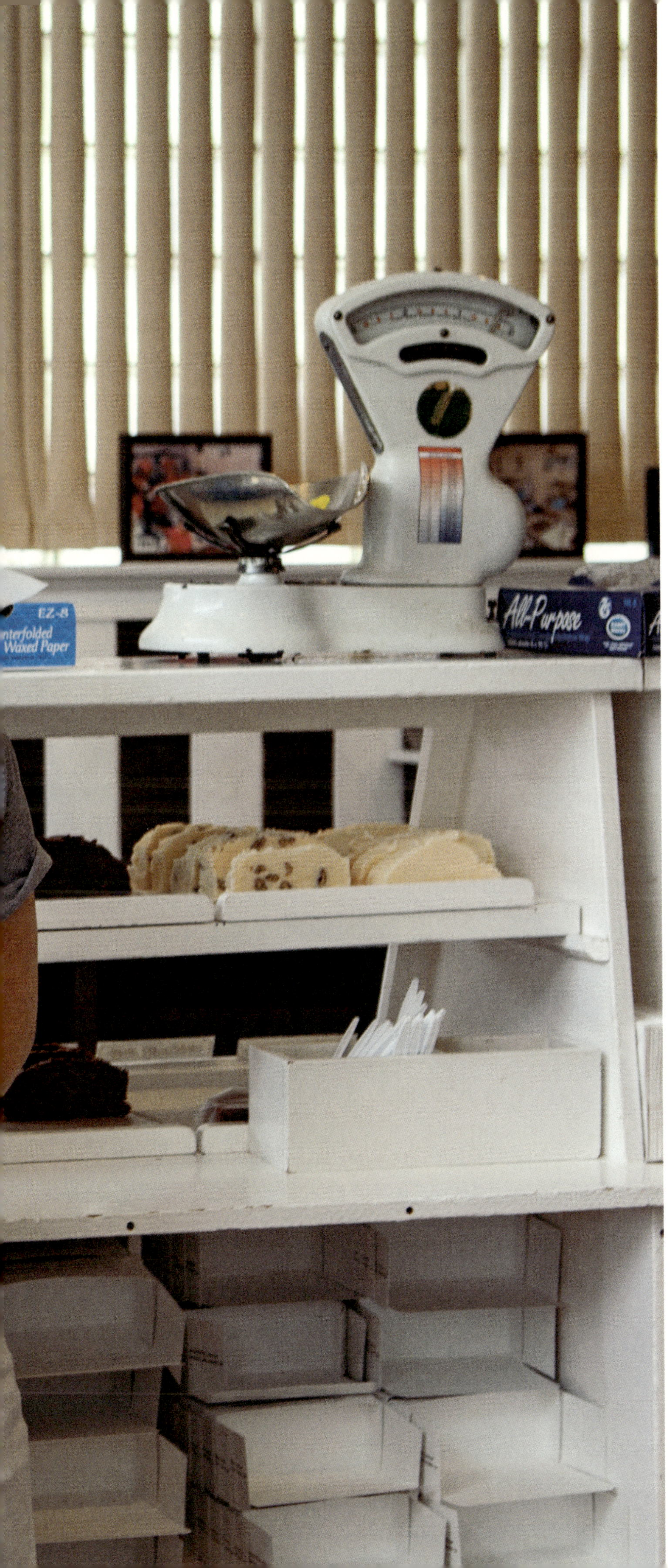

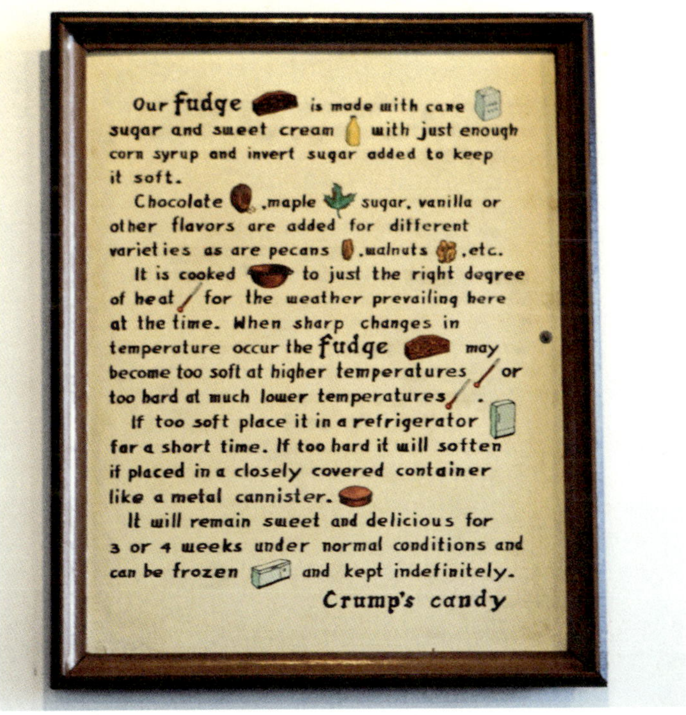

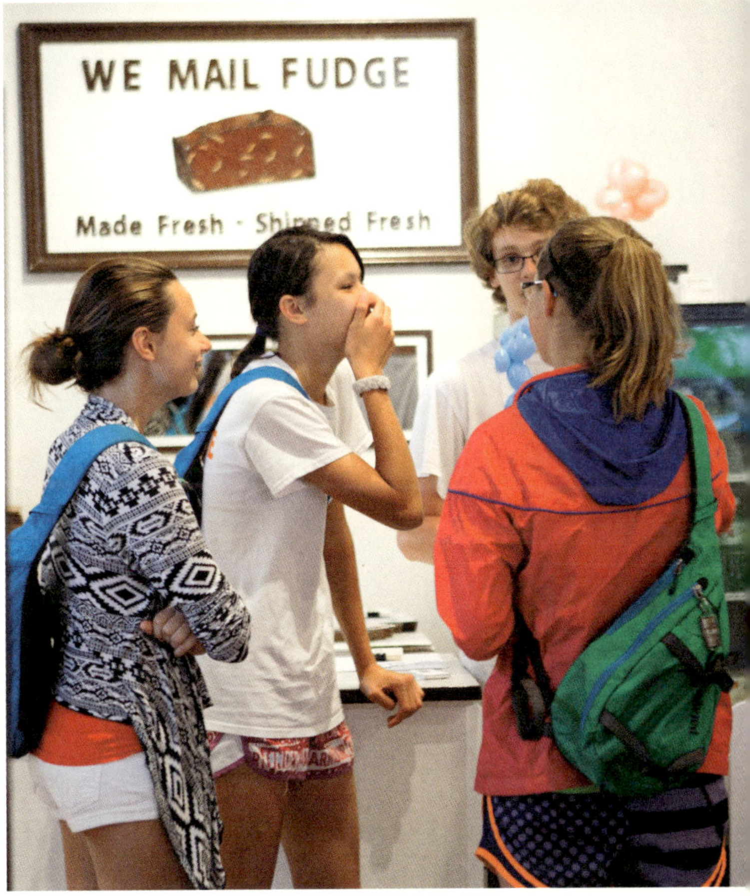

When I photographed Howse's Fudge Shop this year, the owner (and father of 11 children), Chris, told me a great story: "People come in here because they remember the pictures on the wall they saw as kids. They order their same favorite flavor of fudge, which hasn't changed much in the past 55 years. The original owner's grandson walked in here one day—he didn't announce himself, but just stood there staring. It had been years since he visited, and he almost started crying as he reminisced about being 6 years old and visiting his grandpa's candy store. He said it smelled exactly the same. My kids are going to have the same memories. I'd run the place at a loss if I had to, just to keep that tradition alive."

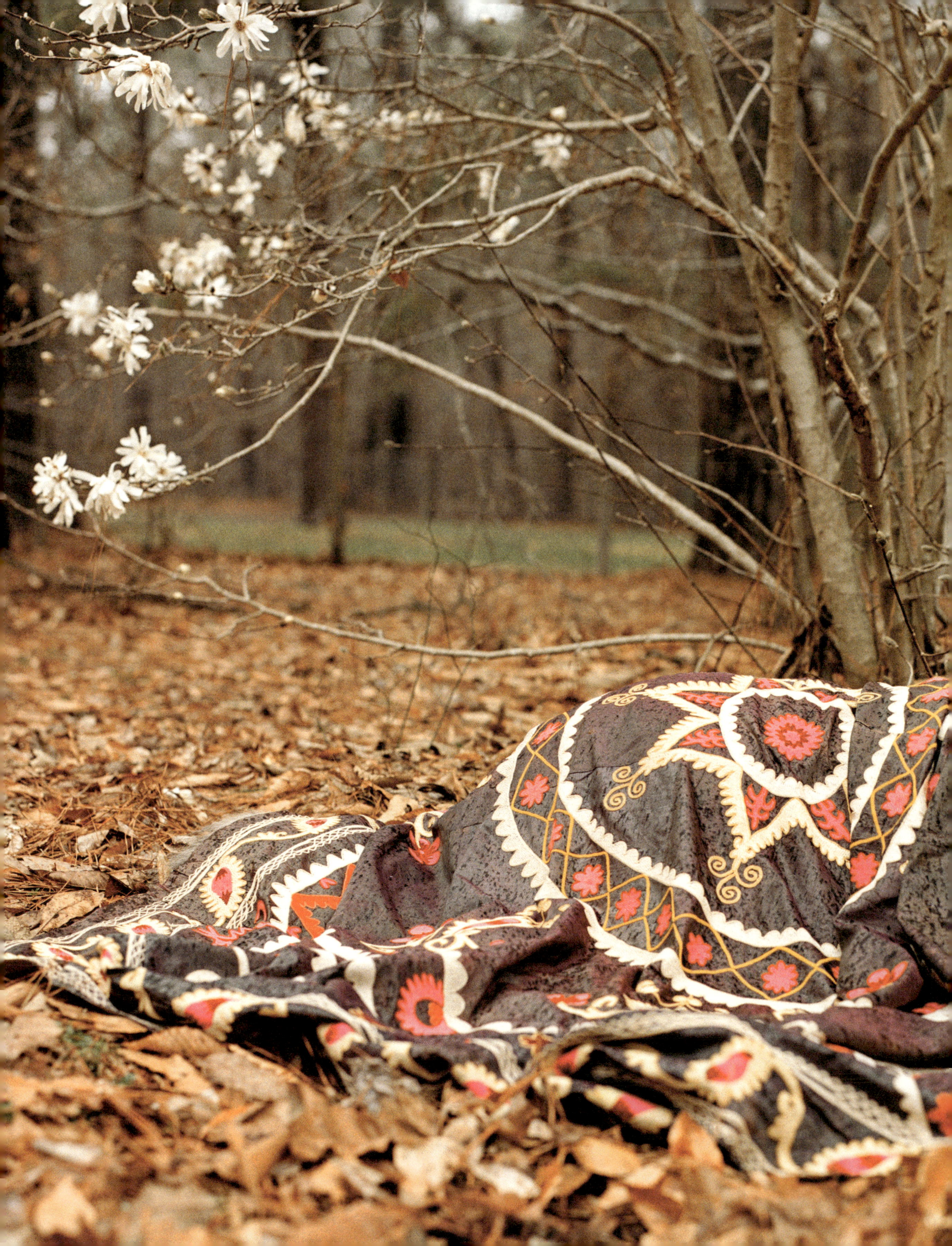

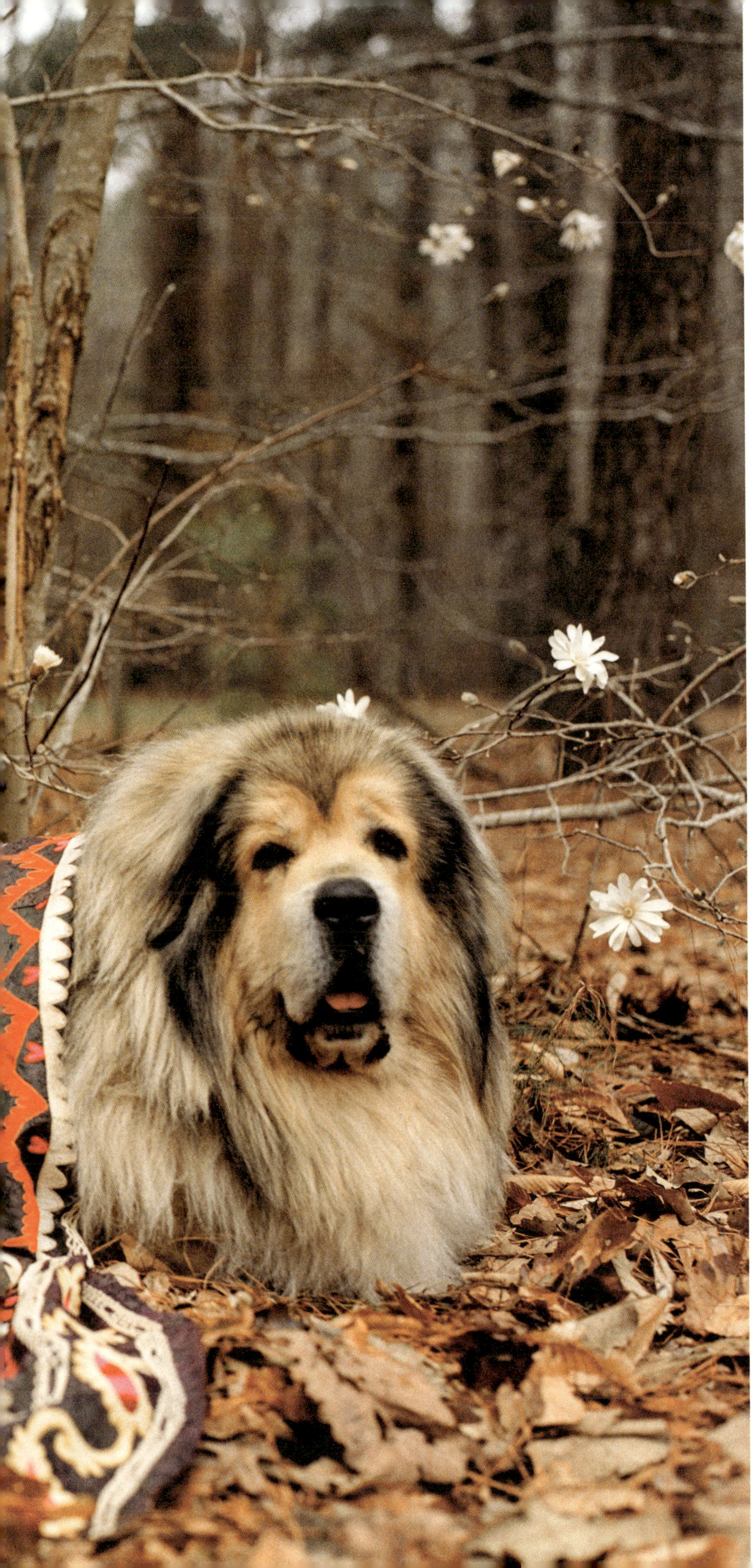

THE DOG WHO *ROARS* LIKE A *LION*

TIBETAN MASTIFFS

PHOTOGRAPHED BY

BRUCE WEBER

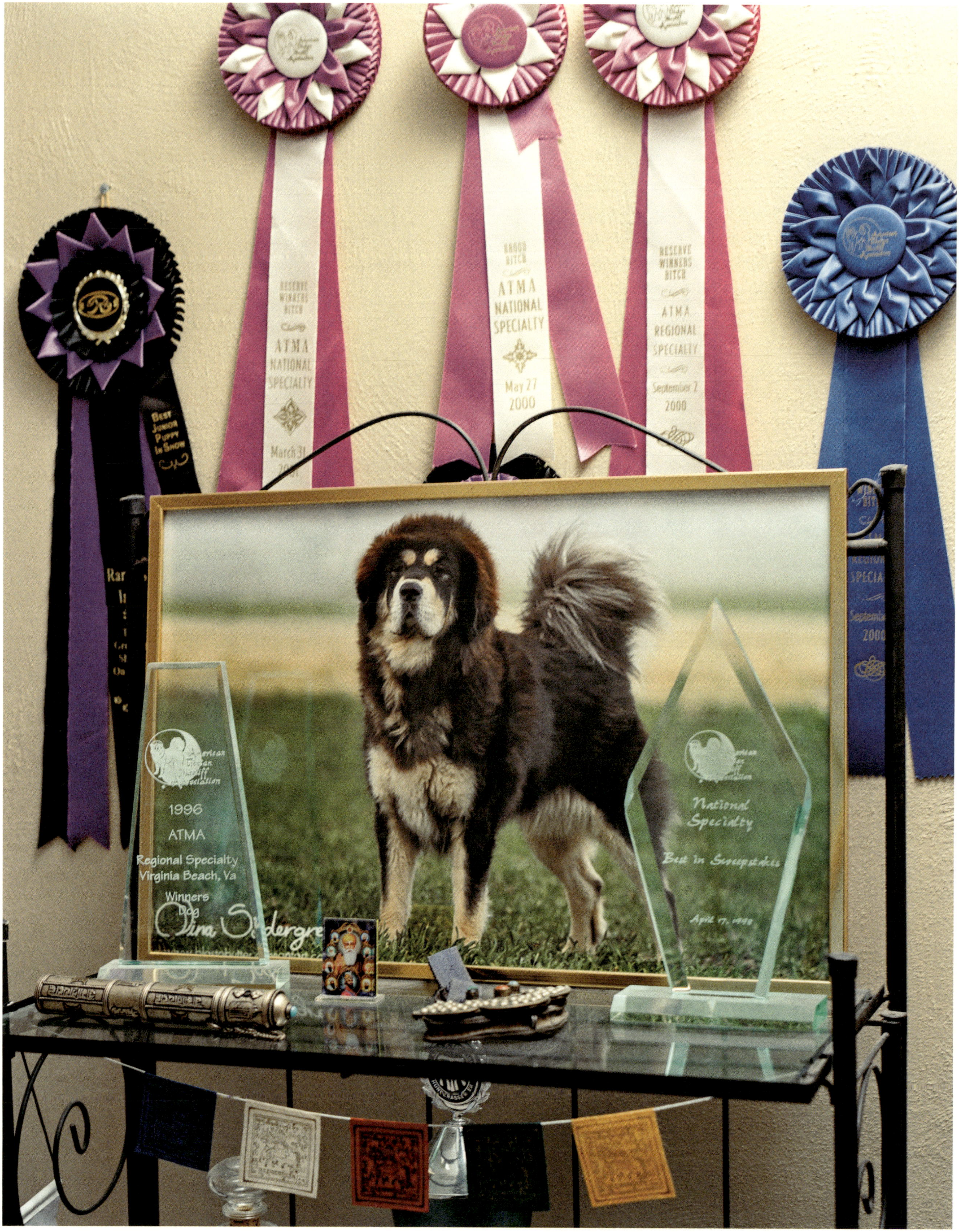
BEST JUNIOR PUPPY IN SHOW
RESERVE WINNERS BITCH
ATMA NATIONAL SPECIALTY
March 31
BROOD BITCH
ATMA NATIONAL SPECIALTY
May 27 2000
RESERVE WINNERS BITCH
ATMA REGIONAL SPECIALTY
September 2 2000
1996
ATMA
Regional Specialty
Virginia Beach, Va
Winners
Dog
National Specialty
Best in Sweepstakes

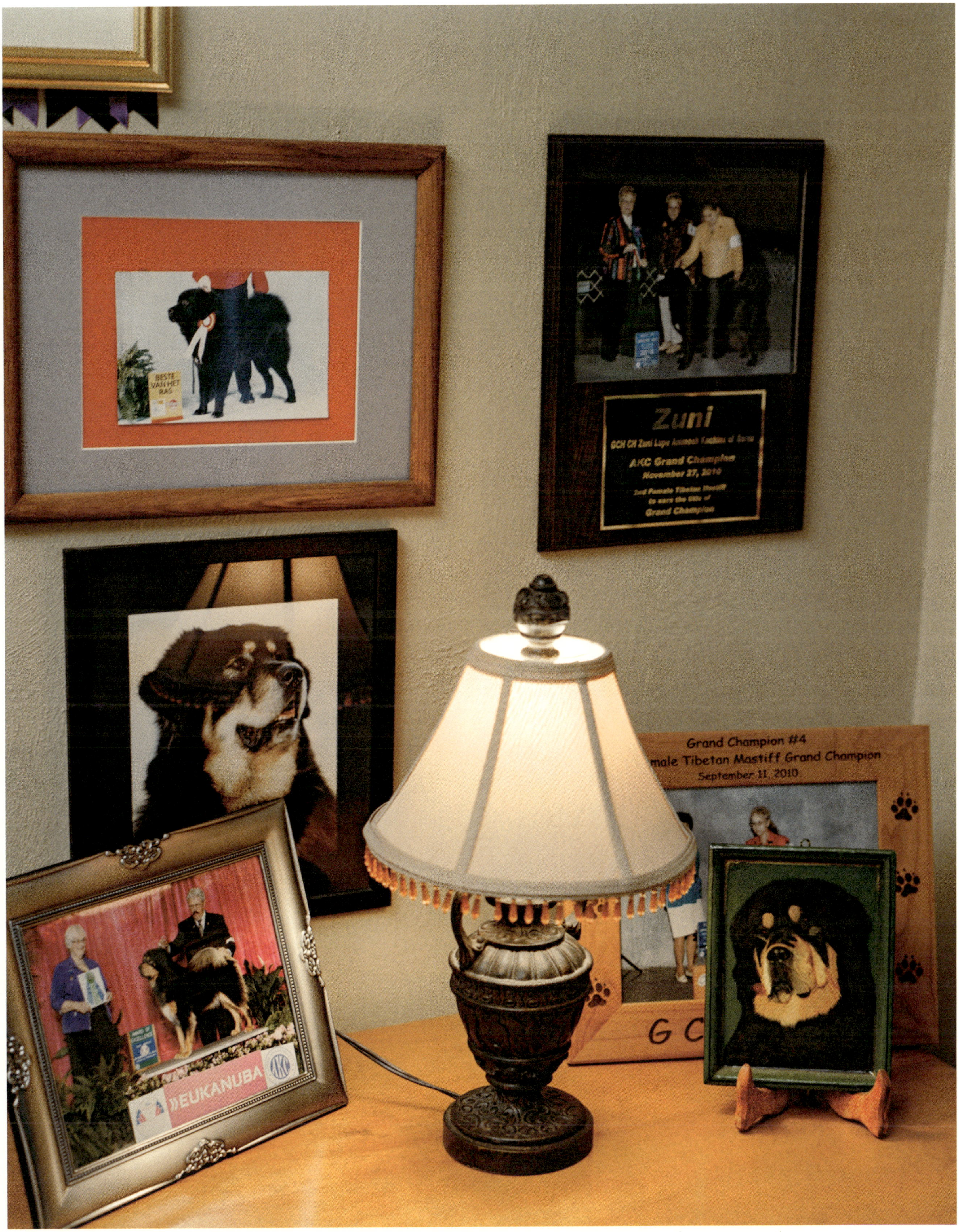
BESTE
VAN HET
RAS
Zuni
AKC Grand Champion
November 27, 2010
Grand Champion
Grand Champion #4
male Tibetan Mastiff Grand Champion
September 11, 2010
G C
EUKANUBA
AKC

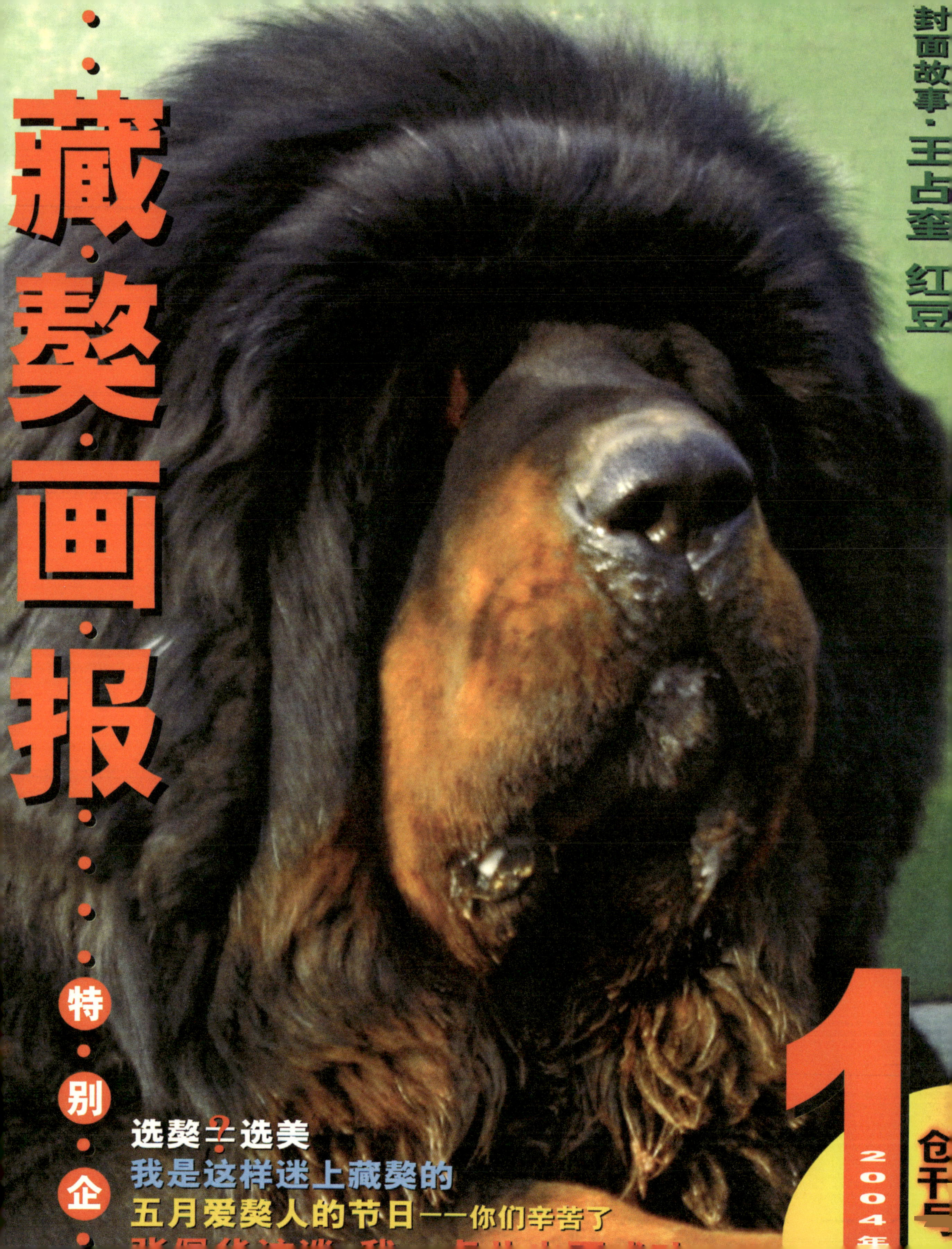
藏·獒·画·报
特·别·企
封面故事·王占奎 红豆
选獒？选美
我是这样迷上藏獒的
五月爱獒人的节日——你们辛苦了
1
2004年

我的名字叫 藏獒

文＼邵杰
图＼任刚

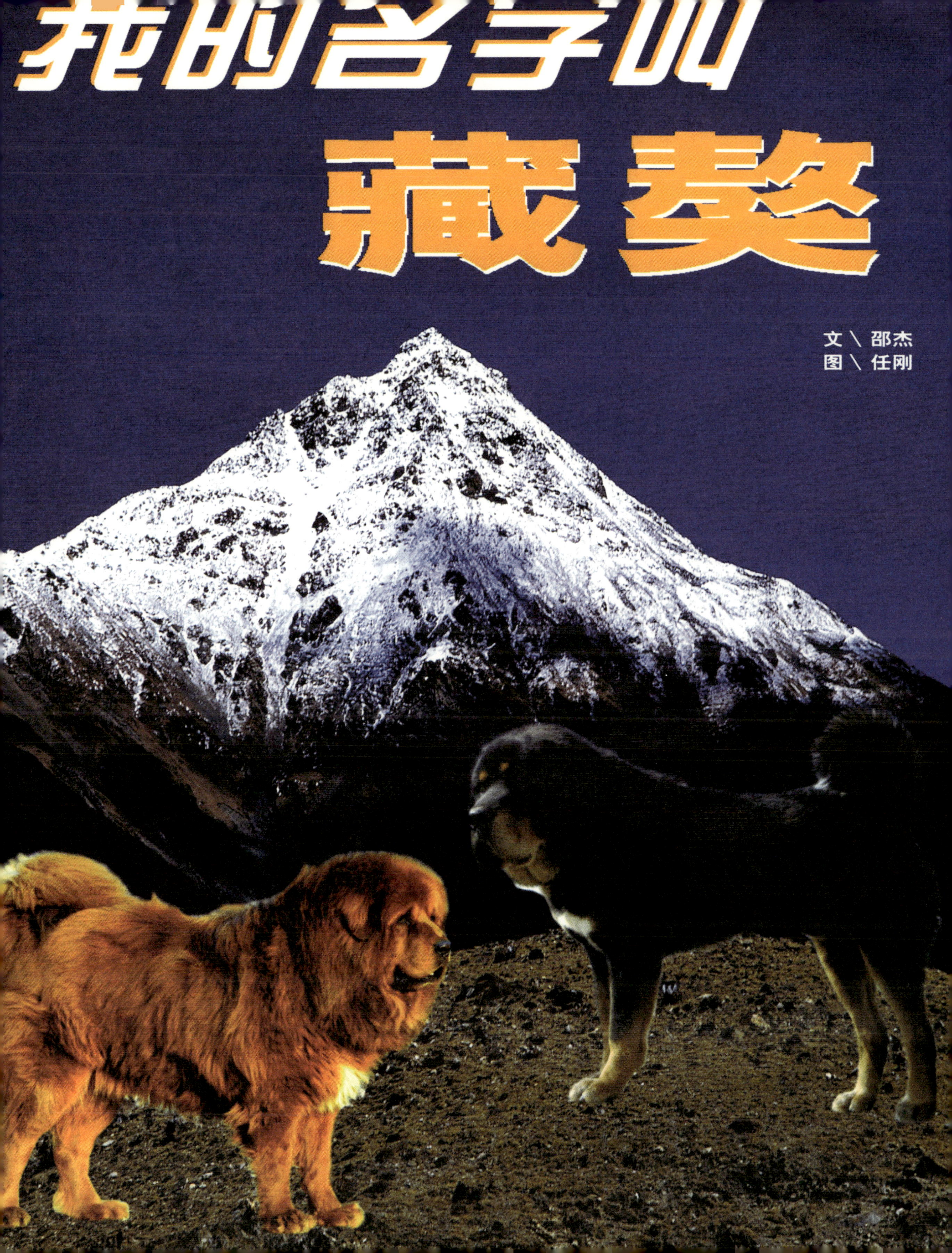

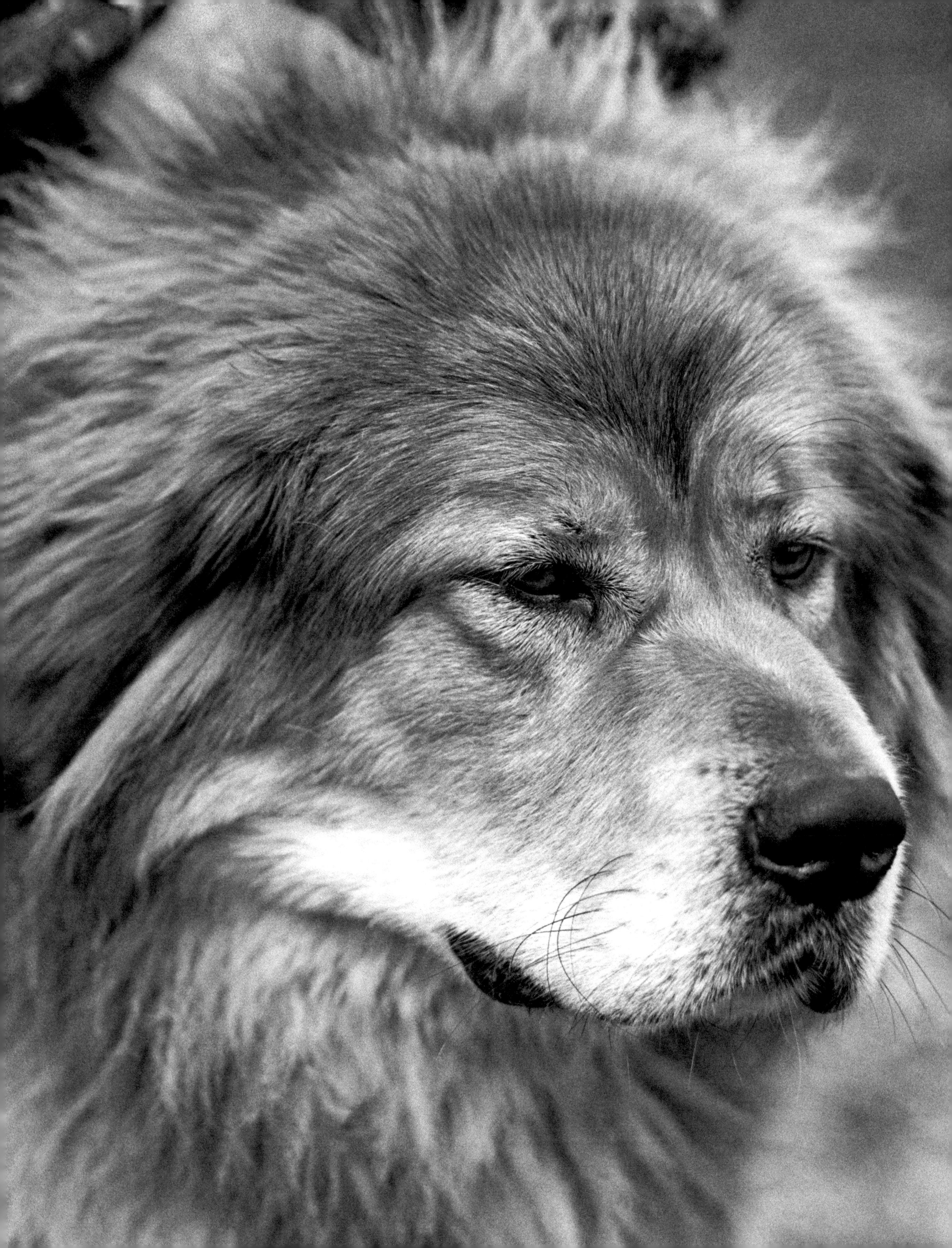

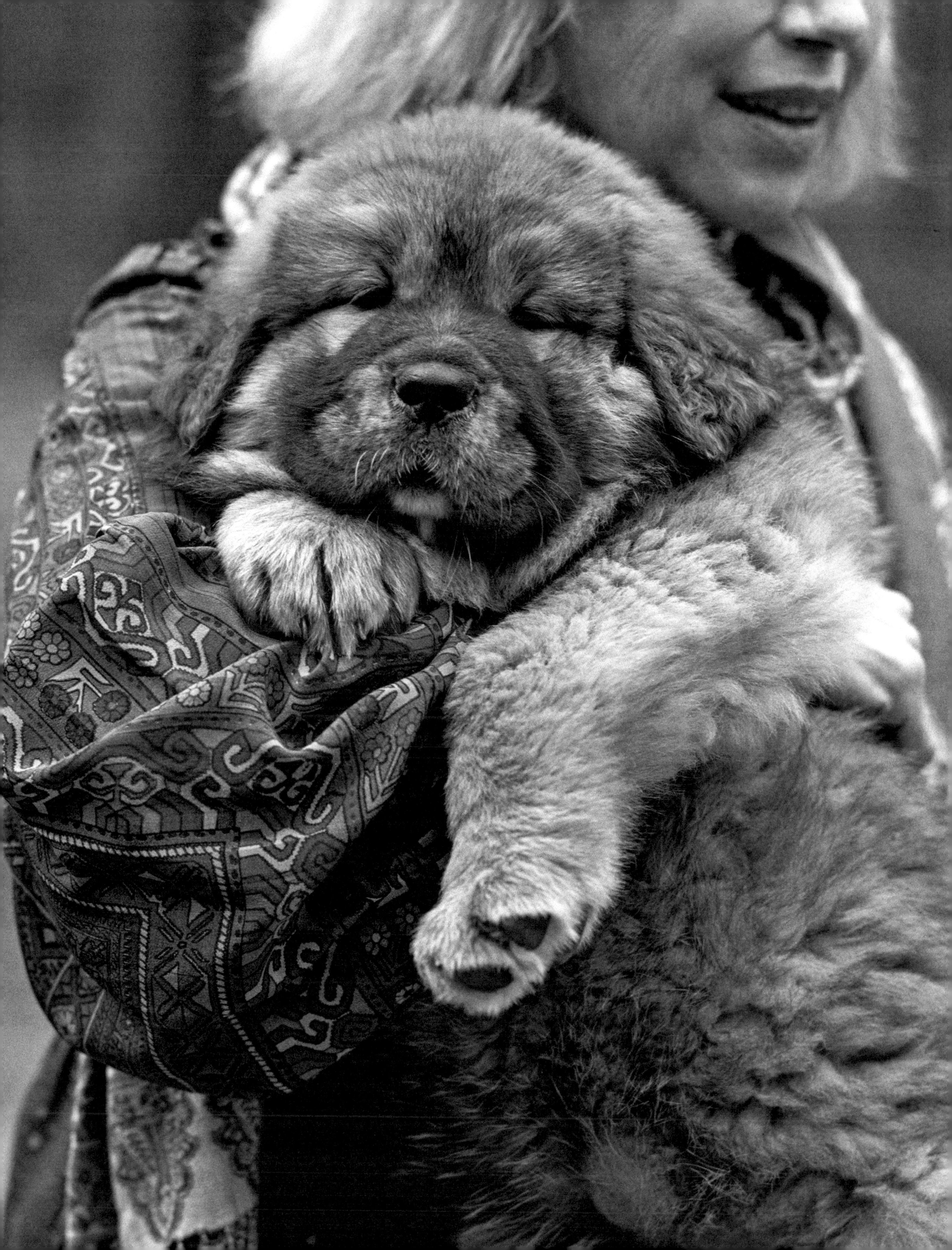

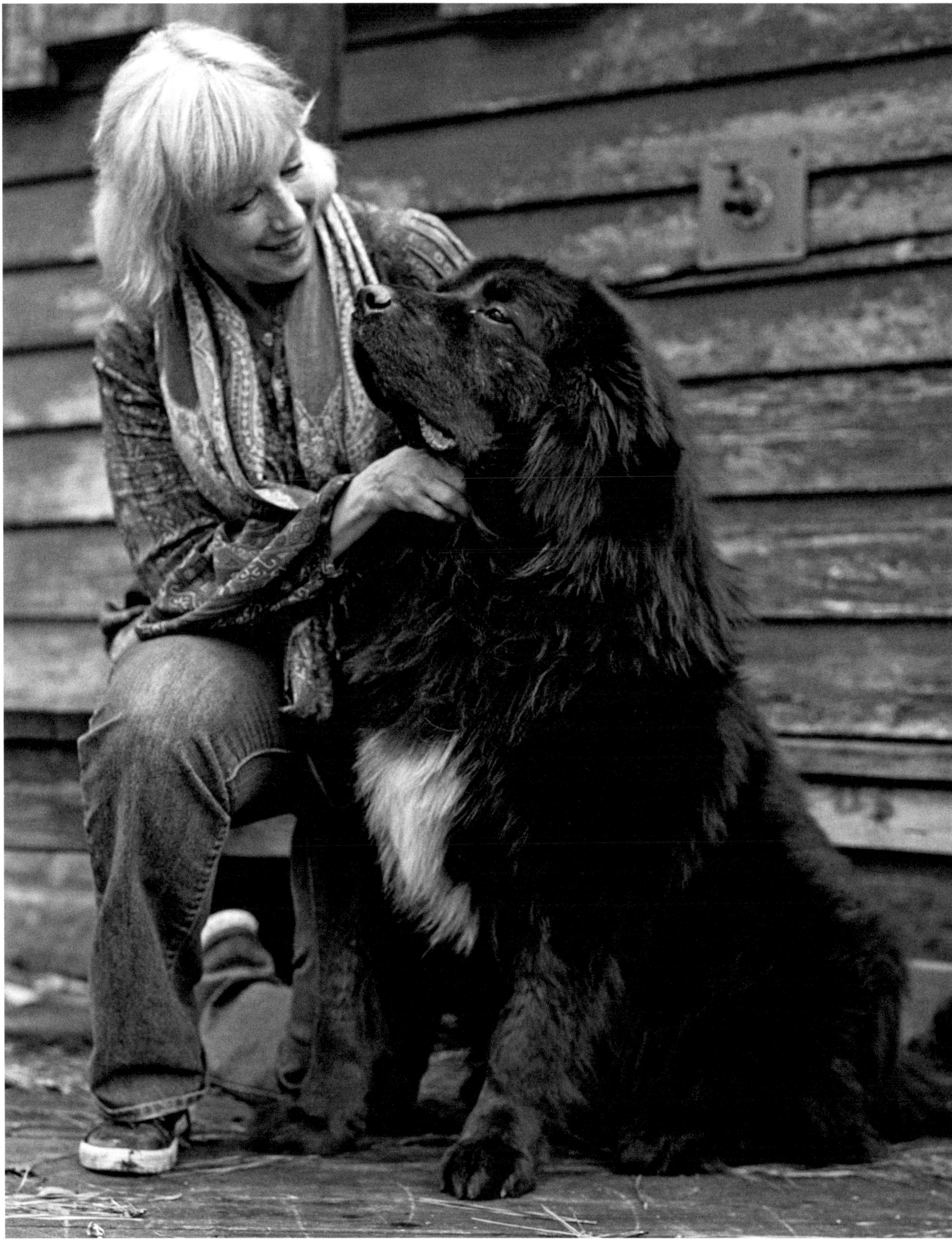

A VERY BIG LIFE WITH VERY BIG DOGS

"IT DOESN'T GET BETTER THAN THIS!"

In the middle of the woods in Chesapeake, Virginia, Susan Ochsenbein lives with 12 Tibetan mastiffs. She has been a breeder of these unique mountain-dwelling dogs for over 25 years. Through her familiarity with the Tibetan mastiff, she has become a well-known judge at dog shows for the breed. Anyone who has been lucky enough to adopt one of her puppies has shaken her hand with gratitude. Susan has traveled the world visiting the people who care for her dogs, as she considers them all her extended family. Upon entering her farm, you can hear the wild roar of a friendly lion on the wind, like the sound of a dungchen, *the ancient Tibetan horn heralding your entrance to the monastery.*

There is a special personality that goes with having a Tibetan mastiff. Most people with dogs have certain expectations of obedience and responsiveness from their pets that are not necessarily attainable with mastiffs. They're quite similar to cats. I have an old book called *The Indian Dog* that was written by a gentleman in the early 1900s, who speculated that mastiffs were actually a hybrid between wolves and tigers. They have very independent personalities and don't feel the need to be adored by everyone. Their spirit suggests, "I'm content within my own skin. I like who I am." People that choose to live with a mastiff really want a dog that's more of an equal—not just a cozy foot warmer.

Although the mastiff breed originates in Tibet, you rarely encounter them there. It's such an impoverished country—people don't have the money to support dogs unless they're really working. Mastiffs are also not as evolved as other breeds—for thousands of years, dogs have been adapting to what people want them to do. They will bring back a bird, chase a ball, or hunt prey. Tibetan mastiffs do a different kind of job—they're a guardian breed, so their temperament is to protect property. But in reality, they're just here to love.

Mastiffs need to be approached with a great deal of respect. If someone is unkind to their Tibetan mastiff, they will never have a healthy and full relationship with them. If you develop that trust, then everything else is effortless. You can't be heavy-handed with this breed. When I need to correct my dogs, I do it very gently, in an understated way. One thing I have learned over the years is that the foundation of trust is particularly important for young dogs. When you're stable and have a routine, they can trust you. That carries over to when they're older—if they feel they can't trust you, they're going to go their own way. Consistency and fairness are key. In some ways, it's the same as with a child—sometimes people try to exert too much control. At the end of the day, it's very similar to relationships elephants have with their trainers. Having worked in a zoo, I would say that elephants and mastiffs share many characteristics—both are extremely independent, nurturing, and hard to figure out. And they both remember *everything*.

When there's a breeding taking place, I've got almost 300 pounds of dogs together. My girls typically grow between 100 to 120 pounds, and the boys are typically 130 to 150 pounds. So, it's a lot of dog to handle if they decide they don't want to do what I want them to. I've bred puppies that I've shipped to Poland, Czech Republic, Netherlands, or Finland. When I go to these places to visit, even if it's been 3 or 4 years since the last time they saw me, the dogs I raised always come racing over to me.

One of my great dogs was Vashti, whose name came from the Bible. Vashti was the Queen of Persia—when her husband called her to come to dinner, she refused. Since Tibetan mastiffs don't come when they are called, that seemed like the right name for her. Today, I have Janoo, which in Punjabi means "someone who is full of light and love." He has a daughter who we call Jaan, which is the feminine version of that same name. She looks just like her father and has a sweet and bright spirit. There's Khumba, named after a region in Tibet, and Gazer, named for his beautiful expression. And finally, Elaina, who we call Leila—because she's sort of a little gal, built like a coffee table.

In the Buddhist religion, we believe we are all part of one energy—that's why we don't kill anything. The underlying principle is that we are put here to learn—and as we learn, we evolve towards a higher form of life. Some Buddhists say that because Tibetan mastiffs are so smart, they must have been Buddhist monks that didn't behave very well in a past life and were reborn as these great dogs to get taught a lesson or two before evolving again to a higher level.

When I think about the dogs who have lived with me and been in my family, the ones that made the biggest impression were those that did something that marked time for me: the first mastiff that ran away, the first dog to have a litter here in Virginia. Those are the memories that I consider part of my education of working with this breed. When I think about how much I love them individually, and the dynamics within the pack, I become very sentimental. Just like in any group, whether it's in an office or a family, you've always got a joker, a complainer. All of the different personalities and individual characteristics are wonderful.

I hope I spoil my dogs and give them a life they wouldn't have anywhere else. It won't be long now until breeding season—it's almost time to start all over again.

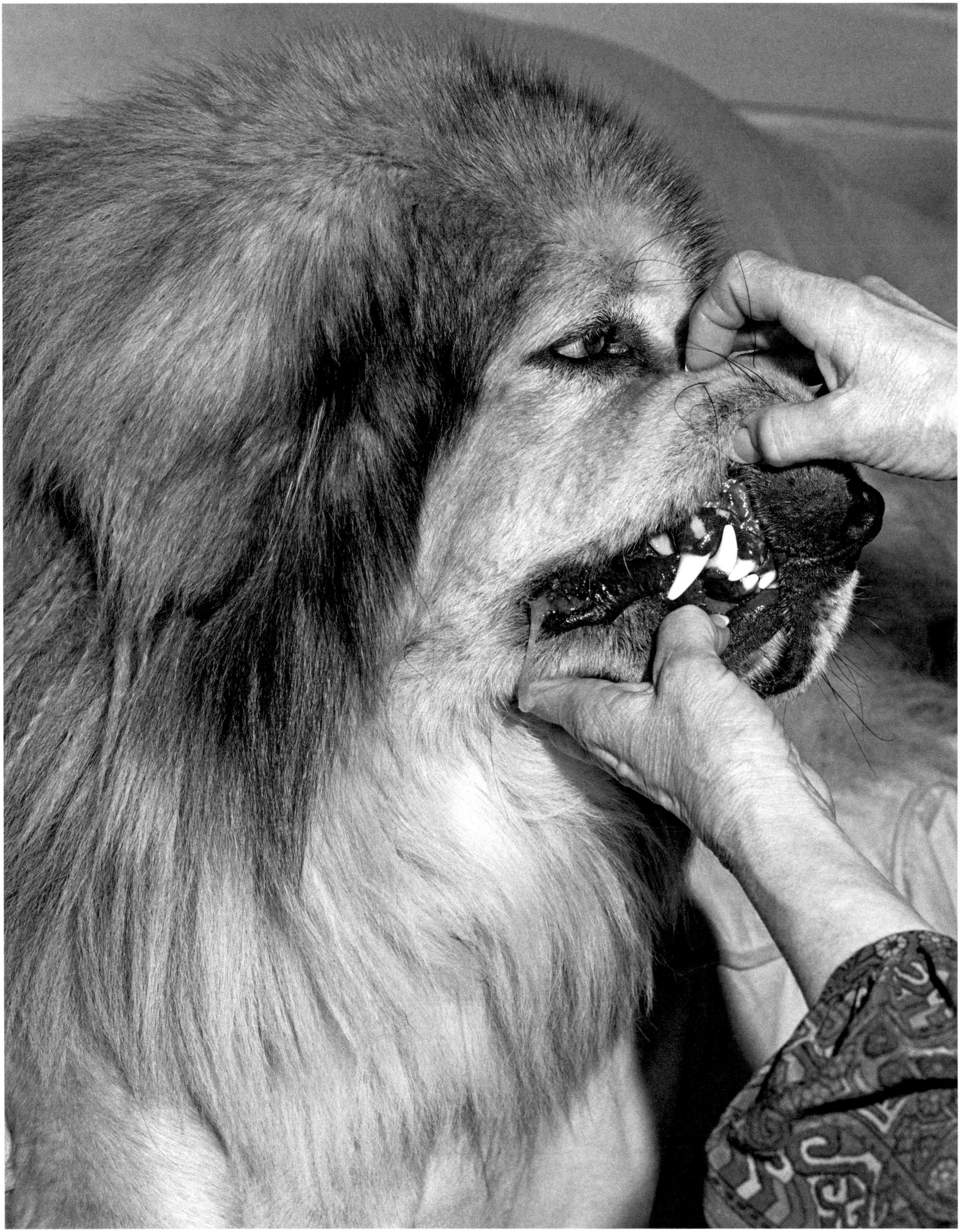

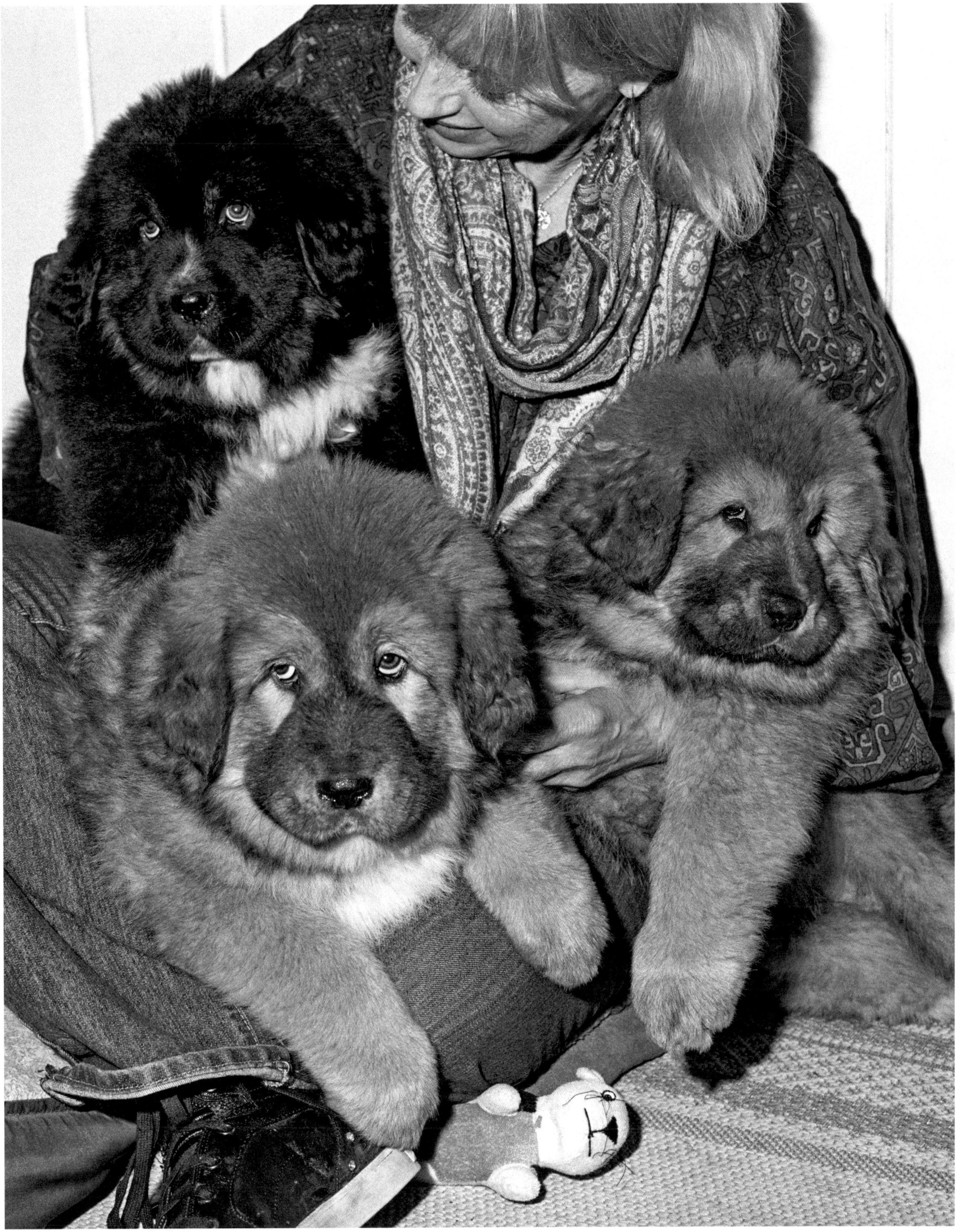

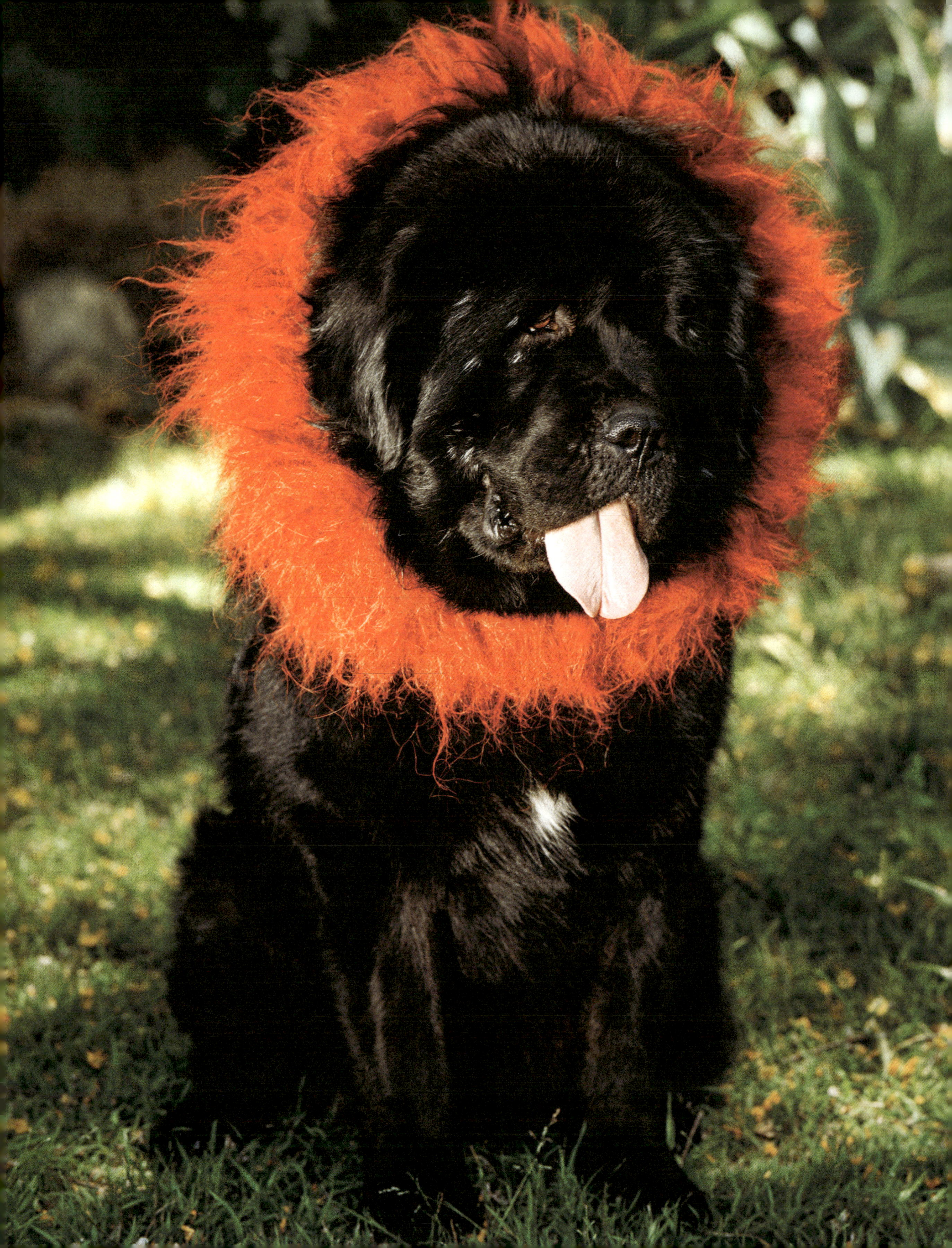

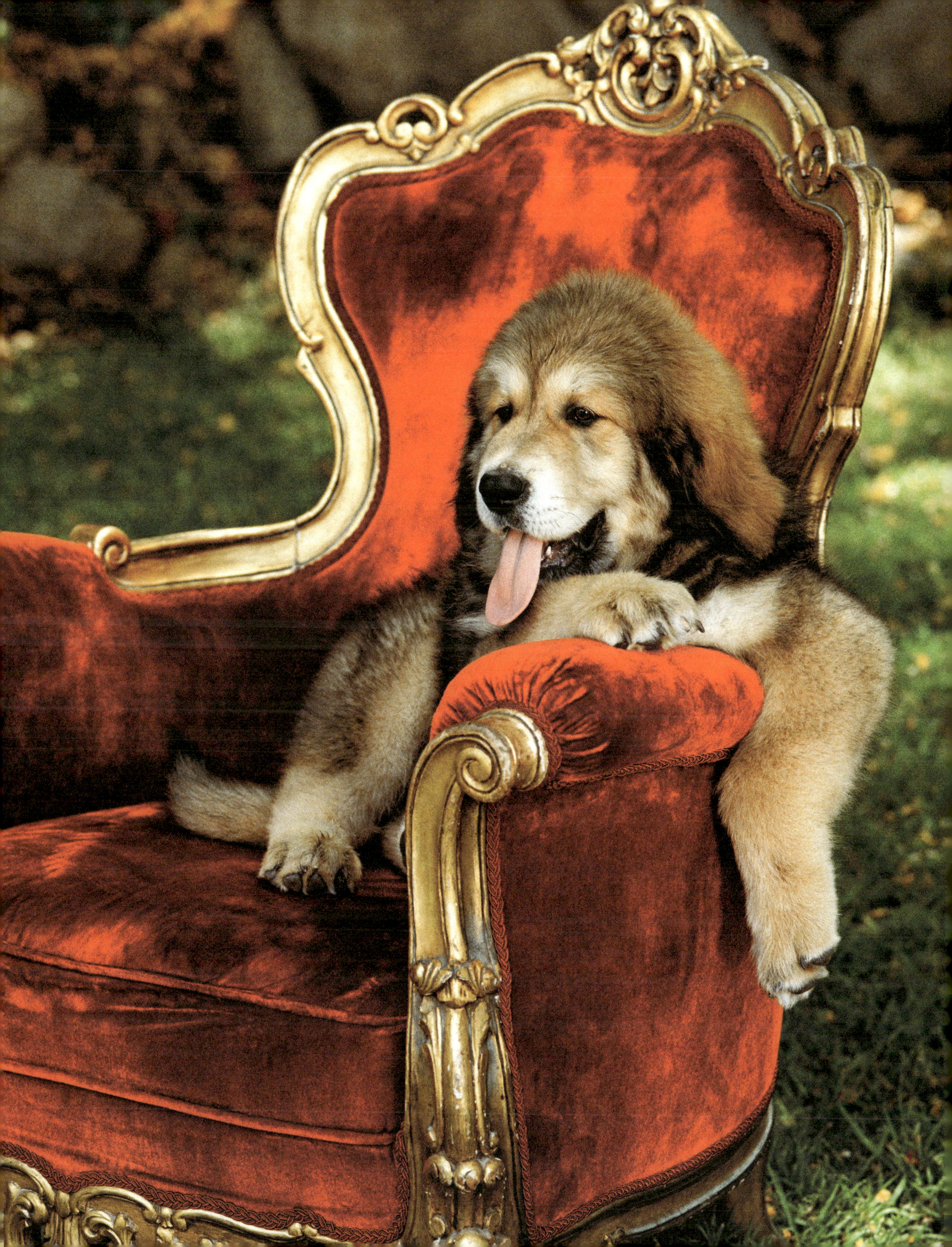

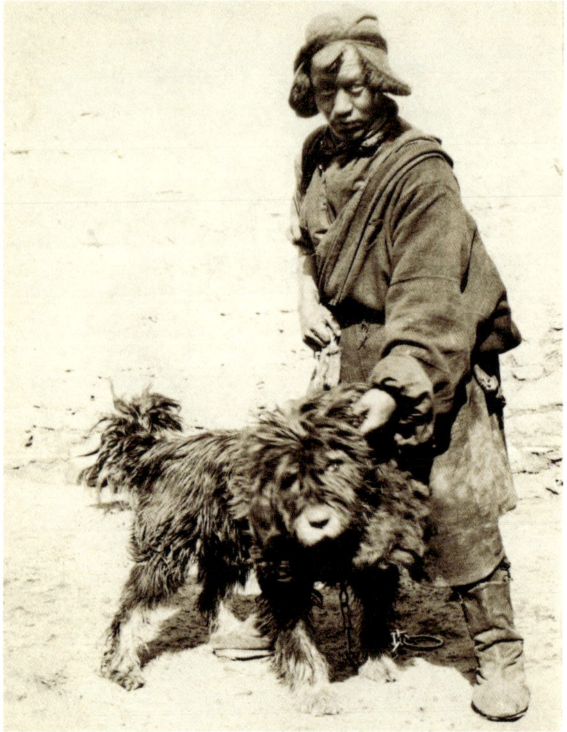

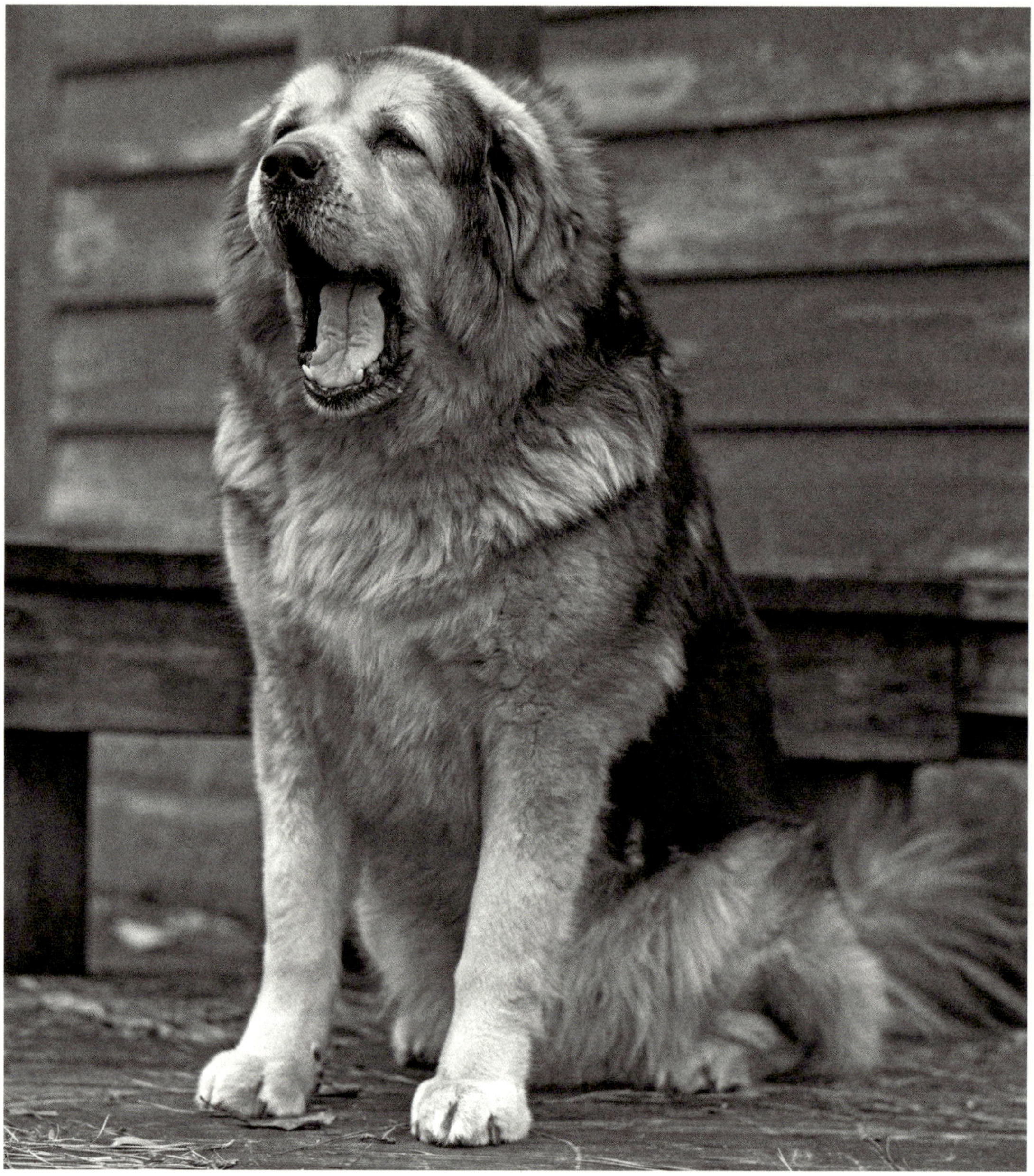

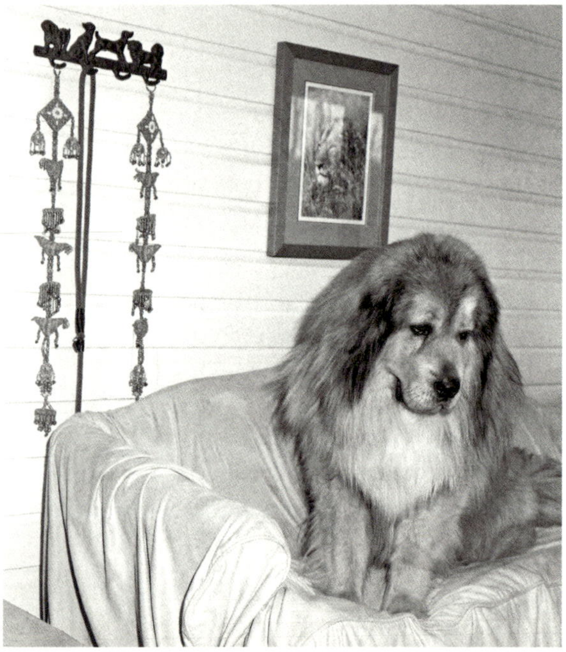

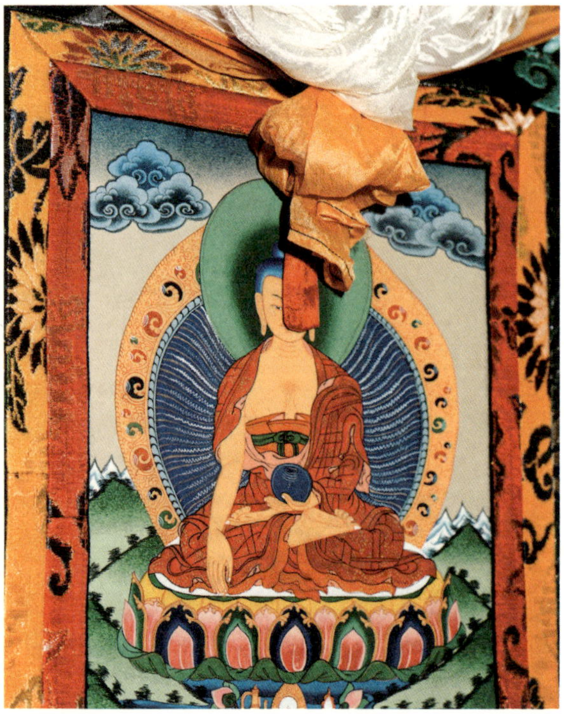

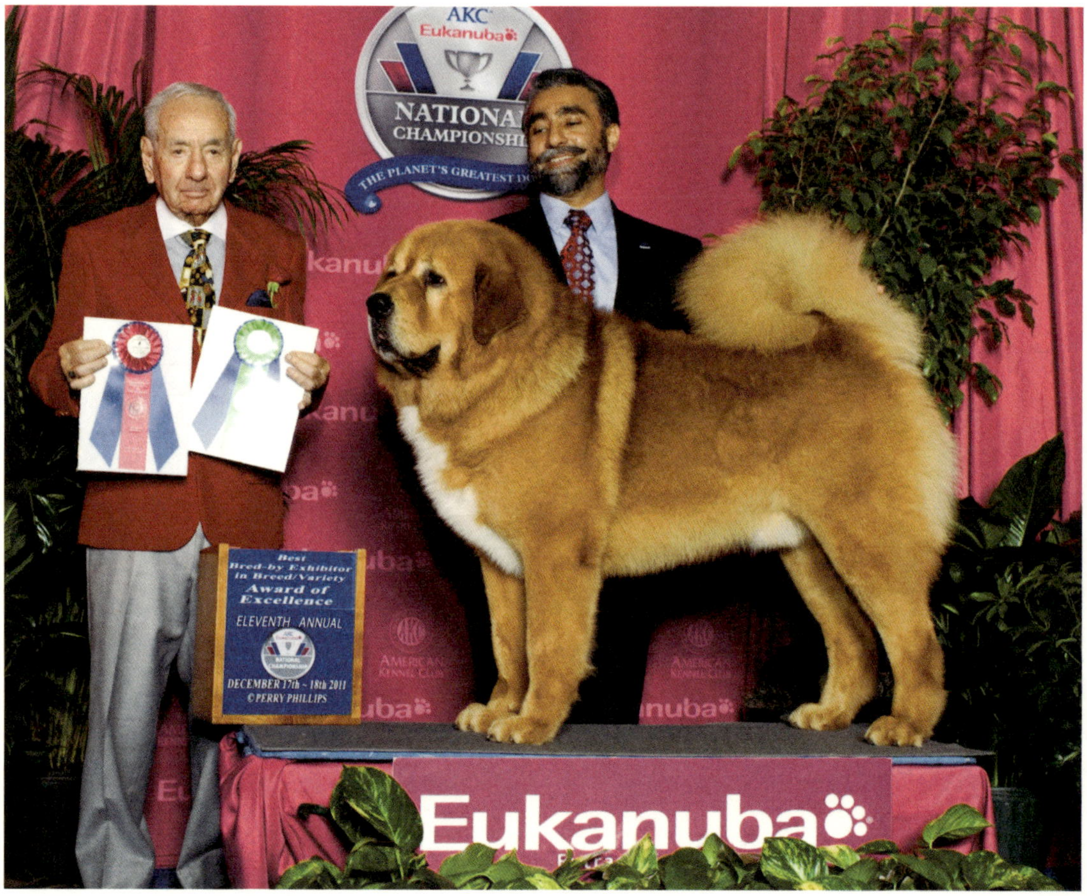
AKC
Eukanuba
Best
Bred-by Exhibitor
in Breed/Variety
Award of
Excellence
ELEVENTH ANNUAL
DECEMBER 17th - 18th 2011
©PERRY PHILLIPS
Eukanuba

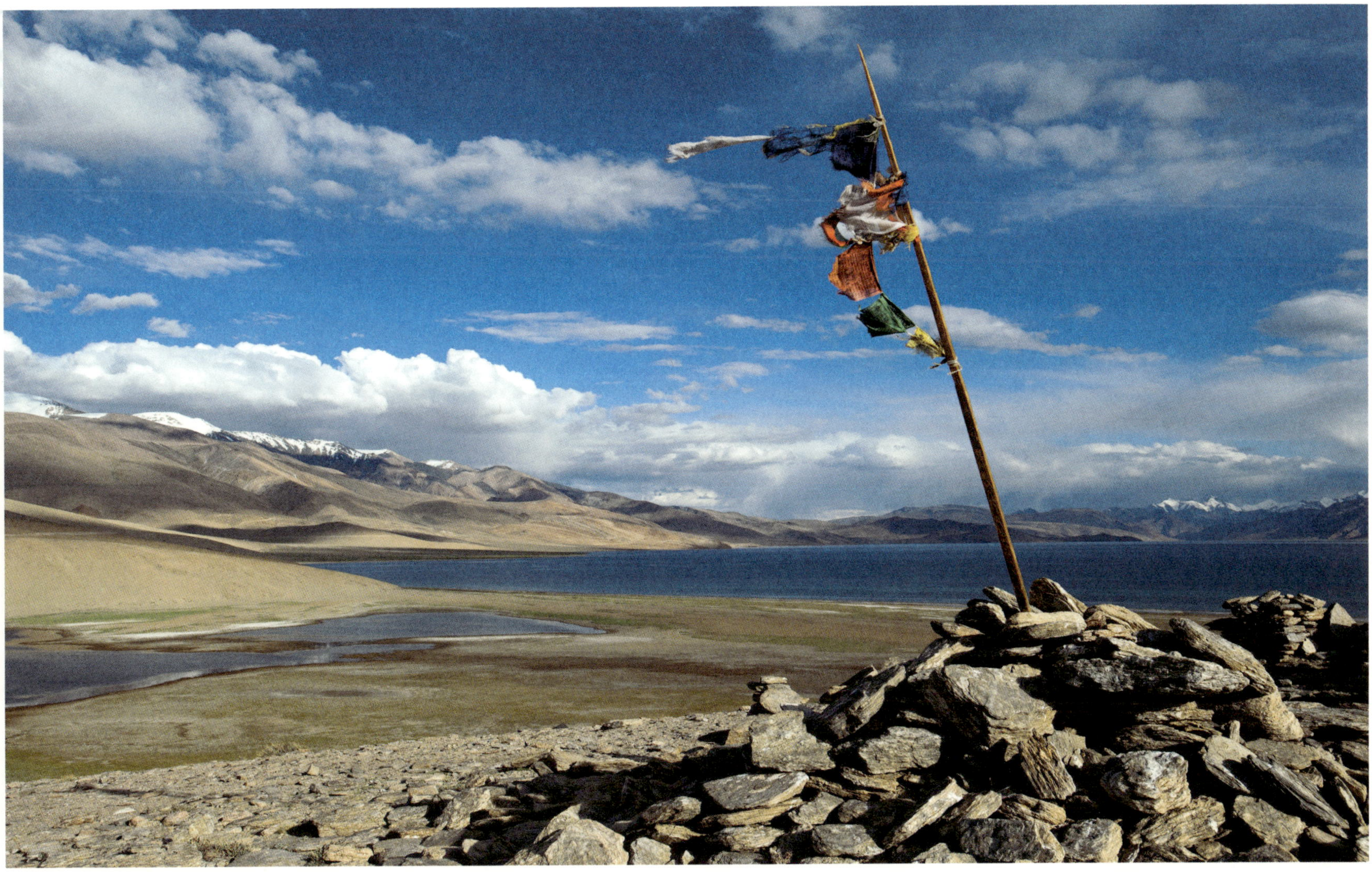

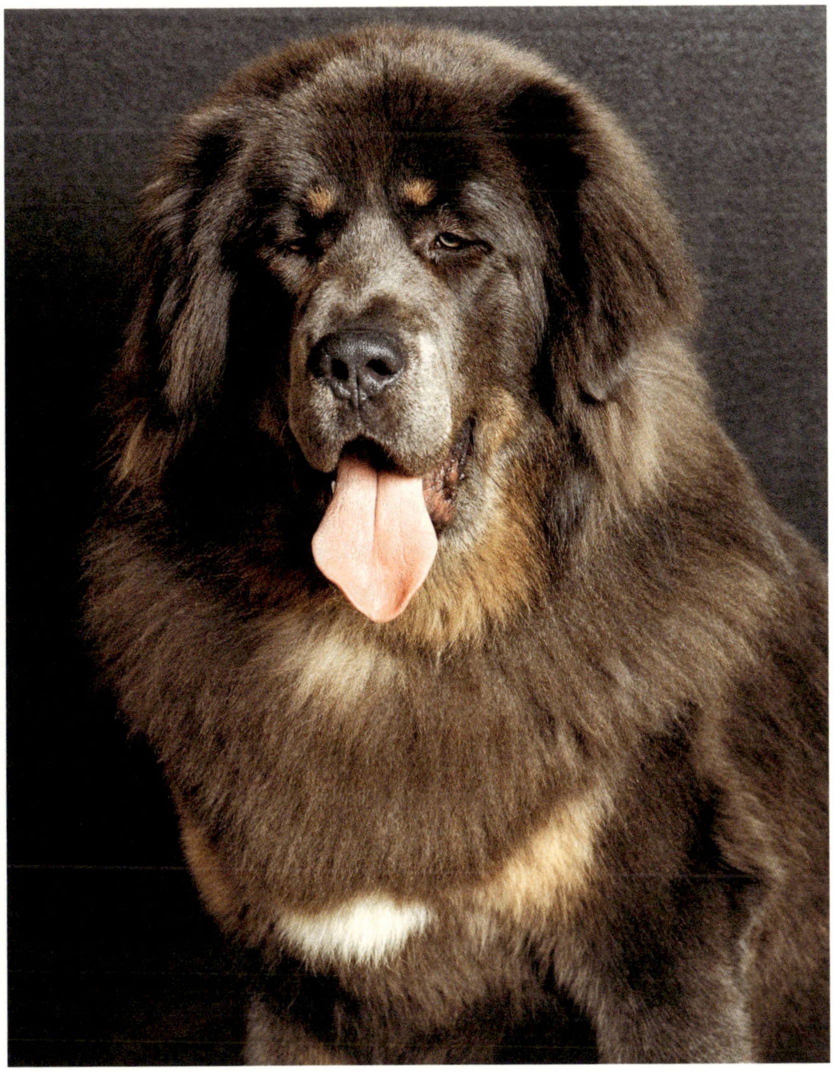

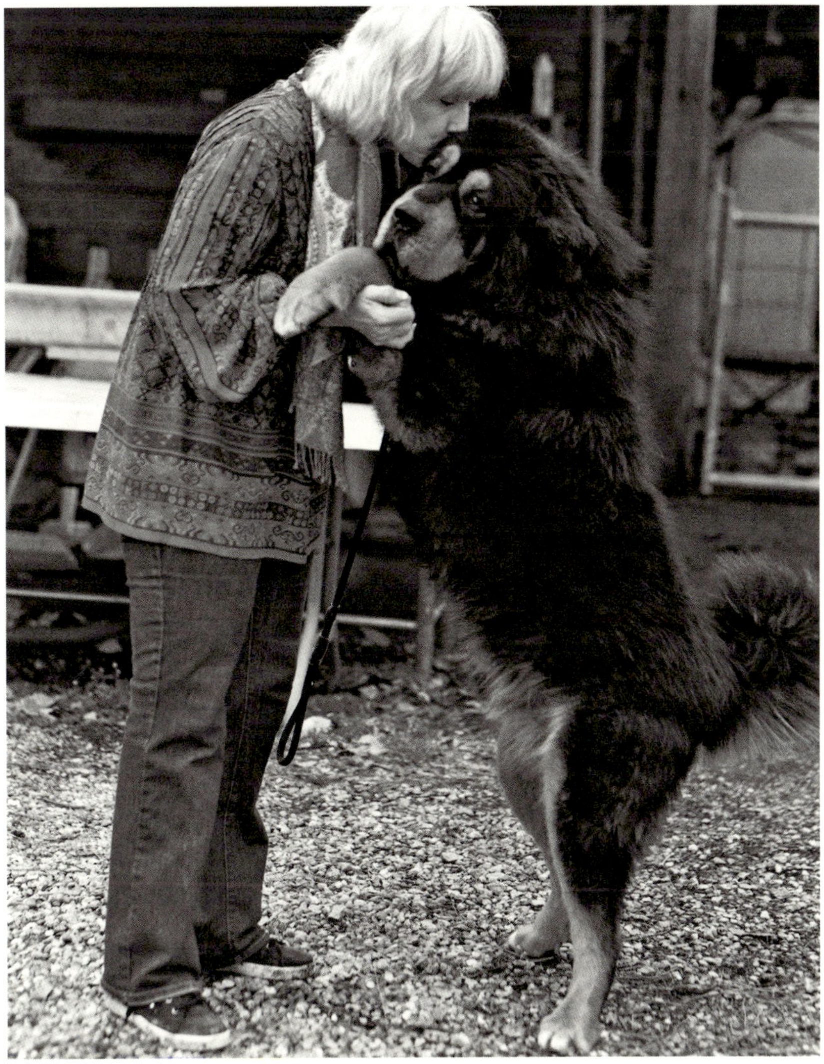

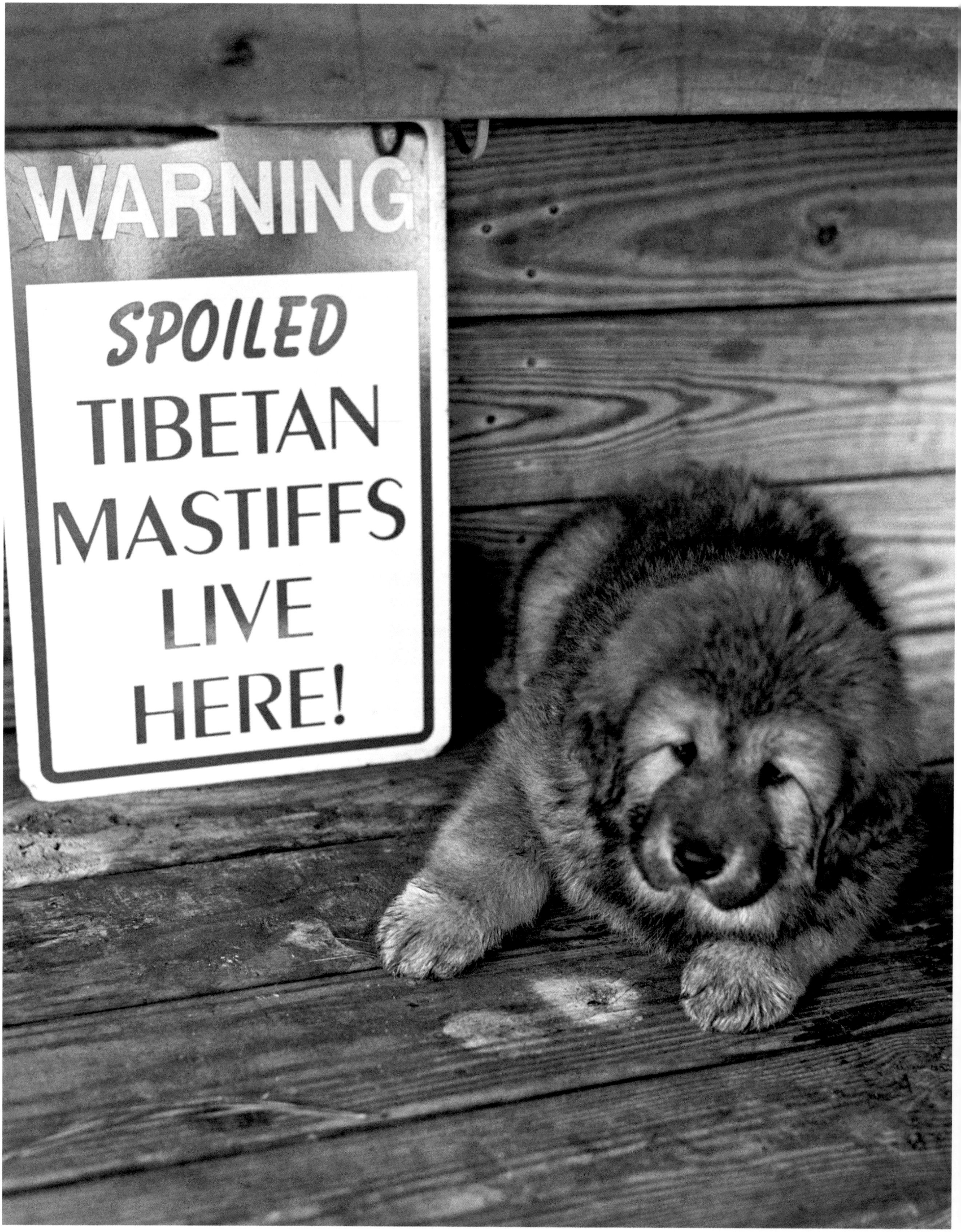
WARNING
SPOILED
TIBETAN
MASTIFFS
LIVE
HERE!

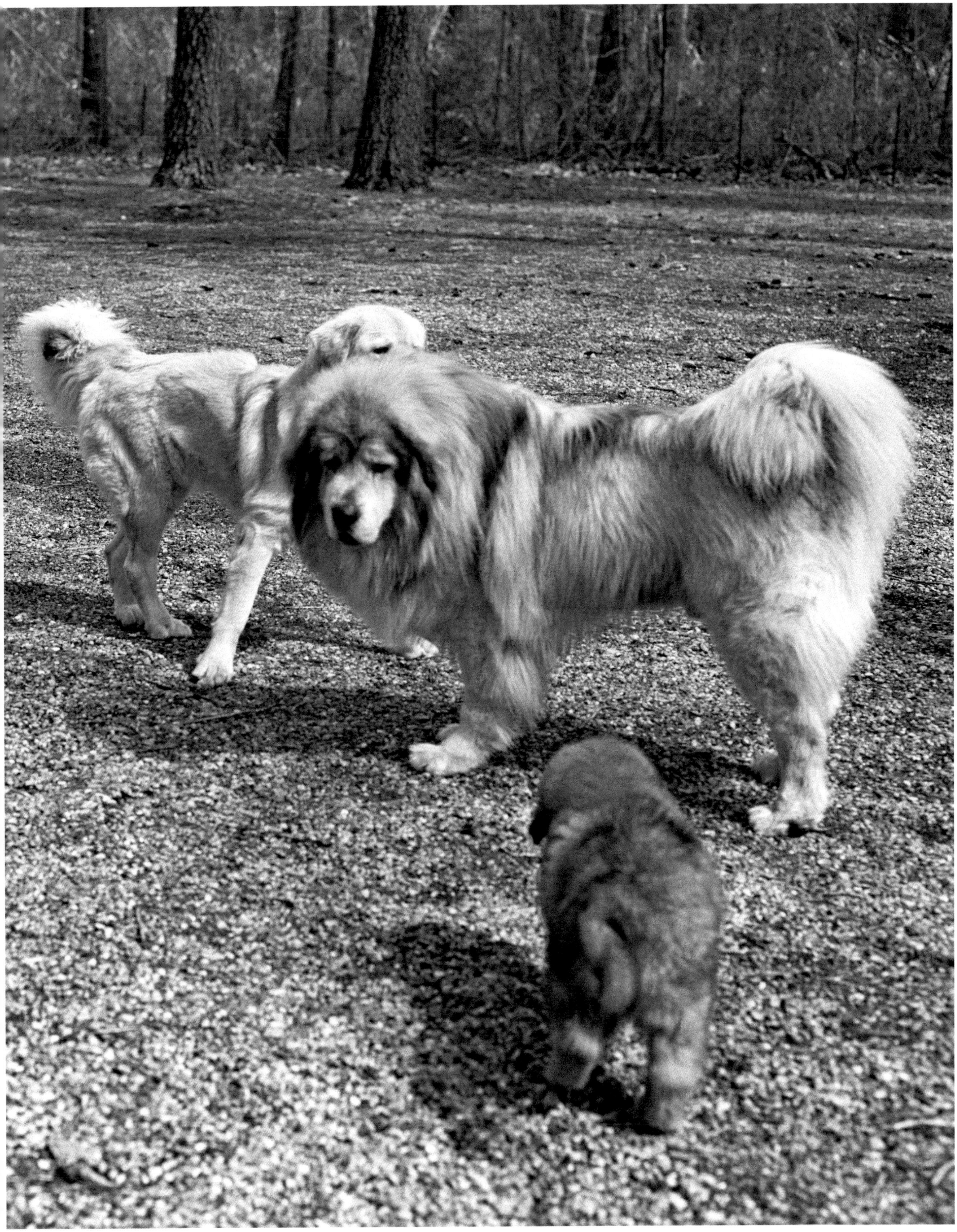

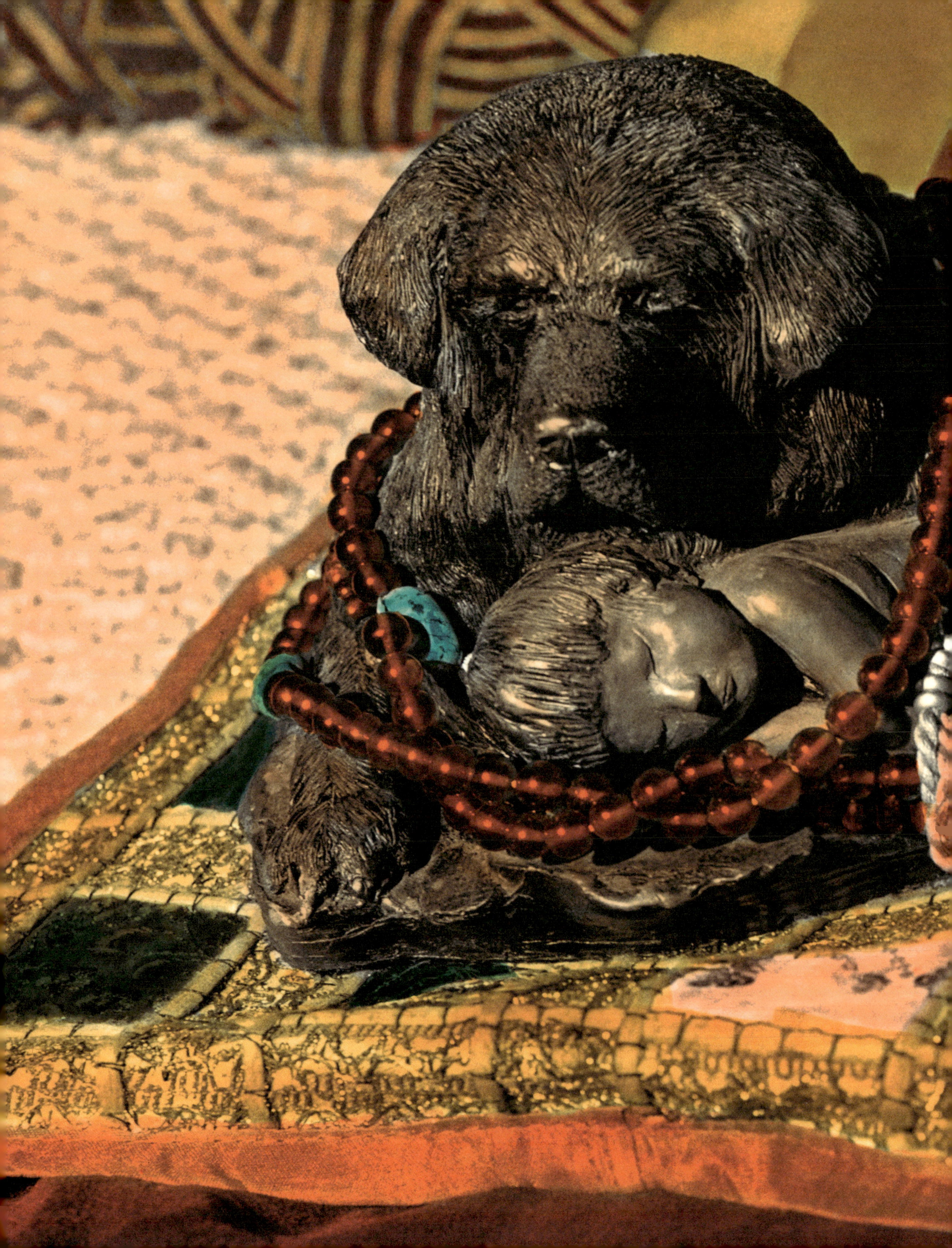

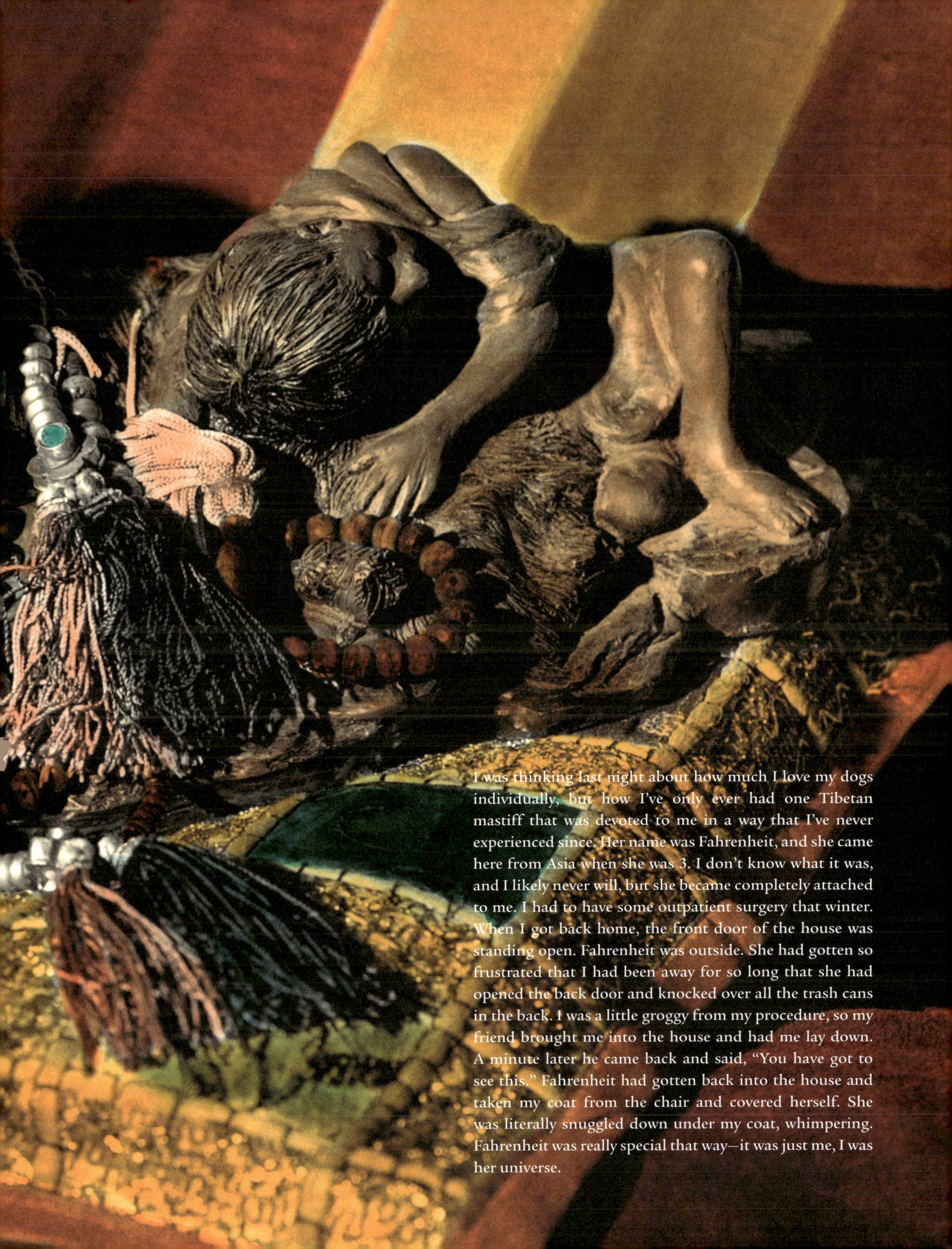

I was thinking last night about how much I love my dogs individually, but how I've only ever had one Tibetan mastiff that was devoted to me in a way that I've never experienced since. Her name was Fahrenheit, and she came here from Asia when she was 3. I don't know what it was, and I likely never will, but she became completely attached to me. I had to have some outpatient surgery that winter. When I got back home, the front door of the house was standing open. Fahrenheit was outside. She had gotten so frustrated that I had been away for so long that she had opened the back door and knocked over all the trash cans in the back. I was a little groggy from my procedure, so my friend brought me into the house and had me lay down. A minute later he came back and said, "You have got to see this." Fahrenheit had gotten back into the house and taken my coat from the chair and covered herself. She was literally snuggled down under my coat, whimpering. Fahrenheit was really special that way—it was just me, I was her universe.

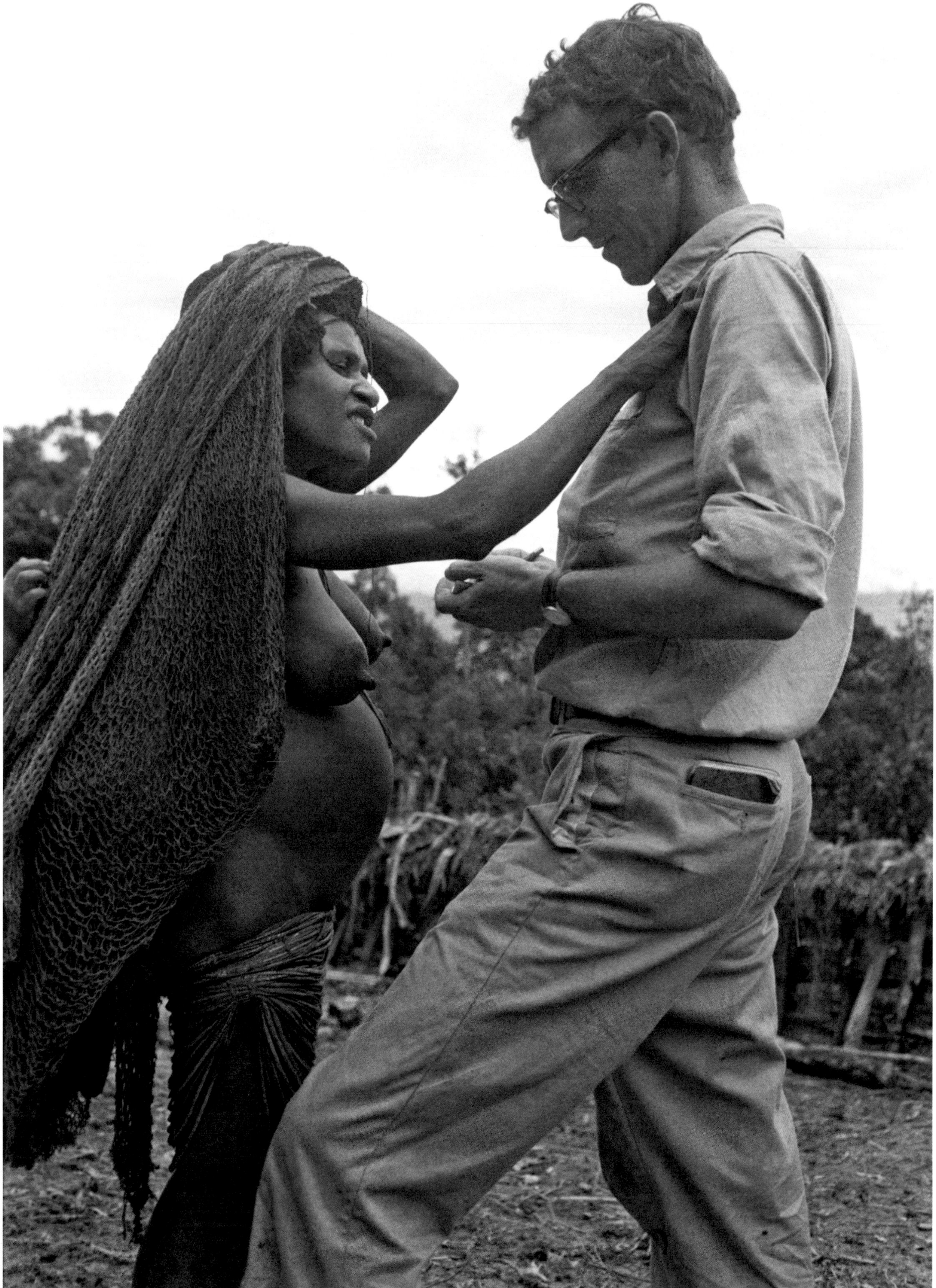

NO SNOWFLAKE EVER FALLS IN THE WRONG PLACE

THE LITERARY QUEST OF PETER MATTHIESSEN

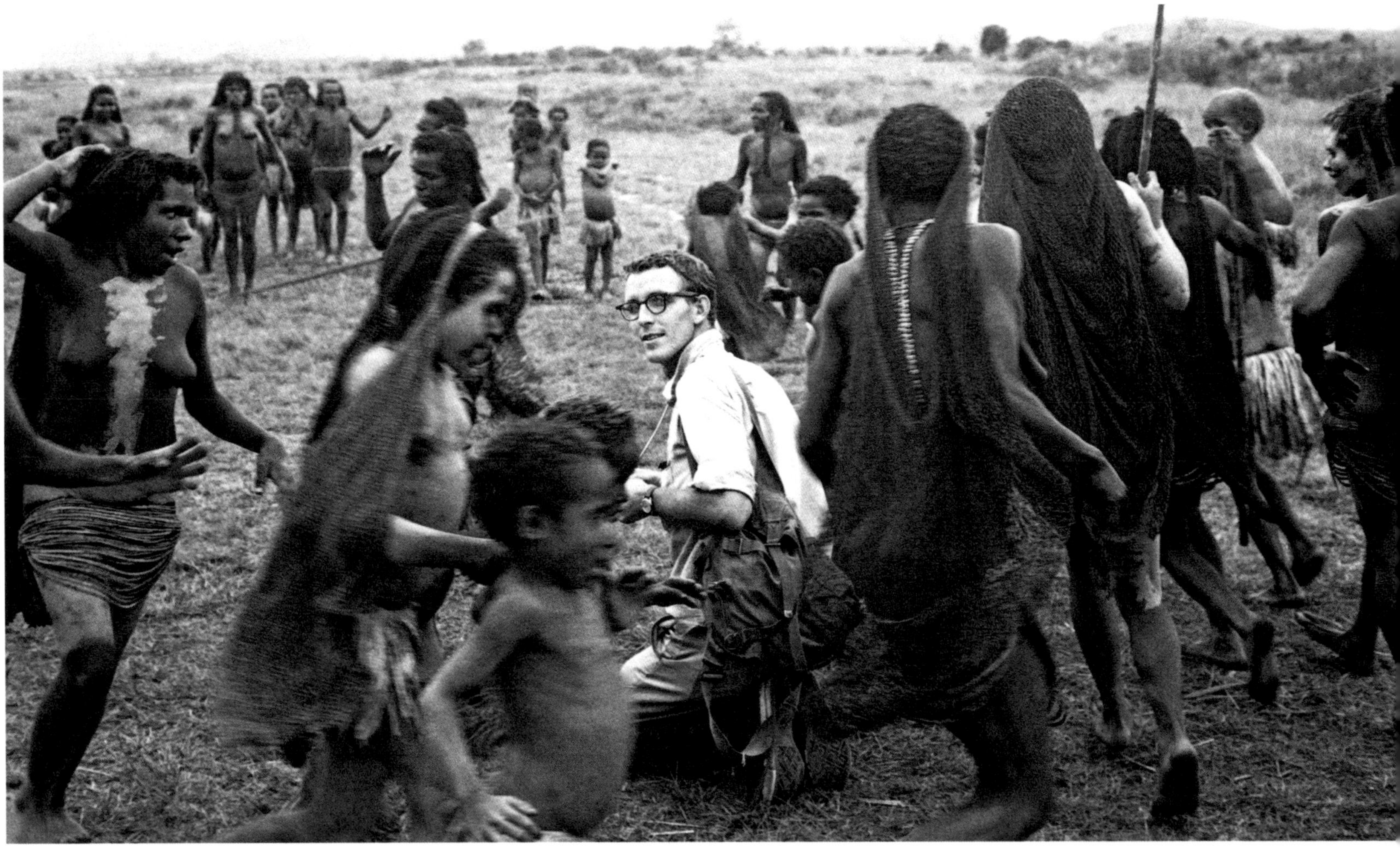

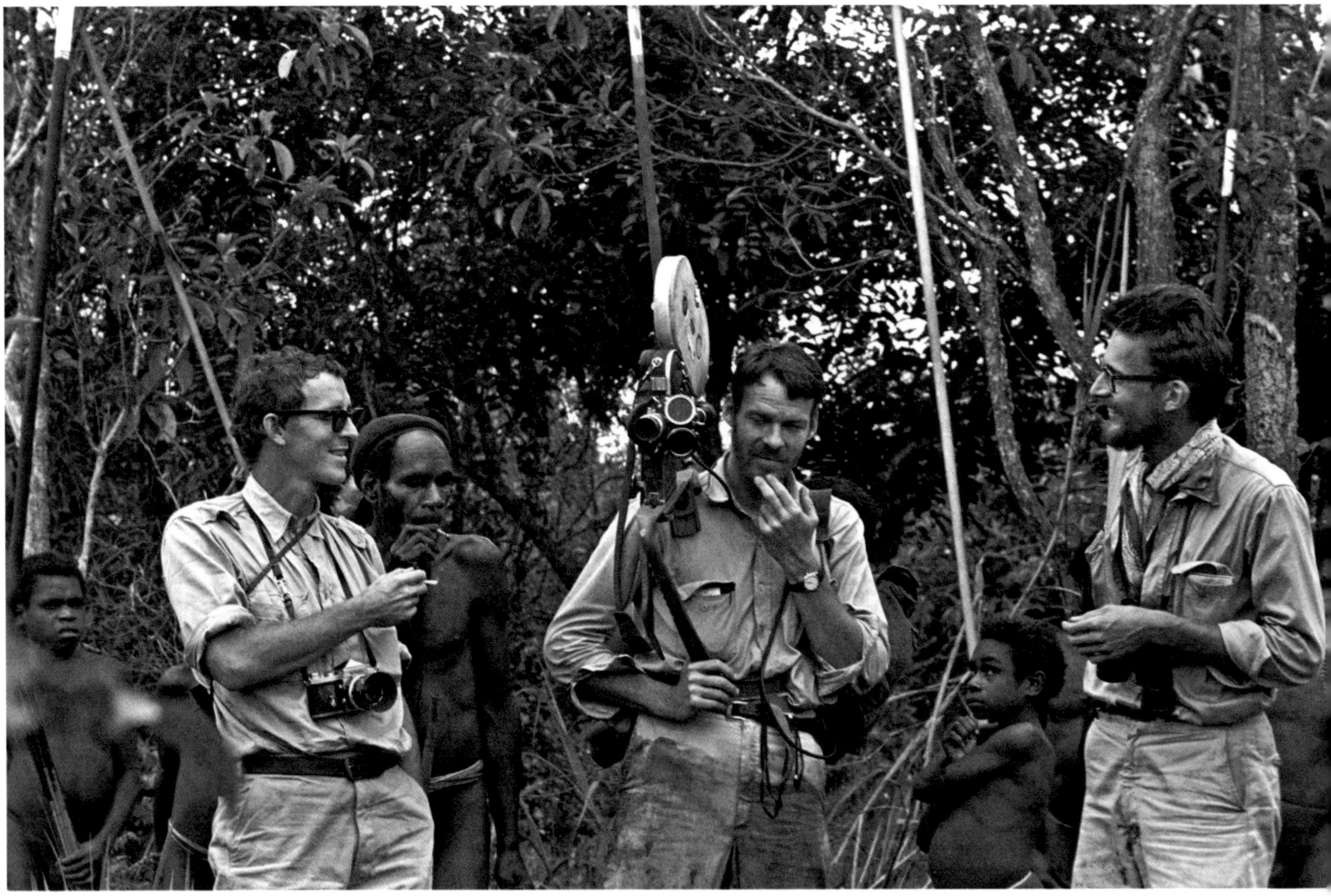

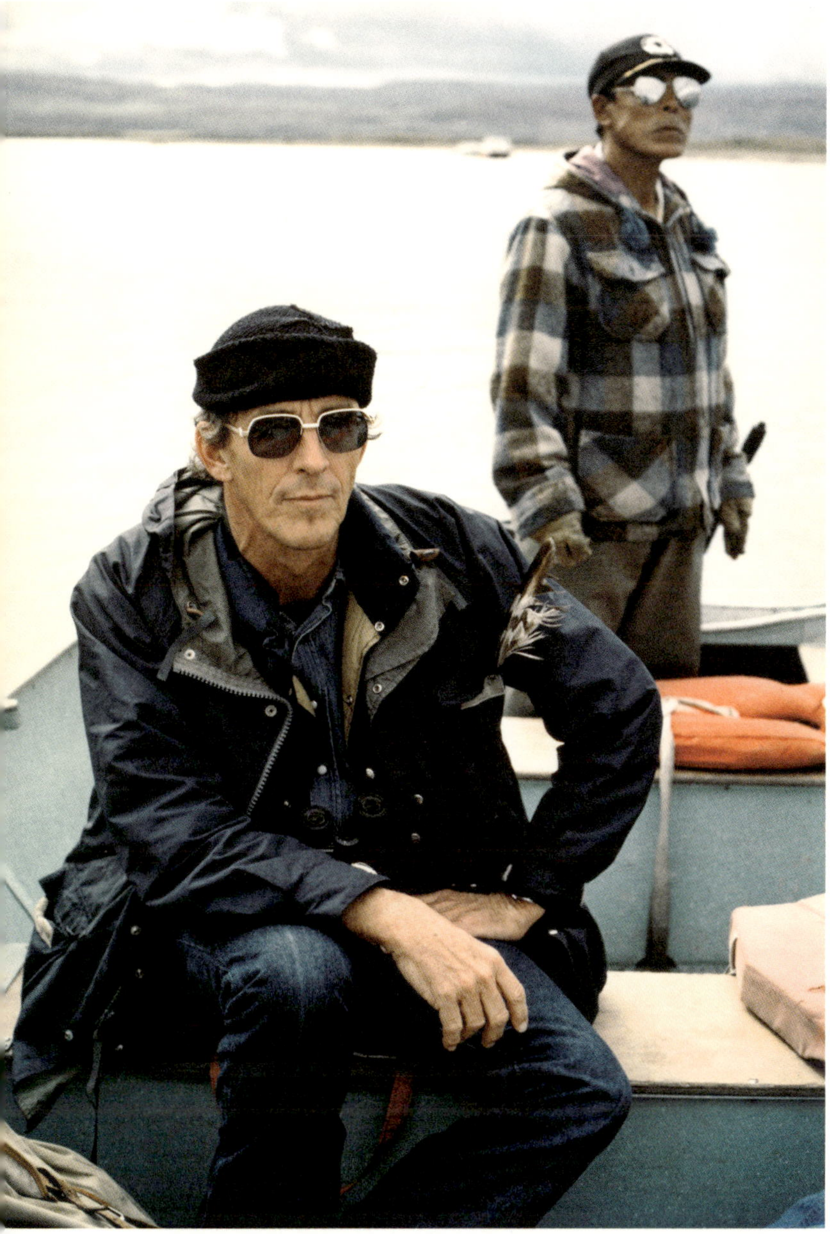

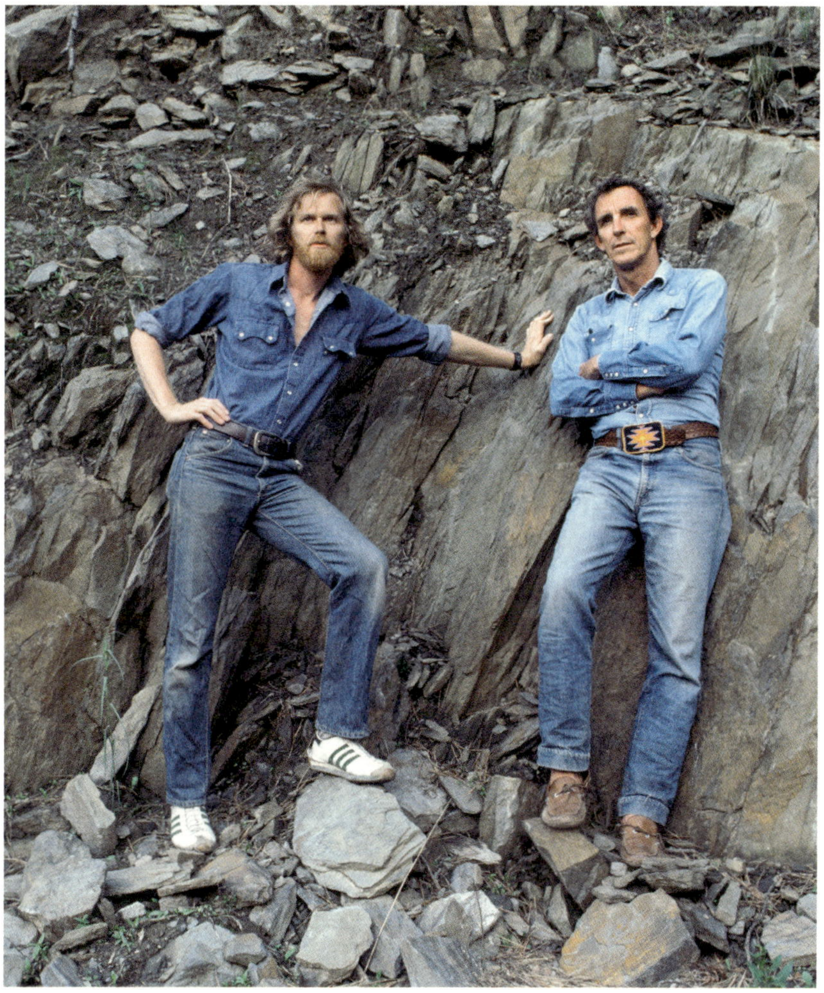

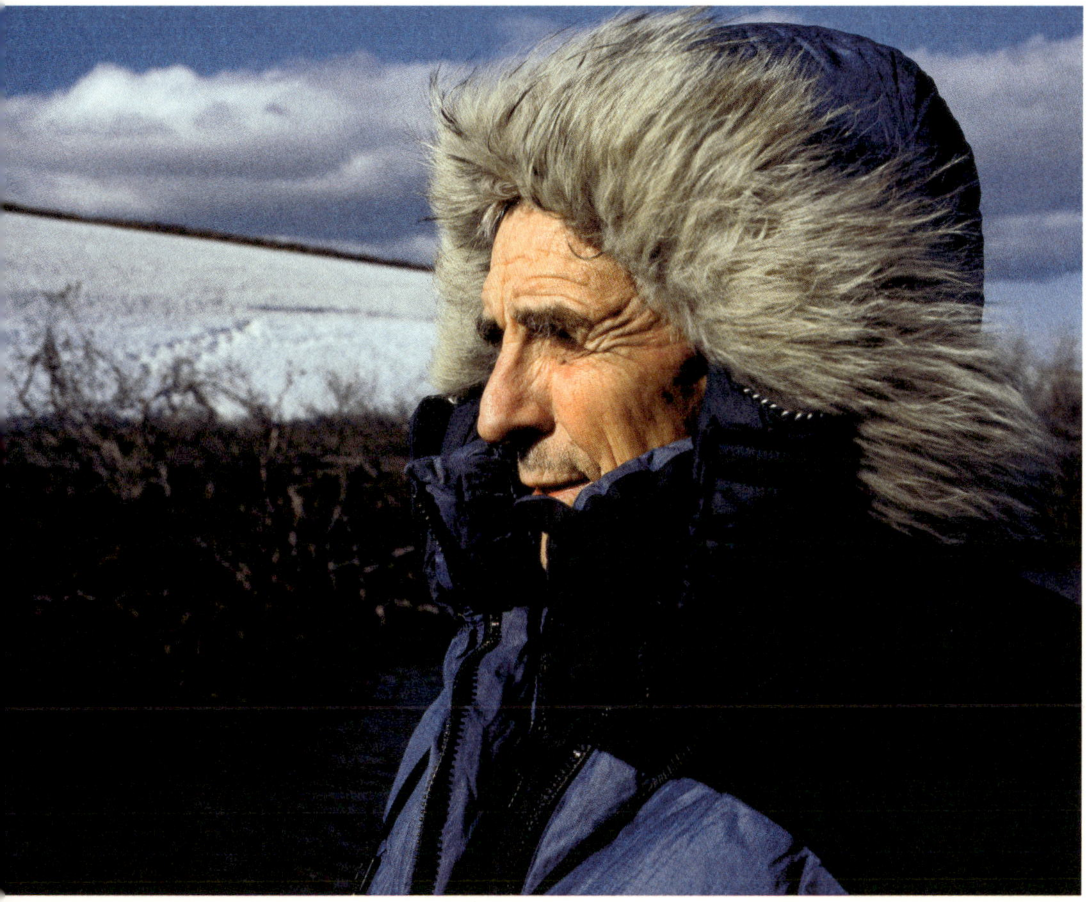

Previous page: Ekapuwe, a native of the Kurelu tribe in New Guinea, with Matthiessen, during a 1961 Harvard-Peabody expedition to the island—Matthiessen's experiences there would form the basis for his 1962 book *Under the Mountain Wall*.

Opposite page–top: Women running around Peter Matthiessen during the Harvard-Peabody expedition; *Bottom*: Matthiessen, Ekali, Wali, Robert Gardner, and Karl Heider waiting to film during the Harvard-Peabody expedition.

This page–clockwise from top left: Matthiessen on the Balhurst Inlet in Canada's Nunavut Territory, 1980; Matthiessen with his friend and fellow naturalist Hans Teensma, founder of *Orion* magazine, in Oglala, SD 1979; Matthiessen in the Arctic Wildlife Refuge, 2002.

"I like to hear and smell the countryside, the land my characters inhabit. I don't want these characters to step off the page—I want them to step out of the landscape."

— PETER MATTHIESSEN

Peter Matthiessen achieved what few writers have by winning the National Book Award in both fiction and nonfiction. His literary legacy continues to inspire future generations to look deeply into the natural world and give consideration to how they will treat our planet. From where did this talent, passion, and conviction arise?

A dyed-in-the-wool New Englander, Peter Matthiessen began life as a child of privilege, with all of the social and professional expectations which that implies. His father imparted a love and respect for the outdoors that would become one of the defining concerns of his son's life and writing. In so doing, he unwittingly set him on a less conventional path. Peter Matthiessen decided at a young age to dedicate his life to his dual and parallel passions: the craft of writing and the study of the natural world.

Peter Matthiessen spent his boyhood between New York City and Connecticut. After completing his degree at Yale, he was recruited by the CIA, who were monitoring the "activities" of expat Americans suspected of Communist sympathizing. Matthiessen took the job, for it gave him the opportunity and means to live abroad and support his writing. As a cover for his CIA work, Matthiessen started the literary magazine *The Paris Review*—which endures to this day as one of the most esteemed publications dedicated to the writer's craft. But disillusionment quickly set in, as Matthiessen realized that his personal beliefs were much more aligned with those he was to be informing on than they were with the CIA. He severed ties with the organization and focused instead on fighting for environmental conservation and justice for those in need.

Travel factored heavily in Matthiessen's creative life, with treks to Asia, South America, Australia, Canada, Africa, and far-flung regions of the United States providing the research for his literary explorations. His fiction depicts the disparate worlds of rain-forest missionaries (*At Play in the Fields of the Lord*, 1965), turtle fishermen of the Caribbean (*Far Tortuga,* 1965), homestead farmers in the Everglades (*Shadow Country*, 2008), and most recently, Zen devotees on retreat at the site of the Auschwitz death camp (*In Paradise*, 2014). His novels are characterized by a vivid, lyrical language that transports the reader to the very places he describes—it stands to reason that his early short story "Travlin' Man" and the novel *At Play in the Fields of the Lord* were adapted into films by Luis Bunuel and Hector Babenco, respectively.

In his nonfiction work, Matthiessen addressed myriad environmental and social concerns he believed deserved awareness and action. A zealous defender of the landscape and wildlife, he became a passionate voice for conservation in the face of growing environmental threats with books like *Wildlife in America* (1959) and *African Silences* (1991). He took a keen interest in the customs and struggles of traditional cultures in books like *Under the Mountain Wall* (1962), and was an early champion of the American Indian movement in his widely lauded volumes *In the Spirit of Crazy Horse* (1983) and *Indian Country* (1984). Throughout his life's work, Matthiessen constantly challenged Western society to look inward, reconsider its values, and eschew destructive material pursuits in favor of a life of conscience.

The spiritual dimension of Matthiessen's critique is unmistakable and deeply personal. Whether through his literature or his Zen Buddhist practice—a devotion he pursued from the mid-1970s—Peter Matthiessen lived his life as a perpetual quest for understanding of the world and his place in it. He joined an illustrious pantheon of American writers who made their homes on the east end of Long Island, including his close friends William Styron, James Salter, John Irving, and Kurt Vonnegut. What set Matthiessen apart was his ability to make us aware of the beat of a bird's wing, the regal presence of a mountain, and the daring knowledge to be found in the remotest corners of the world.

—KELLY FAGAN

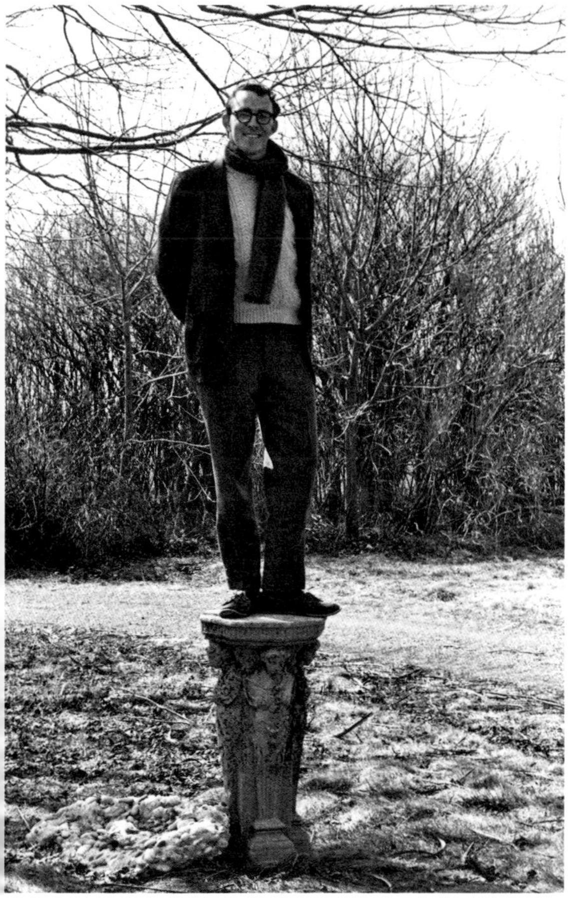

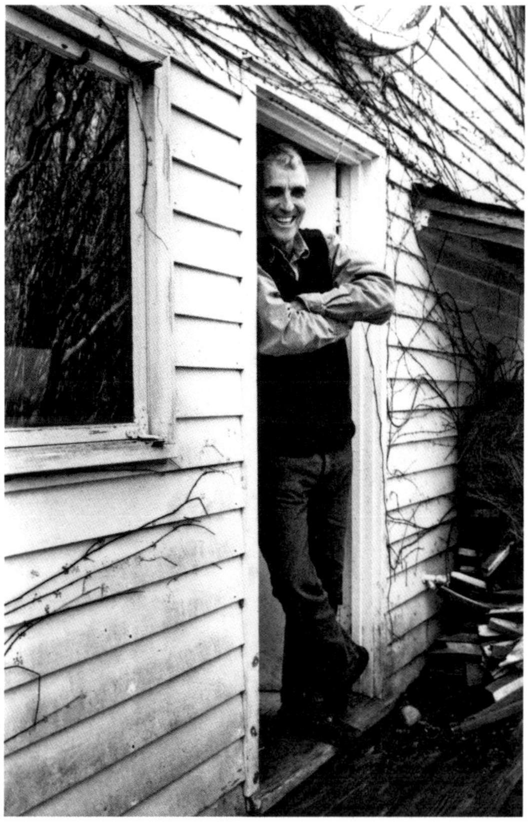

Clockwise from top left: Sagaponack, New York c. 1960s; Matthiessen photographed in the doorway of his Sagaponack writing studio in 1995 by his friend and neighbor, Jill Krementz; A second photograph by Krementz from 1975 showing Matthiessen with George Plimpton at the latter's annual July 4th celebration in Amagansett. A friend of Matthiessen's since childhood, Plimpton served as the first editor of *The Paris Review*.

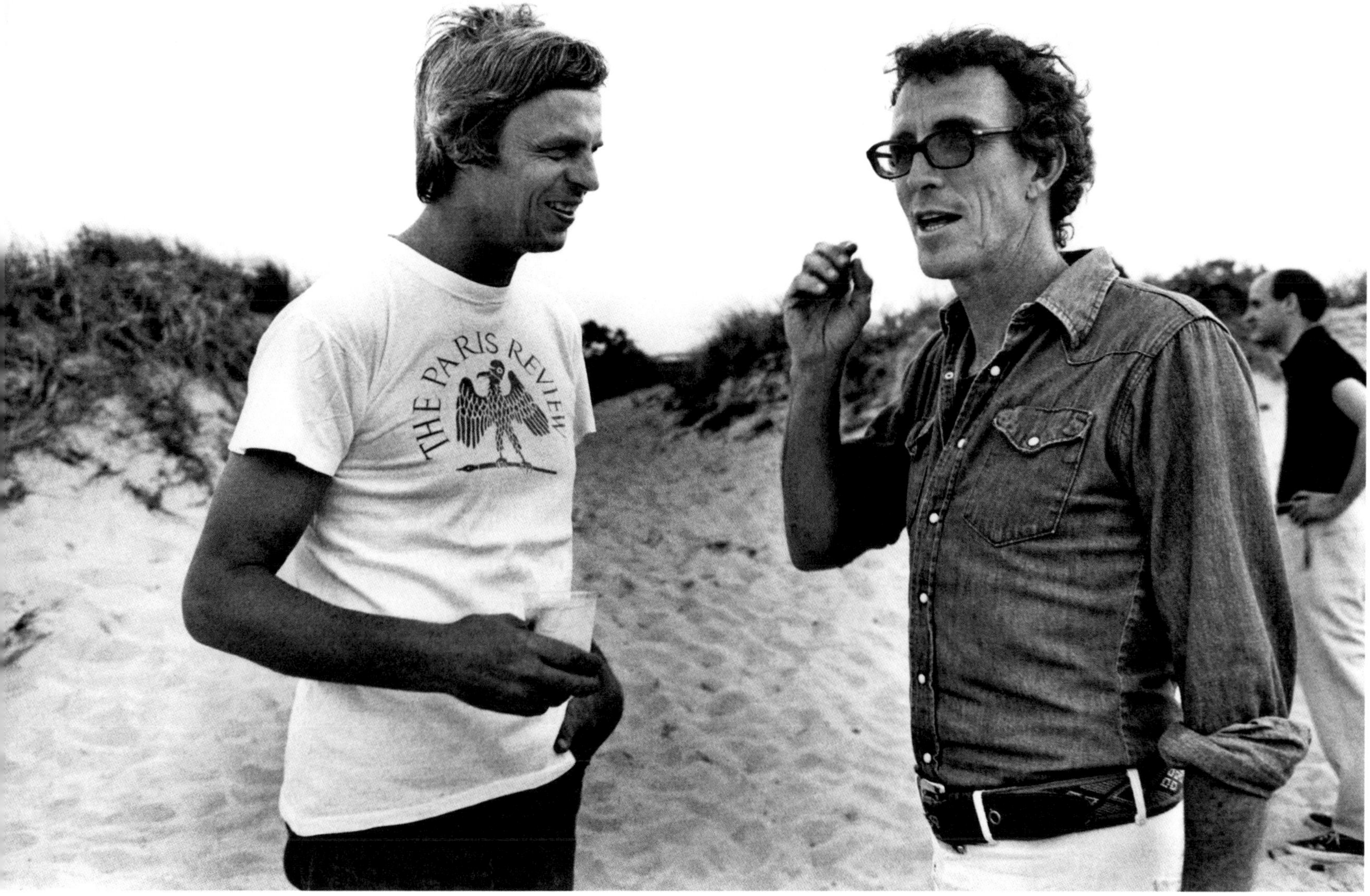

Top right, bottom: Photographs by Jill Krementz

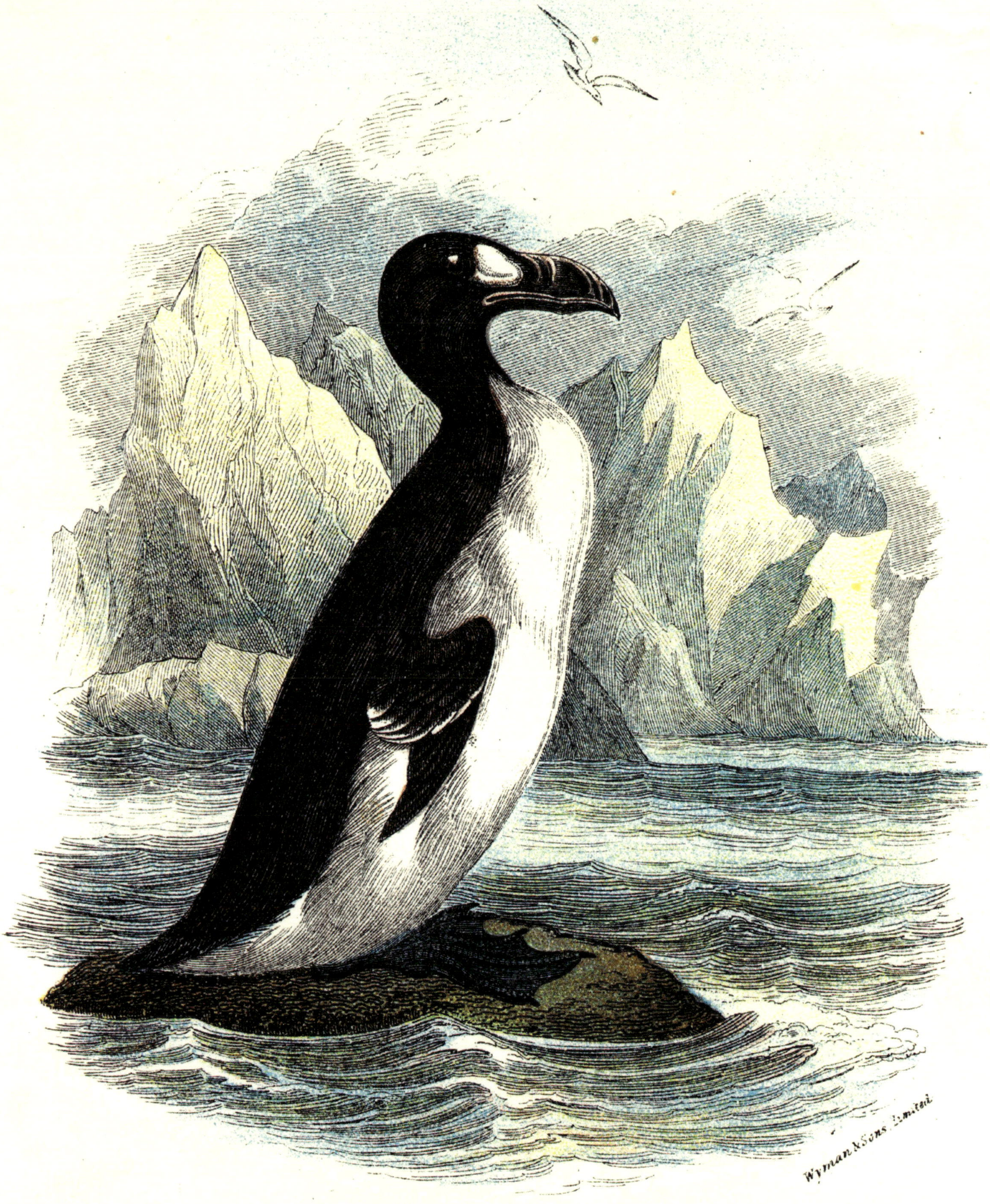

GREAT AUK.

EXCERPT FROM

WILDLIFE IN AMERICA

1959

In early June of 1844, a longboat crewed by fourteen men hove to off the skerry called Eldey, a stark, volcanic mass rising out of the gray wastes of the North Atlantic some ten miles west of Cape Reykjanes, Iceland. On the islets of these uneasy seas, the forebears of the boatmen had always hunted the swarming sea birds as a food, but on this day they were seeking, for collectors, the eggs and skins of the garefowl or great auk, a penguinlike flightless bird once common on the ocean rocks of northern Europe, Iceland, Greenland, and the maritime provinces of Canada. The great auk, slaughtered indiscriminately across the centuries for its flesh, feathers, and oil, was vanishing, and the last birds, appearing now and then on lonely shores, were granted no protection. On the contrary, they were pursued more intensively than ever for their value as scientific specimens.

At the north end of Eldey, a wide ledge descends to the water, and, though a sea was running, the boat managed to land three men, Jon Brandsson, Sigourour Isleffson, and Ketil Ketilsson. Two auks, blinking, waddled foolishly across the ledge. Isleffson and Brandsson each killed a bird, and Ketilsson, discovering a solitary egg, found a crack in it and smashed it. Later, one Christian Hansen paid nine pounds for the skins, and sold them in turn to a Reykjavik taxidermist named Möller. It is not known what became of them thereafter, a fact all the more saddening when one considers that, on all the long coasts of the northern oceans, no auk was ever seen alive again.

The great auk is one of the few creatures whose final hours can be documented with such certainty. Ordinarily, the last members of a species die in solitude, the time and place of their passage from earth unknown. One year they are present, striving instinctively to maintain an existence many thousands of years old. The next year they are gone. Perhaps stray auks persisted a few years longer, to die at last through accident or age, but we must assume that the ultimate pair fell victim to this heedless act of man.

For most of us, its passing is unimportant. The auk, from a practical point of view, was doubtless a dim-witted inhabitant of Godforsaken places, a primitive and freakish thing, ill-favored and ungainly. From a second and more enlightened viewpoint, the great auk was the mightiest of its family, a highly evolved fisherman and swimmer, an ornament to the monotony of northern seas, and for centuries a crucial food source for the natives of the Atlantic coasts. More important, it was a living creature which died needlessly, the first species native to North America to become extinct by the hand of man. It was to be followed into oblivion by other creatures, many of them an aesthetic and economic significance apparent to us all. Even today, despite protection, the scattered individuals of species too long persecuted are hovering at the abyss of extinction, and will vanish in our lifetimes.

The finality of extinction is awesome, and not unrelated to the finality of eternity. Man, striving to imagine what might lie beyond the long light years of stars, beyond the universe, beyond the void, feels lost in space; confronted with the death of species, enacted on earth so many times before he came, and certain to continue when his own breed is gone, he is forced to face another void, and feels alone in time. Species appear and, left behind by a changing earth, they diasppear forever, and there is a certain solace in the inexorable. But until man, the highest predator, evolved, the process of extinction was a slow one. No species but man, so far as is known, unaided by circumstance or climatic change, has ever extinguished another, and certainly no species has ever devoured itself, an accomplishment of which man seems quite capable. There is some comfort in the notion that, however *Homo sapiens* contrives his own destruction, a few creatures will survive in that ultimate wilderness he will leave behind, going on about their ancient business in the mindless confidence that their own much older and more tolerant species will prevail.

EXCERPT FROM

THE SNOW LEOPARD

1978

In a dark grove of mossy oaks, wet camp is made at 9000 feet. Through the ragged treetops, skies are clearing. There is a moon, and cold.

How strange everything seems. How strange everything is. One "I" feels like an observer of this man who lies here in this sleeping bag in Asian mountains; another "I" is thinking about Alex; a third is the tired man who tries to sleep.

In his first summers, forsaking all his toys, my son would stand rapt for near an hour in his sandbox in the orchard, as doves and redwings came and went on the warm wind, the leaves dancing, the clouds flying, birdsong and sweet smell of privet and rose. The child was not observing; he was at rest in the very center of the universe, a part of things, unaware of endings and beginnings, still in unison with the primordial nature of creation, letting all light and phenomena pour through. Ecstasy is identity with all existence, and ecstasy showed in his bright paintings; like the Aurignacian hunter, who became the deer he drew on the cave wall, there was no "self" to separate him from the bird or flower. The same spontaneous identity with the object is achieved in the bold sumi painting of Japan—a strong expression of Zen culture, since to become one with whatever one does is a true realization of the Way.

Amazingly, we take for granted that instinct for survival, fear of death, must separate us from the happiness of pure and uninterpreted experience, in which body, mind, and nature are the same. And this debasement of our vision, the retreat from wonder, the backing away like lobsters from free-swimming life into safe crannies, the desperate instinct that our life passes unlived, is reflected in proliferation without joy, corrosive money rot, the gross befouling of the earth and air and water from which we came.

Compare the wild, free paintings of the child with the stiff, pinched "pictures" these become as the painter notices the painting and tries to portray "reality" as others see it; self-conscious now, he steps out of his own painting and, finding himself apart from things, notices the silence all around and becomes alarmed by the vast significations of Creation. The armor of the "I" begins to form, the construction and desperate assertion of separate identity, the loneliness: "Man has closed himself up, till he sees all things through the narrow chinks of his cavern."

Alex is eight, and already he has shut away the wildness of the world. I lost it, too, in early childhood. But memories would come on wings of light—a shining bird, high pines and sun, the fire in a floating leaf, the autumn heat in weathered wood, wood smell, a child, soft lichen on a stone—a light-filled imminence, shimmering and breathing, and yet so fleeting that it left me breathless and in pain. One night in 1945, on a Navy vessel in Pacific storm, my relief on bow watch, seasick, failed to appear, and I was alone for eight hours in a maelstrom of wind and water, noise and iron; again and again, waves crashed across the deck, until water, air, and iron became one. Overwhelmed, exhausted, all thought and emotion beaten out of me, I lost my sense of self, the heartbeat I heard was the heart of the world, I breathed with the mighty risings and declines of earth, and this evanescence seemed less frightening than exalting. Afterward, there was a pain of loss—loss of *what*, I wondered, understanding nothing.

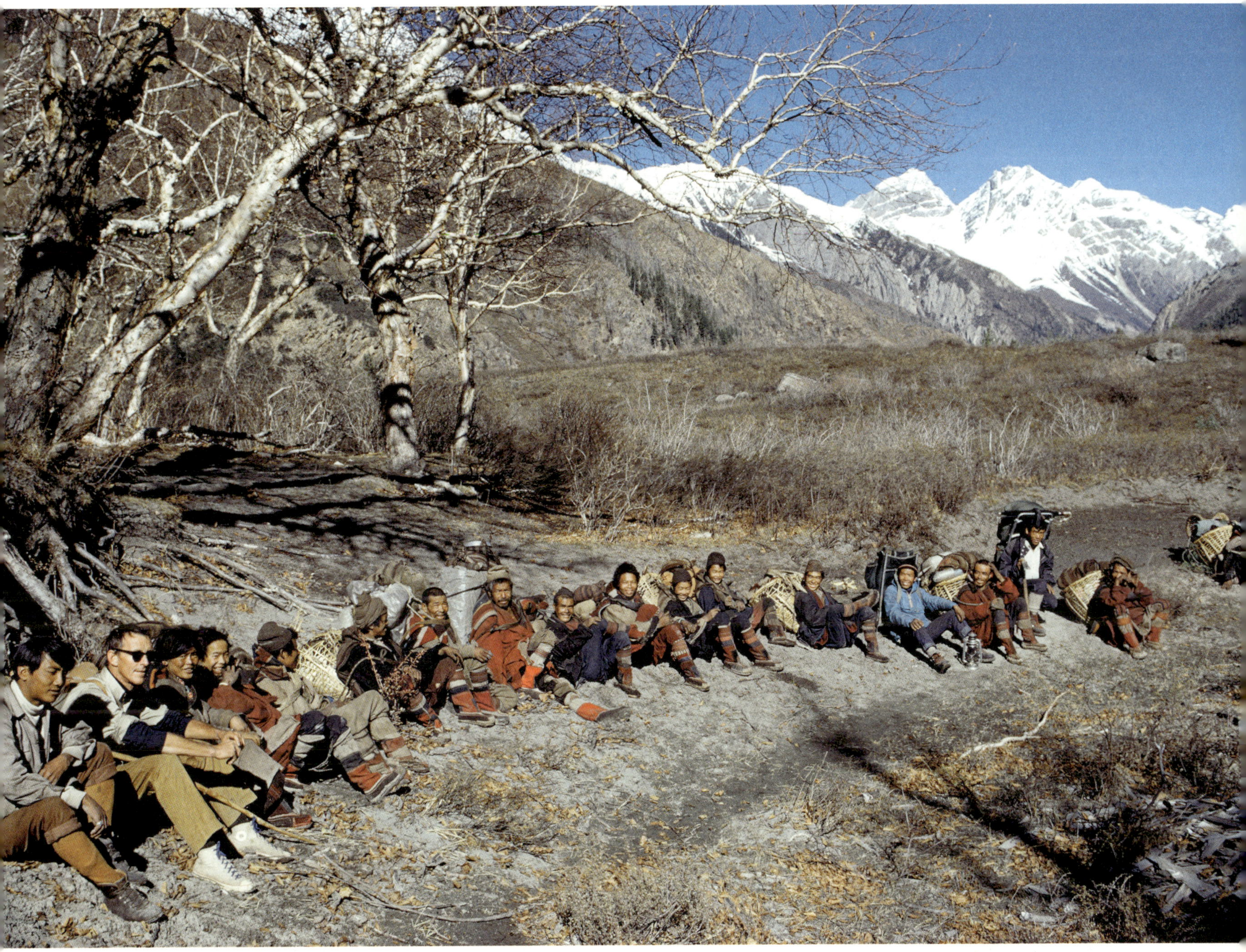

This page: Porters, Sherpas, and Peter Matthiessen at Ringmo, Nepal, at the beginning of his week-long trek over the pass to Shey with George Schaller in October, 1973. Matthiessen's experiences on this trip would form the basis for his acclaimed novel, *The Snow Leopard.*

Following spread: From the same trip, Peter in the Saldang Pass with the sherpas Tukhten, Jang-bu, Gyaltsen, and Dawa.

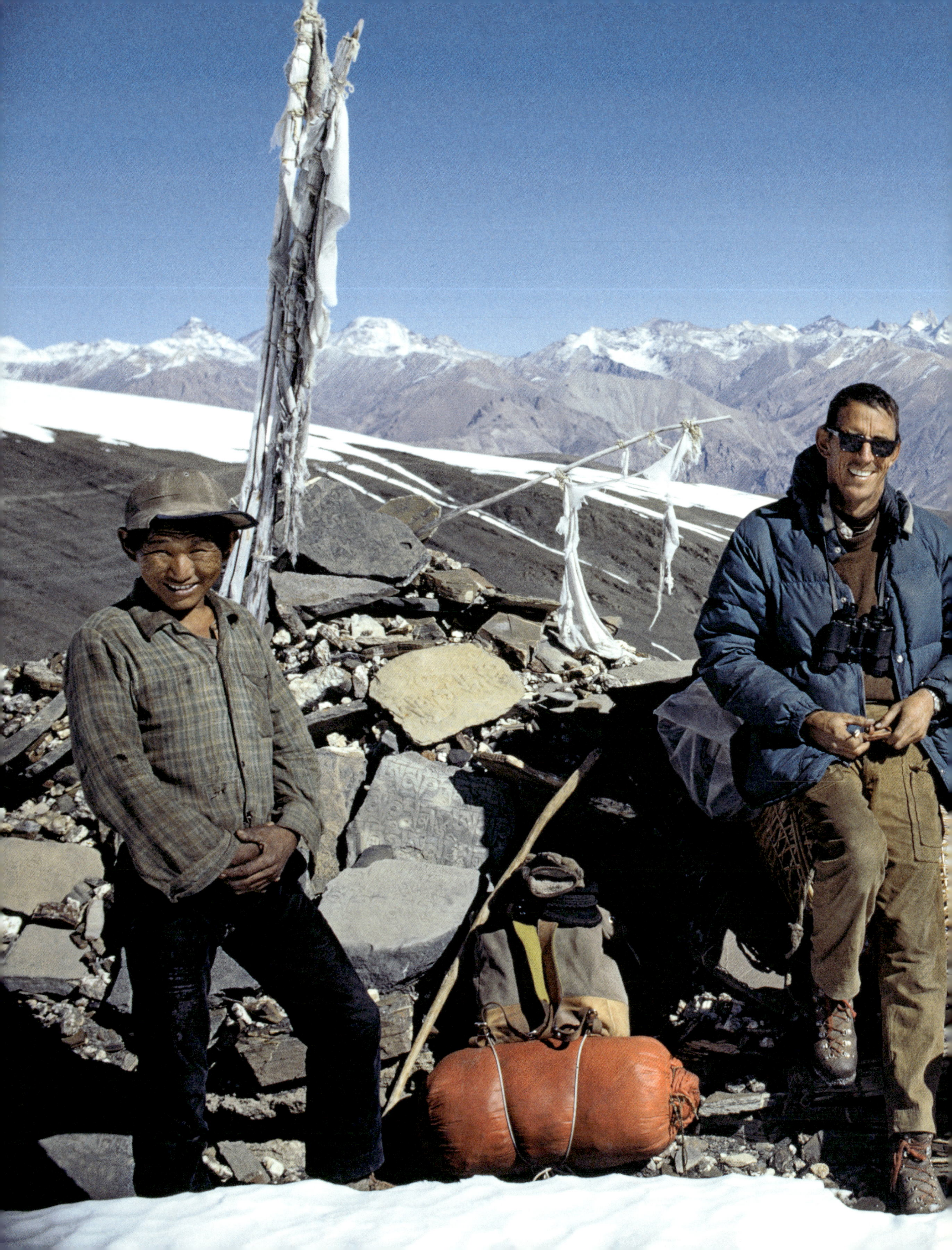

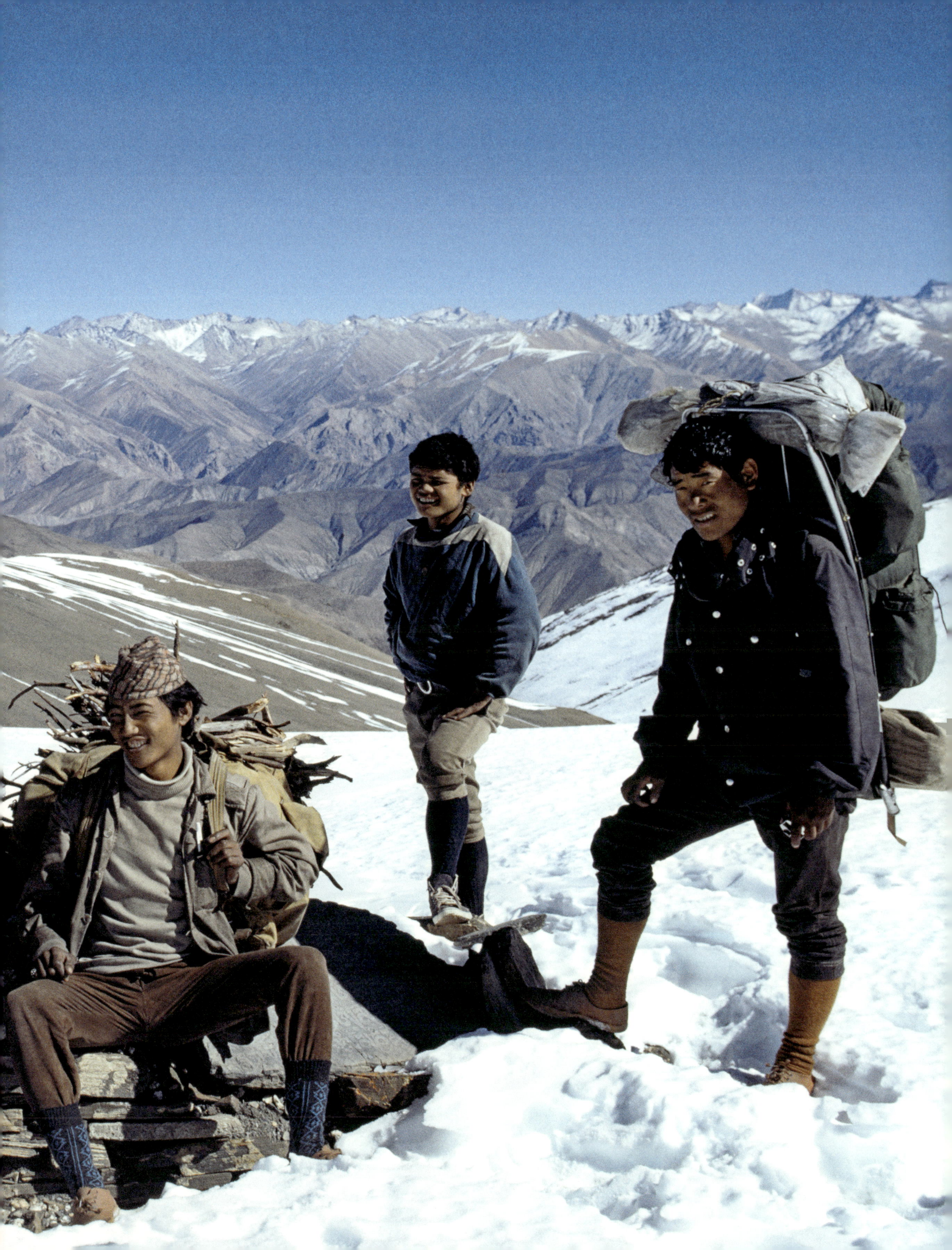

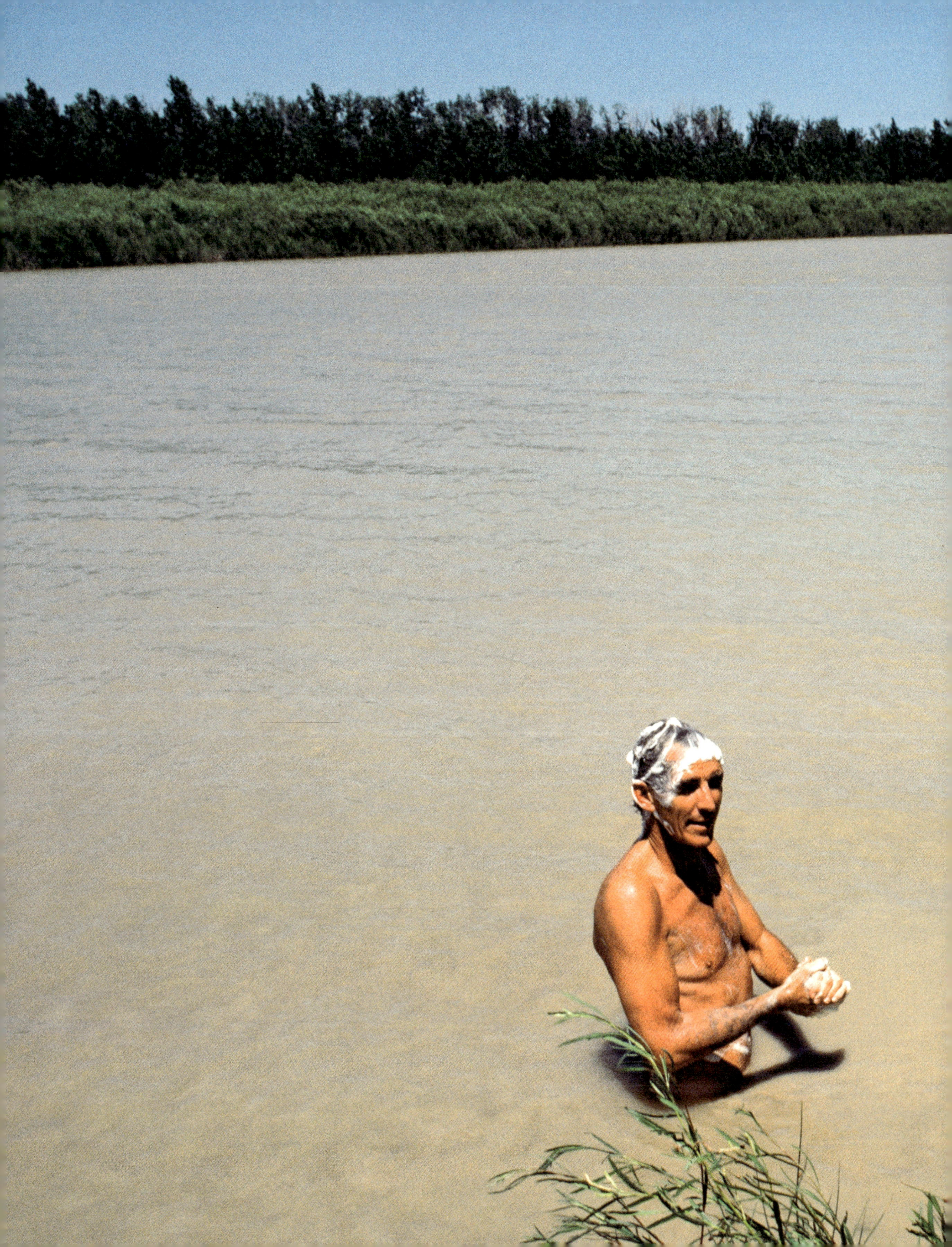

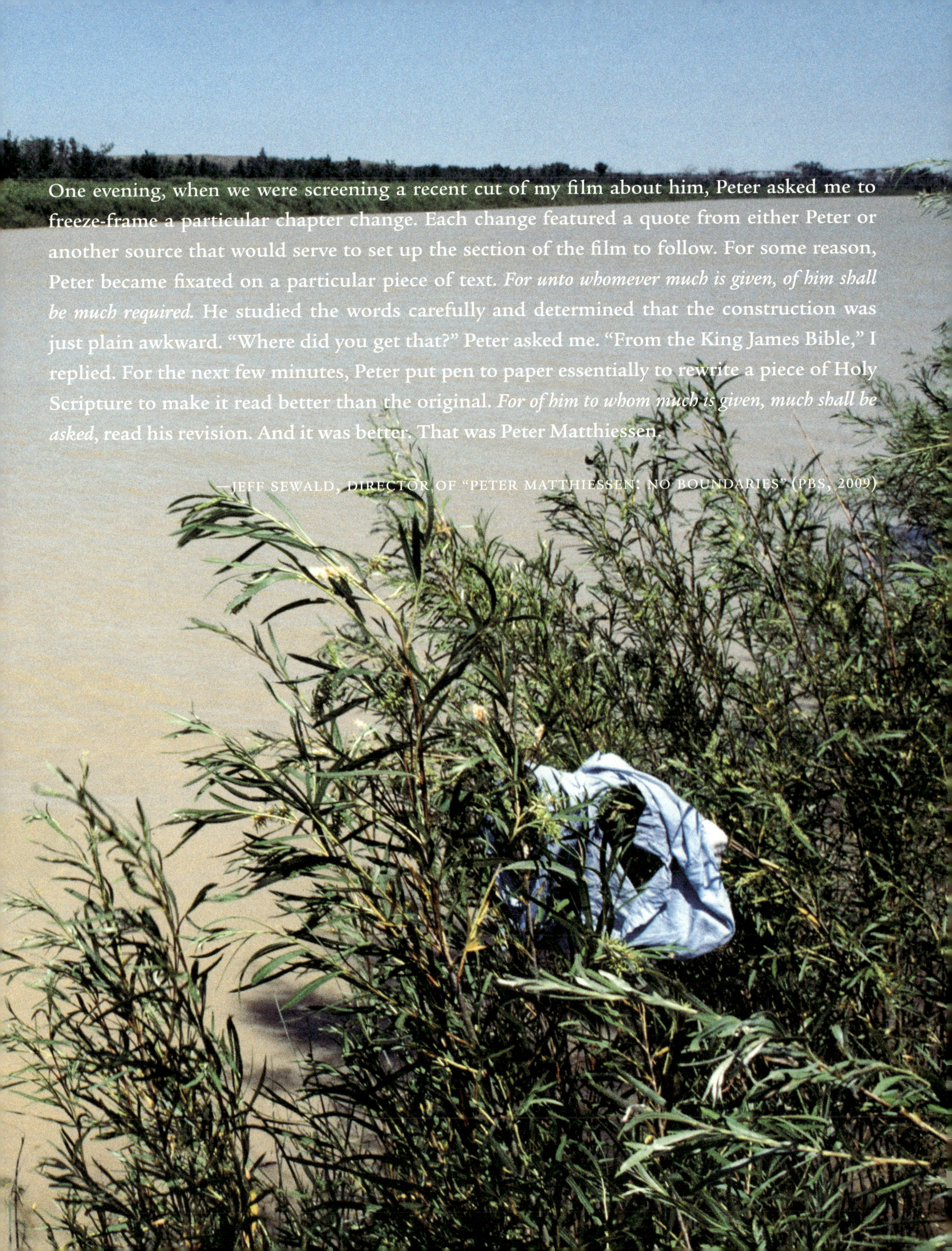

One evening, when we were screening a recent cut of my film about him, Peter asked me to freeze-frame a particular chapter change. Each change featured a quote from either Peter or another source that would serve to set up the section of the film to follow. For some reason, Peter became fixated on a particular piece of text. *For unto whomever much is given, of him shall be much required.* He studied the words carefully and determined that the construction was just plain awkward. "Where did you get that?" Peter asked me. "From the King James Bible," I replied. For the next few minutes, Peter put pen to paper essentially to rewrite a piece of Holy Scripture to make it read better than the original. *For of him to whom much is given, much shall be asked*, read his revision. And it was better. That was Peter Matthiessen.

—JEFF SEWALD, DIRECTOR OF "PETER MATTHIESSEN: NO BOUNDARIES" (PBS, 2009)

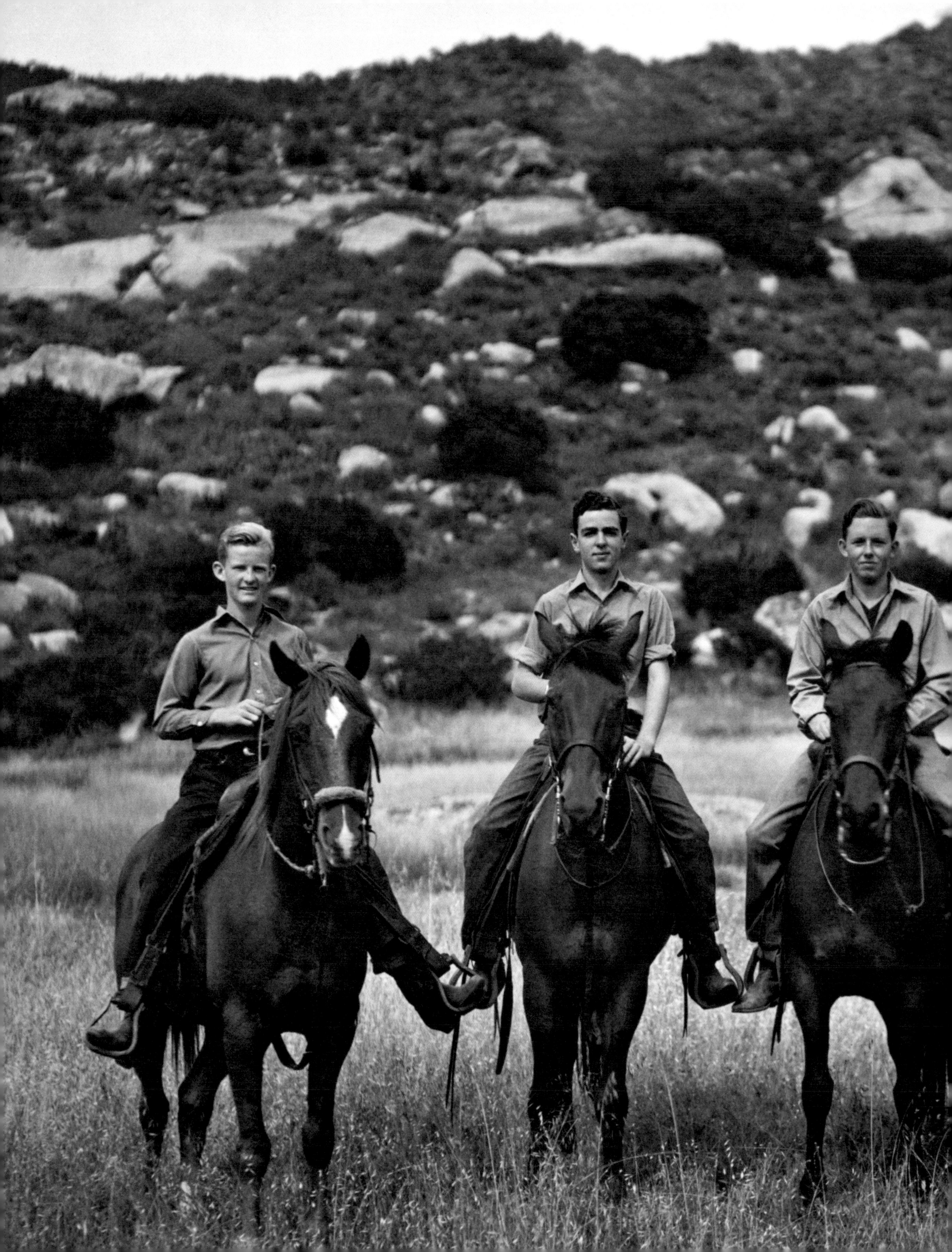

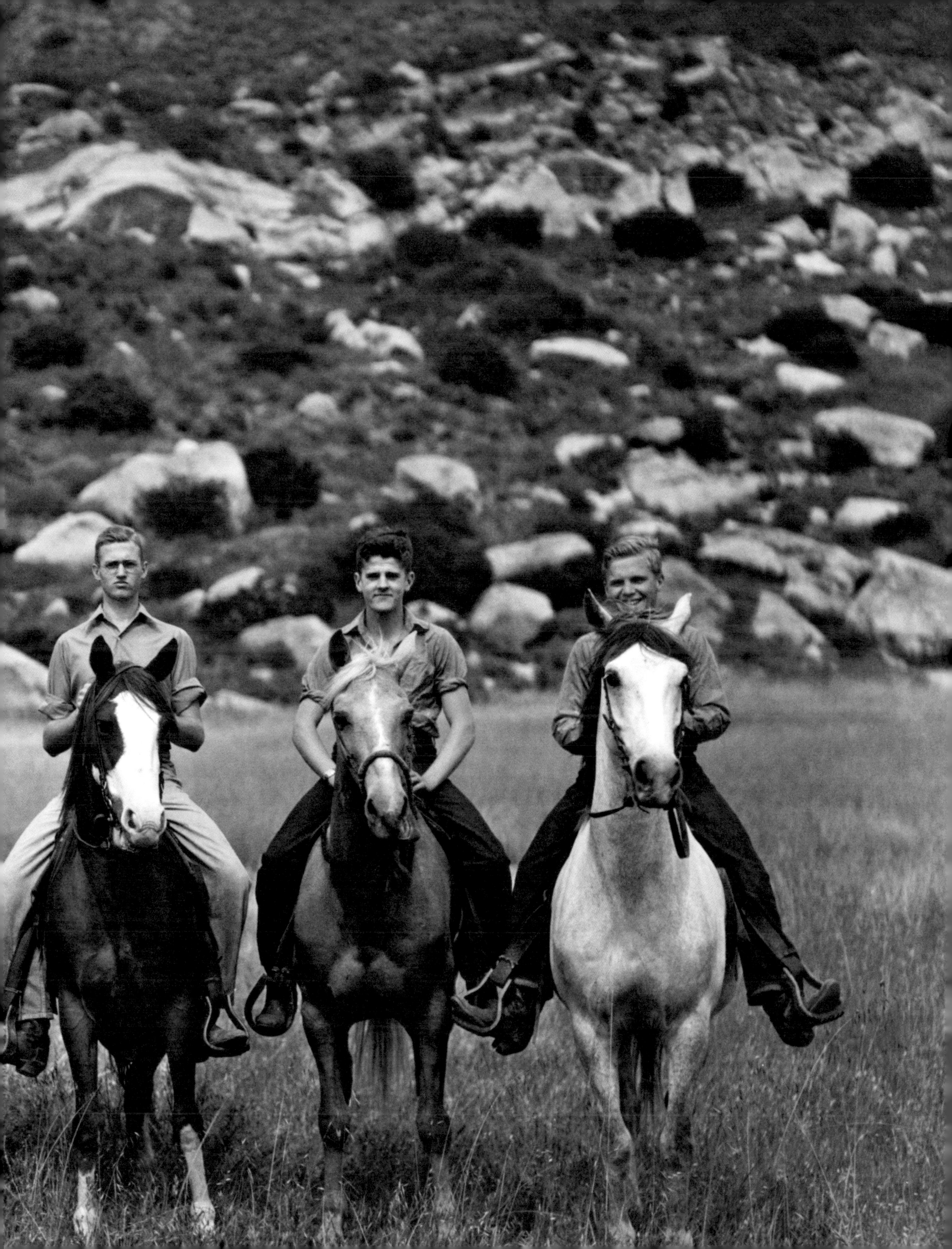

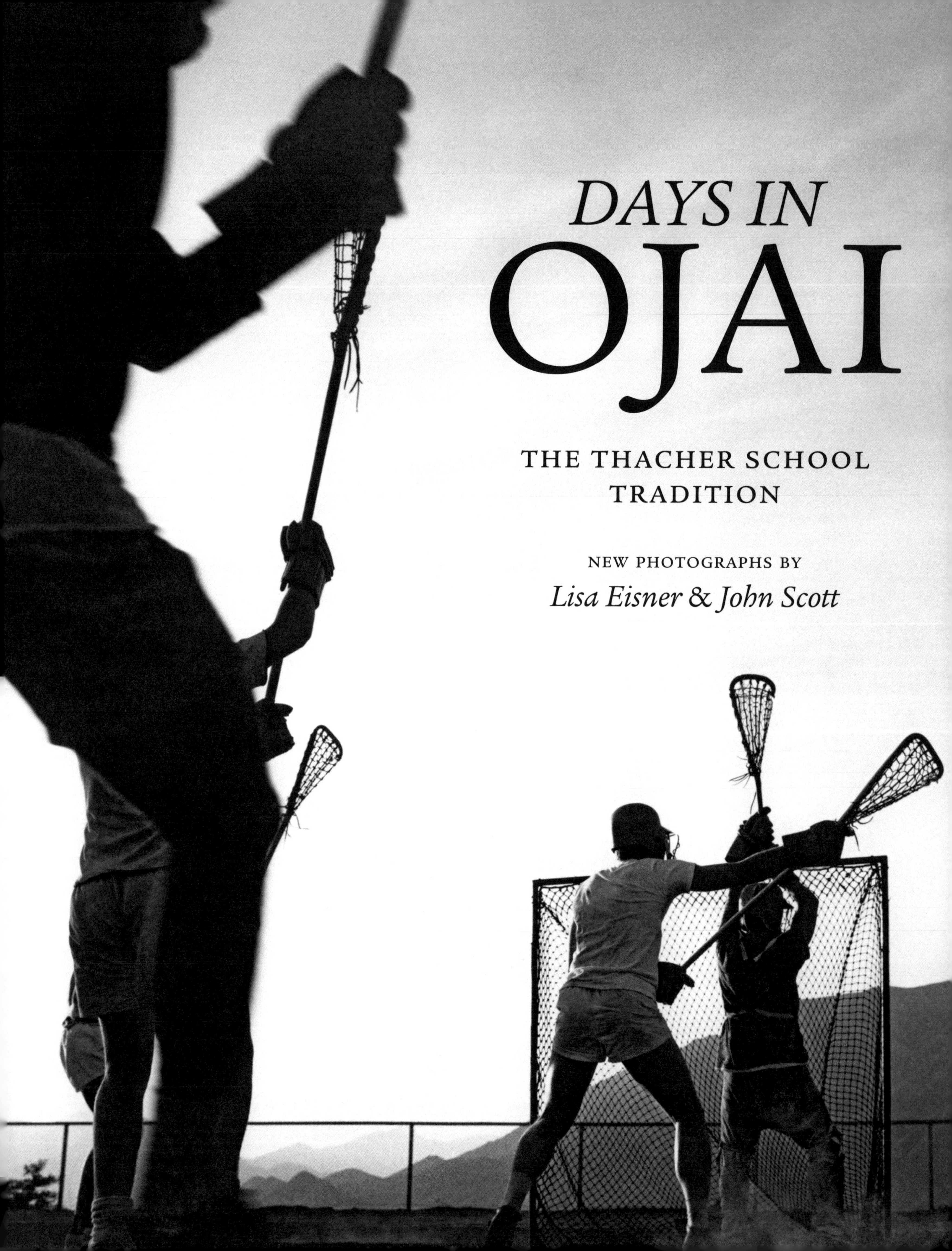

DAYS IN OJAI

THE THACHER SCHOOL TRADITION

NEW PHOTOGRAPHS BY

Lisa Eisner & John Scott

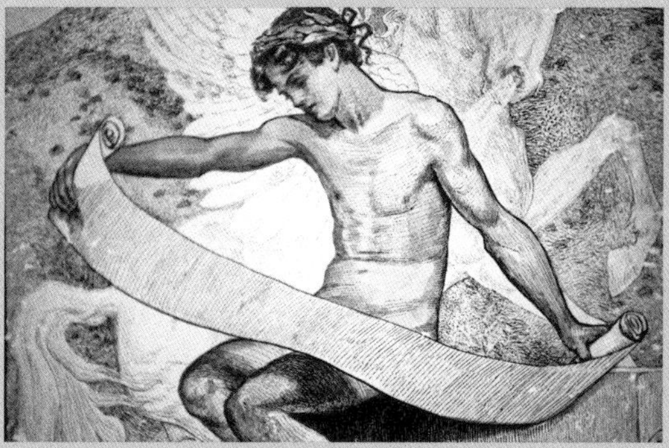

Nestled in a picturesque corner of the Los Padres Mountains of Southern California, among the orange groves and dusty sagebrush of the Ojai Valley, lies the campus of Thacher, a private college preparatory school. We were initially drawn to visit the campus after learning of a distinctive and rather unusual feature of its academic program: Upon admission to the school, each freshman is assigned a horse that they spend the year caring for. They feed and groom their horses every morning, cleaning their stalls and riding for several hours each afternoon under the careful instruction of educators versed equally in equine science and a distinctively Western spirit of self-reliance. As the following pages will attest, the effects of this program are quite profound, imbuing the students with patience, determination, maturity, and trust—values that sociologists often mourn the loss of in teens of the millennial generation.

But the horse program is just one aspect of life at Thacher, and in the time we spent wandering its bucolic grounds, chatting with teachers and students alike, something even more ineffable and ambitious emerged as a guiding principle of the institution. The story of Thacher is, of course, the story of a school, with all the aspirations of 21st century pedagogy and competitive academic pursuit very much front and center. The kids we met were whip smart, articulate, and confident, with big dreams for their college lives and beyond. But they also knew how to build a fire, pack for a trip, and camp in the snow. They spoke about their honor code, the close bonds of the student community, and a shared feeling of responsibility to one another and the world they inhabit in completely sincere and personal terms. The Thacher education is just as much a conversation about the pursuit of character, a desire to instill in students an engaged, connected, mindful way of being in the world. Taken out of context, the self-proclaimed principles of the school—honor, fairness, kindness, and truth—seem rather old-fashioned, throwbacks to a time when horses were actually the common mode of transportation. But speaking to Thacher students and witnessing how they practice those ideals makes them feel nothing less than essential. After a couple of days on campus, we all thought, *We could learn something from these kids...*

"Tradition" is a favorite word at schools like this. But at Thacher, programs established in the early years continue to influence student life in real ways today. The Horse Program, the importance placed on physical wellness, the orchestration of authentic experiences with the natural world through the school's outdoor program—all of these distinguishing features are rooted in the vision set forth originally by the school's founder, Sherman Thacher. Though trained as a lawyer, Thacher spent his early years after graduating from Yale drifting about, looking for an opportunity to seize his energies and interests. He first visited the Ojai Valley in 1887, ostensibly to help his invalid brother with his orange ranch. When Henry Farnam, a colleague from his Yale years, asked Sherman to help tutor his nephew to prepare him for the rigorous academic world back East, Thacher accepted, thinking the assignment would be a good way to keep his own orange ranch solvent. But word of Thacher's presence quickly spread, and soon he had a number of families requesting his services. By 1899, Sherman Thacher was advertising "Outdoor Life and Study for Boys"—with the three stated aims of "health and enjoyment...unselfish manly character...and thorough, self-reliant habits of thought and study" in the local paper. Drop the manly bit, and you have a fairly accurate description of the Thacher mission today.

As early as 1899, the school had classrooms and dorms, as well as a riding program, tennis courts, stables, and a swimming reservoir to encourage physical rigor together with the life of the mind. Sherman Thacher served as headmaster until 1931, overseeing the school's expansion to 90 students, incorporating it as an independent institution, and rebuilding the campus after two fires—a regrettable consequence of the arid locale. The school continued to grow through the middle part of the century, surviving the Great Depression and the wild days of 1960s to become one of the leading prep schools in California. It became coed in 1977, and since 1993 has been guided by the widely regarded leadership of one Michael Mulligan.

We encountered Mulligan early in our visit, chatting with students in a baseball cap and hiking boots while walking with a determined gait through the Pergola, a campus gathering spot that has endured from the early days. Mulligan's easy familiarity with the students belies the passion and intensity of his leadership, which during his tenure has been focused on ensuring the longevity of the institution and diversifying its student body, all while maintaining a commitment to the school's core values and traditions. He seemed the perfect person to ask a nagging question: *How does an experience like Thacher, albeit unique, relate to the technologically obsessed world outside? With ever-shorter attention spans and the challenges posed by the barrage of social media, what can things like caring for a horse and participating in a camping expedition mean for kids today?* Mulligan's reply was persuasive and compelling:

"Who is telling our sons and daughters who they should be? In my opinion, if you leave it to the broader culture, our kids get lost. The culture is always attempting to sell them a message of, *You're not good enough, you're not beautiful enough, you're not thin enough, you're not smart enough, you don't have enough cachet. Do this, buy this, look like this, and you will get it.* Add to that the pressure of a rapid-firing, technological world, and it's no surprise that kids are experiencing a dislocation between how they understand who they are and what they can be relative to all that is coming at them.

"At Thacher, we're trying to create an environment where kids come to know who they are by virtue of hard work they undertake for positive goals. It may seem counterintuitive to the world we live in—why would you learn to saddle a horse, why would you spend a week camping in a snowstorm? But we're trying to teach these young people that what they bring intuitively to their experience often matters the most. We want our students to understand that nature can be an important, healing aspect in their lives. They wake up in the morning and smell the pepper trees and eucalyptus; they have the physical experience of putting their hands on an animal they care for. All of that is healing. We can't hand out self-esteem or good feeling to these kids. But we can help them by saying, *'Stop. Wait. Look at yourself. Look at what you're doing. Look at where you can go. Look at what you can do.'* The horses, the nature, the outdoors, and the adult role models are all powerful tools for helping kids move past the ego, to help them find a healthy path and move the boundaries of their emotional understanding.

"If access to information were the cure for society's ills, our cultural problems would have been solved millennia ago with the invention of the printing press. Technology is a useful tool, but we do not want it to dominate the consciousness of our students. Instead, we challenge them to make their own meaning around every experience. As we say in horsemanship training, 'How do you make the right thing easy and the wrong thing difficult?' The same holds true when working with teenagers today—if you create a situation where success is the right thing and their own idea, then it works."

Judging by the students we met during our days in Ojai, Sherman Thacher's hopeful vision is certainly succeeding.

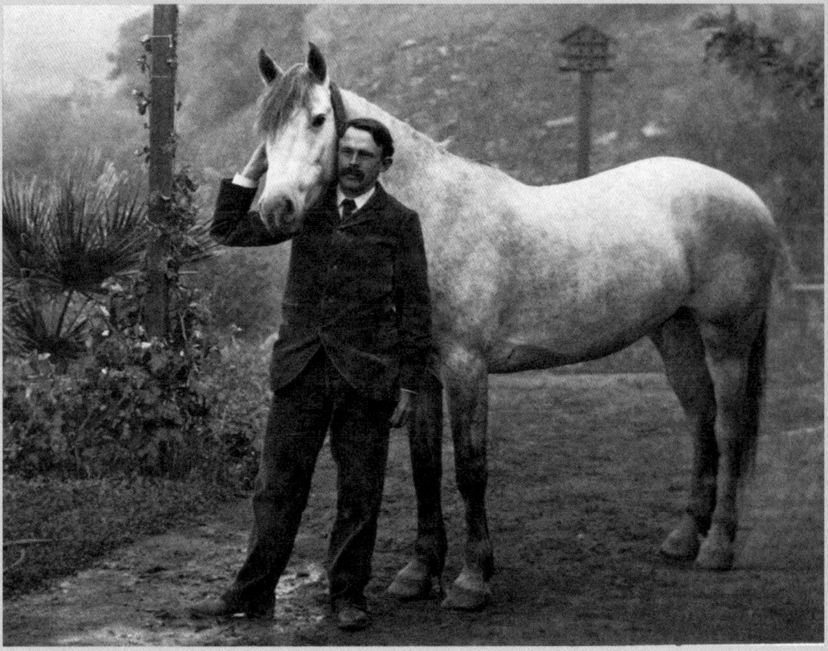

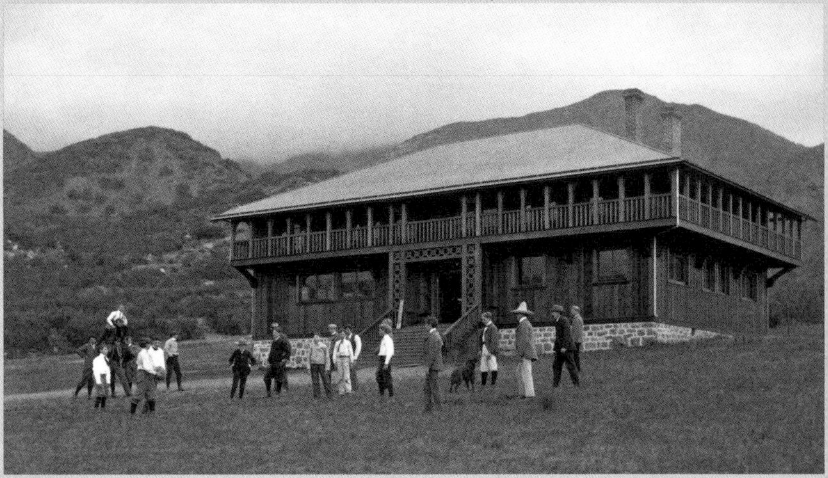

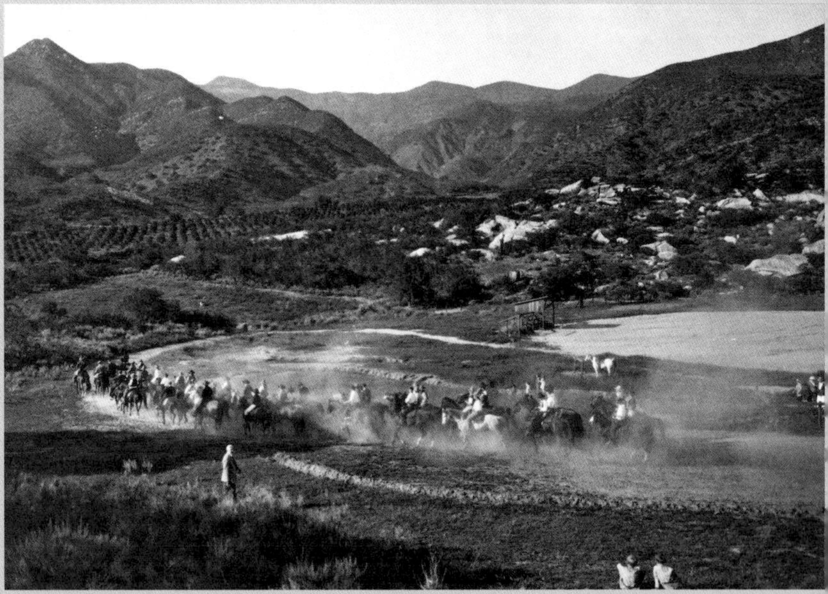

This page—top: Sherman Thacher, the founder of the school, with his horse, c. 1890s; *Center*: The school's Main Building in 1895—today, the lower floor is used as the dining hall and administrative offices occupy the upper floors. *Bottom*: The parade starting off the 1920 Gymkhana—the annual stunt and riding competition that culminates the freshman year Horse Program; *Opposite*: The entry procession for the 2010 Gymkhana.

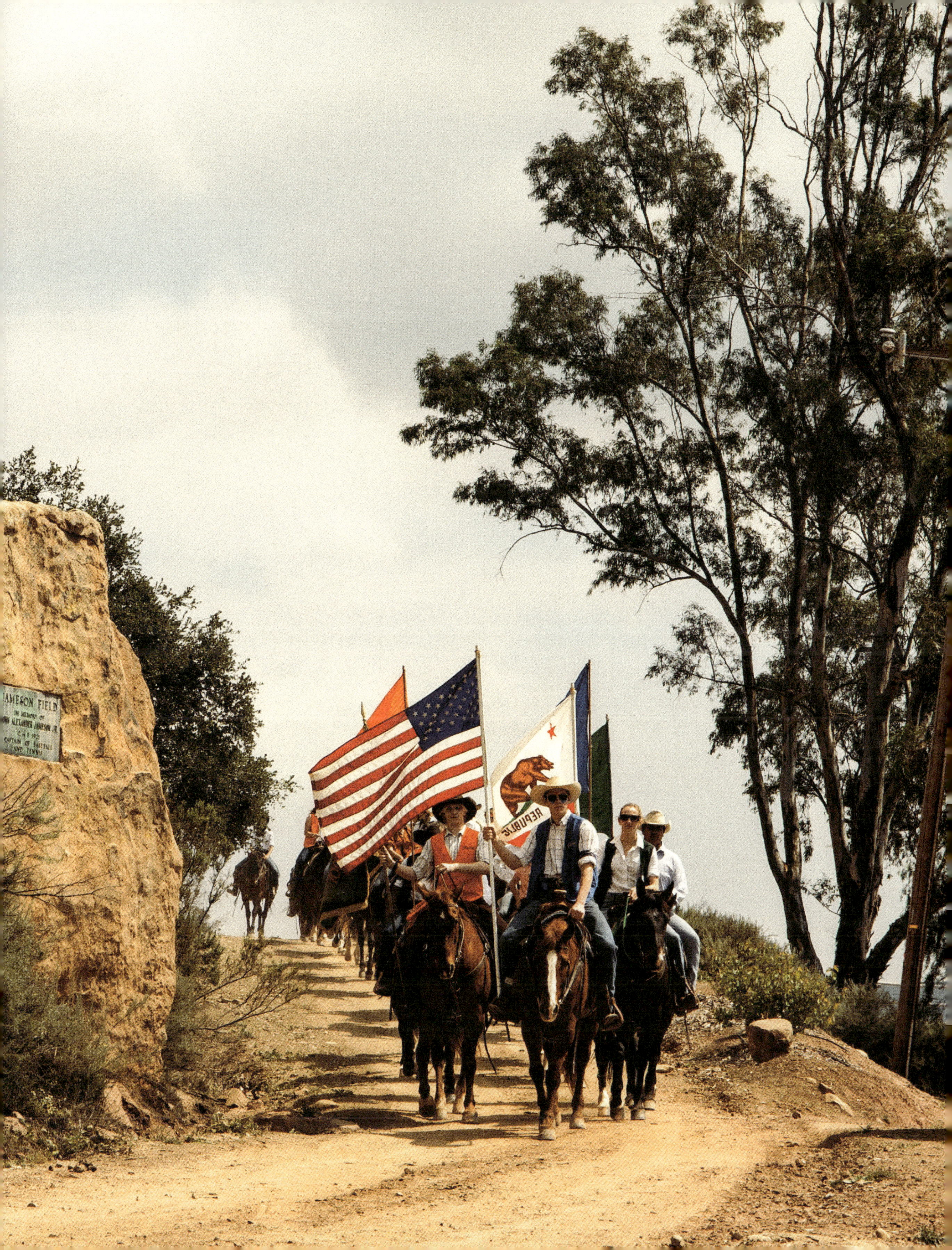
JAMESON FIELD
CAPTAIN OF BASEBALL
AND TENNIS

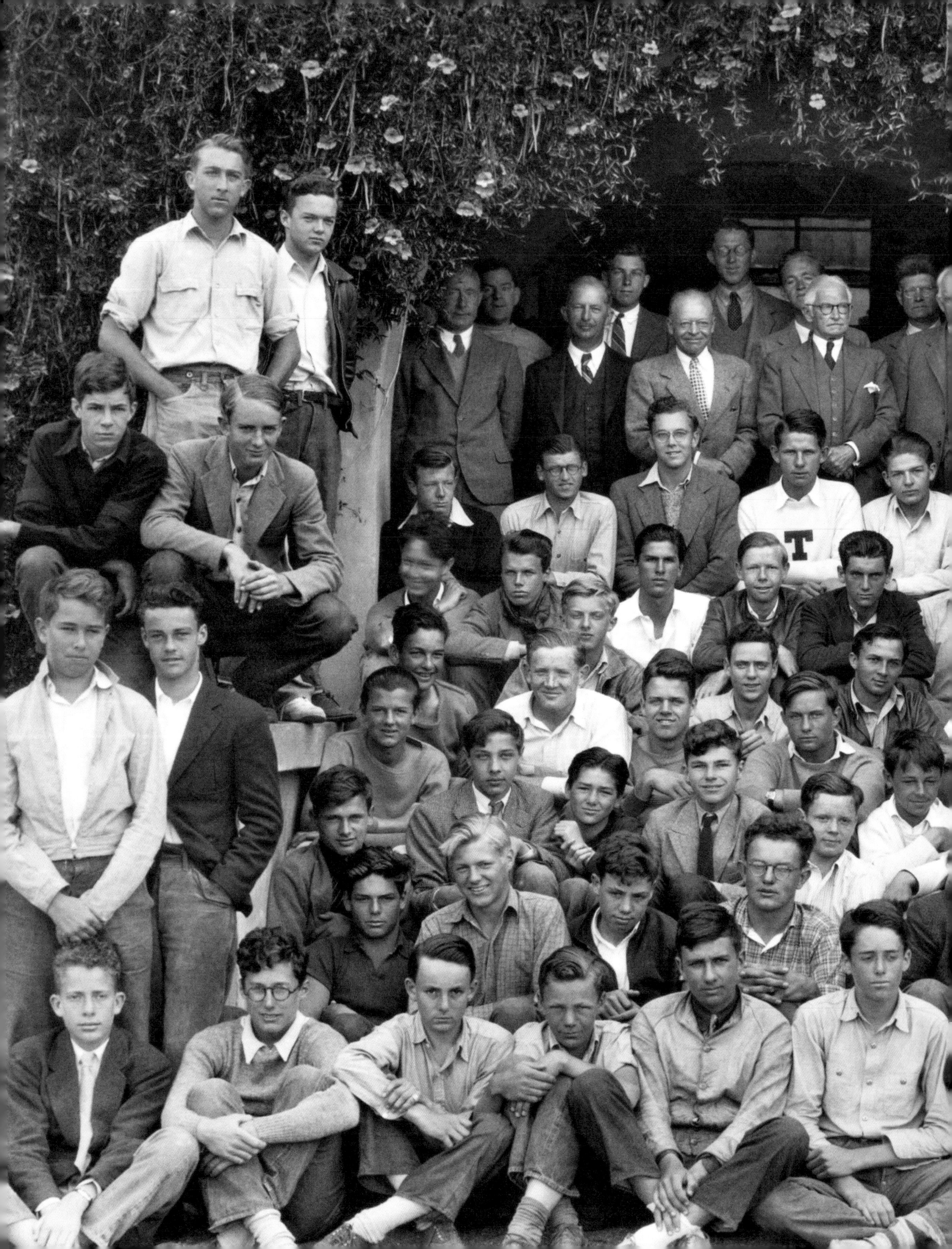

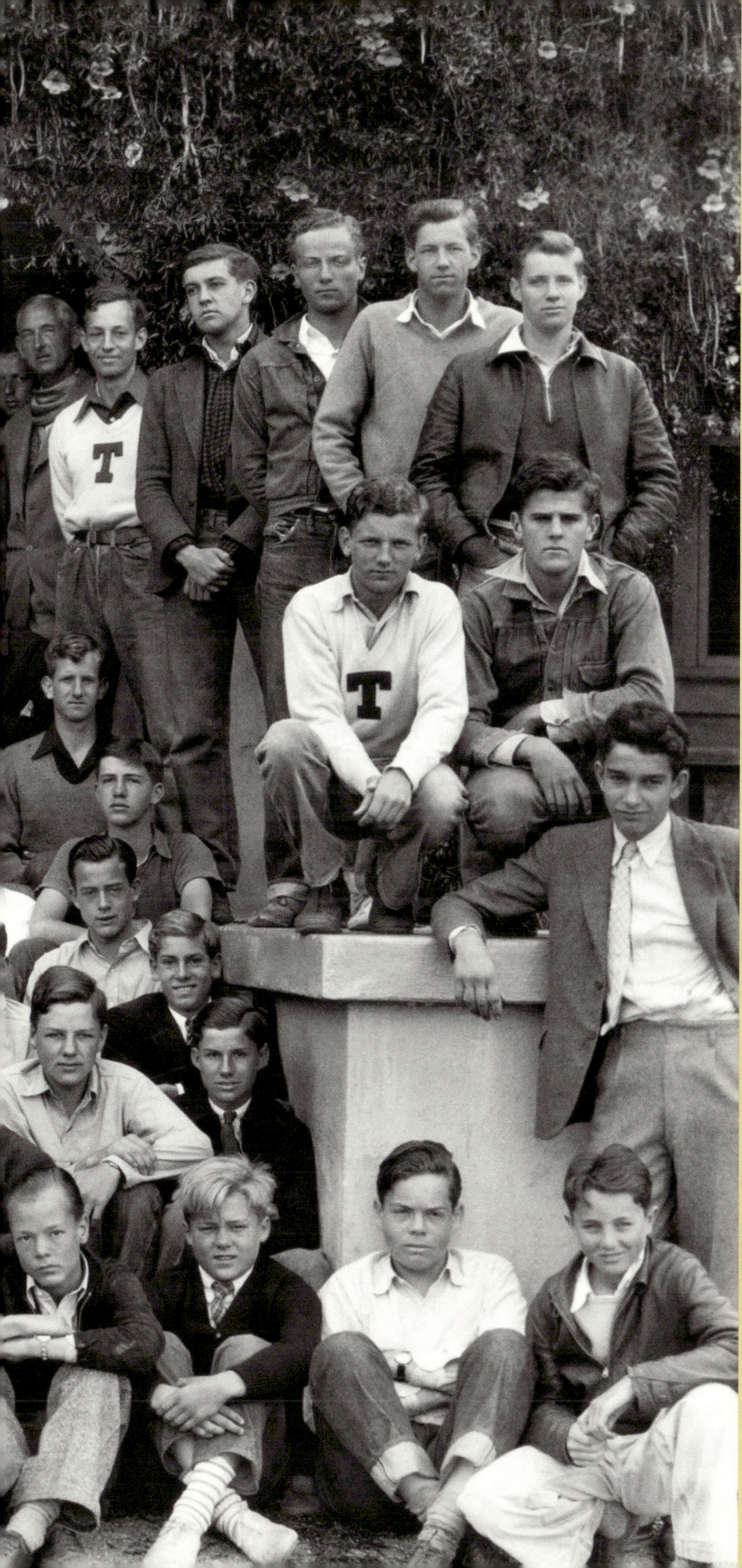

The Thacher School Class of 1935

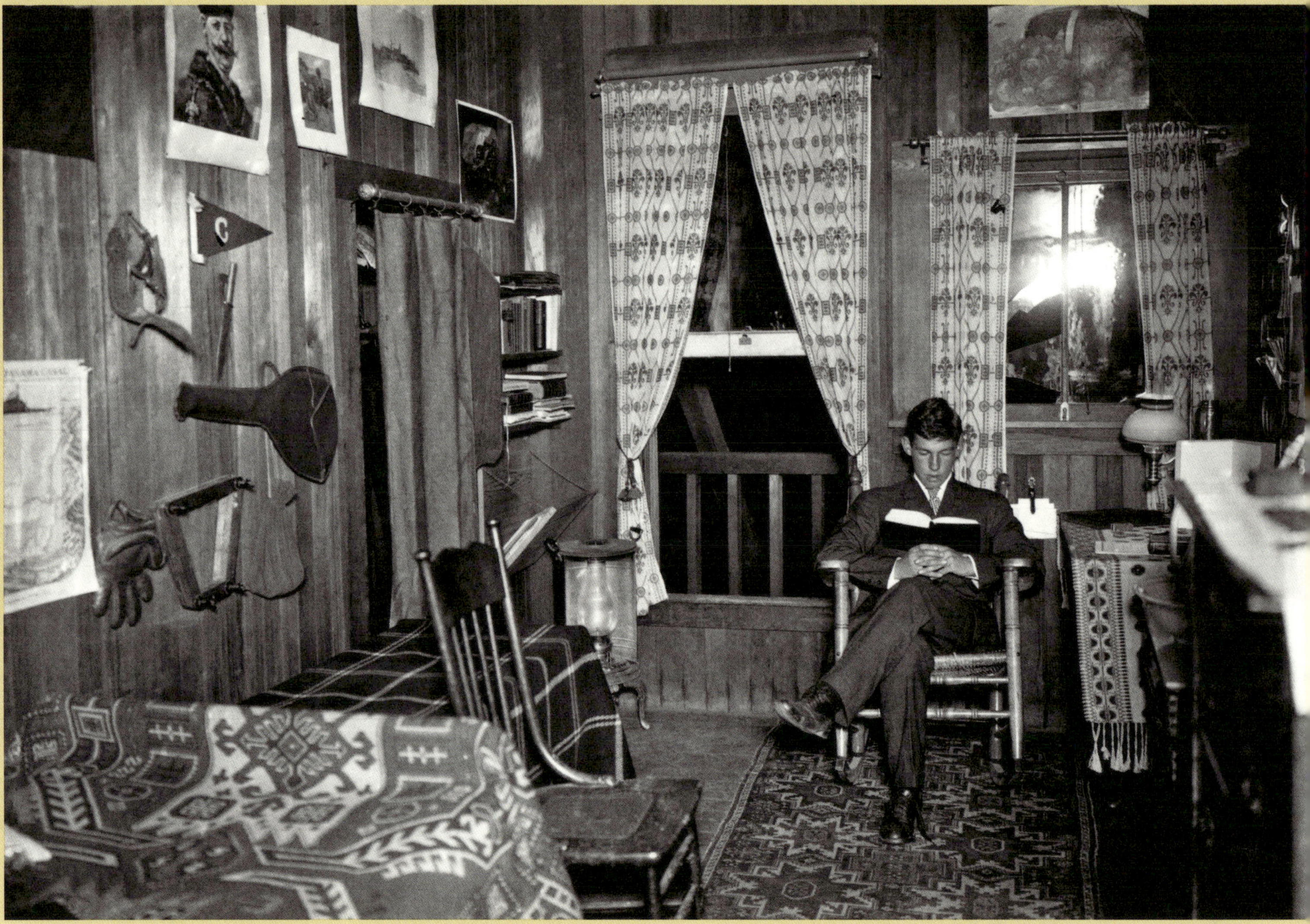
C

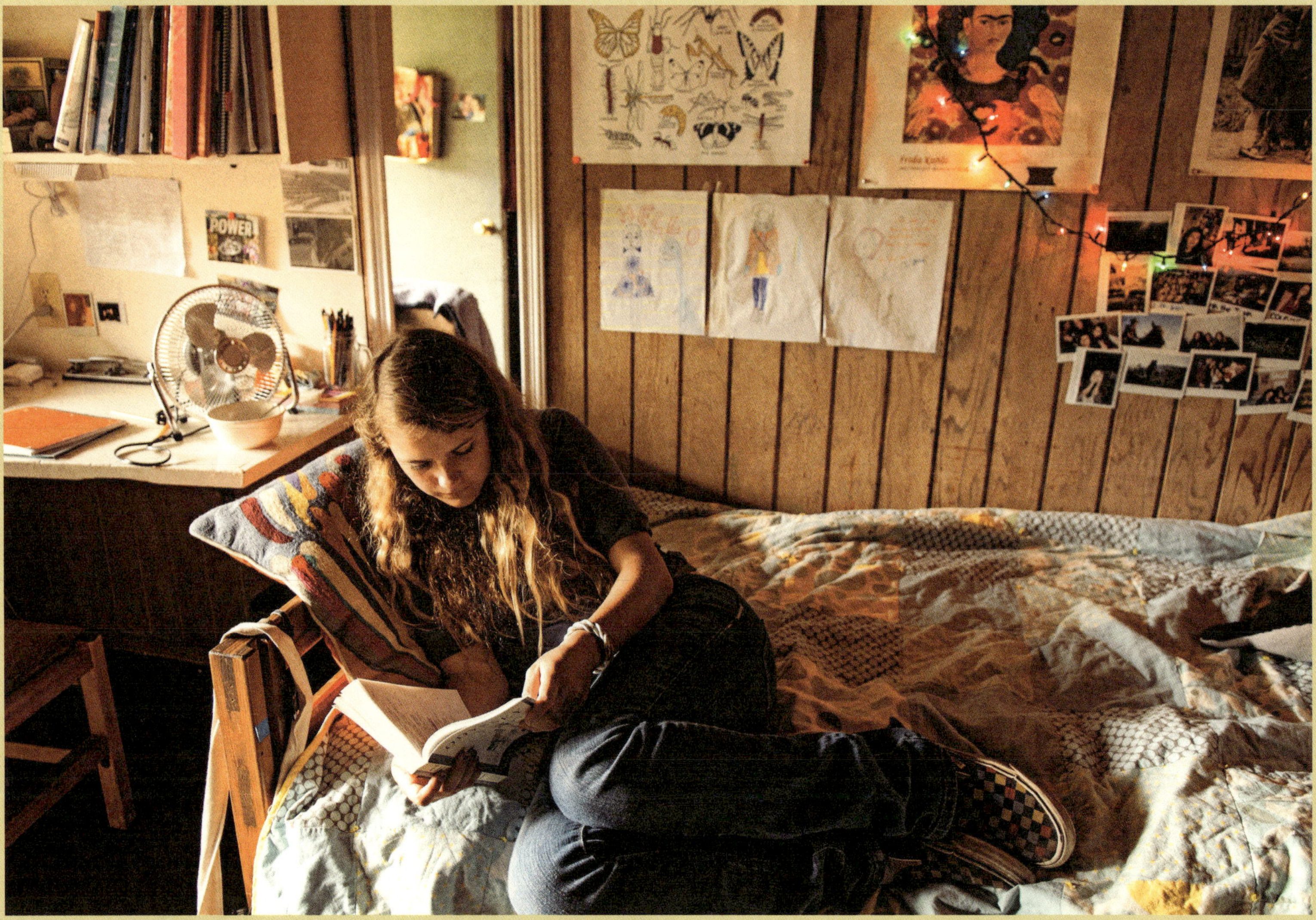
POWER

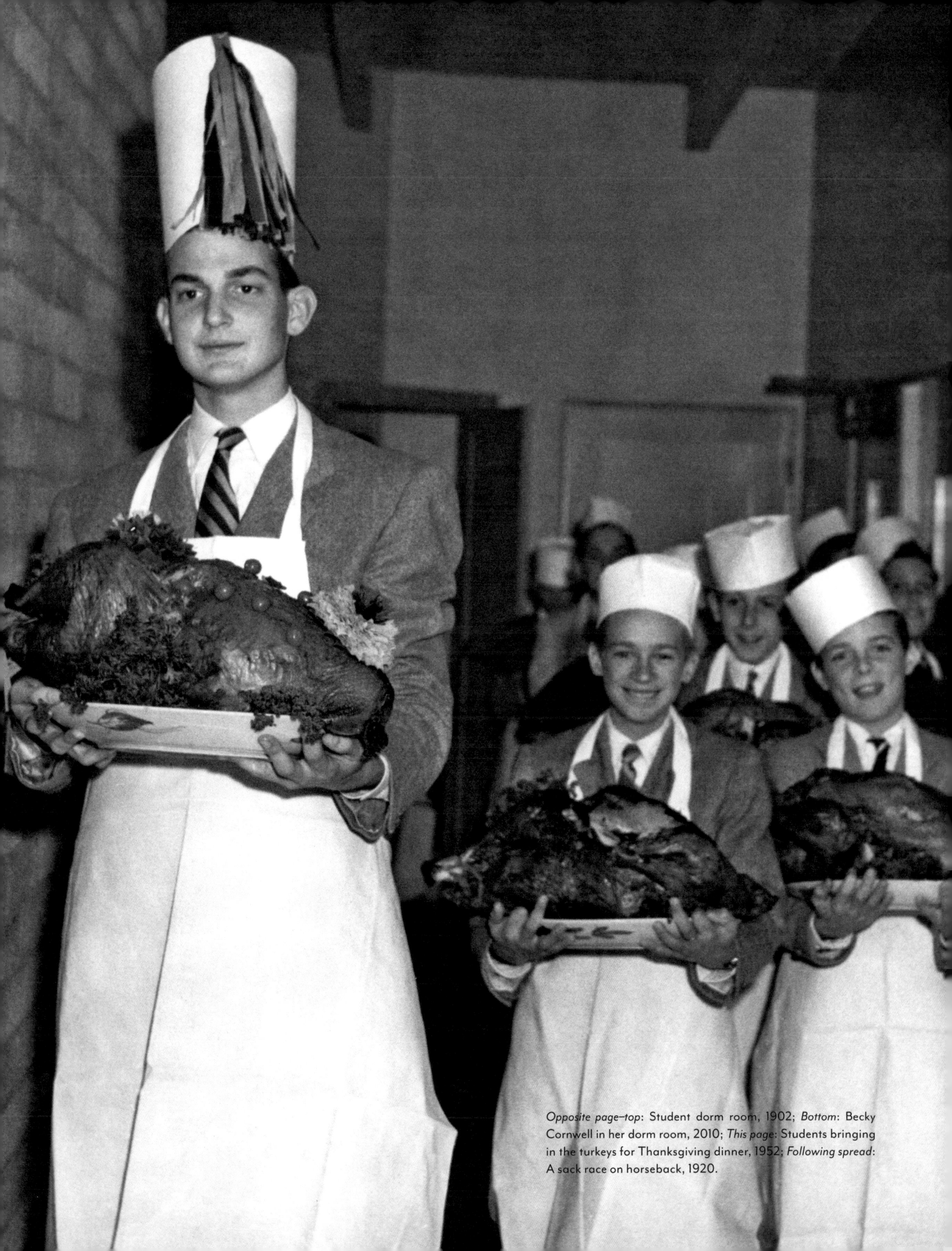

Opposite page–top: Student dorm room, 1902; *Bottom*: Becky Cornwell in her dorm room, 2010; *This page*: Students bringing in the turkeys for Thanksgiving dinner, 1952; *Following spread*: A sack race on horseback, 1920.

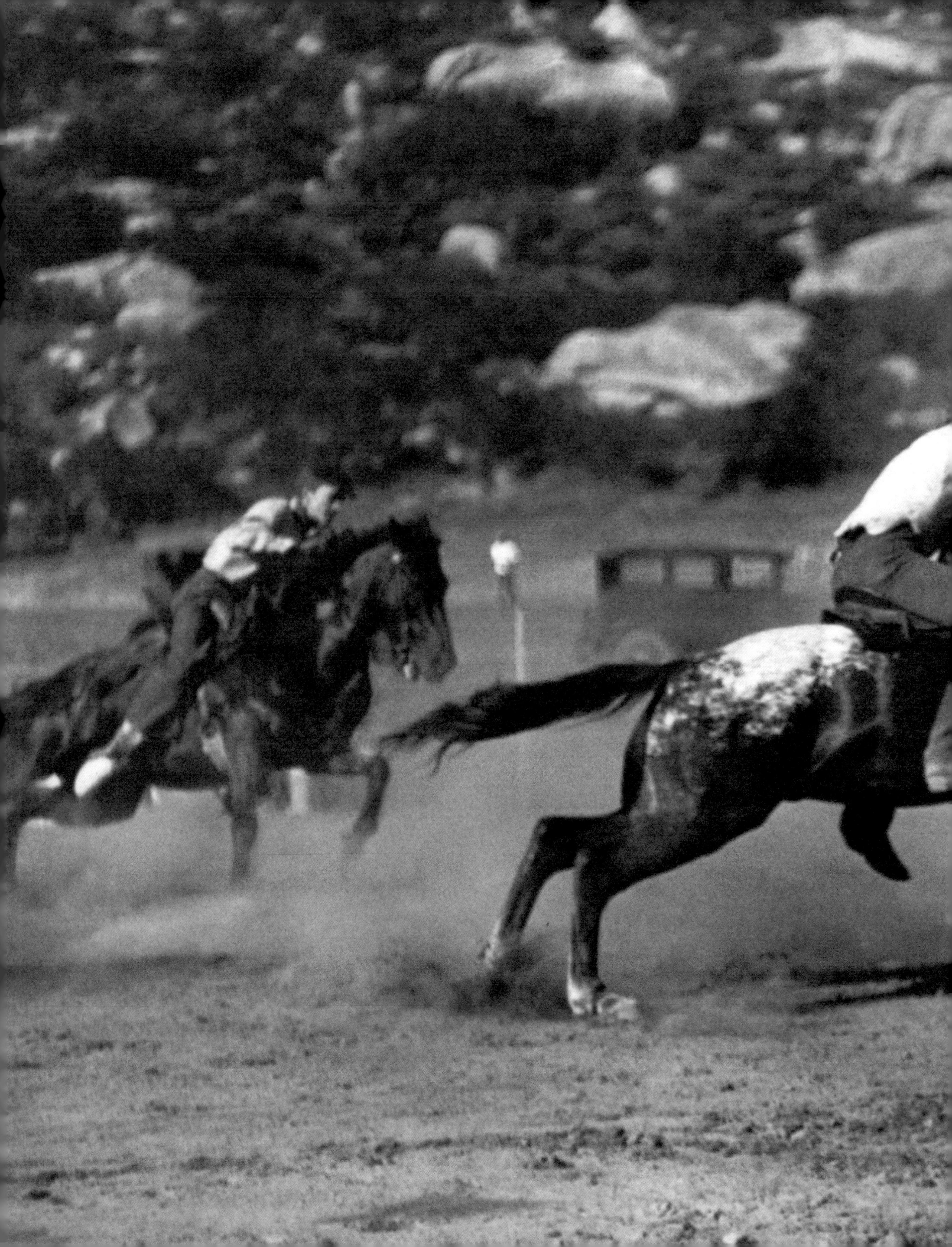

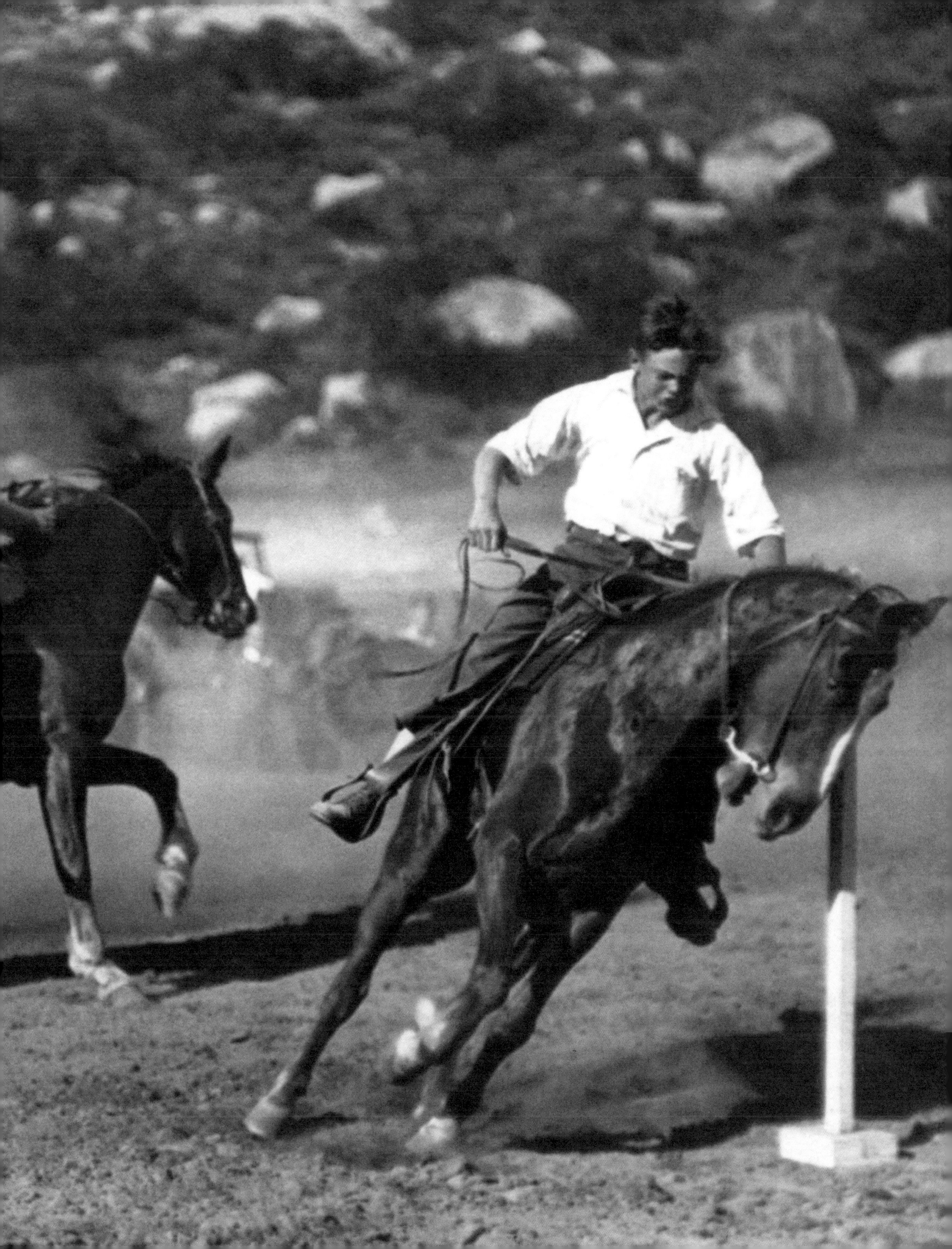

KATHERINE HALSEY

This is my 19th year at Thacher School—I teach French and English, and I work in the Horse Program. When I first started teaching here, I didn't ride at all—so I'm kind of the adult "poster child" for the program. At the beginning of any given school year, we have roughly 50 to 60 students in the freshman class, most of whom have never been near a horse before. We divide them into groups of about 10 and teach them how to ride. These groups of novices then progress through the winter term together. Once they pass their rider's test, they compete in Gymkhana in the spring. It's phenomenal what they accomplish in terms of basic riding skills over the course of the school year.

On the first day of school, the freshmen come through the barn to meet us and the horses. As each kid steps into the space, we gauge their interest, past experience, fear factor, and their natural balance and physical precision. Afterwards, the teachers from the Horse Department sit down together and match the kids to the horses.

Then every morning, seven days a week, the students have to feed, clean, and groom their horse by a certain hour. During the week, it's before classes at 8 a.m. At the beginning of the year, it takes them half an hour or 45 minutes to get it done properly. By the end of the year, it takes them eight minutes—they really learn to do it efficiently.

The kids ride five days a week for about two hours—that's roughly what they are expected to commit to. Some kids get deeply connected to their animal and will come out to the stables to just hang out with their horse on their own.

The lessons of this program carry over into all aspects of a student's life. It offers kids a chance to think about and process emotions differently. The horse is a simple creature in some ways, but it's also a deeply soulful creature. It can help calm the turbulent internal landscape of many kids. Inevitably, they develop a deep emotional response to this thousand-pound creature that they're trying to learn to communicate with. In doing so, they learn to recognise their own emotional response—they have to in order to be successful with their horse. Then they can manage and use those emotions in productive ways.

One of the great gifts of the program is that it offers the students the skills to deal with almost anything in life. In the Horse Program, the kids are pushed out of their comfort zone every day—no matter how skilled they are as riders. It's a daily lesson for them, because whether they want to or not, they have got to come and care for this living creature they are responsible for. They are forced to dig deep in ways that they've never done before. It's not about formulating the "great argument" that's going to convince their parents to

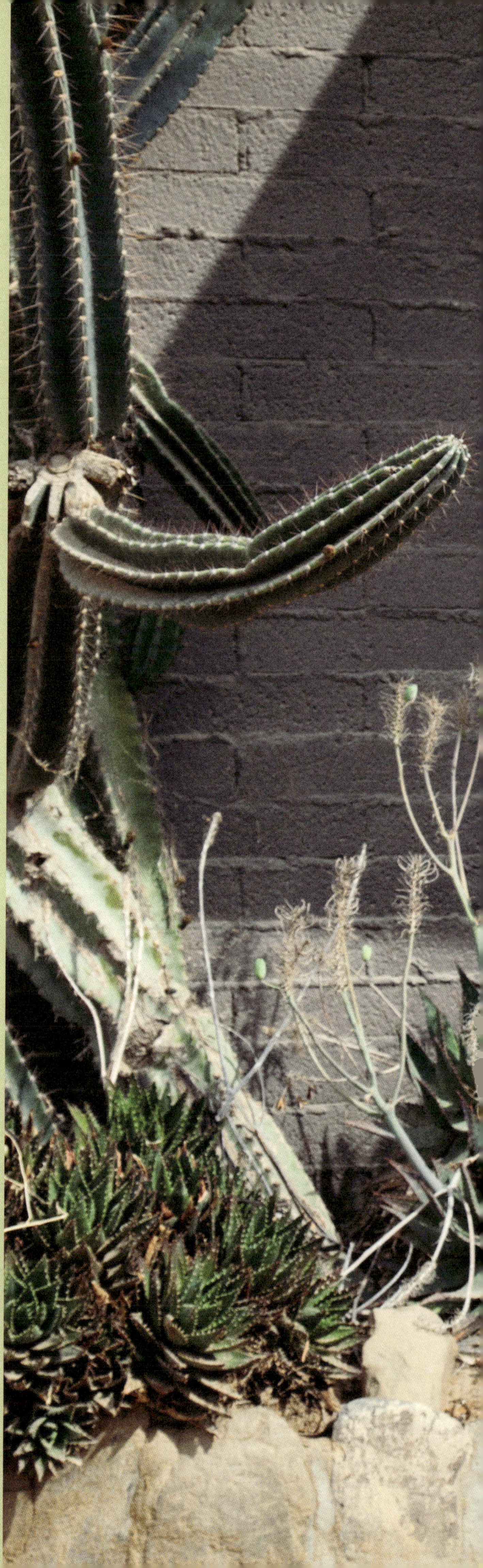

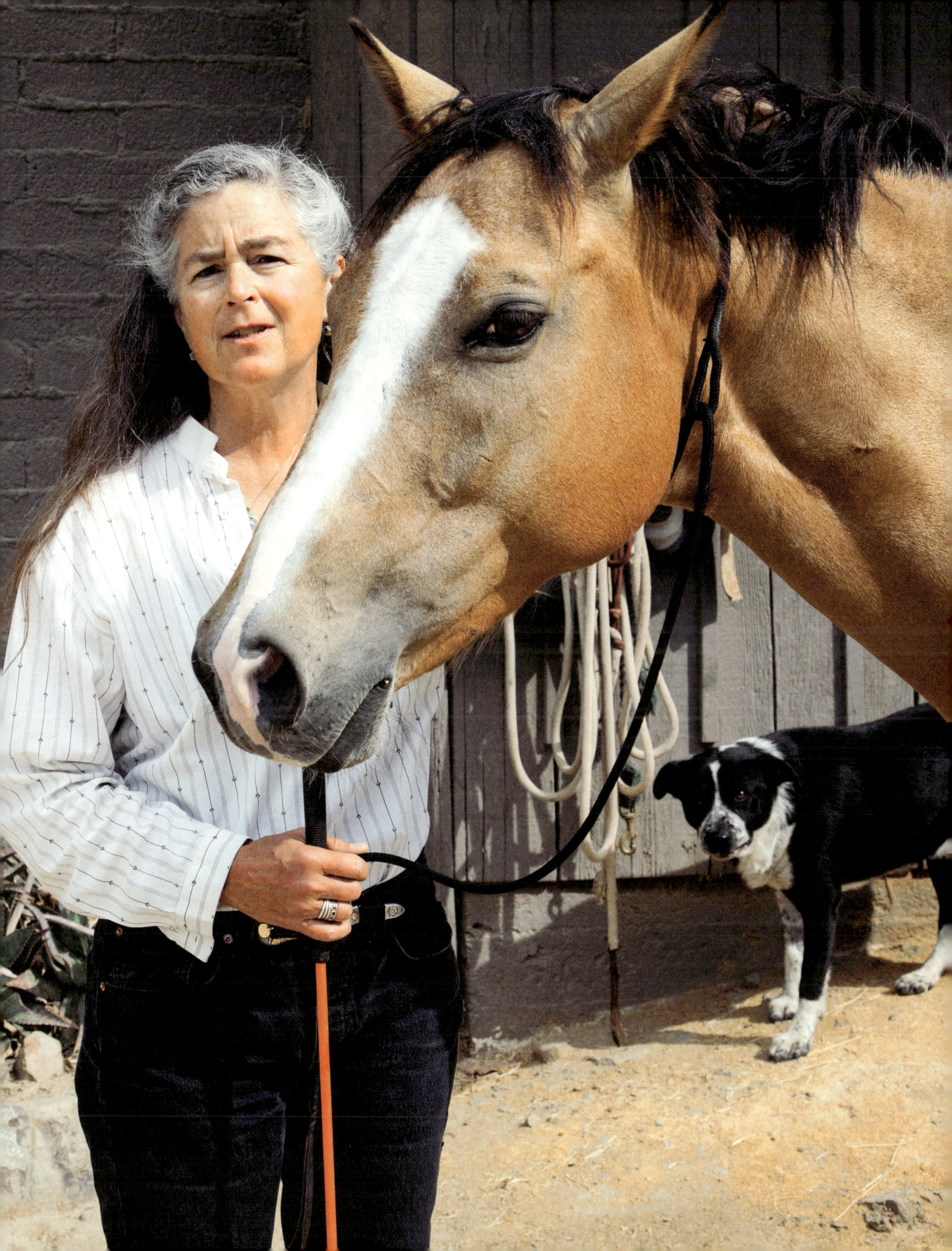

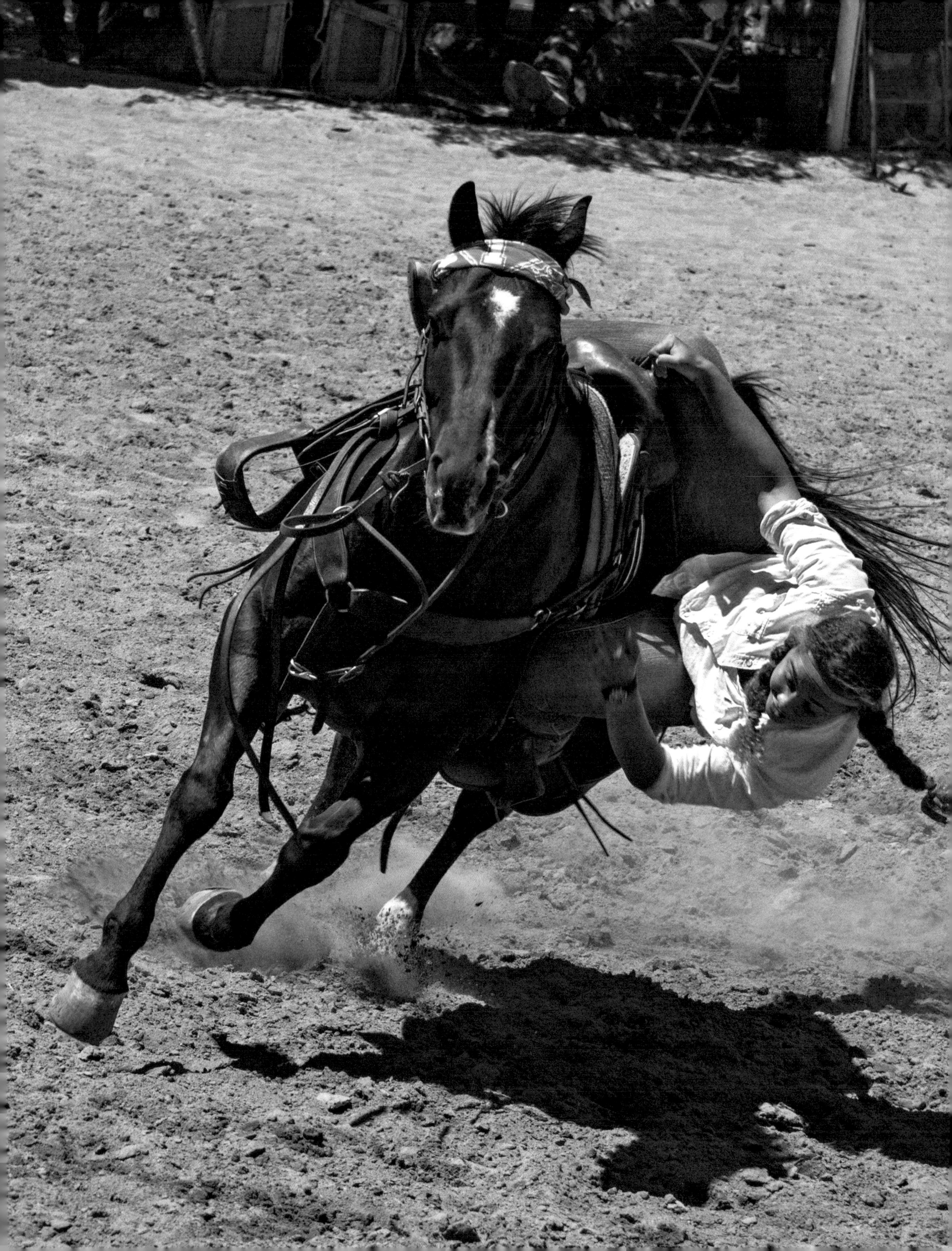

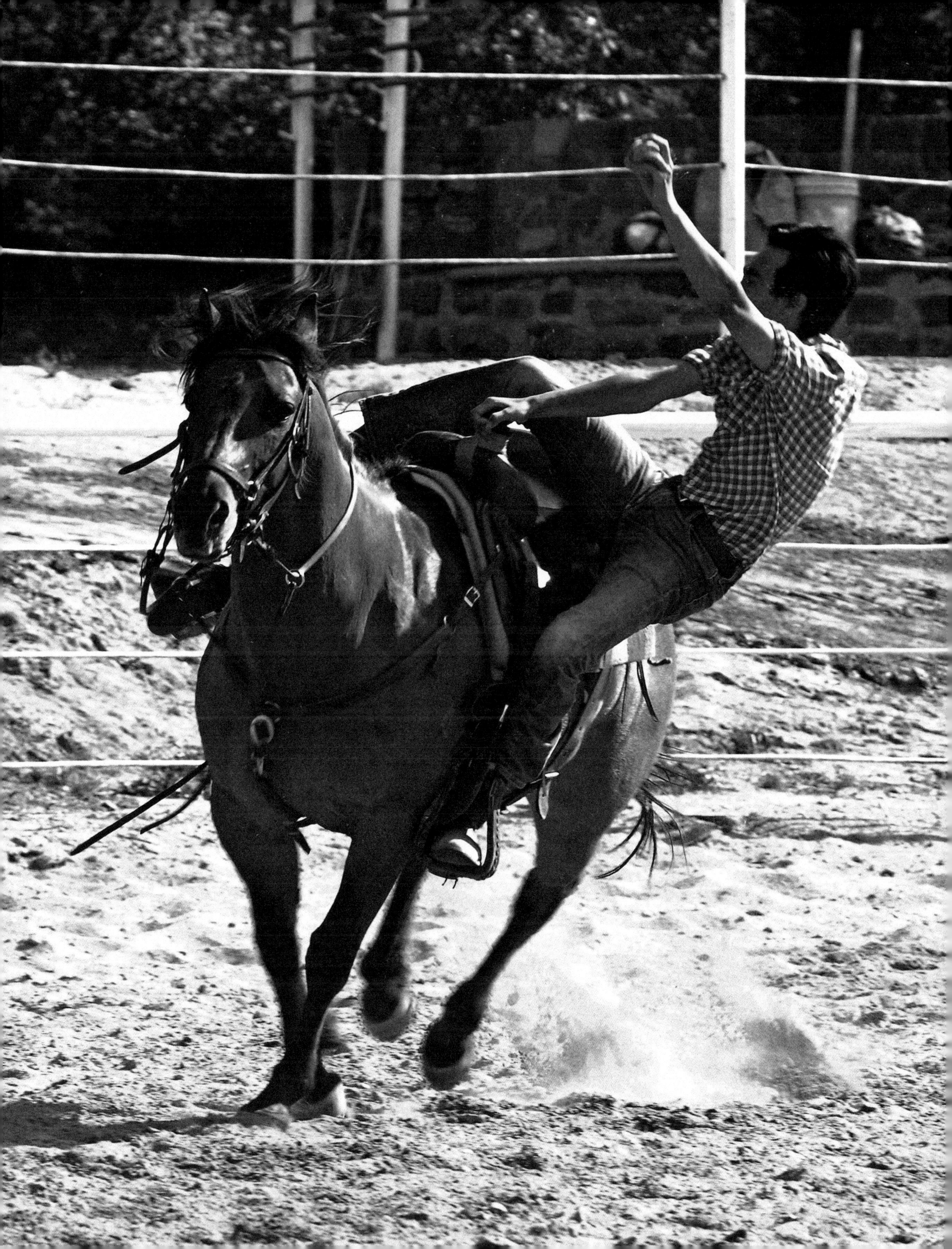

say yes to something. There's a horseman's adage "the horse is always a mirror." That is, the horse offers you a glimpse into your own being. In this program, there is no arguing with the truth of that mirror. It can take the kids a while to understand and accept that. Once they build a trusting relationship with their horse, they learn that their horse needs to be able to trust them for the partnership to work. It can take some time to understand what that exactly means—how you establish trust and nurture trust. These lessons also carry over into the classroom and the relationships that kids forge with the adults that they're working with. That emotional maturity enriches the whole academic experience here. It makes the job of teachers so much more rewarding, because we've got these incredible relationships in place with thoughtful, smart, engaged kids who want to figure out how to be good people—even though they're doing those weird adolescent things too. The horse program creates the most extraordinary environment in which to work and play with these kids.

Our program is grounded in this idea of the West, but it transcends the West, which is why it's still compelling in 2014. It's part of our philosophy to believe in kids—and help them to realize that they are invested with genuine trust and responsibility through the care of these incredible creatures. It helps them, in the moment, to be the best person they can be and to envision themselves as people who are independently honorable and connected to other people in a way that is meaningful. Trust isn't something that just happens—although one of the powers of our model is that we extend that trust from the moment the kids get here. Still, it's our job to help the students understand that our trust in them is a conscious choice that we're making as educators. The kids feel empowered by taking ownership of their school culture and they're proud of it. What happens out here is deeply moving. It's the most powerful model I've encountered as an educator.

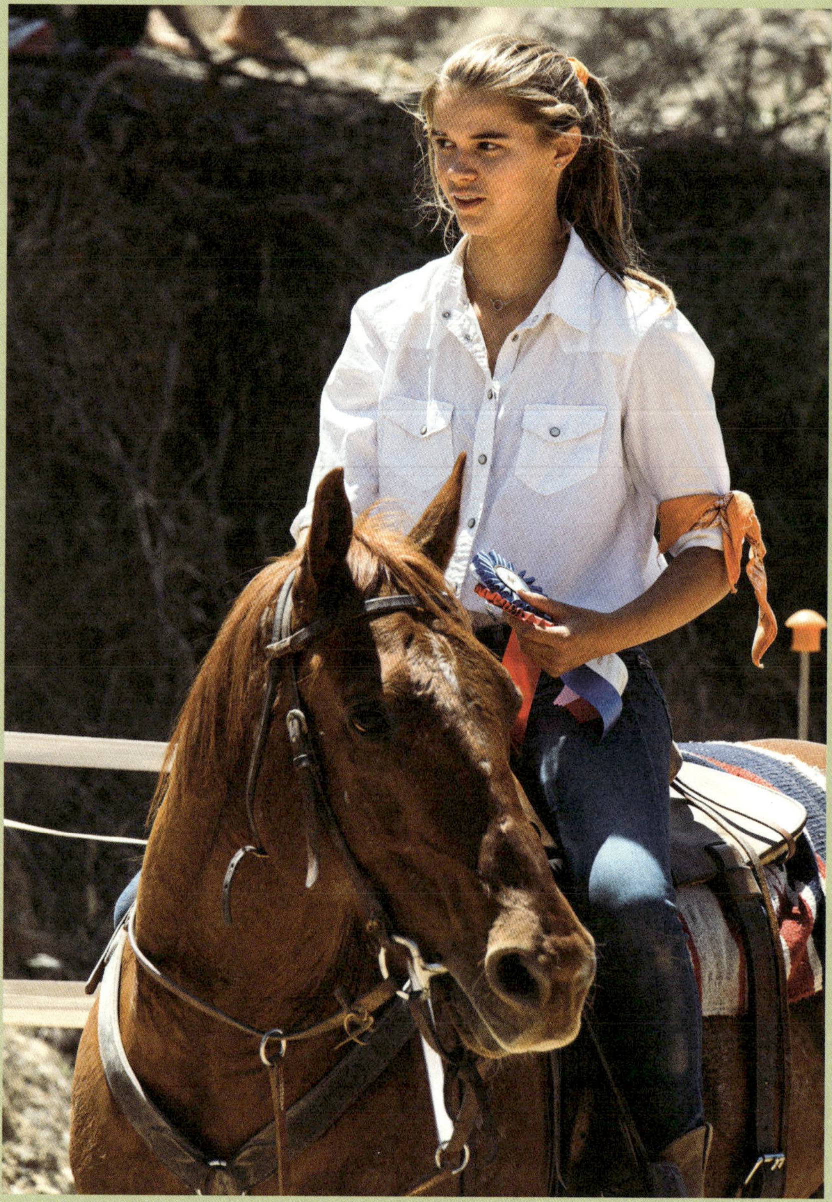

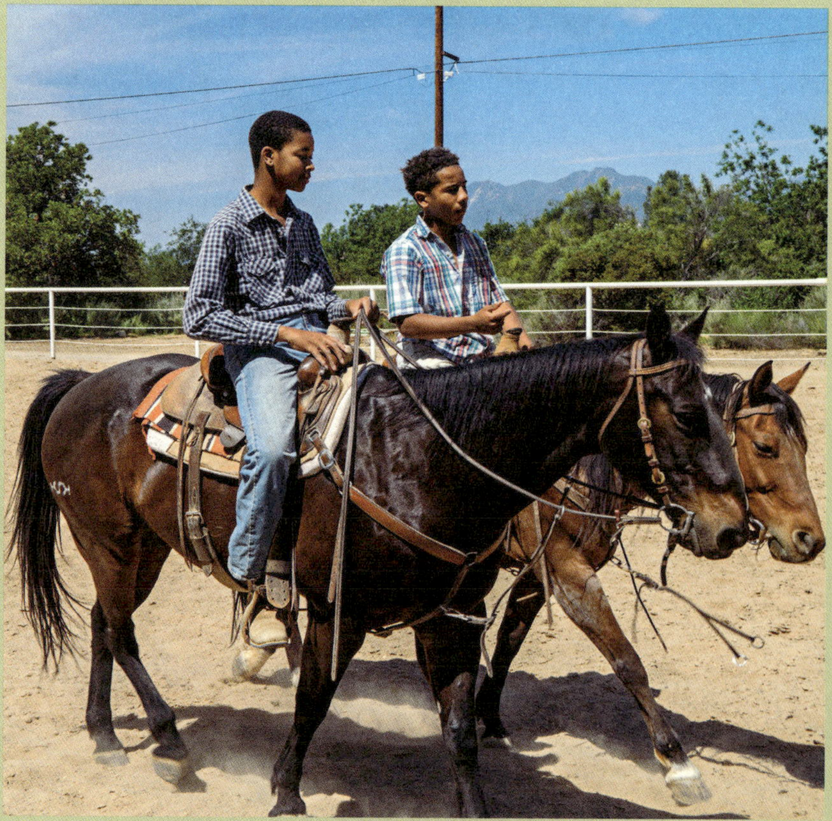

Previous spread: Jordan Perry and Maximilian Damon practicing for Gymkhana, 2014.

This page—top: Isabelle Doubleday, 2010; *Bottom*: Tobi Oyinlola and Jackson Carroll, 2014; *Opposite page—top left*: Horse Camping Director Rene Duykaerts, 2014; *Top right*: Wade Warren grooming his horse, 2010; *Bottom*: Competitors taking a break during Gymkhana, 2014.

Following spread: Peter Ammon and friends during Gymkhana, 2014.

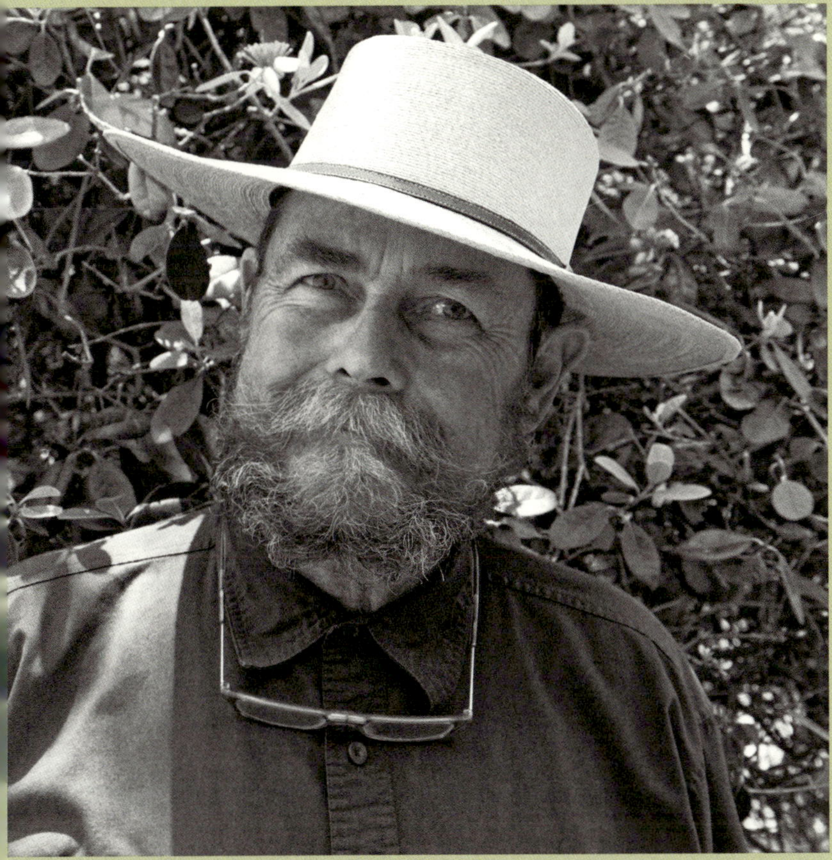

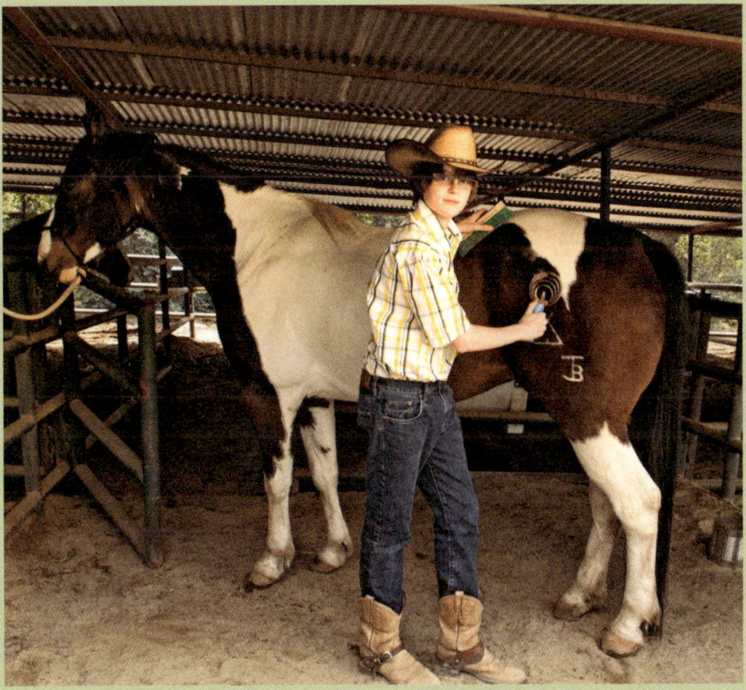

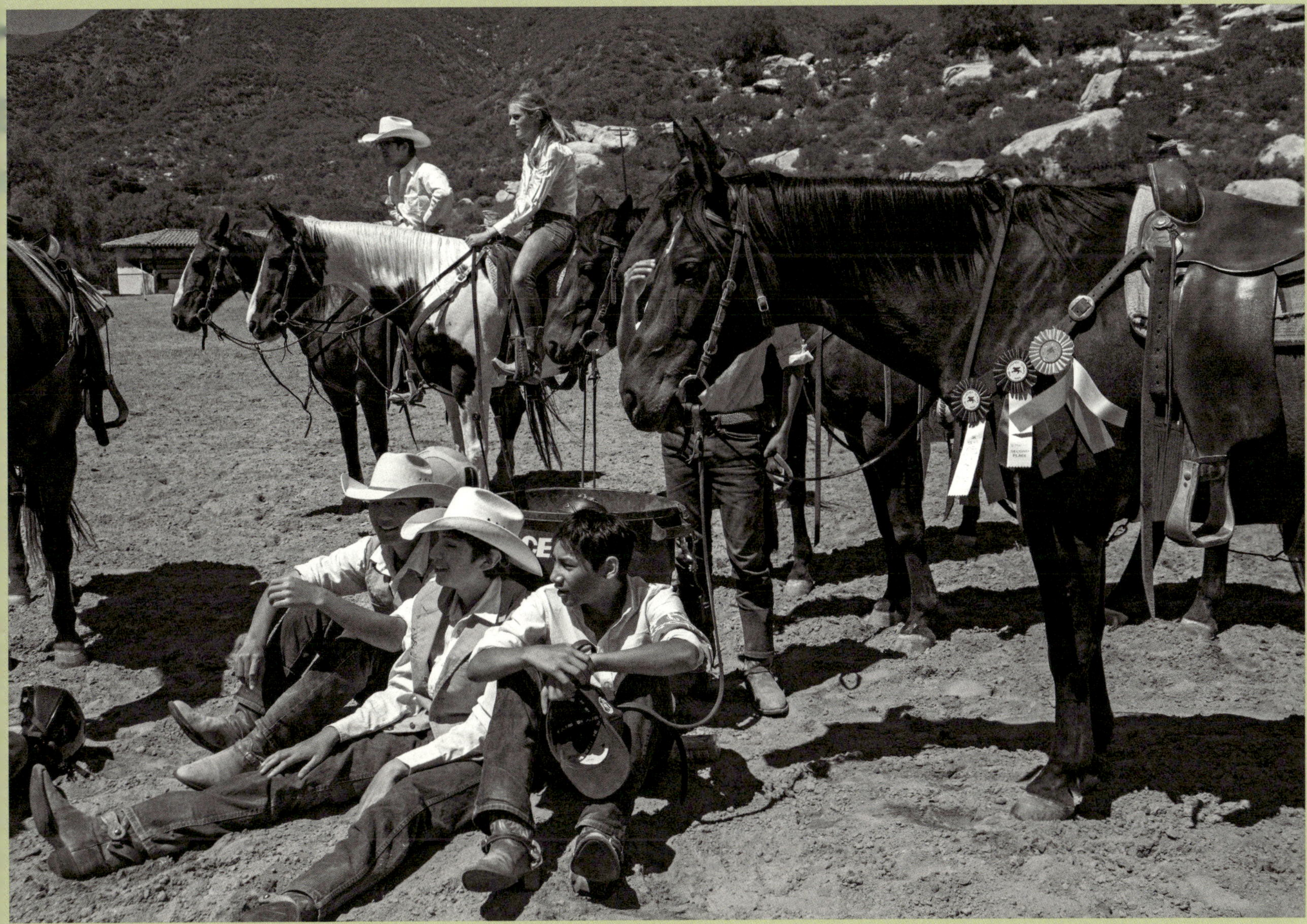

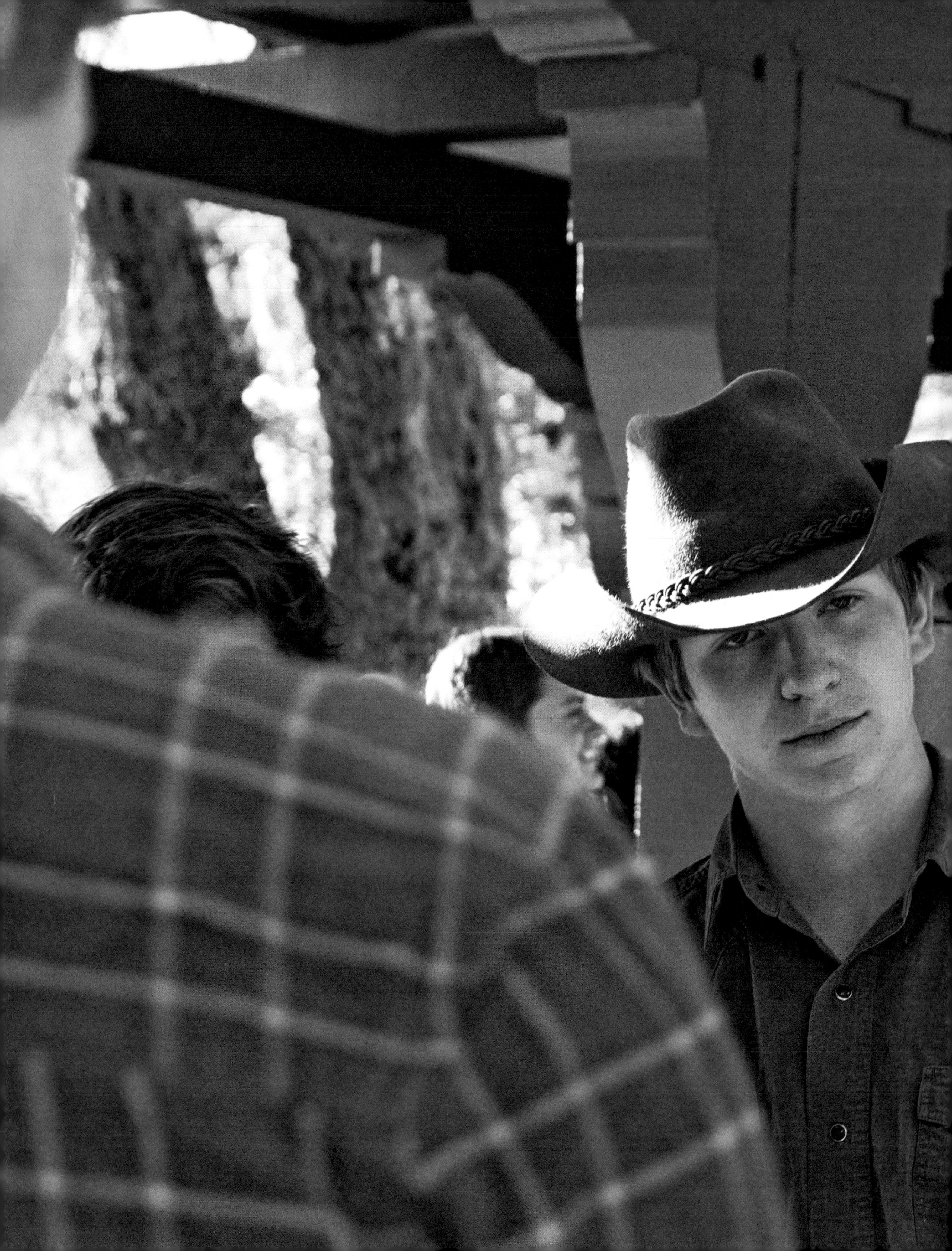

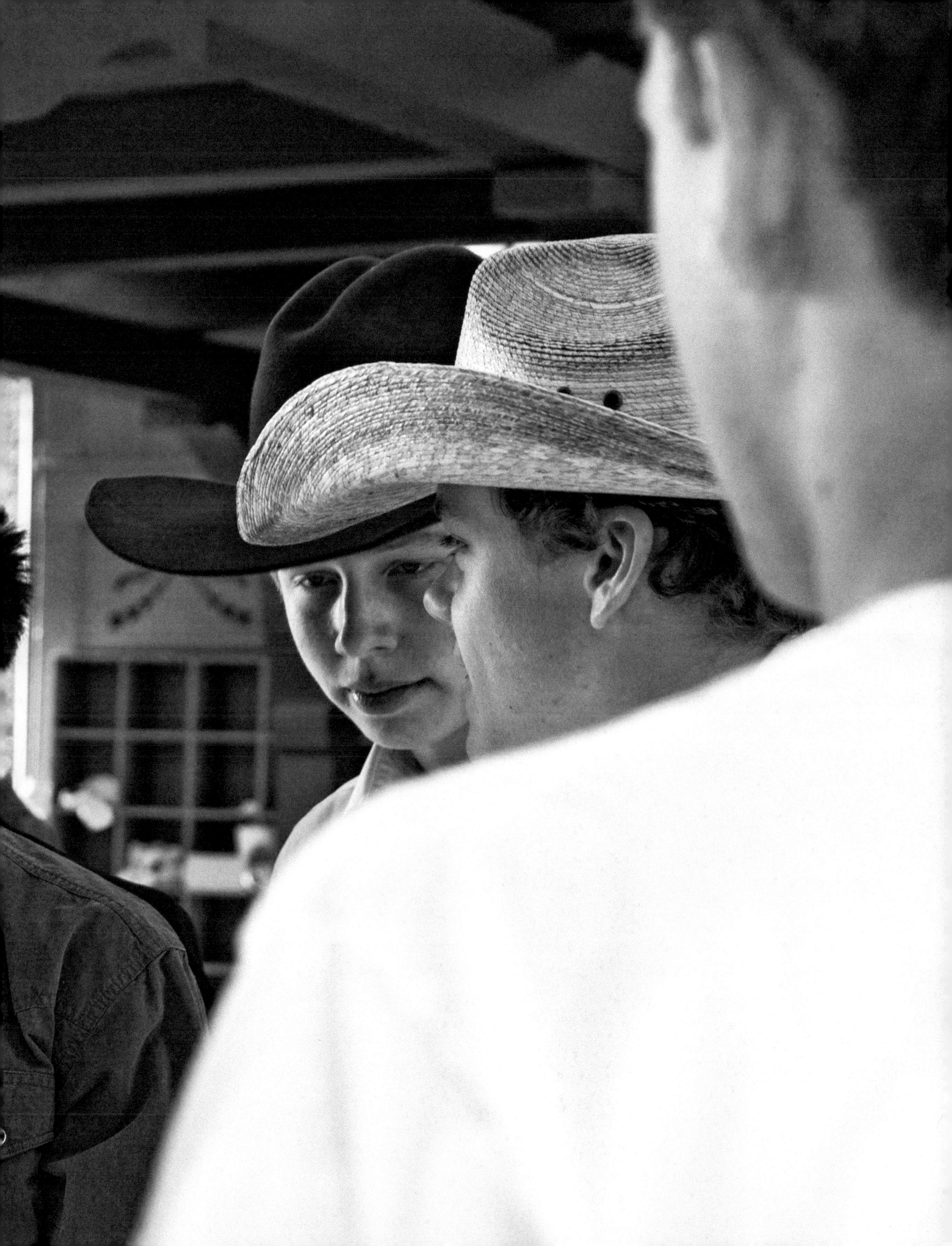

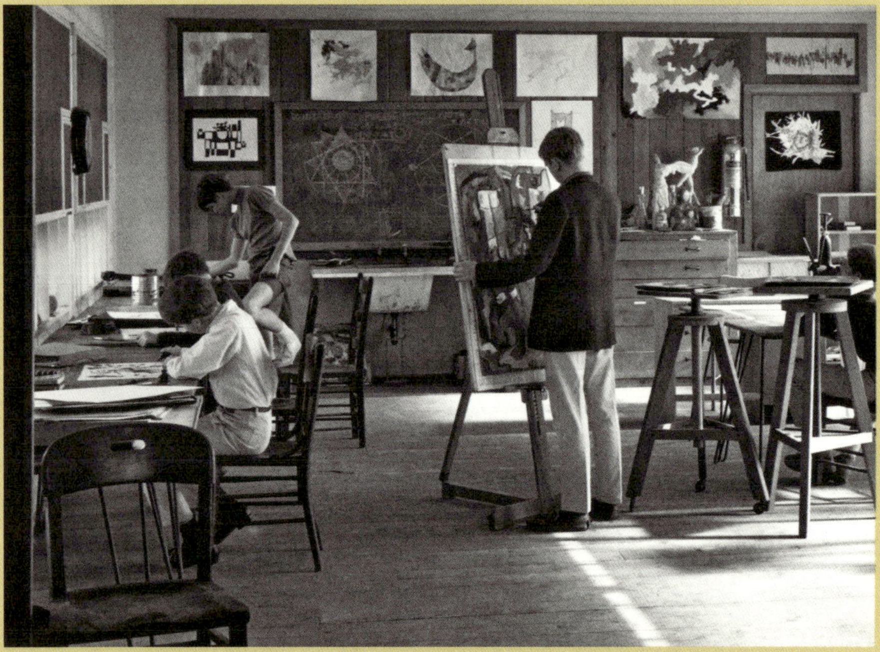

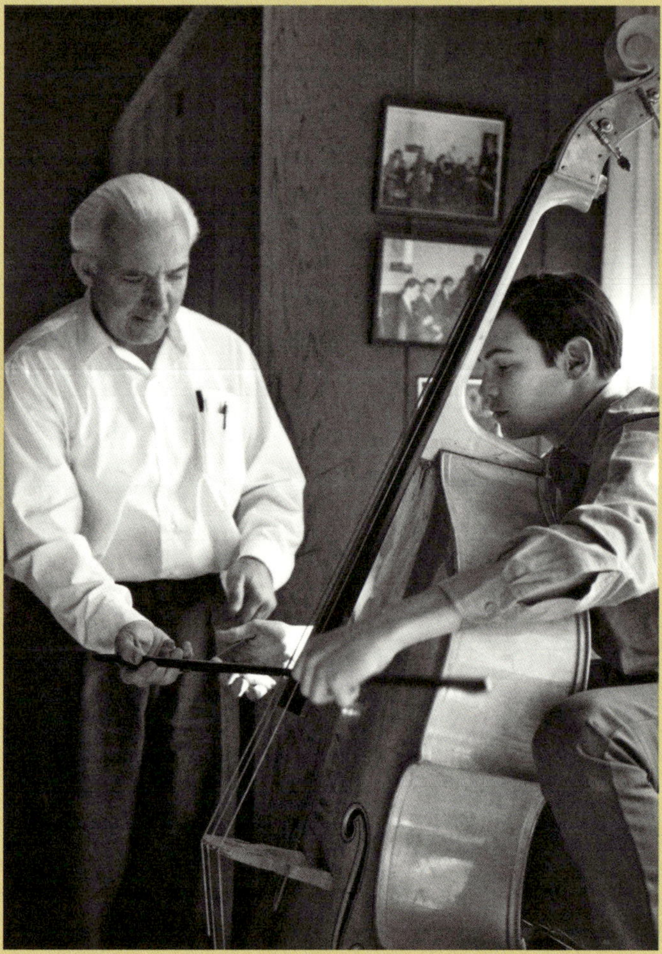

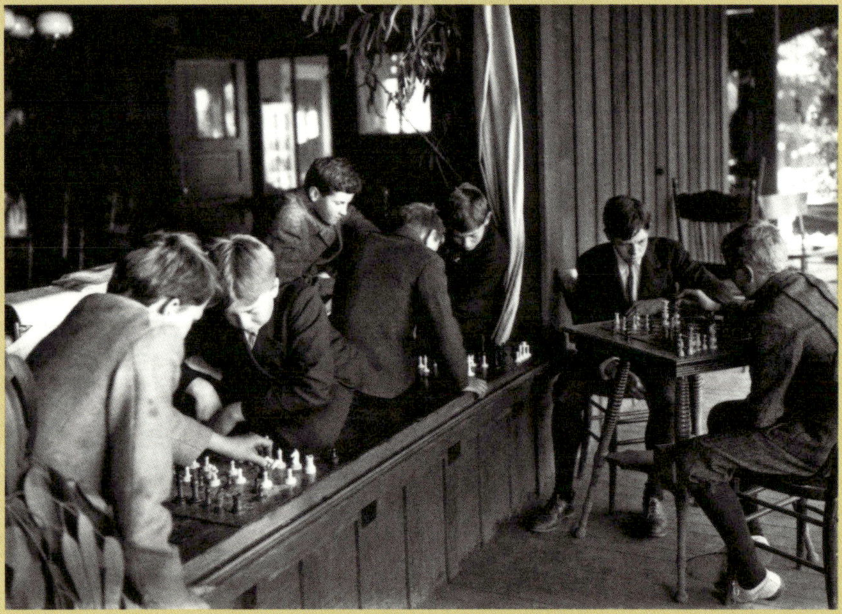

Clockwise from top left: Students of art teacher Gui Ignon in the Art Studio, 1967; Music Instructor, Michael Ehrhardt, teaching a classical bass lesson, c. 1960; Jack Huyler, faculty member since 1949, pictured with a group of students at Patton's Cabin—a school owned property in the Los Padres National Forest, c. 1950's; Avery Hellman in her dorm room, 2010; Students playing chess in the Parlor, 1893–today, the parlor is part of the dining hall.

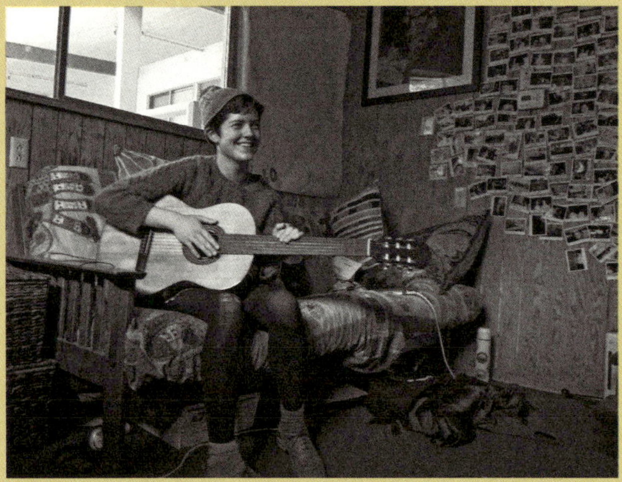

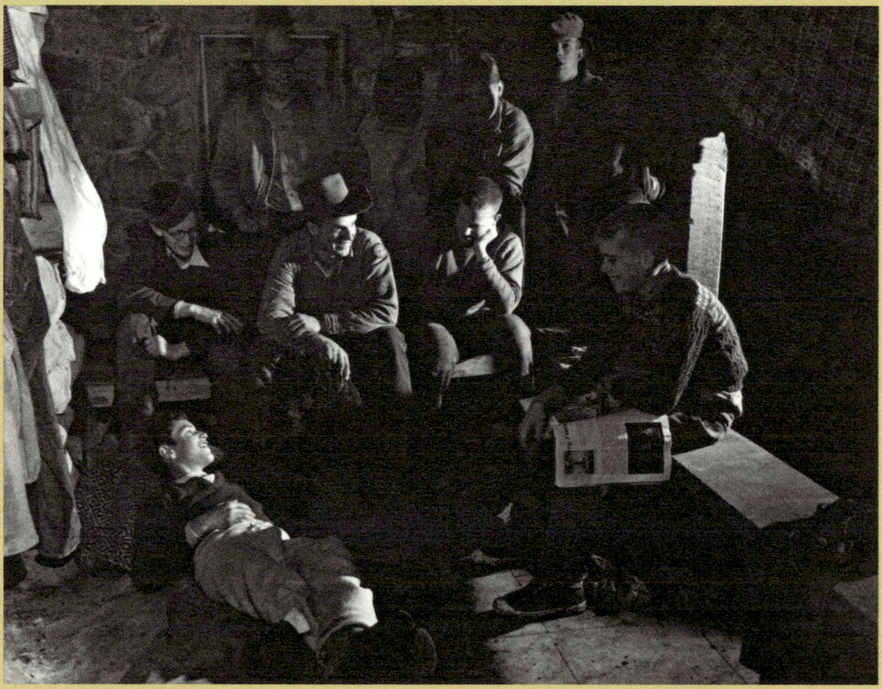

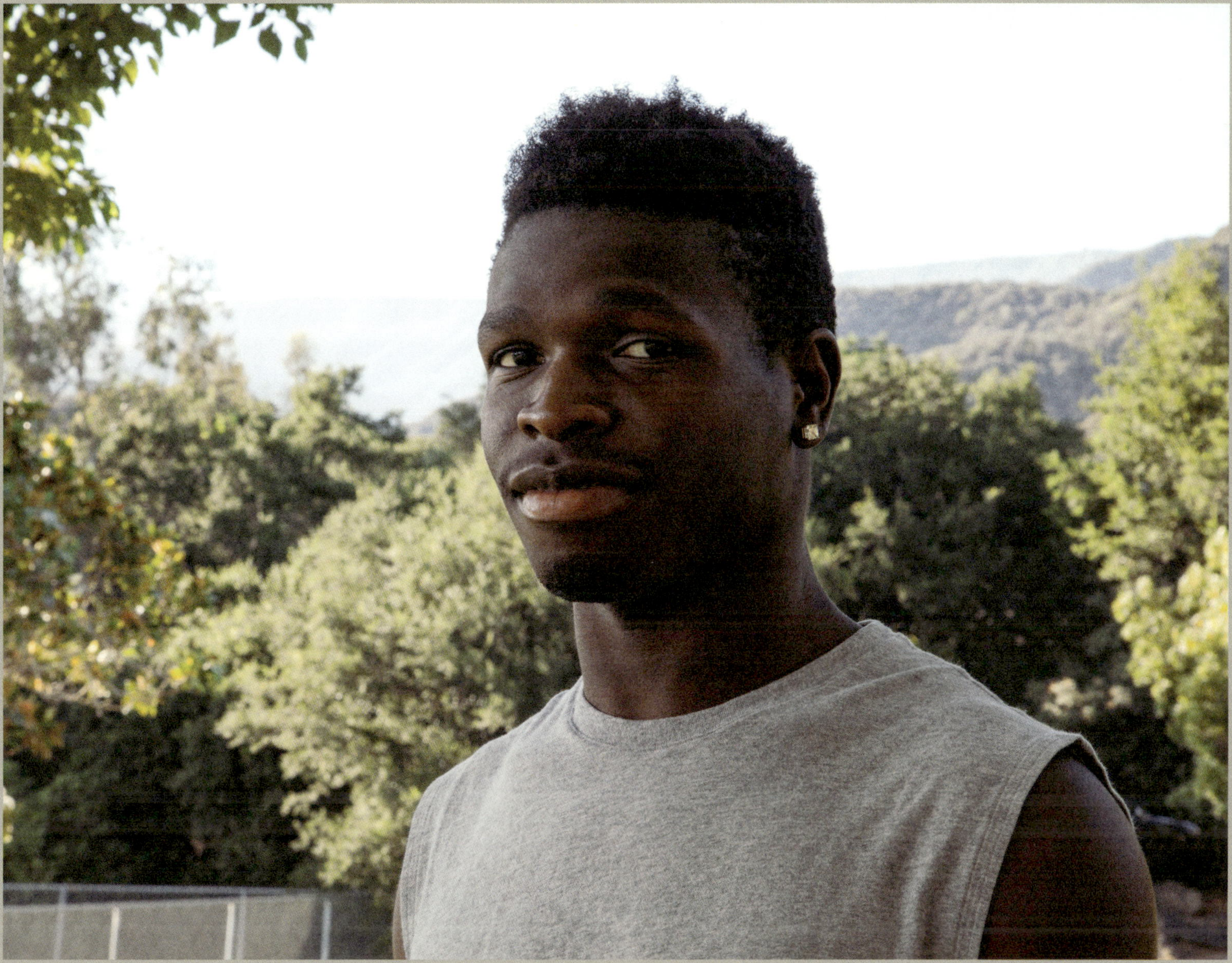

MOMO LEWIS

I grew up in Harlem in New York City. Coming to Ojai was definitely a transition, but I soon appreciated the differences from life back home. I like to think of coming from New York and going to Thacher as living the best of both worlds. The culture here was really different from anything I had experienced before. I had never sat on a horse or touched a horse even—and you have to do those things right away as a freshman. My horse's name was Clifford. When I told my friends back home about him, they just laughed, "What, is he big and red?" Clifford was tough with me at first, but after some time we got to like each other. He and I were tight by the time the program ended and I had to let him go.

The thing about the Horse Program is you have to go into it with an open mind-set. You're working with a creature that's not human and doesn't think the way you do, doesn't have the same emotions you do. But at the same time, they have their own emotions—they do have a brain and they do think. You have to set aside any problems you're experiencing—even if you've had a hard day, you can't go into the experience angry. The horse doesn't know how your day went and probably doesn't care. I feel like that's a great way to approach life in general. When you go into the real world, you'll be working with people who have their own situations to deal with, and if you bring all this extra baggage, it isn't going to end well.

I'm going to Occidental College in Eagle Rock, California next year, and I'm going to double major in Economics and Philosophy. That's mostly an individual decision—over the years I've wanted to get into business, but I also love reading philosophy and thinking about all those different ideas. I'll really miss my history teacher, Mr. McGowan, who I have been lucky to have for all four years. He's the kind of person who is willing to allow the kids to go about learning in their own fashion, while giving them the keys and tools to get there. Mr. McGowan has never tried to impose his own views and values on us, because history can be interpreted in so many different ways. He really allows us to do that.

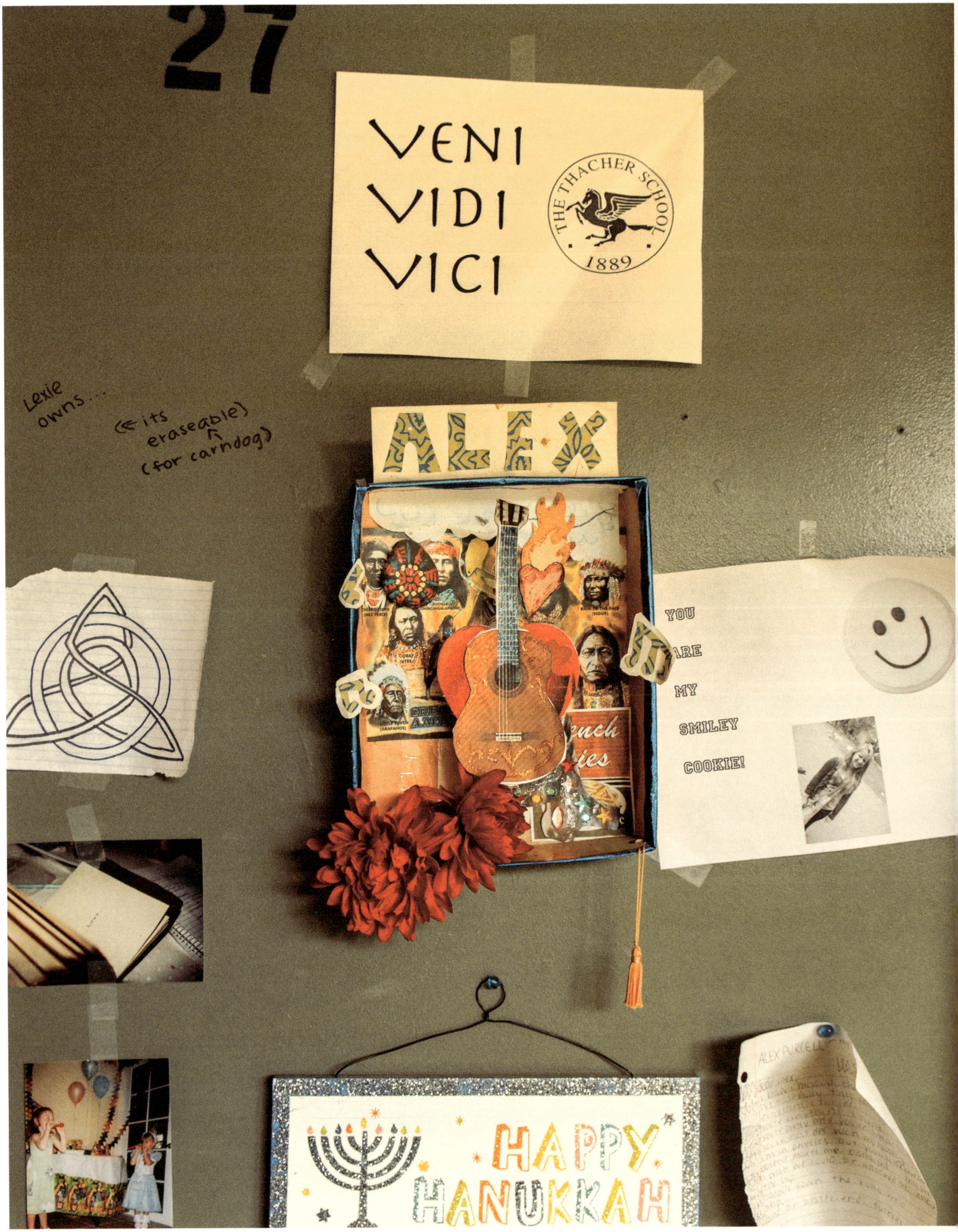
27
VENI
VIDI
VICI
THE THACHER SCHOOL
1889
Lexie owns...
(⇐ its erasable)
(for carndog)
ALEX
YOU
ARE
MY
SMILEY
COOKIE!
HAPPY
HANUKKAH

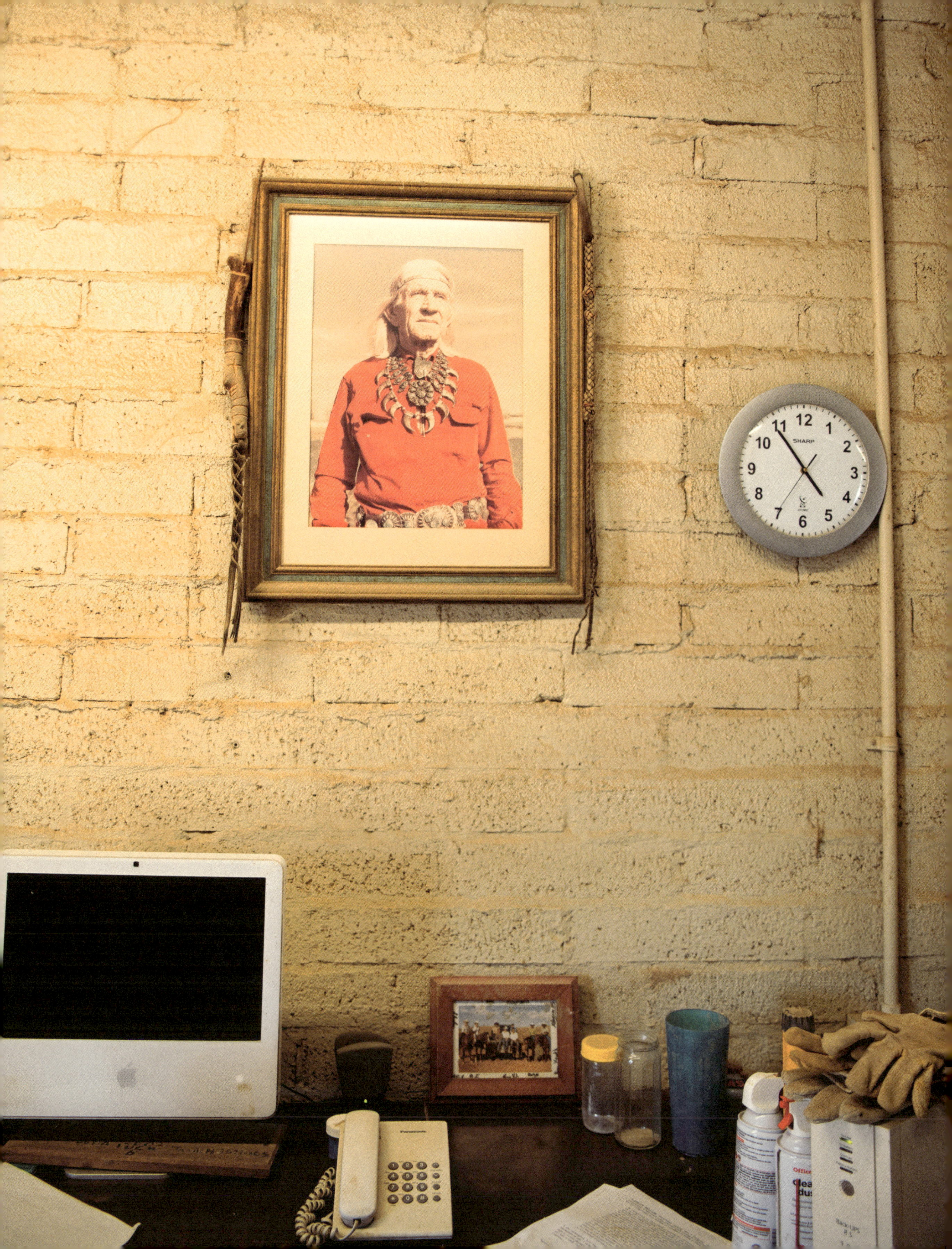
SHARP

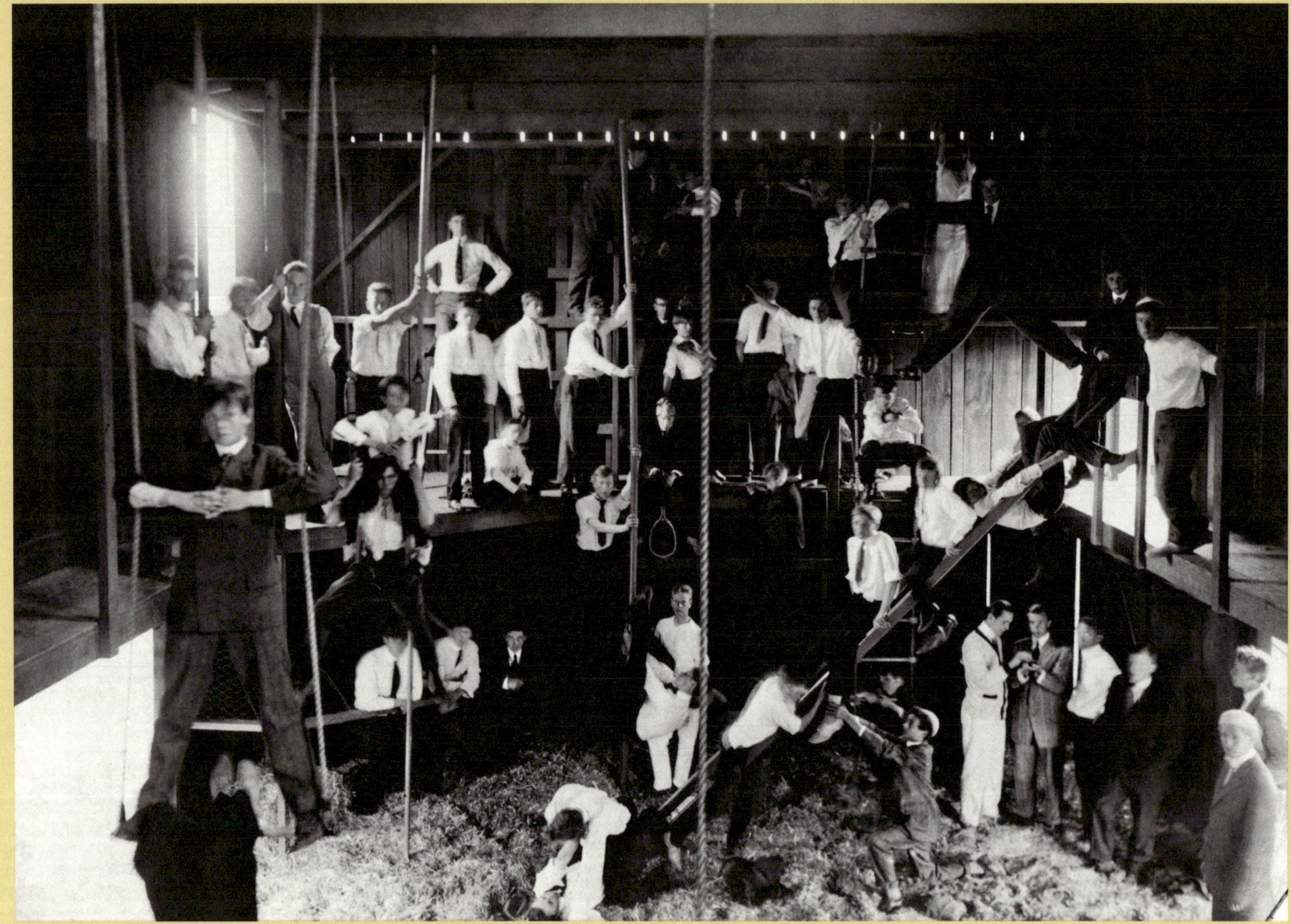

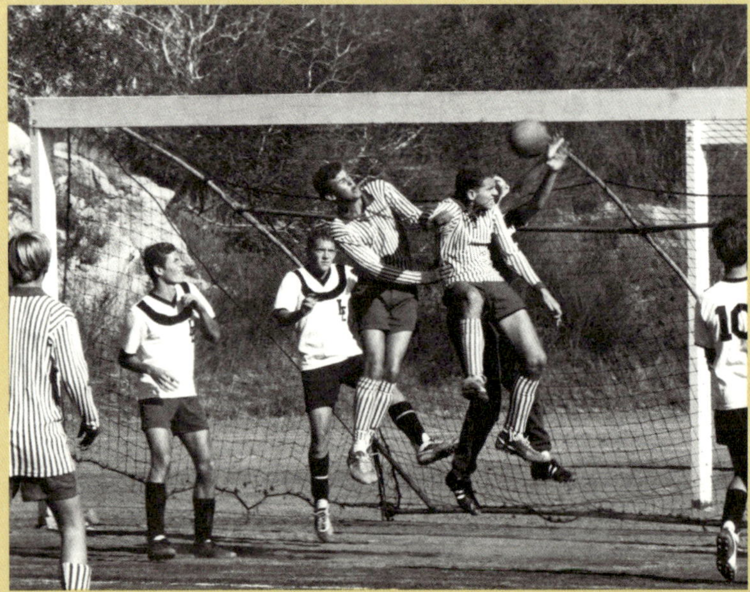

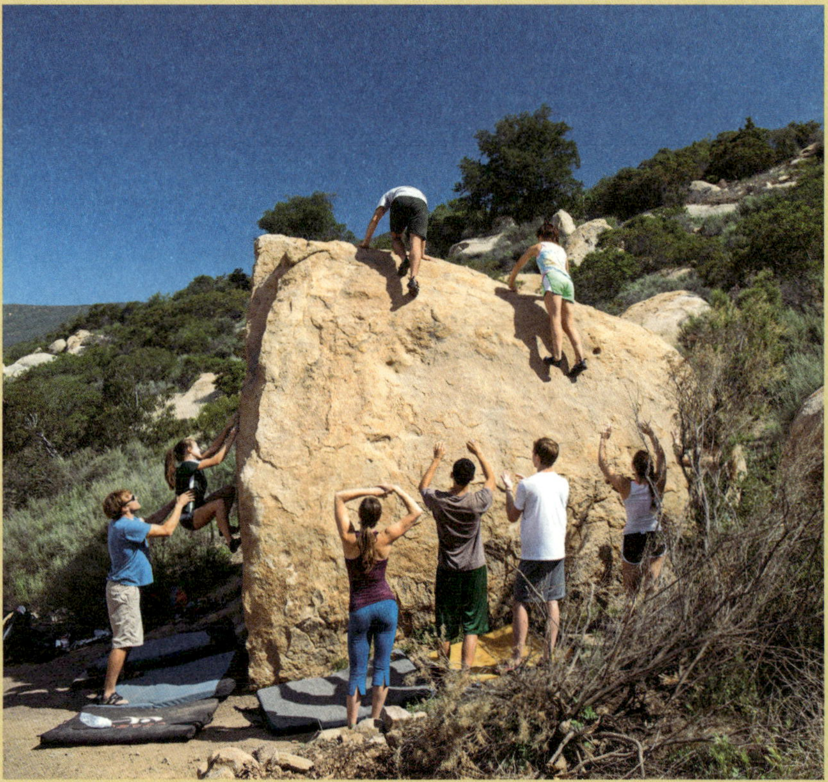

Clockwise from top left: Students in The Rough House, a barn-sized jungle gym built in 1906 and equipped with ropes, ramps, chutes and ladders—it quickly became a favorite place for students to burn off steam; Outdoor Program Director Brian Pidduck assists students with climbing instruction; A soccer game from 1967.

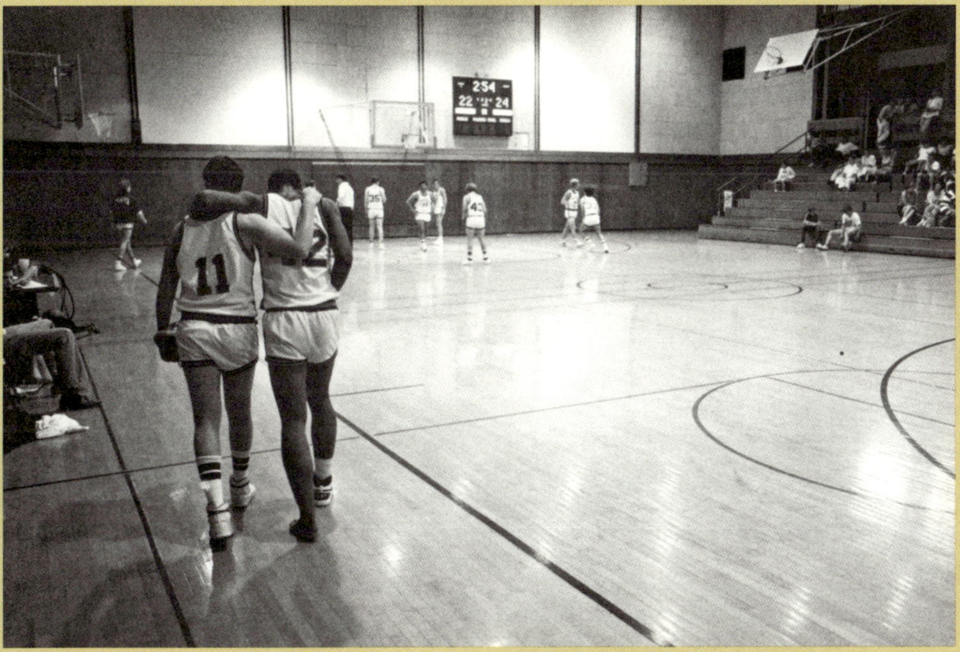

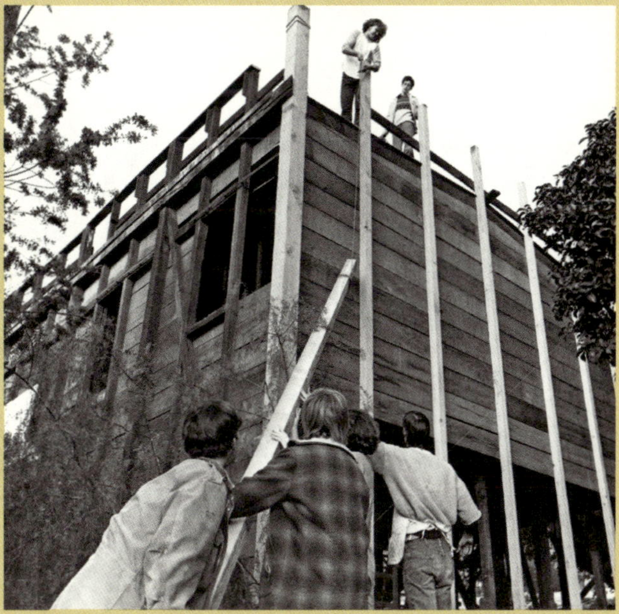

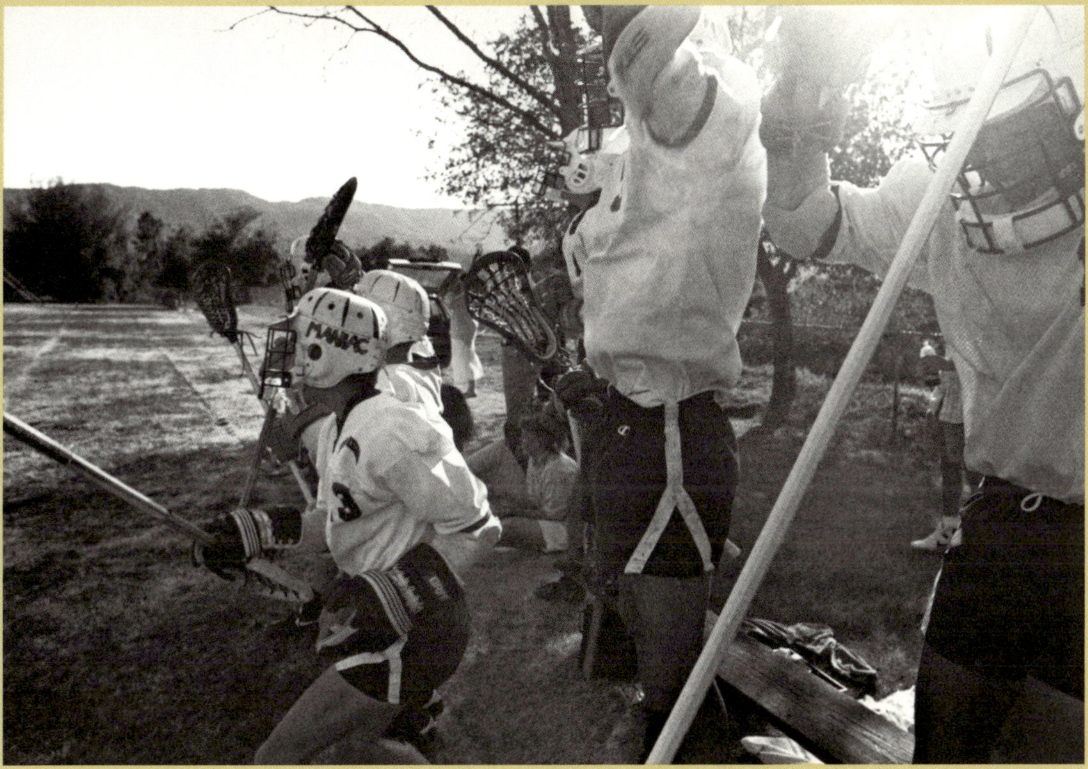

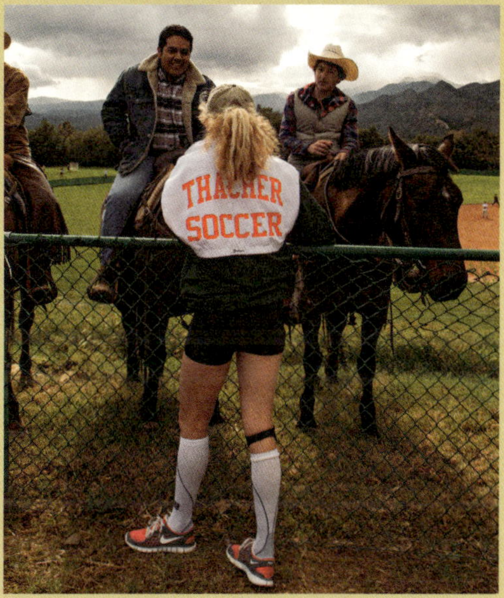

Clockwise from top left: Basketball game, 1970s; Constructing a new Roughhouse, 1970; Lacrosse meets riding, 2010; Swimming in the old resevoir; Girl's basketball game, 1985; Boy's lacrosse team victory, 1989.

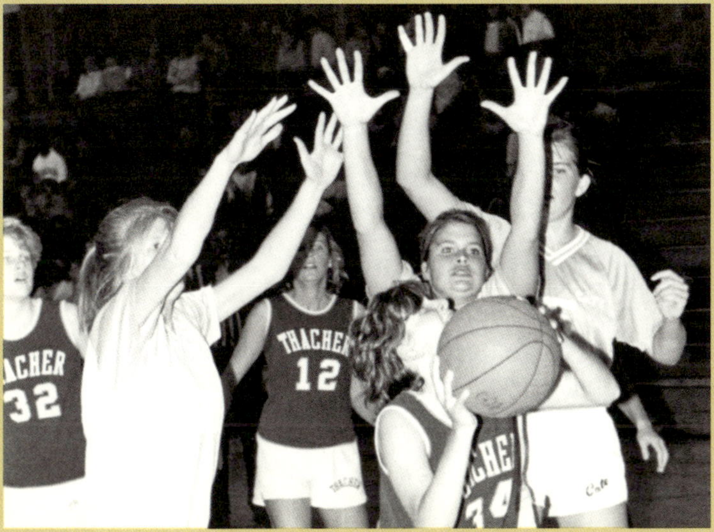

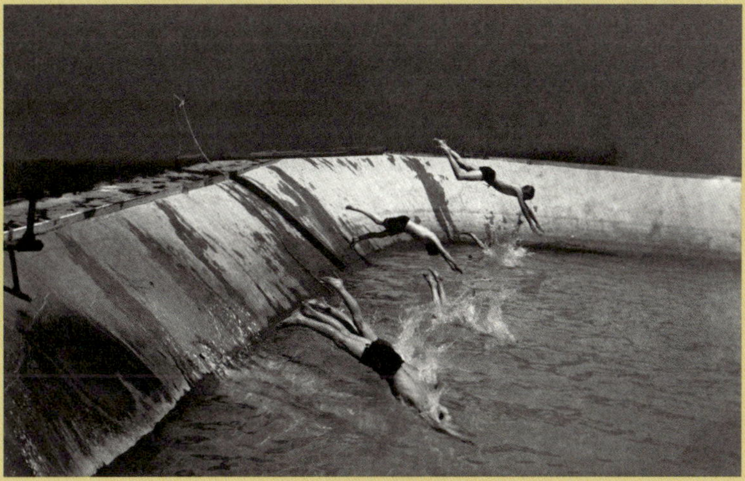

HAYDEN HOWARD

I came to Thacher in part to get out of Los Angeles for a little while. My dad always told me—and I've found this to be true—that when you leave a familiar place you get a fresh perspective on things. Distance allows you to look back and see who your real friends were, for example. Leaving the city also helped me to stop being preoccupied with all the superficial stuff and just focus on my education. That's something people often take for granted here, but it's harder to accomplish in most places.

When I visit my friends back home, I see the ways in which I've changed at Thacher. I've become more mature and learned how to cope on my own. My friends back home certainly don't study like we do here. Not that I'm going to be an academic, but Thacher gives you a great work ethic, for sure. People here are also less sarcastic, a little more genuine, so it took them a while to realize I wasn't being rude—it was just the way we talked back in L.A. The fact that it's so sheltered here took some getting used to. It's safer, in a good way, though it was difficult for me to trust people and just relax at first.

Sometimes I miss my friends back home, but I don't really mind the fact that we aren't allowed to use our phones outside the dorms. It's one of our policies. When I talk to my friends back in L.A., their heads are always down, constantly texting. I used do the same thing—check my phone every 5 seconds—but now when I'm home, I find it really frustrating. Occasionally I miss that immediate connection, but we do socialize a lot here—play games, watch movies, do sports all the time. Look at where we are—it just feels so much healthier, mentally and physically.

Lots of kids, especially where I'm from, are used to just not doing what they don't want to do. Many of them are spoiled, and I can't say I wasn't a little bit too when I first came here. But the horse program is mandatory, and I quickly understood there are just some things you *have* to do. It was so hard at first. Adults always say, "You can do it if you try." I used to doubt that, or argue about it. But working with Tigger—my horse—taught me that you really can overcome most difficulties if you put in the effort. Tigger also walked really funny—pretty much always to the side—so he was super easy to ride, a horse for the "very special" riders. I think they assigned him to me because I fell into that category.

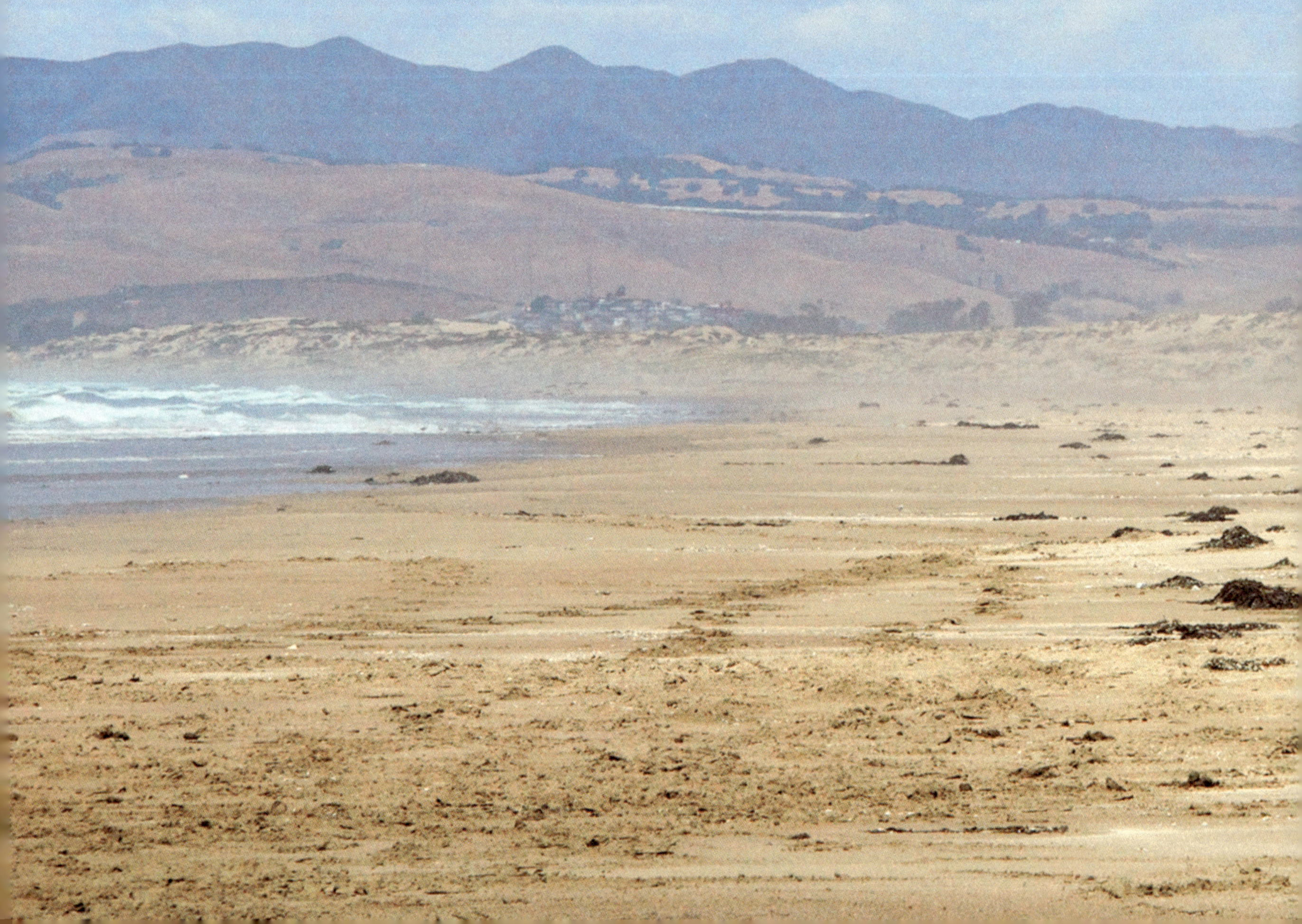

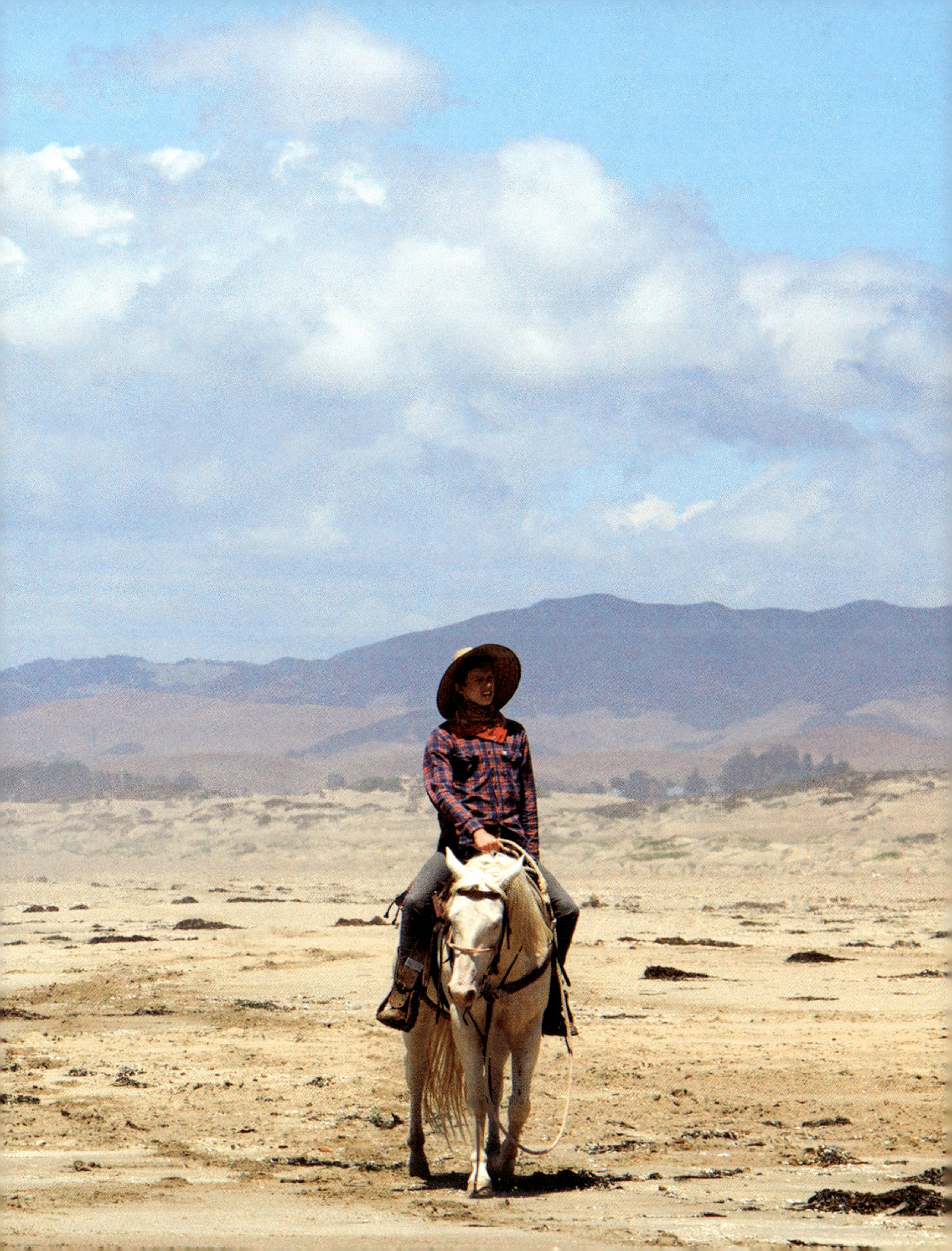

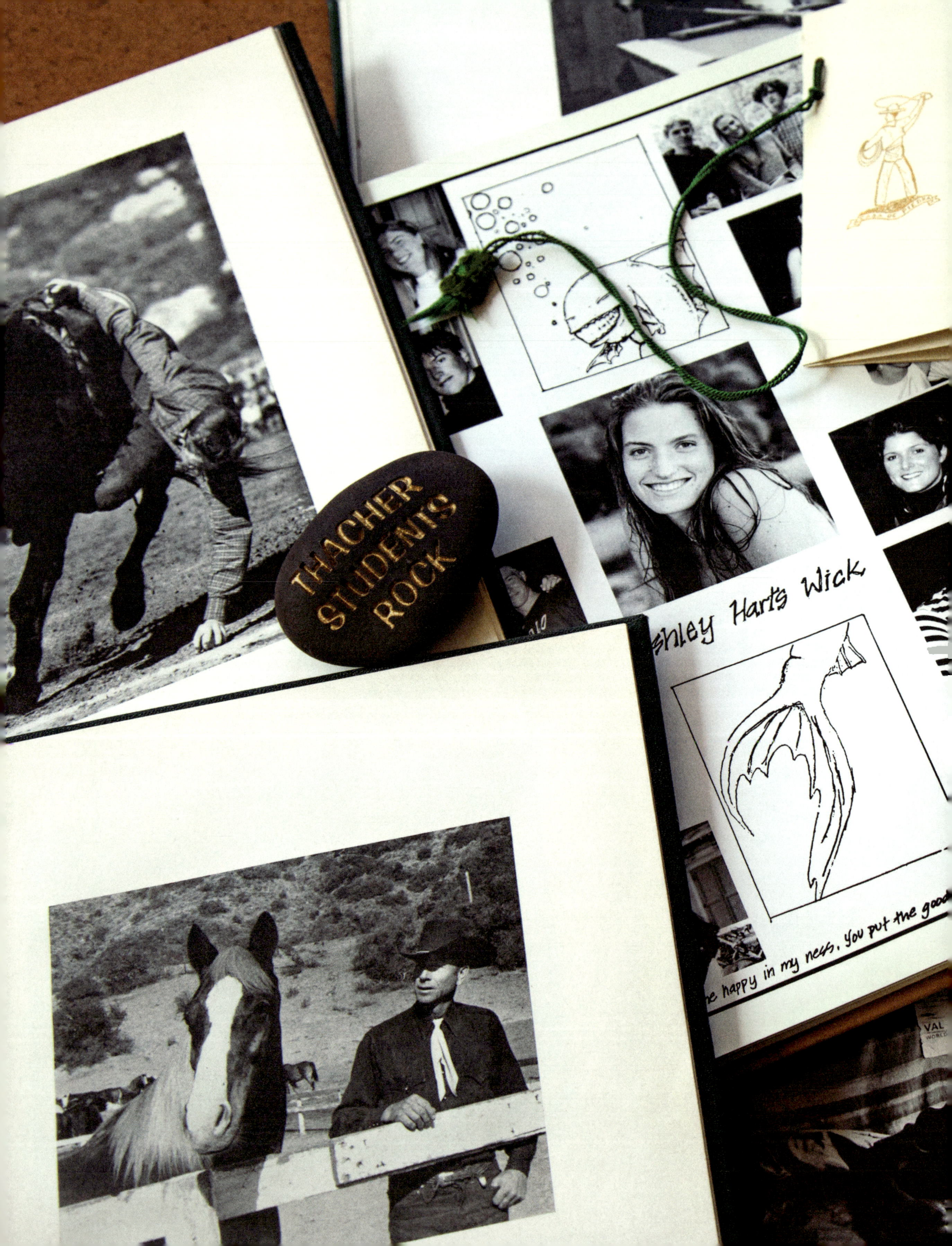

THACHER STUDENTS ROCK
shley Harts Wick
e happy in my ness. You put the good

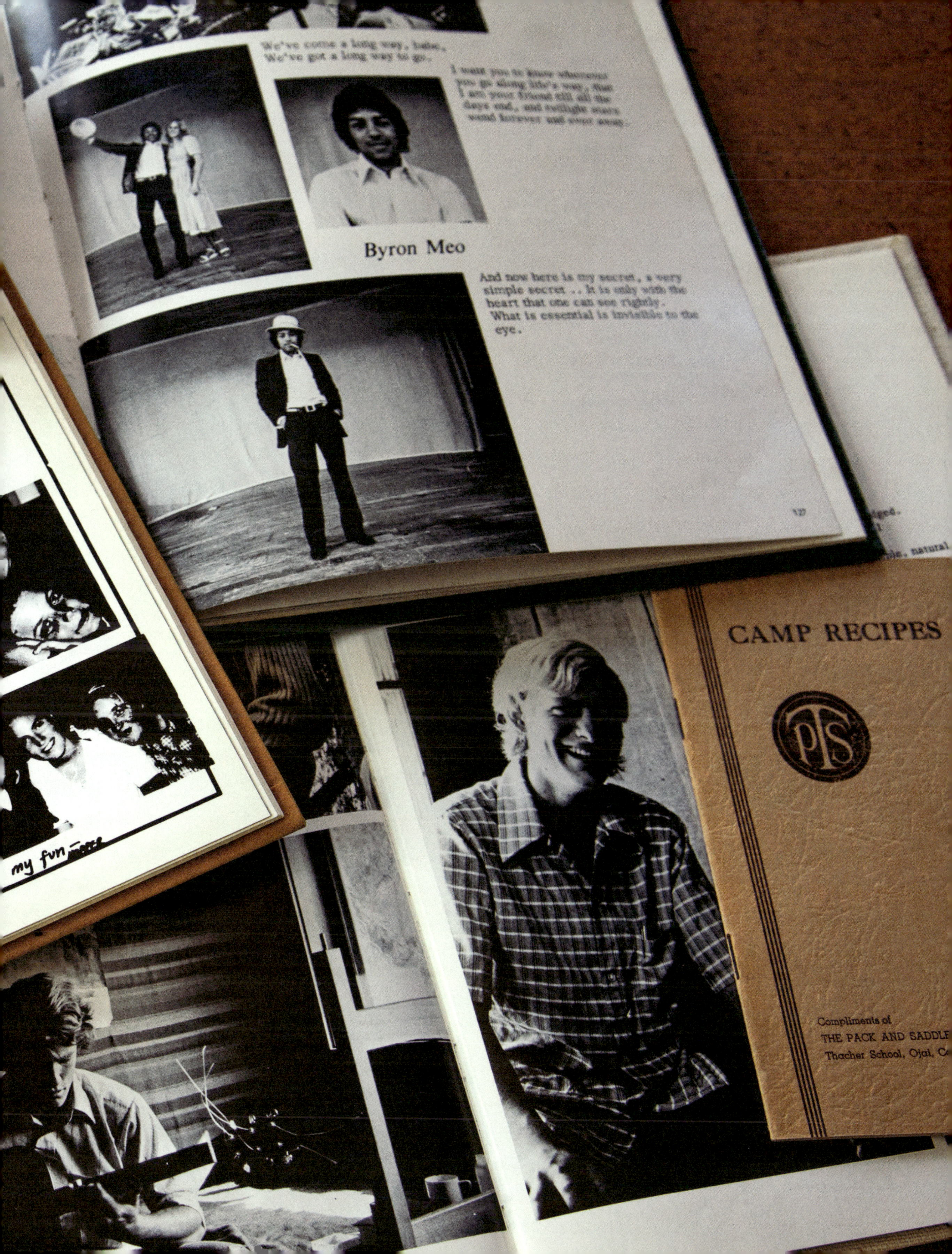
We've come a long way, babe,
We've got a long way to go.
Byron Meo
And now here is my secret, a very simple secret .. It is only with the heart that one can see rightly. What is essential is invisible to the eye.
127
my fun
CAMP RECIPES
Compliments of
THE PACK AND SADDL
Thacher School, Ojai, C

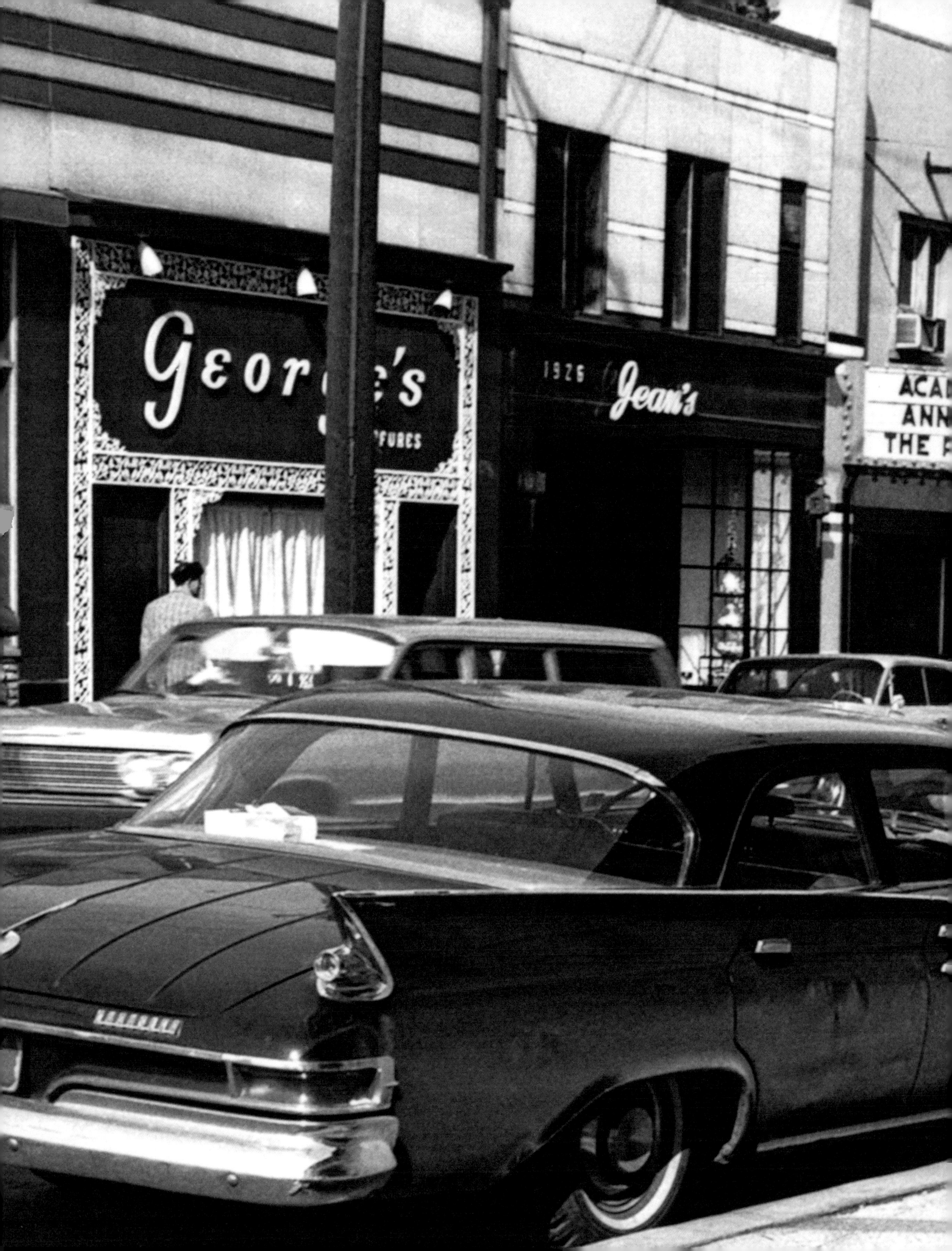
1926
Jean's

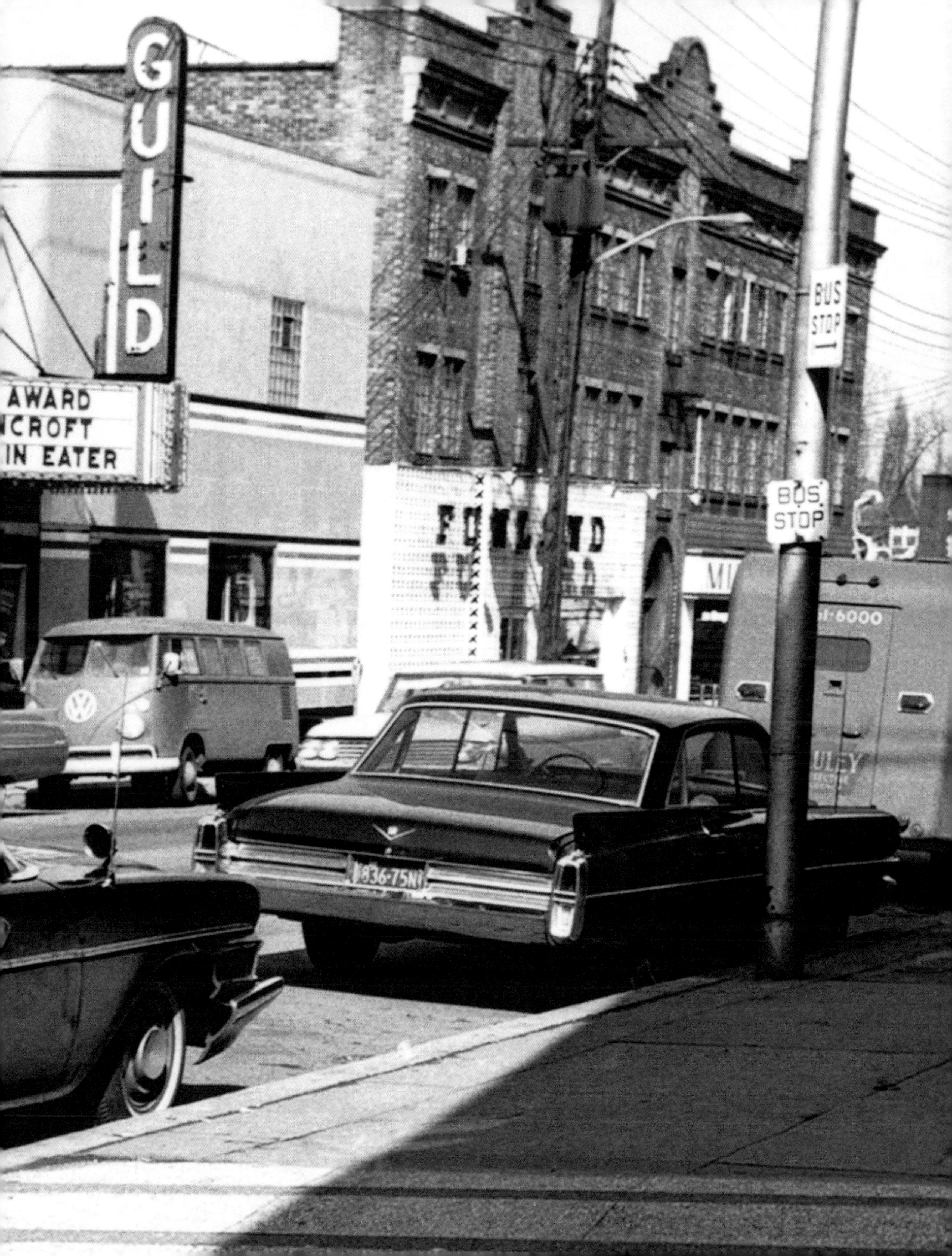
GUILD
AWARD
NCROFT
IN EATER
BUS STOP
BUS STOP

A couple of years ago, Nan and I were walking along Via della Reginella in Rome with our friend Alessia d'Amico as our guide. She explained that the neighborhood had been a Jewish quarter that was turned into a ghetto during World War II. We went into a little gallery called Il Museo Del Louvre and met Giuseppe Casetti, the owner, and Giosetta Fioroni, his favorite artist. We talked about photography as we looked around his room covered with prints by Francesca Woodman. I took Giosetta outside to take her portrait, and we were suddenly surrounded by mothers and babies and cooks in their aprons. Nan came outside to show me some photographs Guiseppe had of all my favorite actors and directors from the European cinema: Marcello Mastroianni, Giulietta Masina, Monica Vitti, Michelangelo Antonioni, Pier Paolo Pasolini, Luchino Visconti, Vittorio De Sica—and so many others. And there on the back of each print was the name: *Paolo di Paolo*.

Since that day, we've been lucky to have many of his photographs become part of our collection. When I look at them now, I am reminded of being a kid, captivated by the flickering images on the screen at the Guild Movie Theater in Pittsburgh, Pennsylvania, where I would go every other Sunday night to watch the European classics with my mom, dad and sister, Barbara—who would grow up to speak perfect Italian and lived most of her later years in Capri. After the movie ended, we would all go next door to Weinstein's deli in Squirrel Hill. As I ate my double brisket on pumpernickel with Russian dressing, never could I have imagined that years later I would rediscover that enchanted world once again, seen through the lens of Paolo di Paolo.

—BRUCE WEBER, MONTAUK, NY, 2014

PHOTOGRAPHS BY

PAOLO DI PAOLO

OUR FRIEND IN ROME

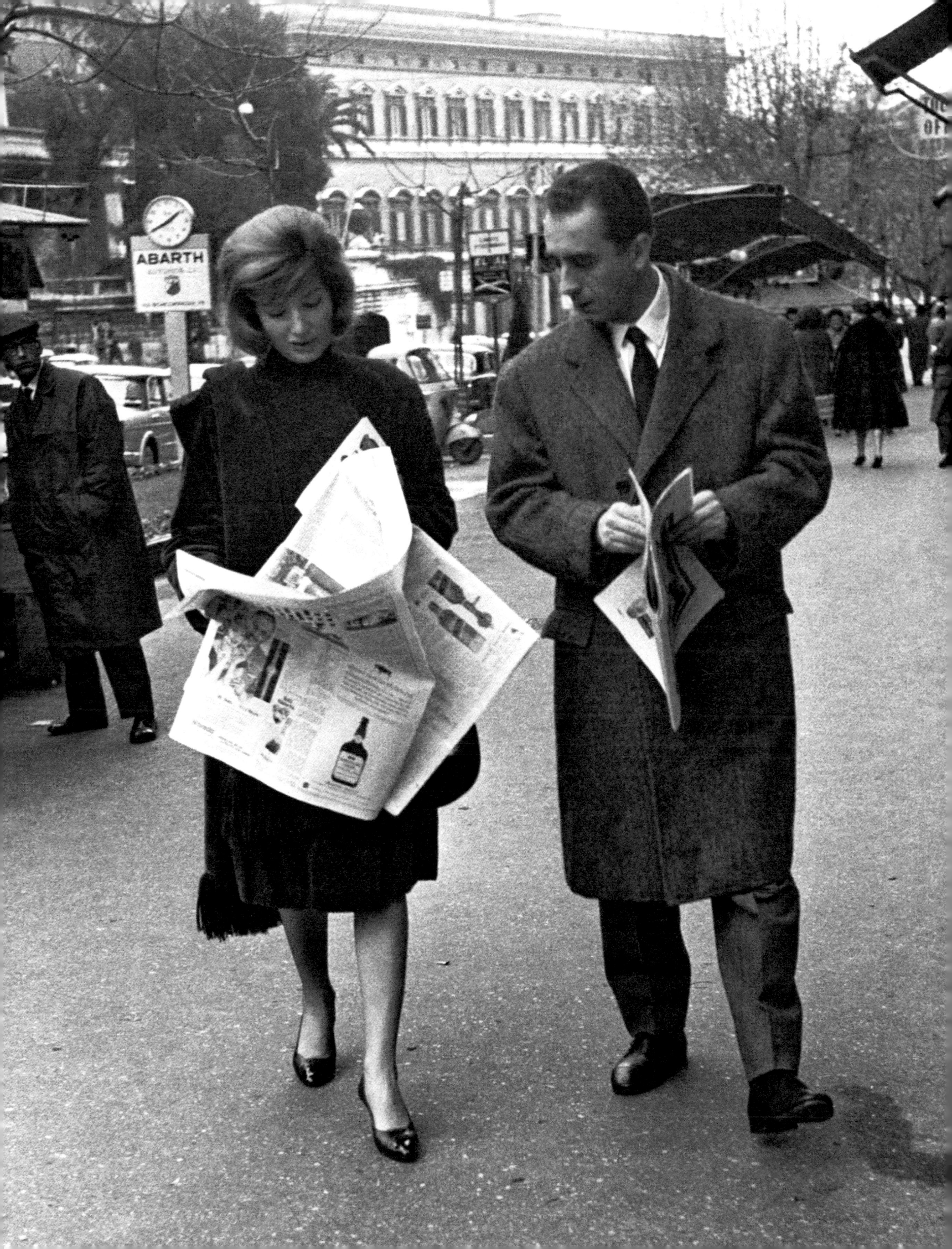
ABARTH

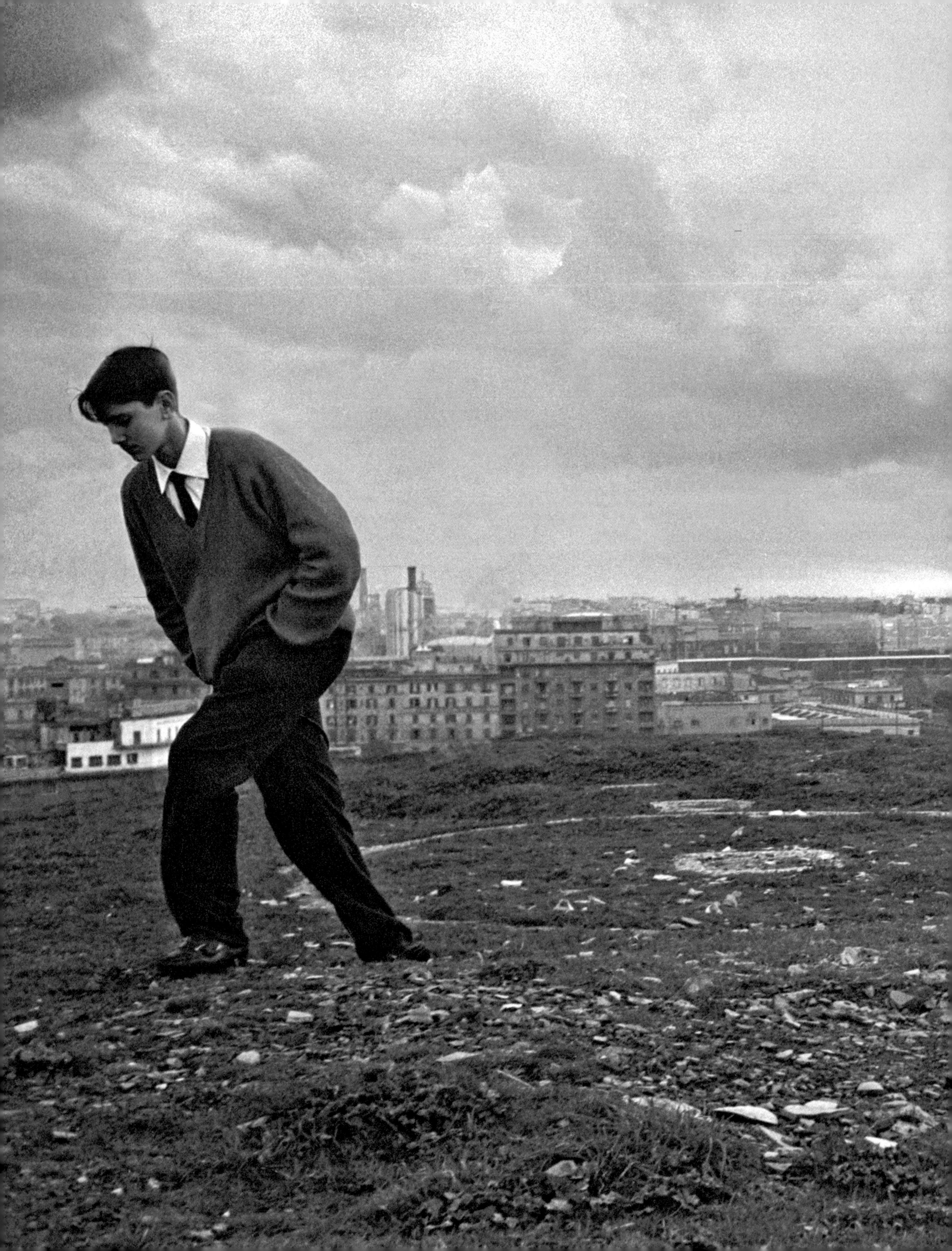

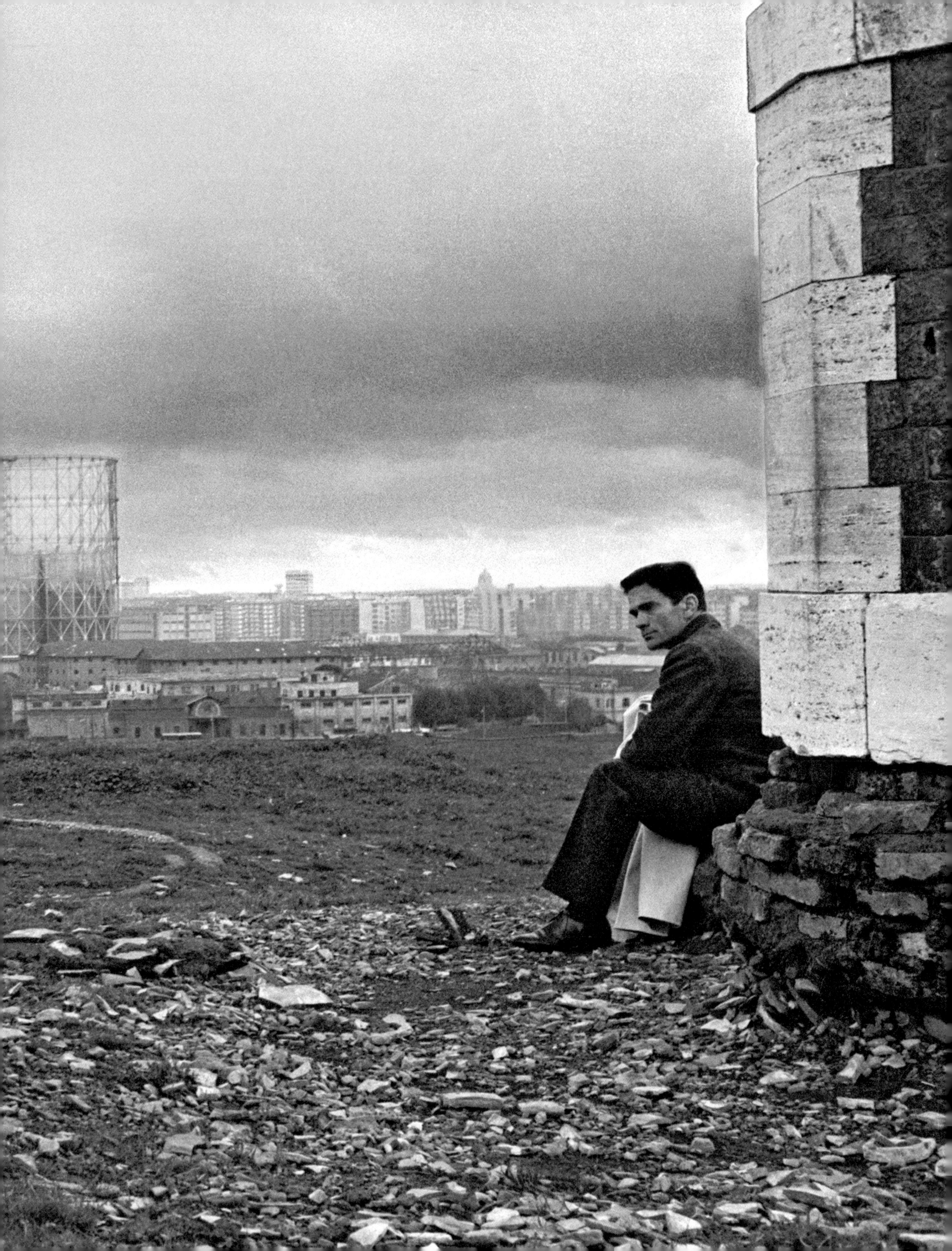

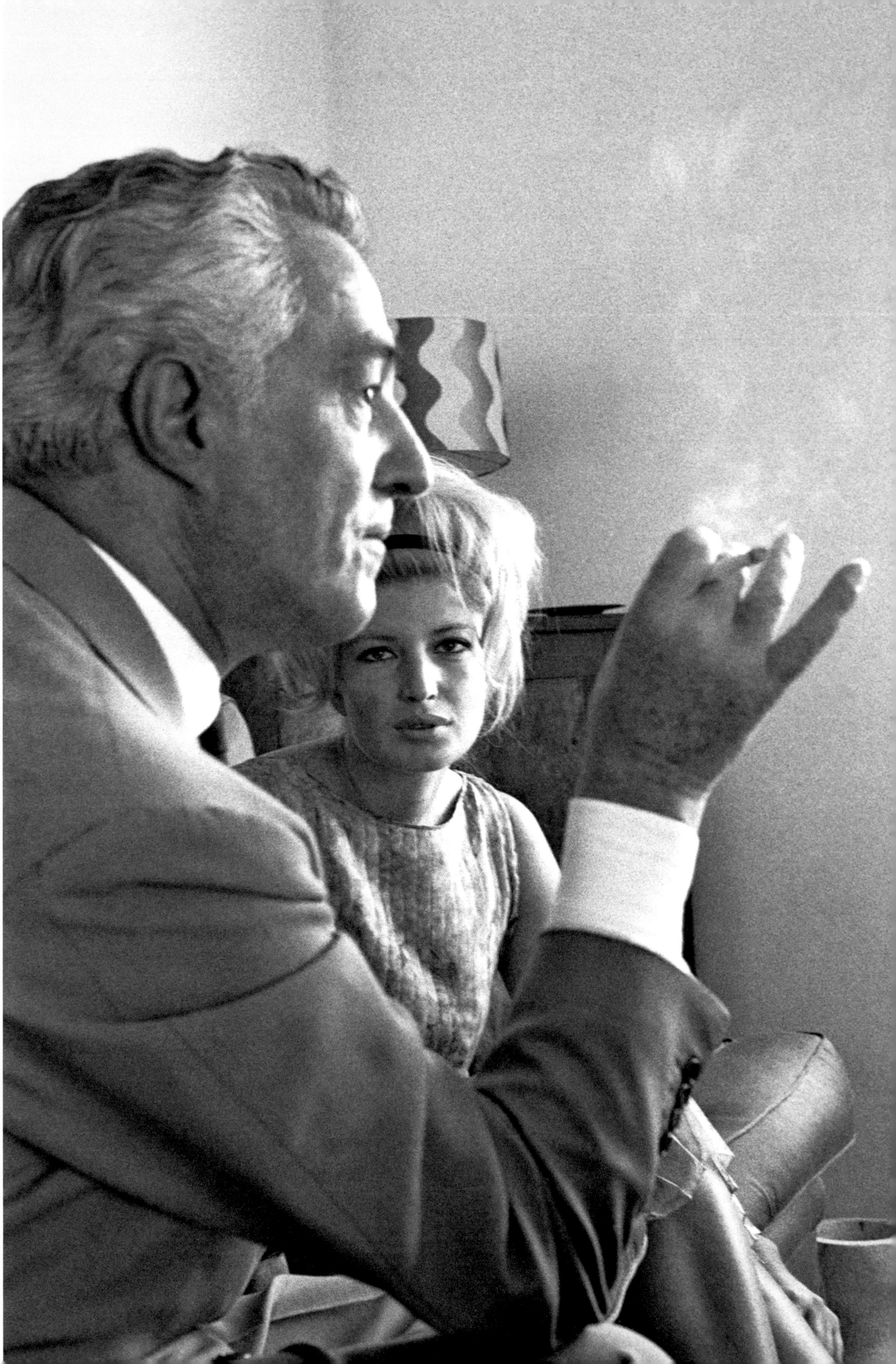

MY FATHER

BY SILVIA DI PAOLO

About 15 years ago, I was in the basement of my parent's house searching for my skis. As I was looking around, I discovered a filing cabinet stuffed with negatives and orange Agfa boxes filled with prints. I went to my father and asked, "What are these pictures?" He said, "Well, I was a photographer once." I was 17 years old at the time, and he had *never once* mentioned this to me. I had always known my father as a writer and historian—that had been his profession all of my life. "Oh, you know, that's all in the past," was all he said. But I love photography and his pictures are beautiful, so little by little I got him to tell me the full story.

My father was born in 1925 in a little village in the south of Italy called Larino. When he turned 18, he left home with his cardboard suitcase and moved to Rome to study philosophy. He paid for his studies by delivering newspapers and working as a typesetter. In Rome, he became very good friends with a small but important group of artists known as Gruppo Forma Uno. This was right after World War II, so all of them were really poor—they would often pay for their restaurant bills with artworks. With the little money he made, my father bought a Leica M6 so he would have a way to express his artistic impulses. He taught himself how to use the camera, and someone suggested he submit his photographs to a cult magazine that all the intellectuals were involved with called *Il Mondo*. He quickly became its most published photographer.

The photos he did for *Il Mondo* were not related to famous people—instead they had a very distinct feeling and atmosphere, reflecting the difficult conditions people were facing in Italy after the war. *Il Mondo* didn't pay much for his photos, so my father eventually started working for a bigger magazine called *Tempo Illustrato*. They commissioned him to do stories all over the world, including portraits of the Neorealist actors and directors. As my father put it, "*Tempo Illustrato* sent me places, but I was always thinking of the one photo I would bring back for *Il Mondo*."

I think the secret of my father's pictures is their intimacy, because these people really became his friends. He would have lunch with Vittorio Gassman and Alberto Sordi. When Kim Novak or Gloria Swanson came to Rome, he would send flowers to their rooms at the hotel with a note inviting them to his studio. He traveled with Pasolini, went to the beach with Anna Magnani and her son. My father always used natural light and favored spontaneity over a carefully constructed image. He considered himself an amateur—taking photographs out of love and passion—who was fortunate that it became his profession.

Il Mondo closed in 1966, and for my father, that was the end of an era. The times began to change—people were buying televisions; the paparazzi style took hold in Italy. For my father, the camera had always been the source of his art, but with the rise of the paparazzi, it became seen as something vulgar and aggressive. Then the magazines he worked for started asking him for gossip about his friends who were actors and actresses. My father of course refused to betray them, and so after a couple of months of being asked for scandals, he decided to leave photography behind altogether. The poetry of those early days in Rome had disappeared.

So my father went back to his roots, to a very simple way of life. As he says, "It's better to leave the scene when you're at your best." When he decided to close his studio in Rome, he married his assistant, Elena—my mother—and moved to the country. She was 22 years younger than him, and I think a little removed from his glamorous past—he'd had all these love affairs with actresses and princesses. She was likely just as happy that my father completely stepped away from his *Dolce Vita* life. He went back to studying history and philosophy, wrote many books about the *carabinieri* (Italian military police), tended the garden, and worked on his many sports cars.

My father is almost 90 years old, and today he's very happy about the ways I try to bring attention to his work, to give it a life again. He feels proud to be thought of as an artist in a way that he never considered himself. From my perspective, it was an incredible life he decided to leave behind. But he speaks of it differently: "I was doing it because I loved to."

Previous spread: Pier Paolo Pasolini
Left: Vittorio De Sica and Monica Vitti

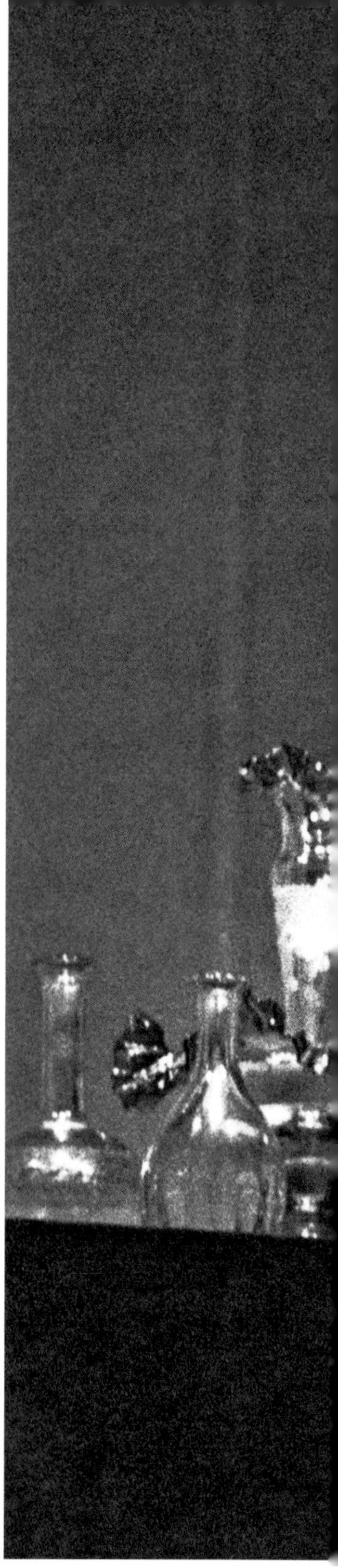

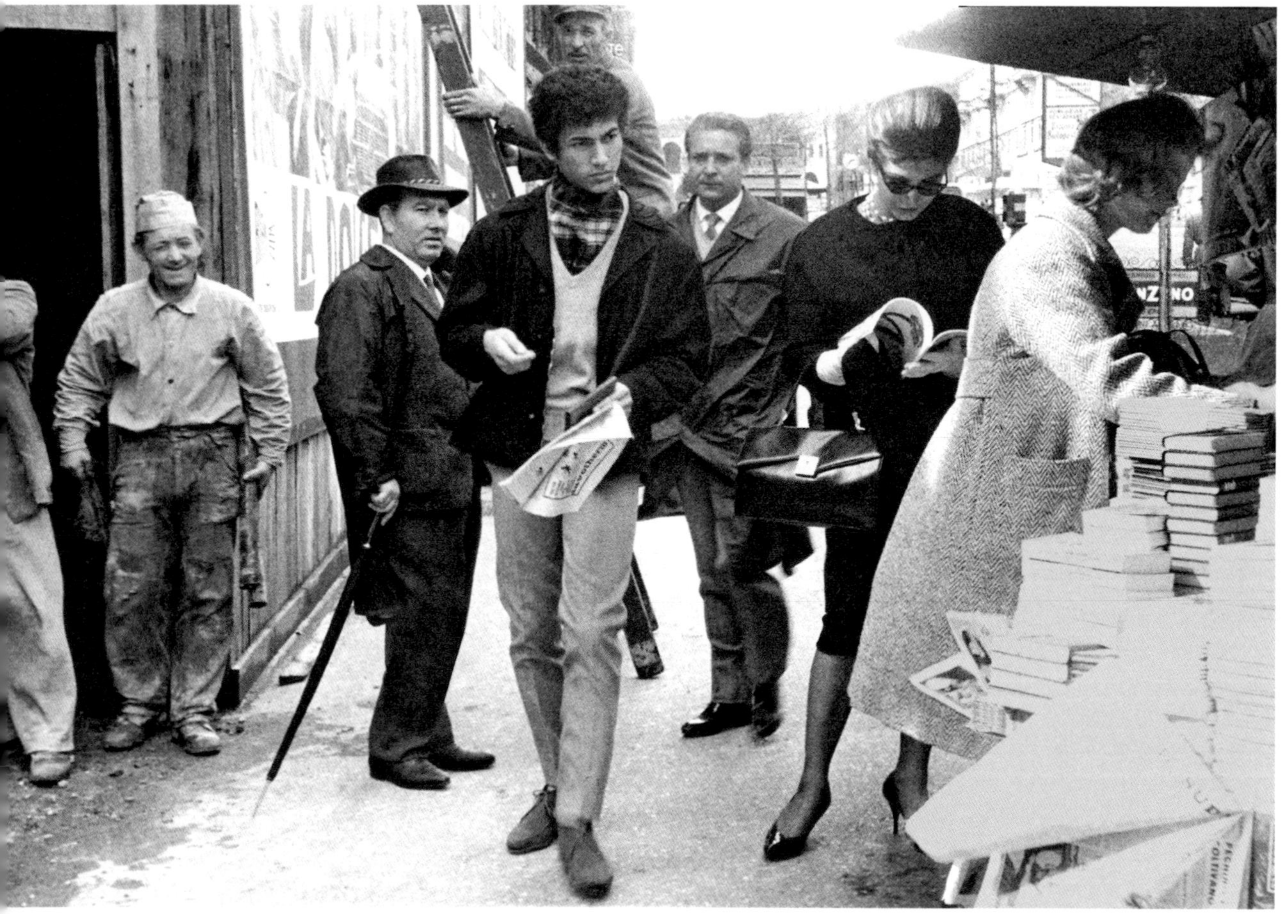

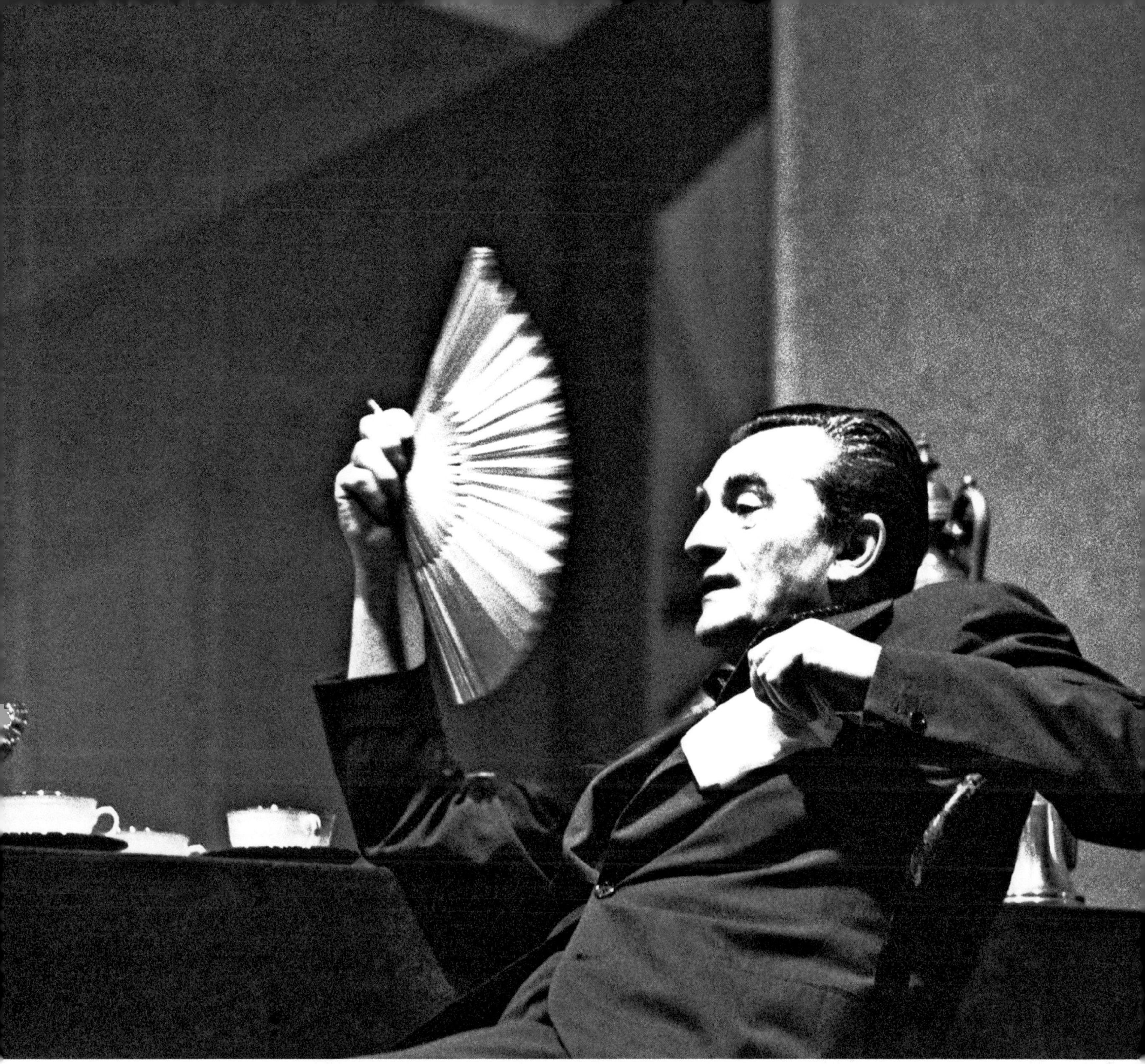

This spread–left: Via Veneto, Rome; *Right*: Luchino Visconti
Following spread: Anna Magnani

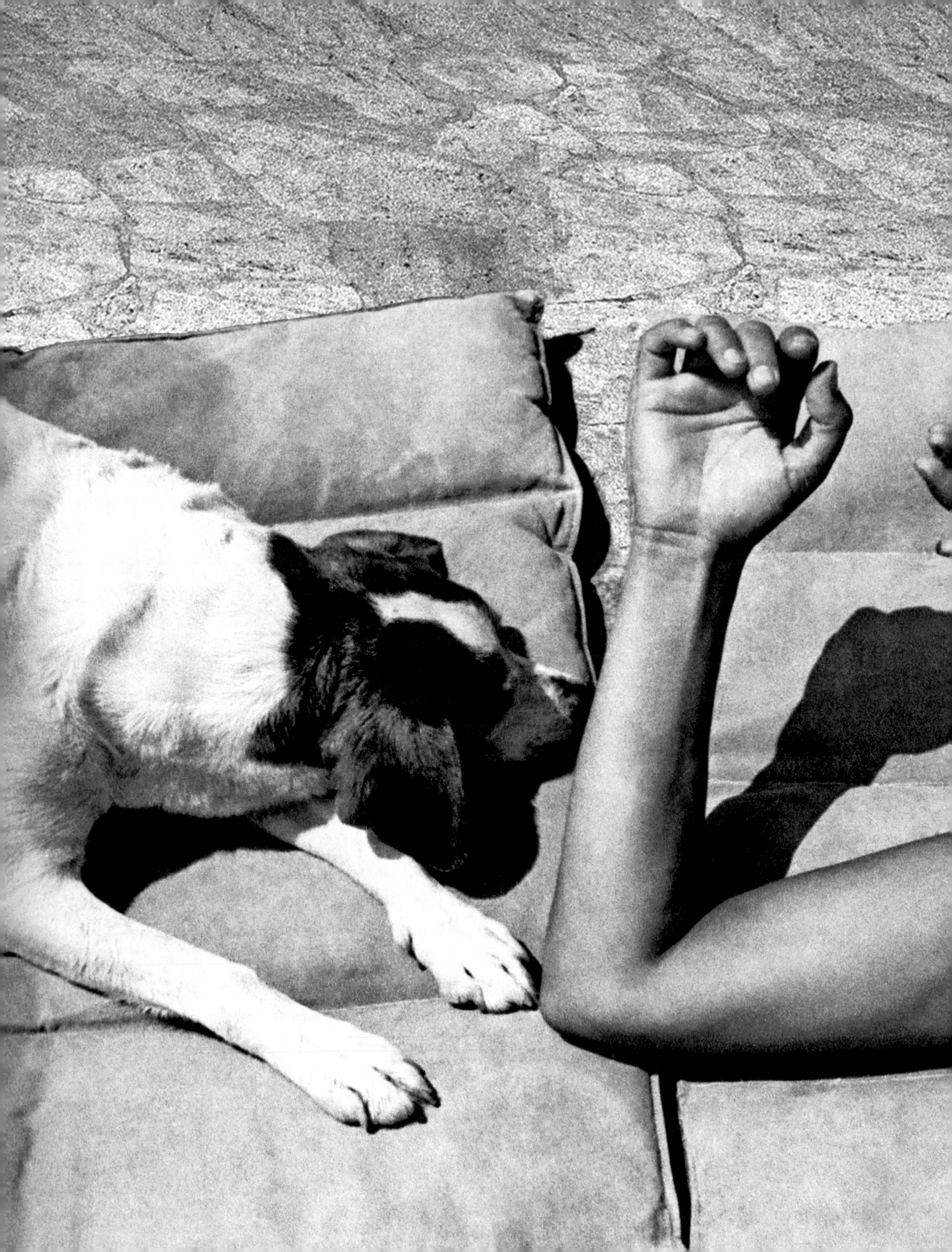

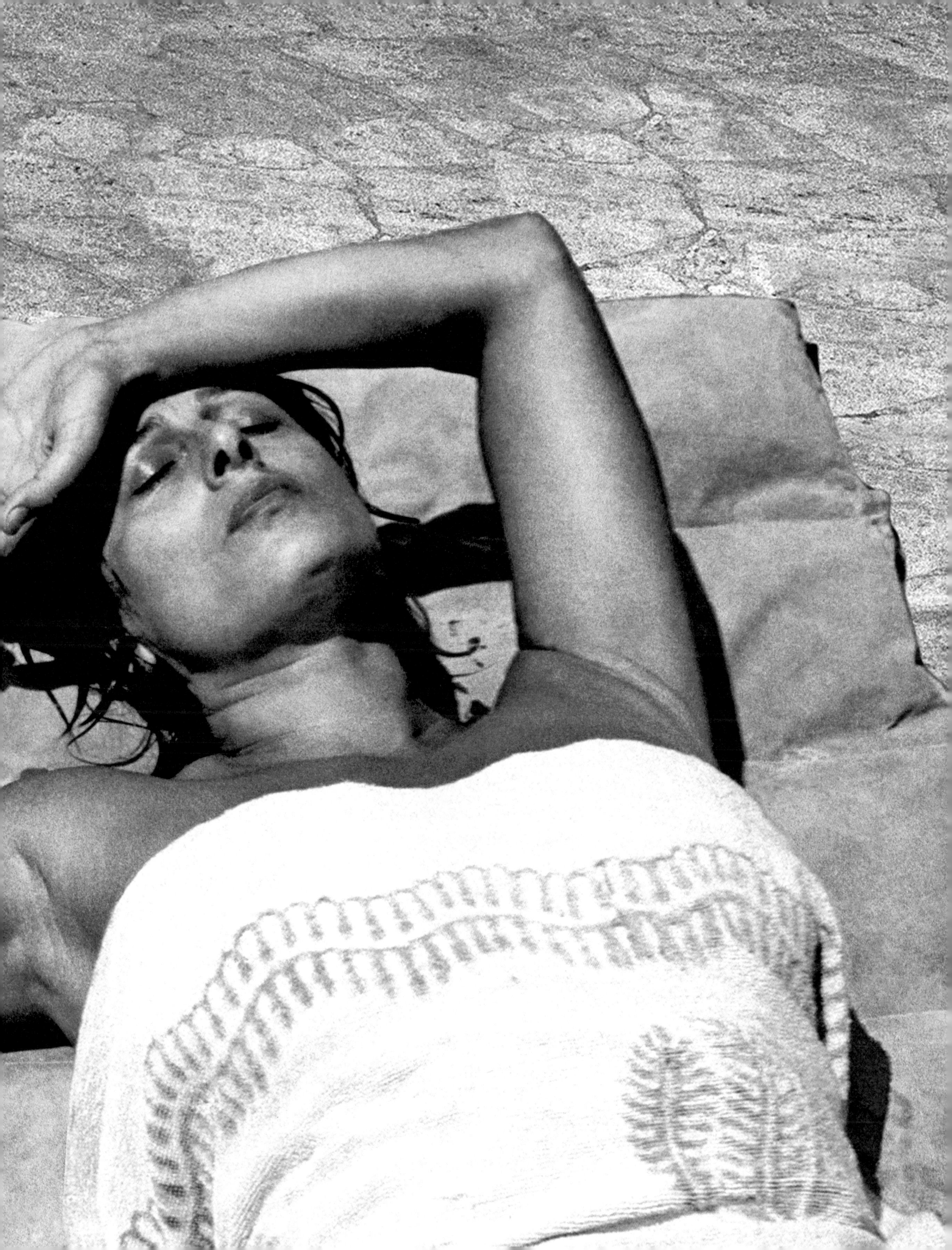

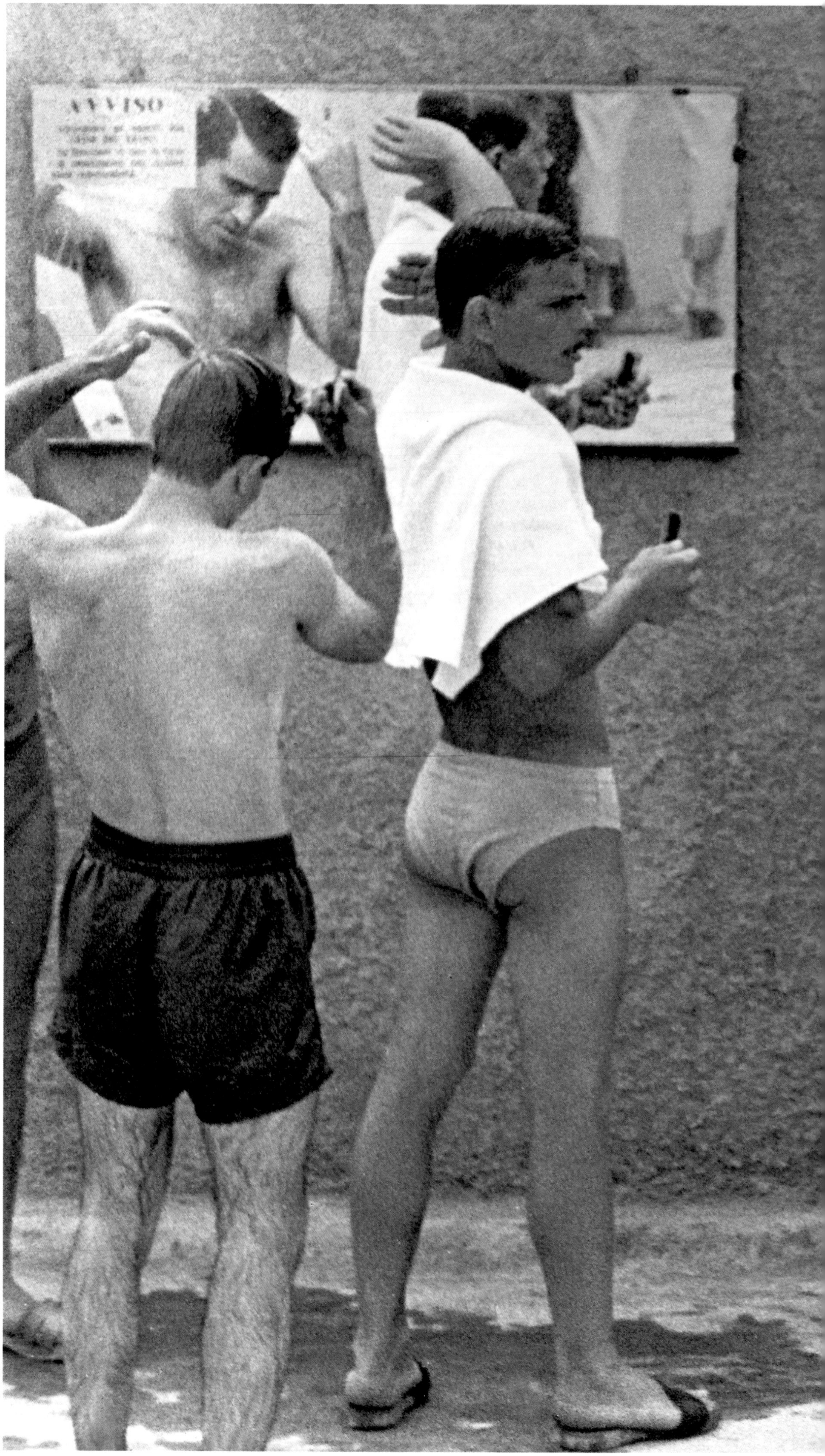

Beach club in Naples

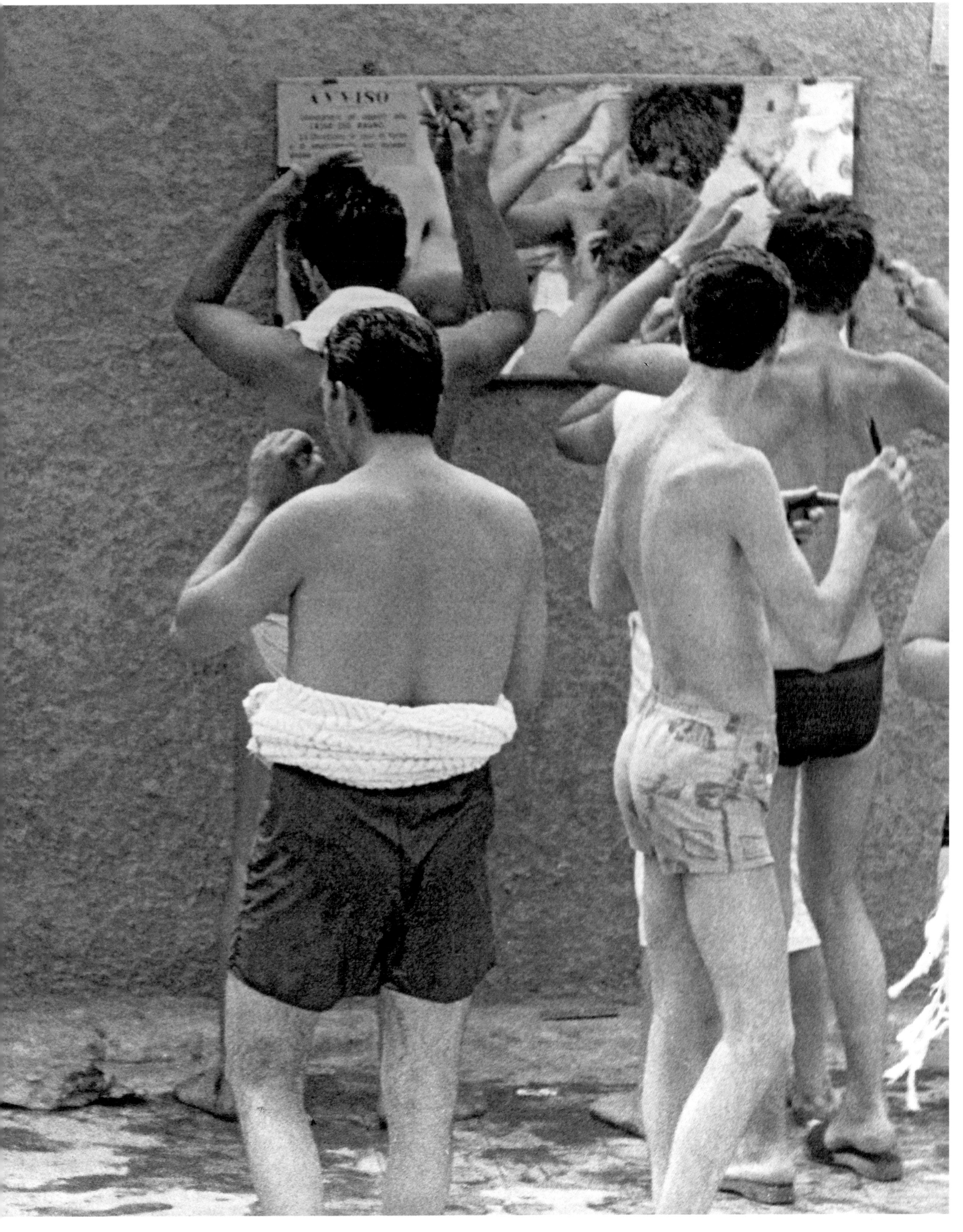
AVVISO

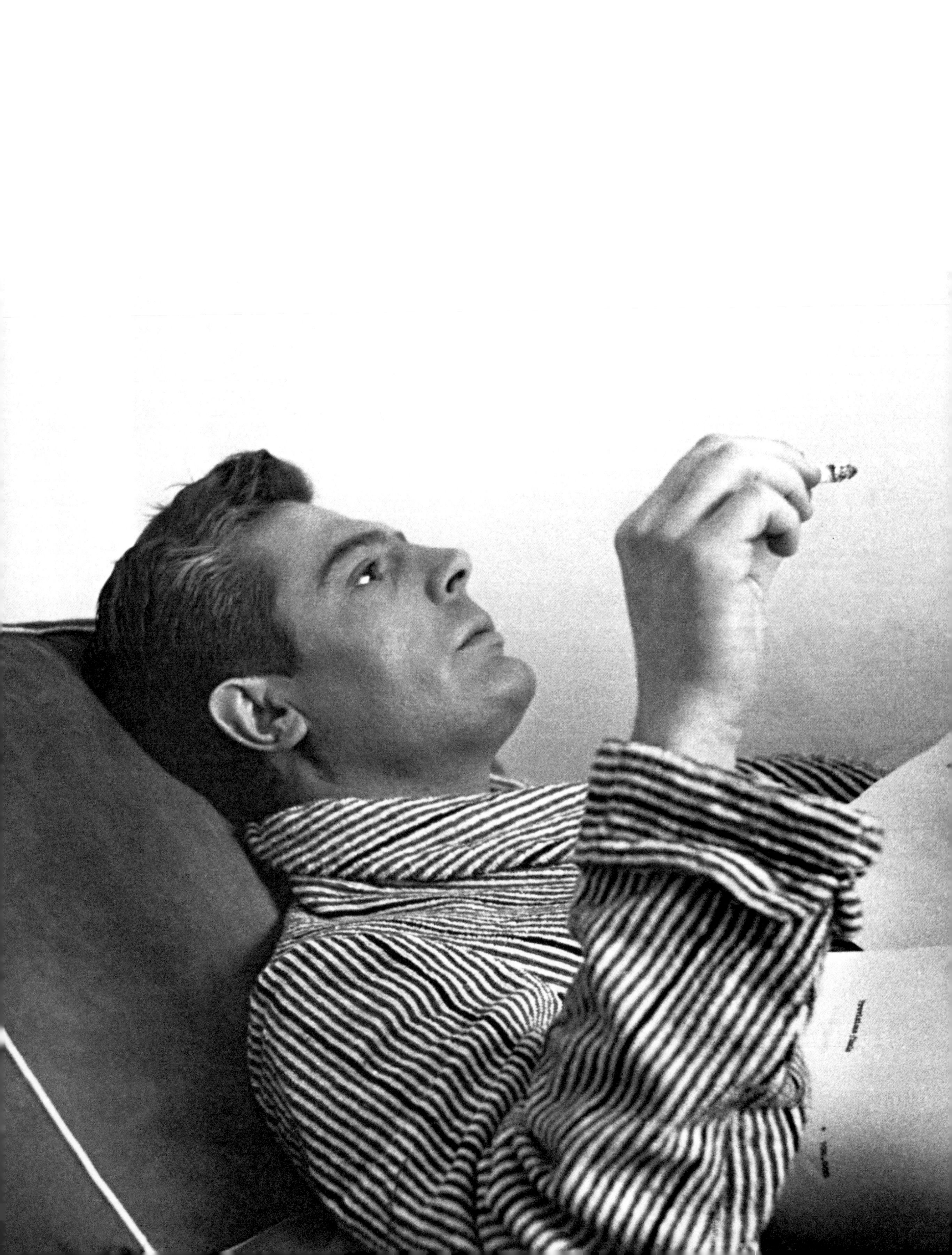

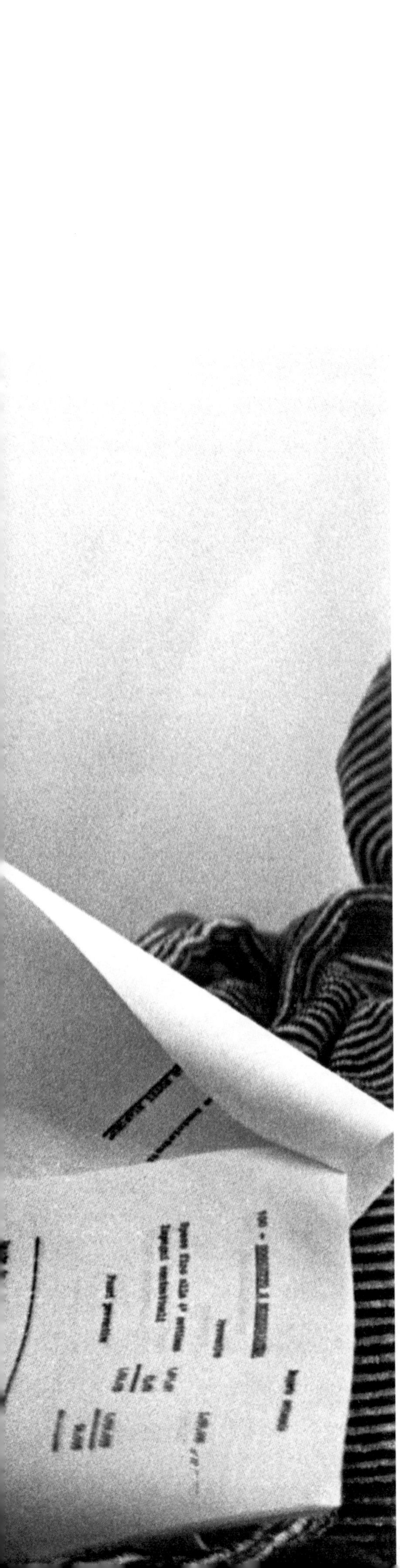

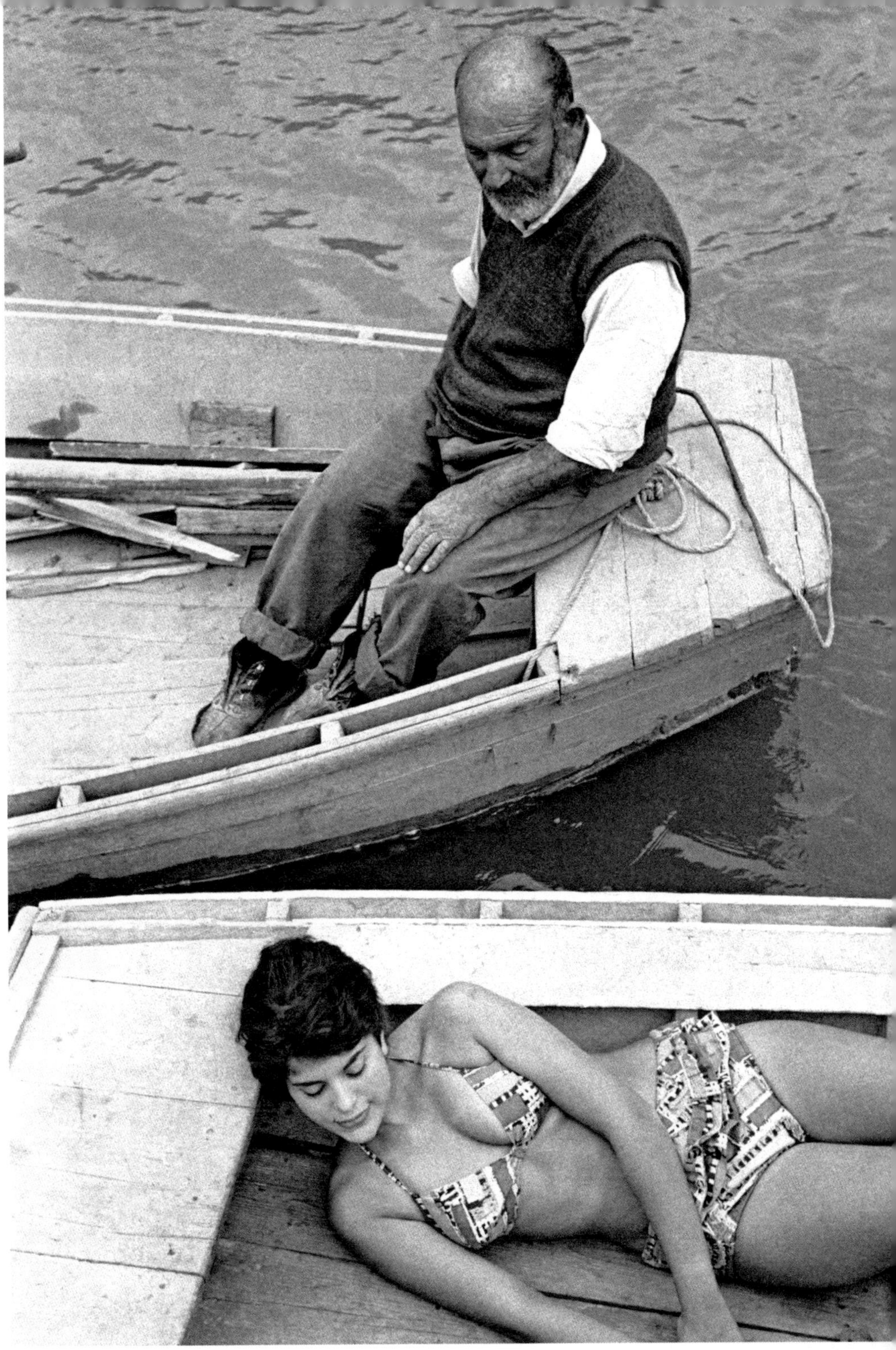

Left: Marcello Mastroianni
Right: Tiber River, Rome

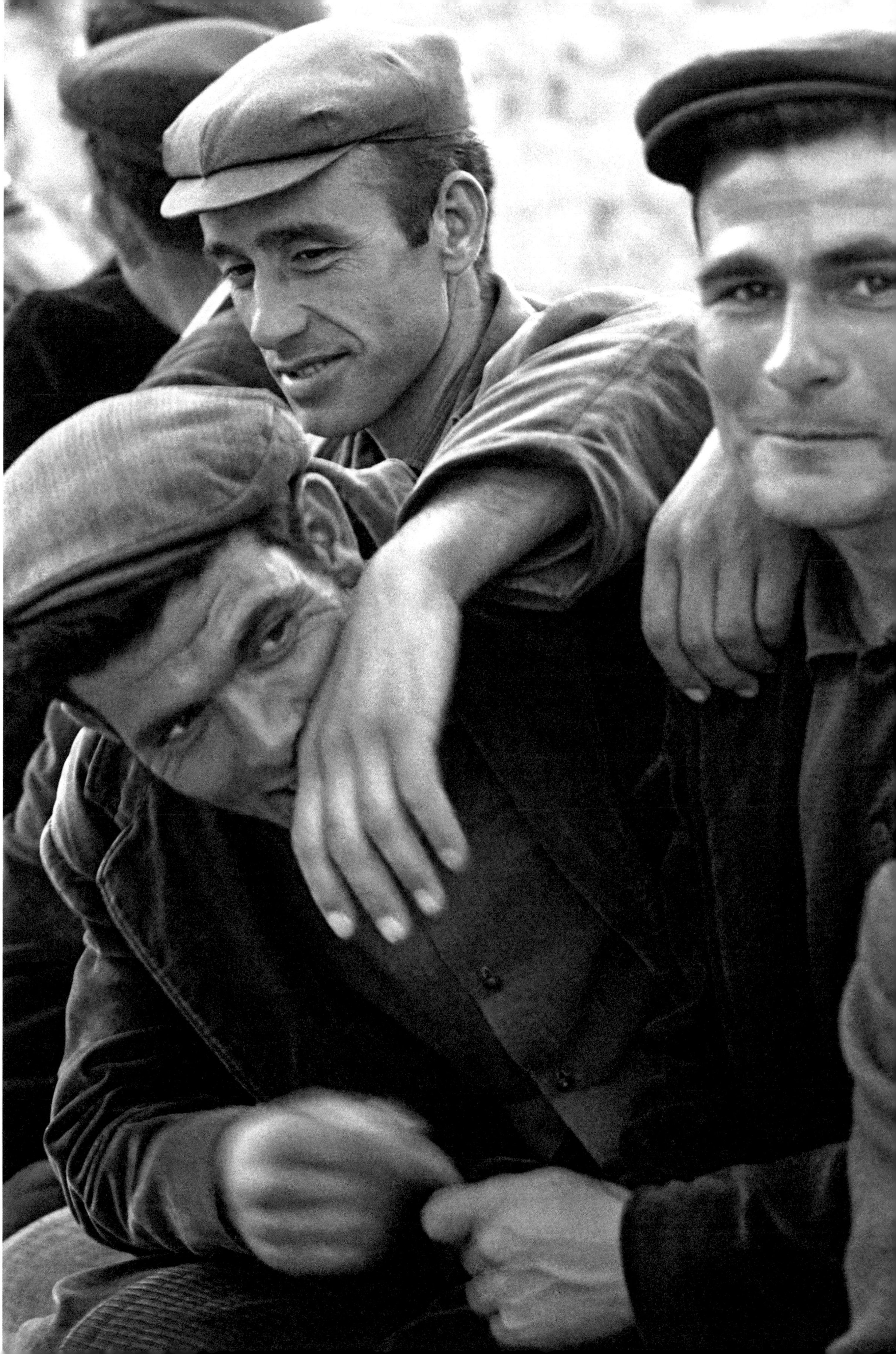

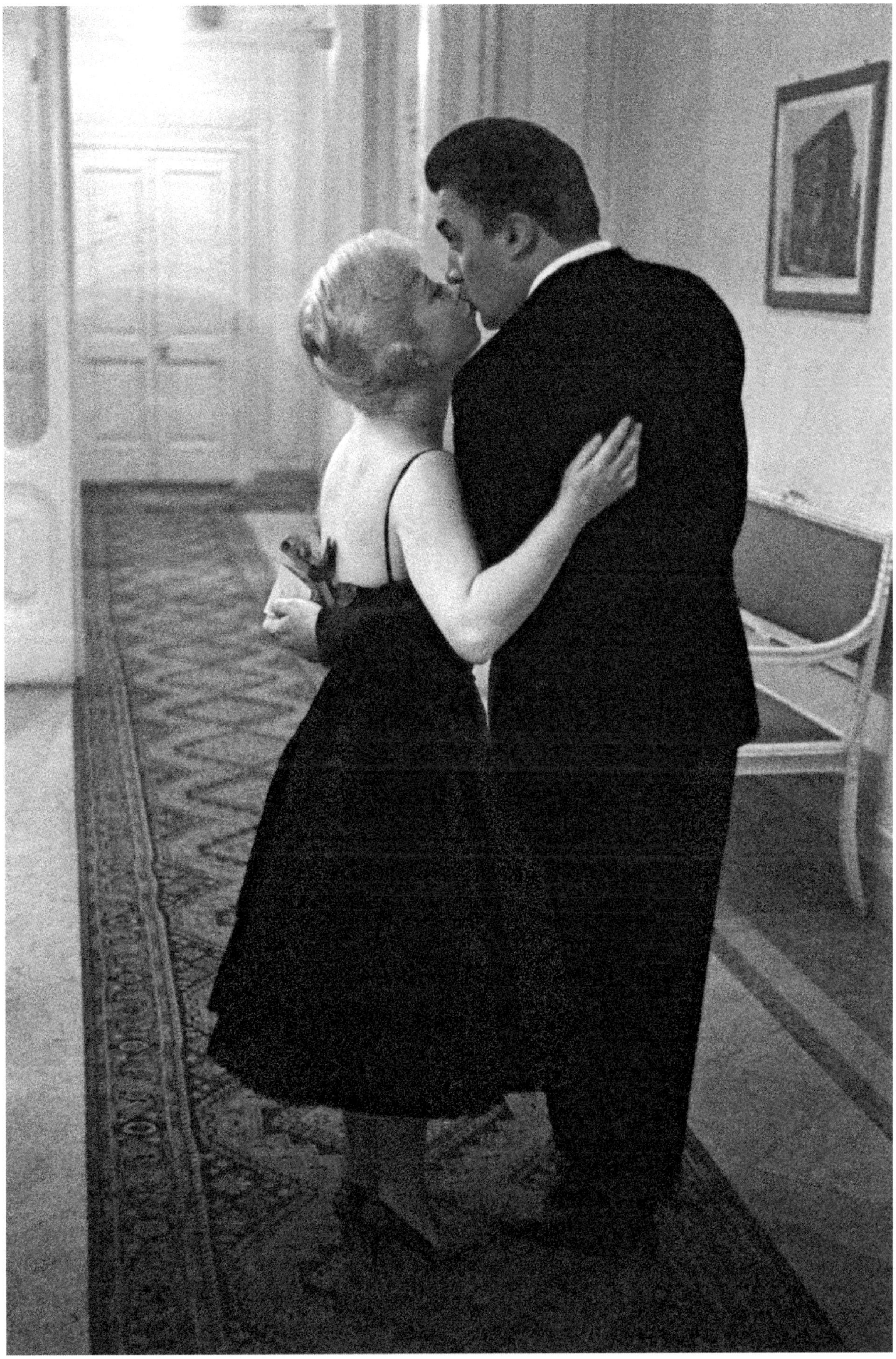

Left: Orgosolo, Sardinia
Right: Giulietta Masina and Federico Fellini

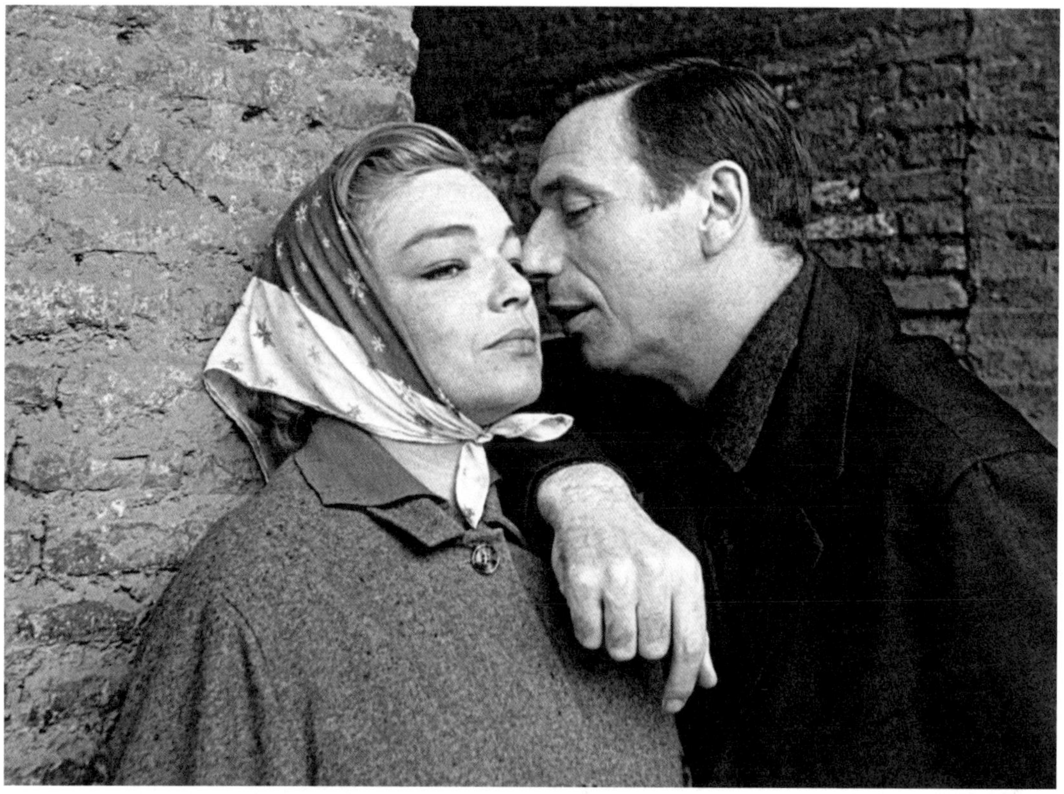

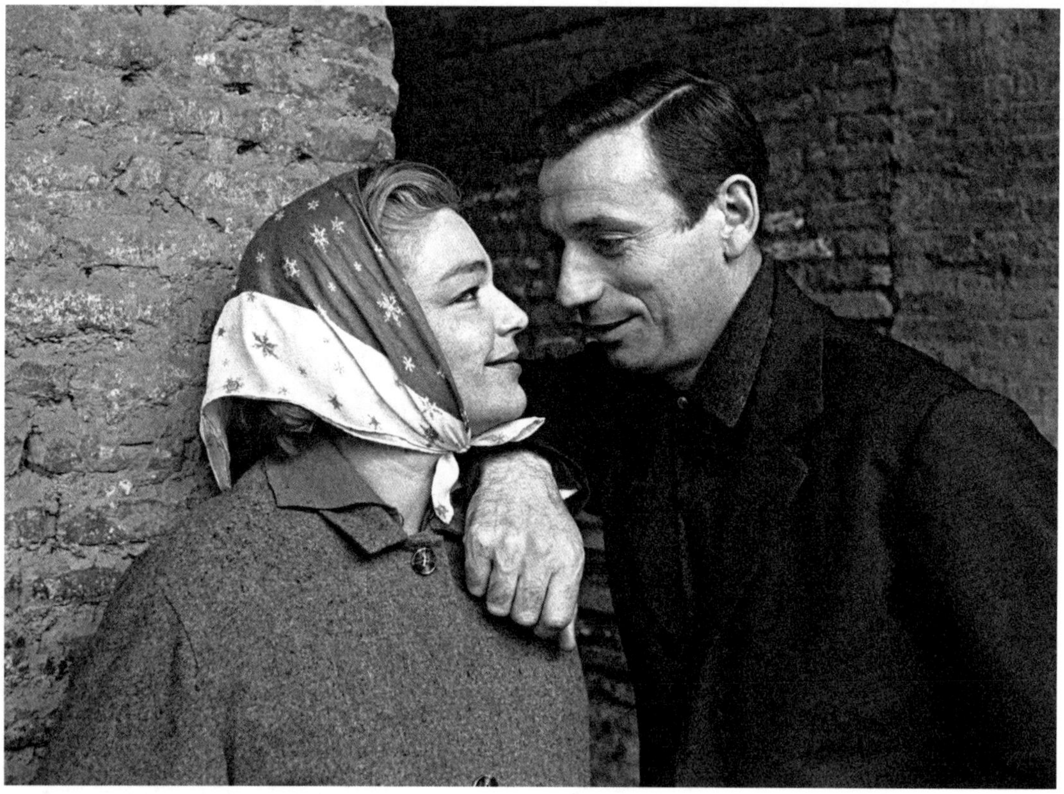

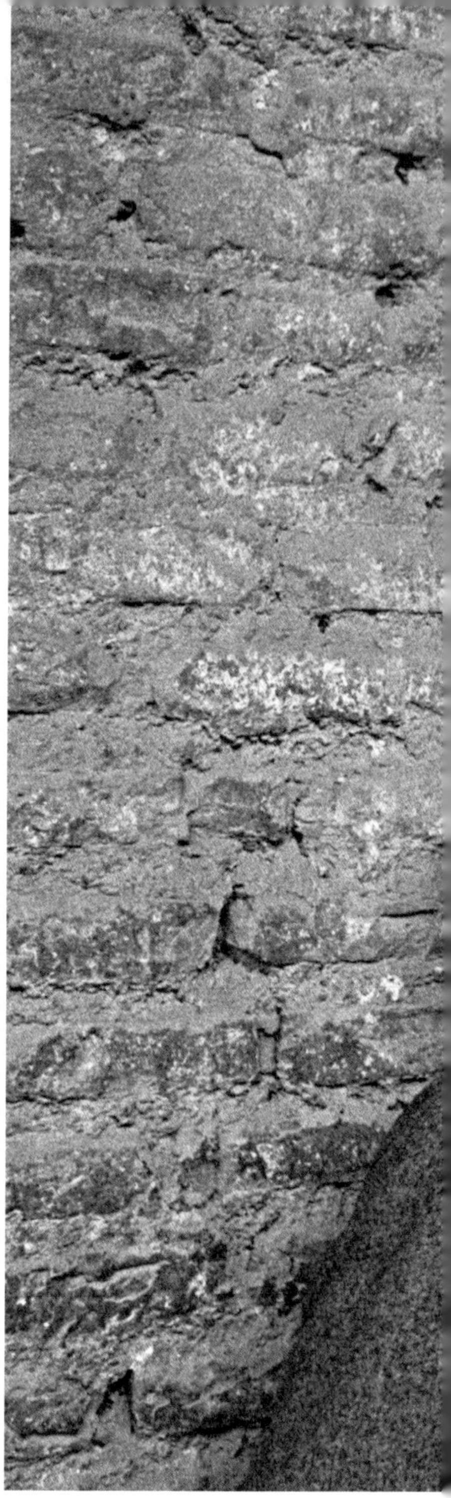

Simone Signoret and Yves Montand

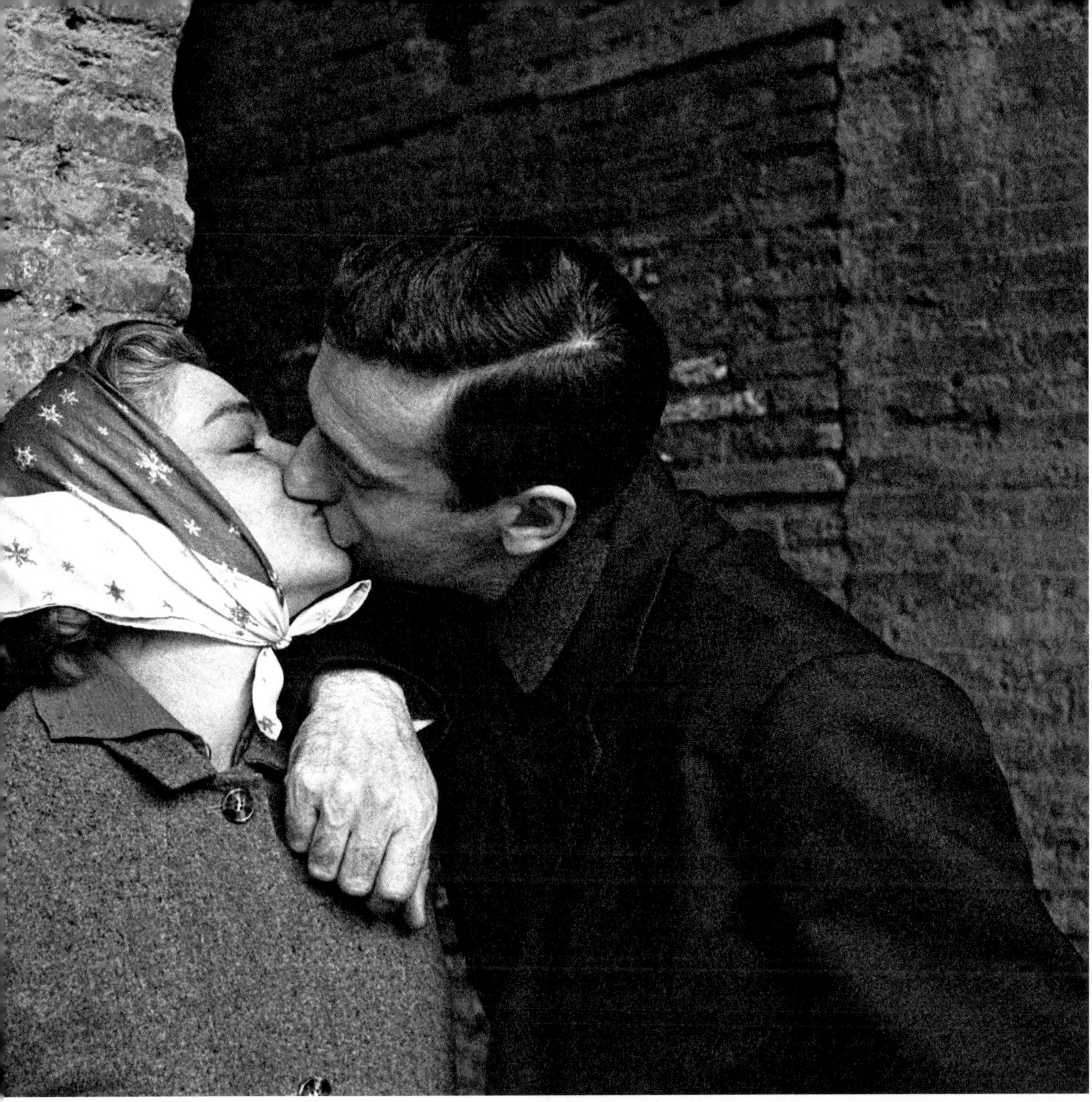

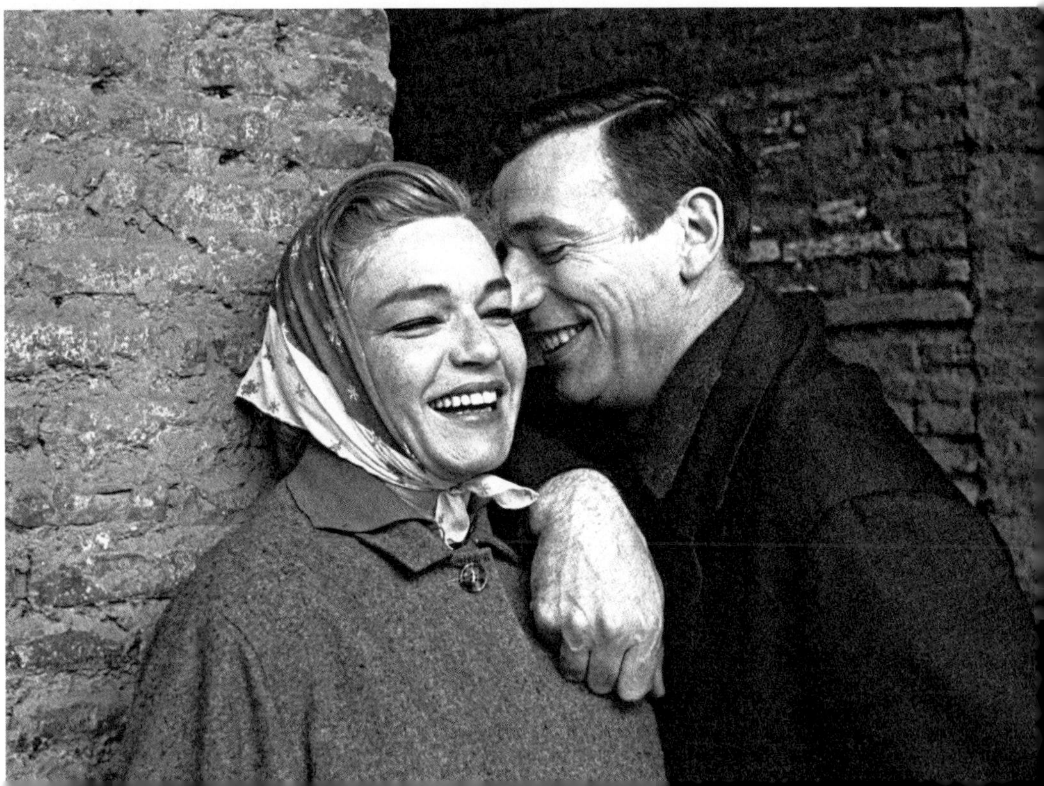

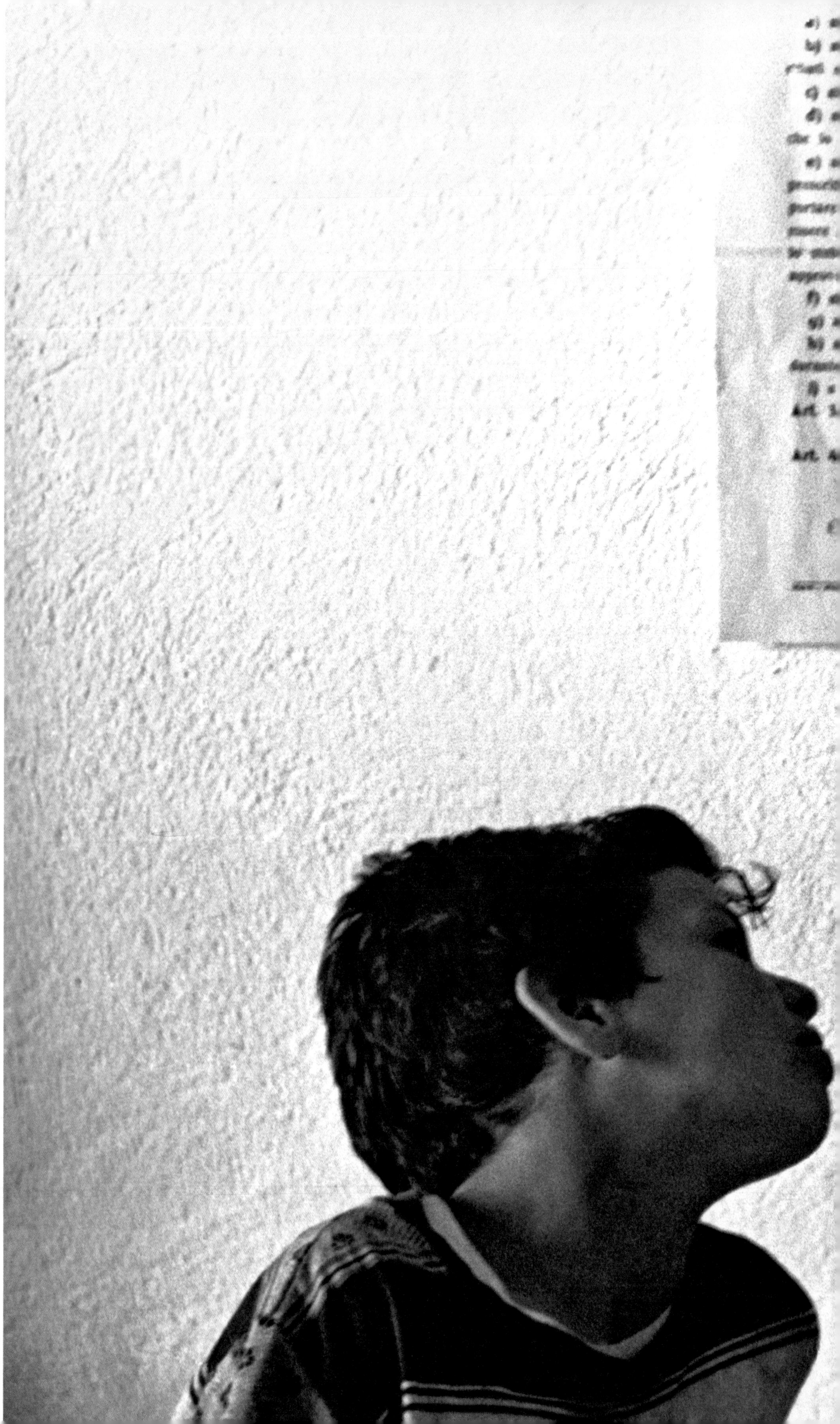

Sophia Loren

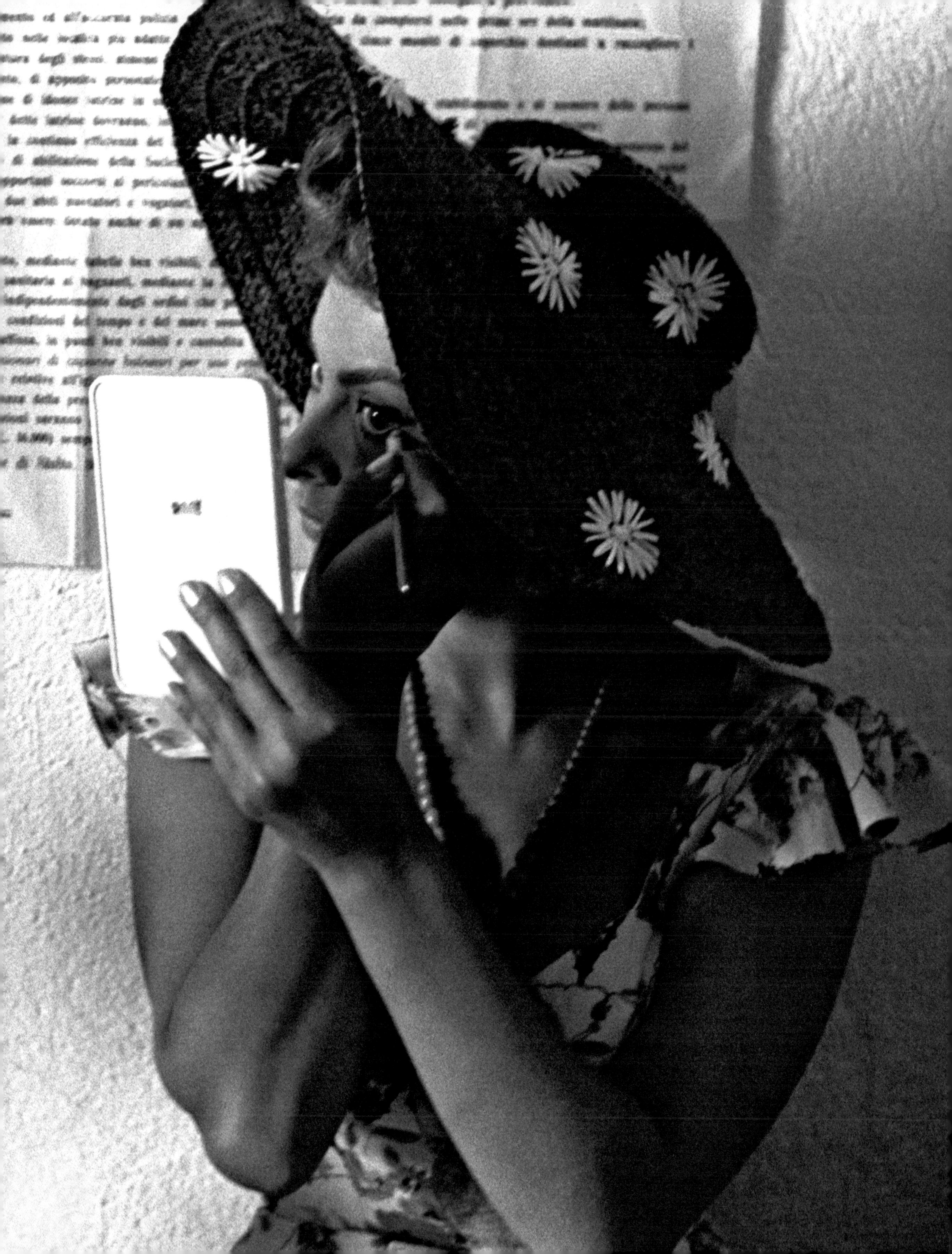

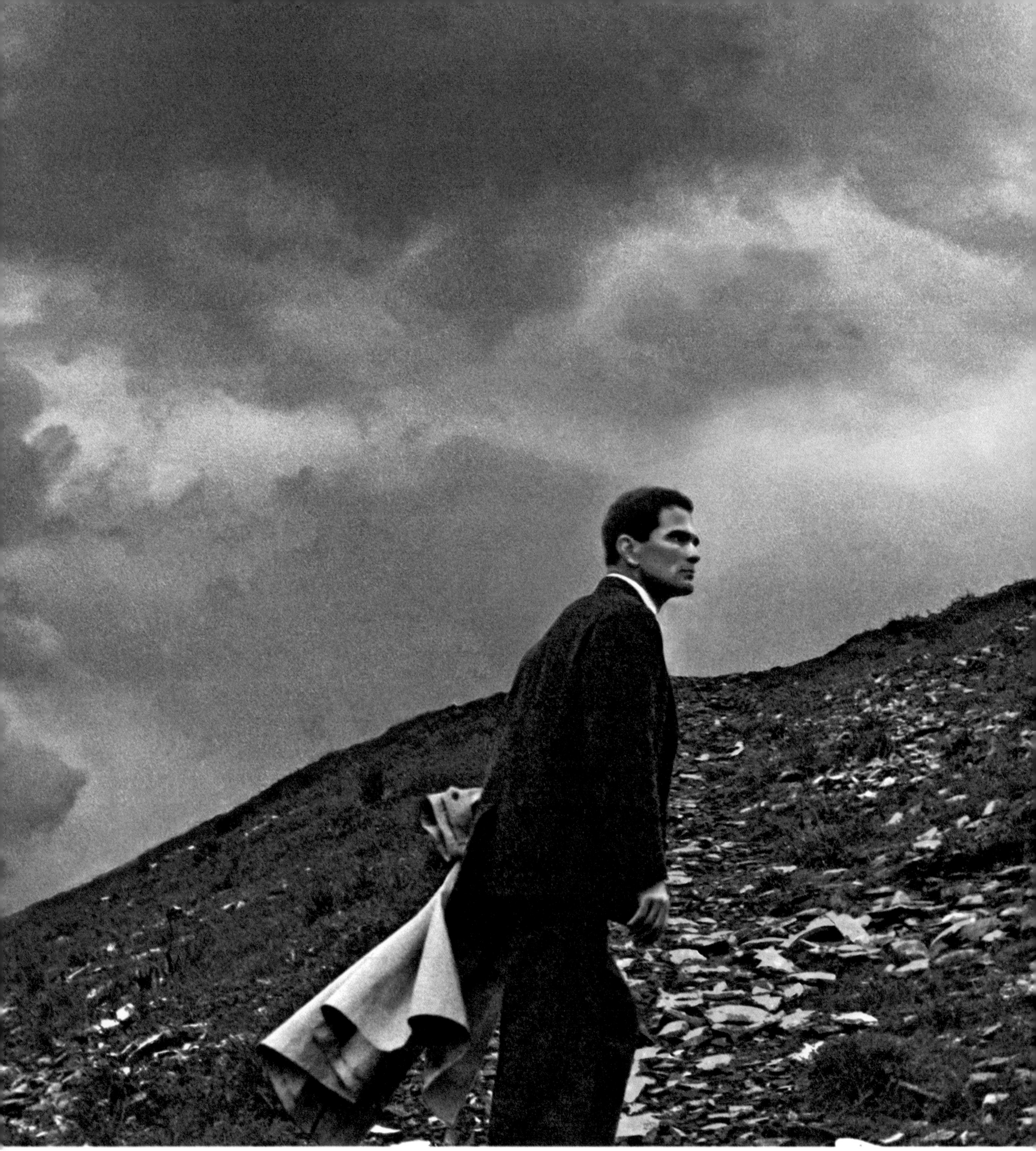

This spread—left & right: Pier Paolo Pasolini
Following spread: Wedding in Abruzzo

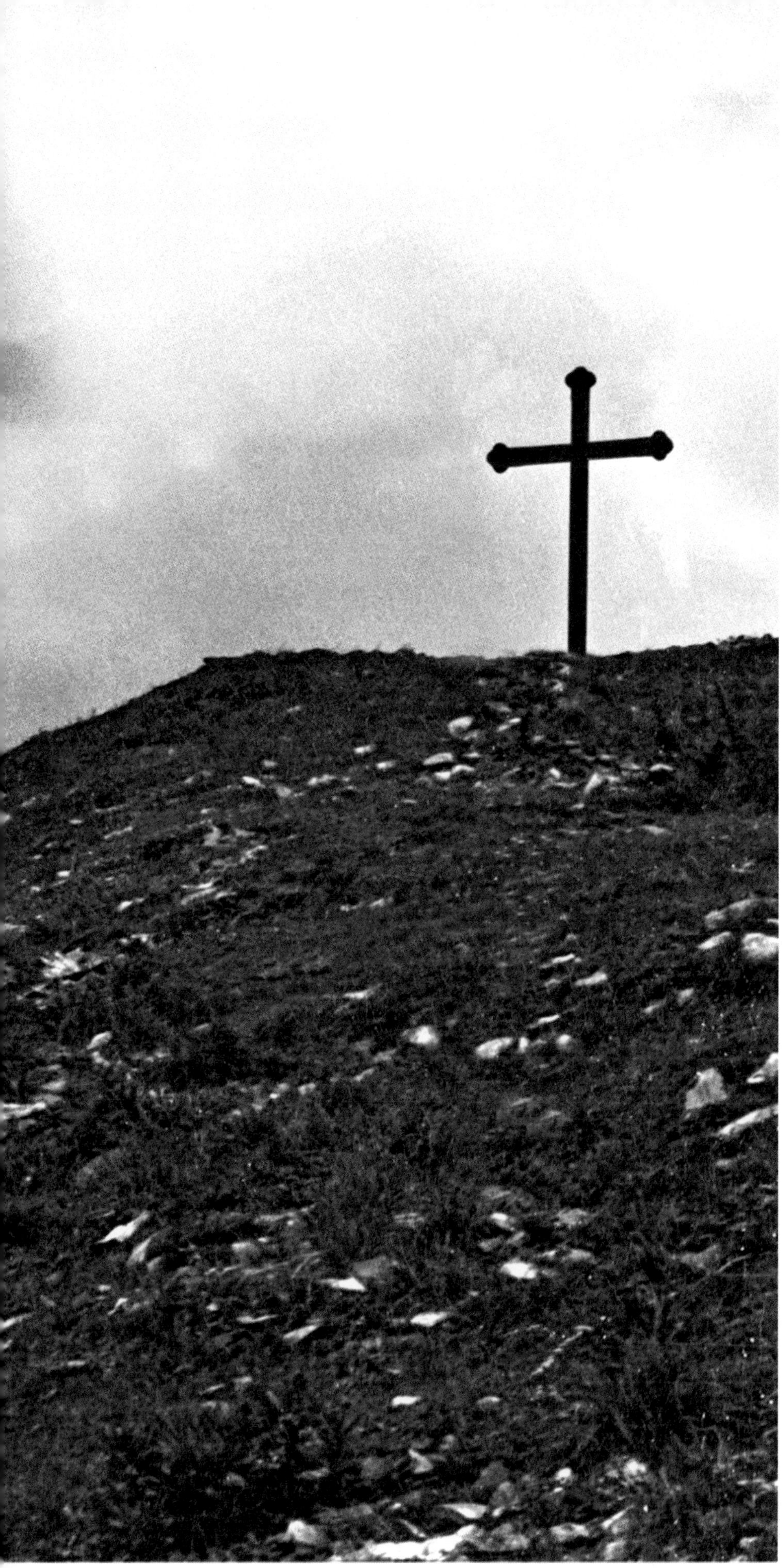

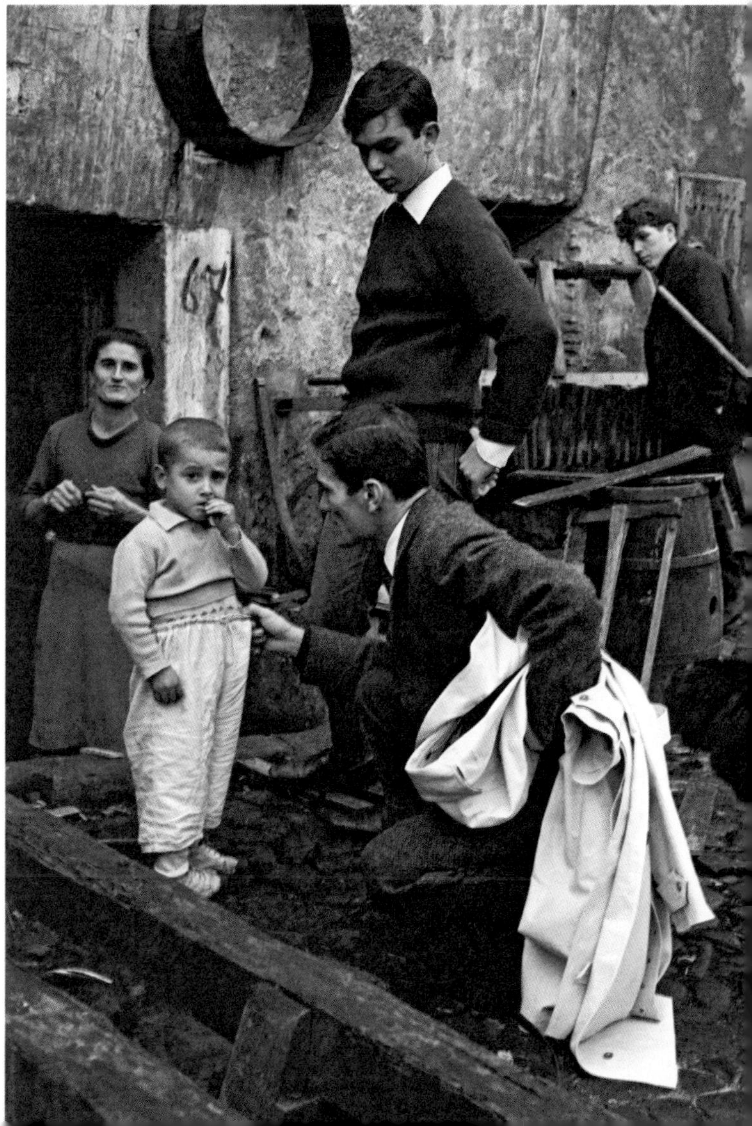

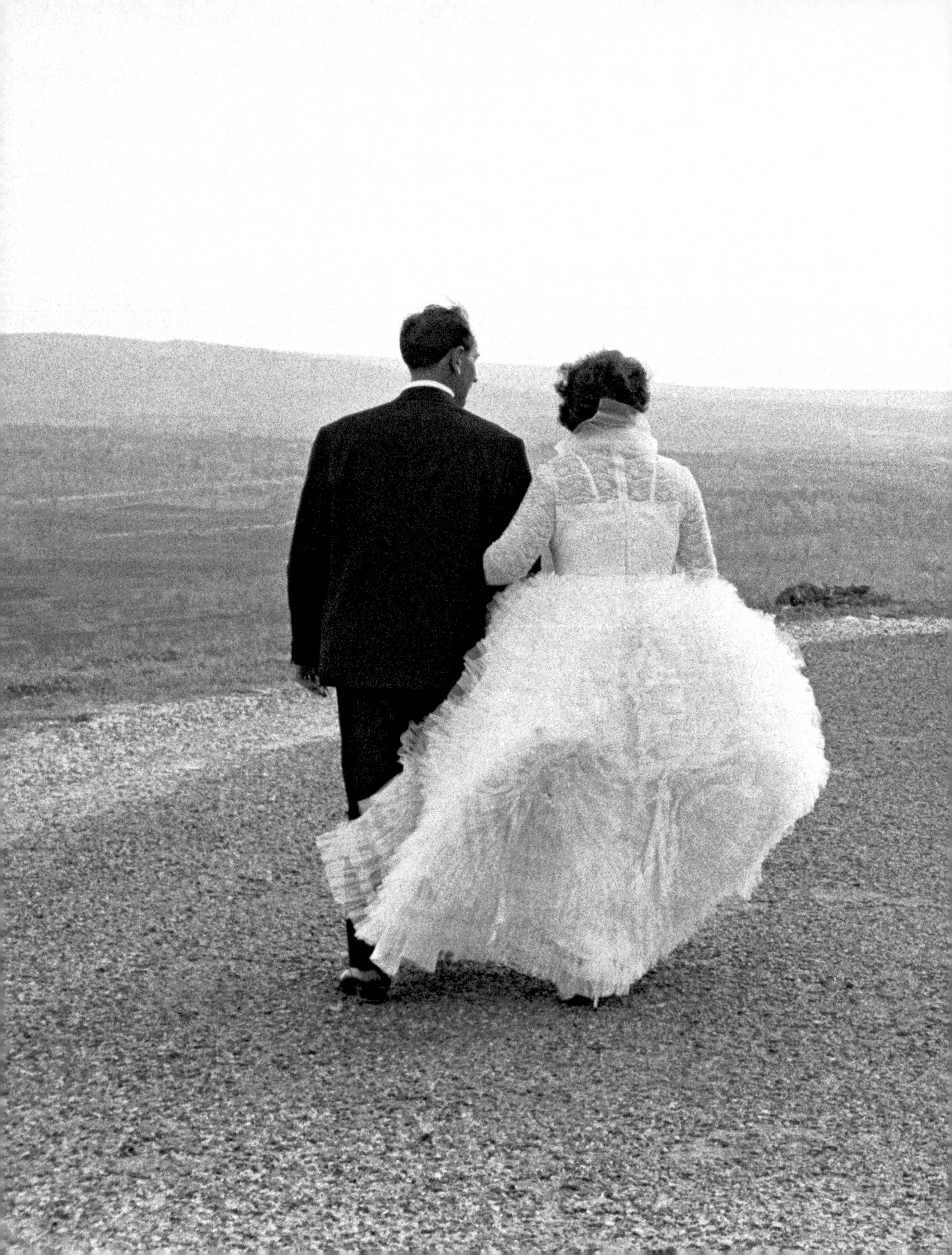

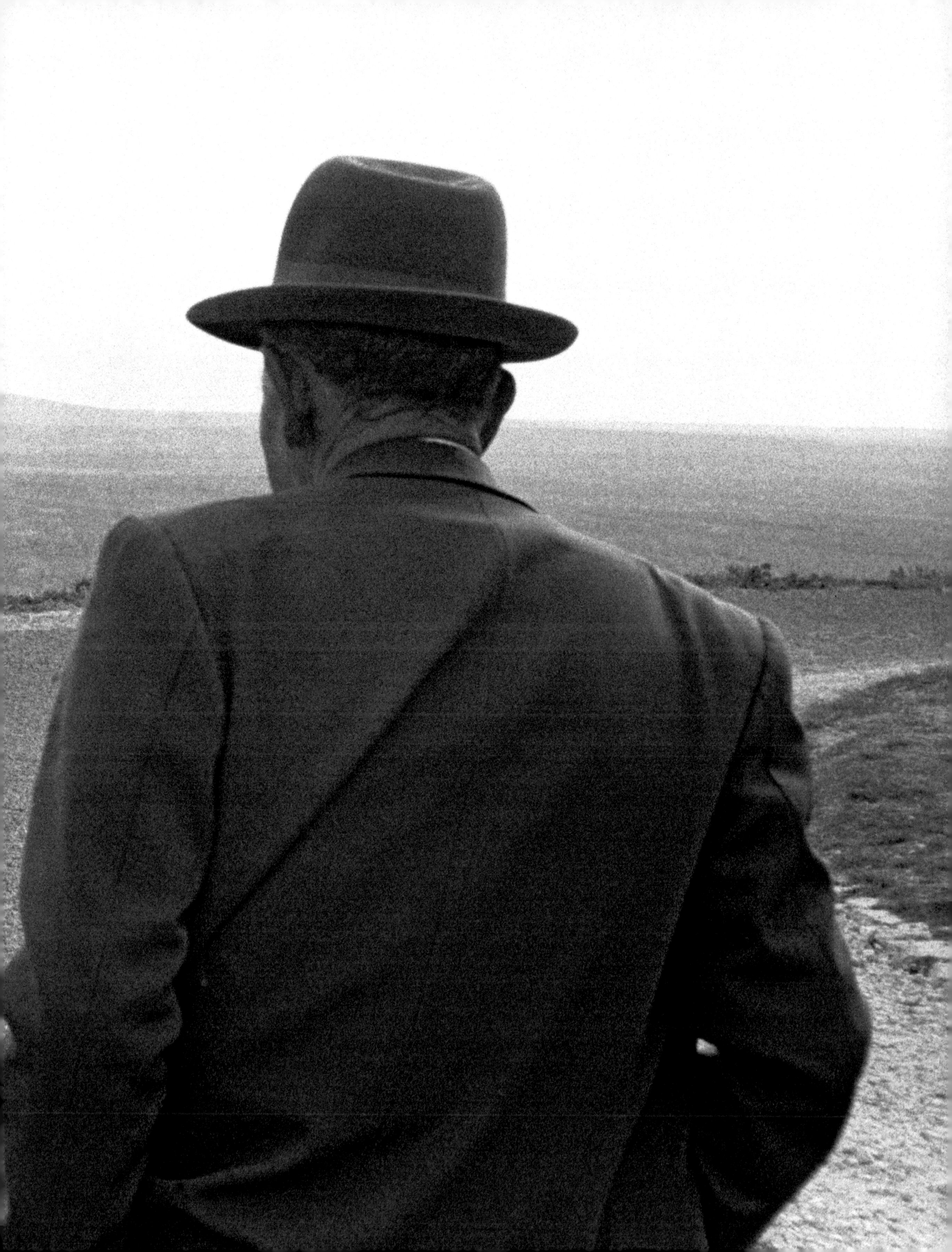

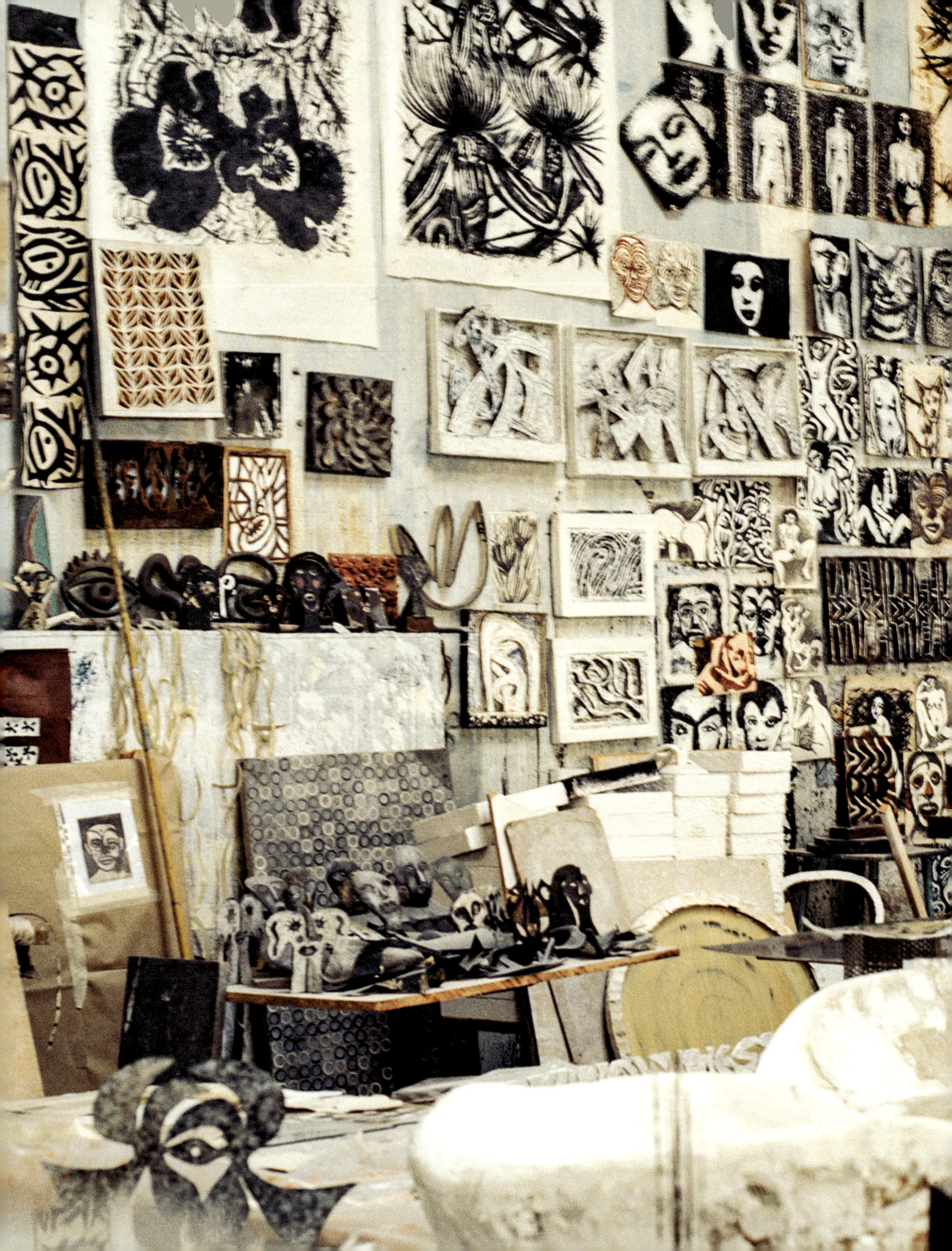

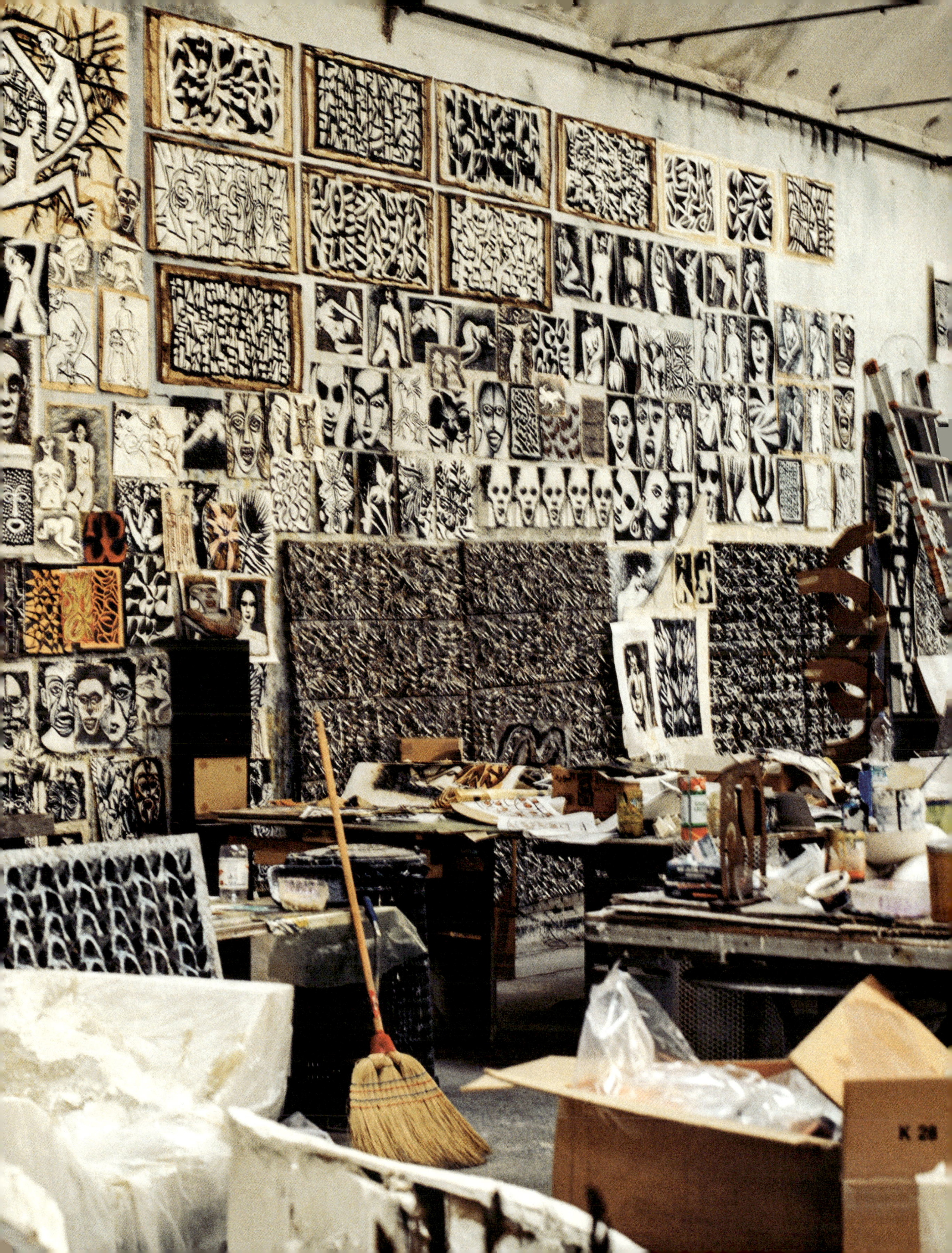
K 28

IT *WAS* A LOVE STORY *I GUESS* YOU COULD SAY

PAINTER, DESIGNER & SCULPTOR

Kris Ruhs

IN CONVERSATION WITH THE ARTIST

Michele Oka Doner

PHOTOGRAPHS BY

Bruce Weber

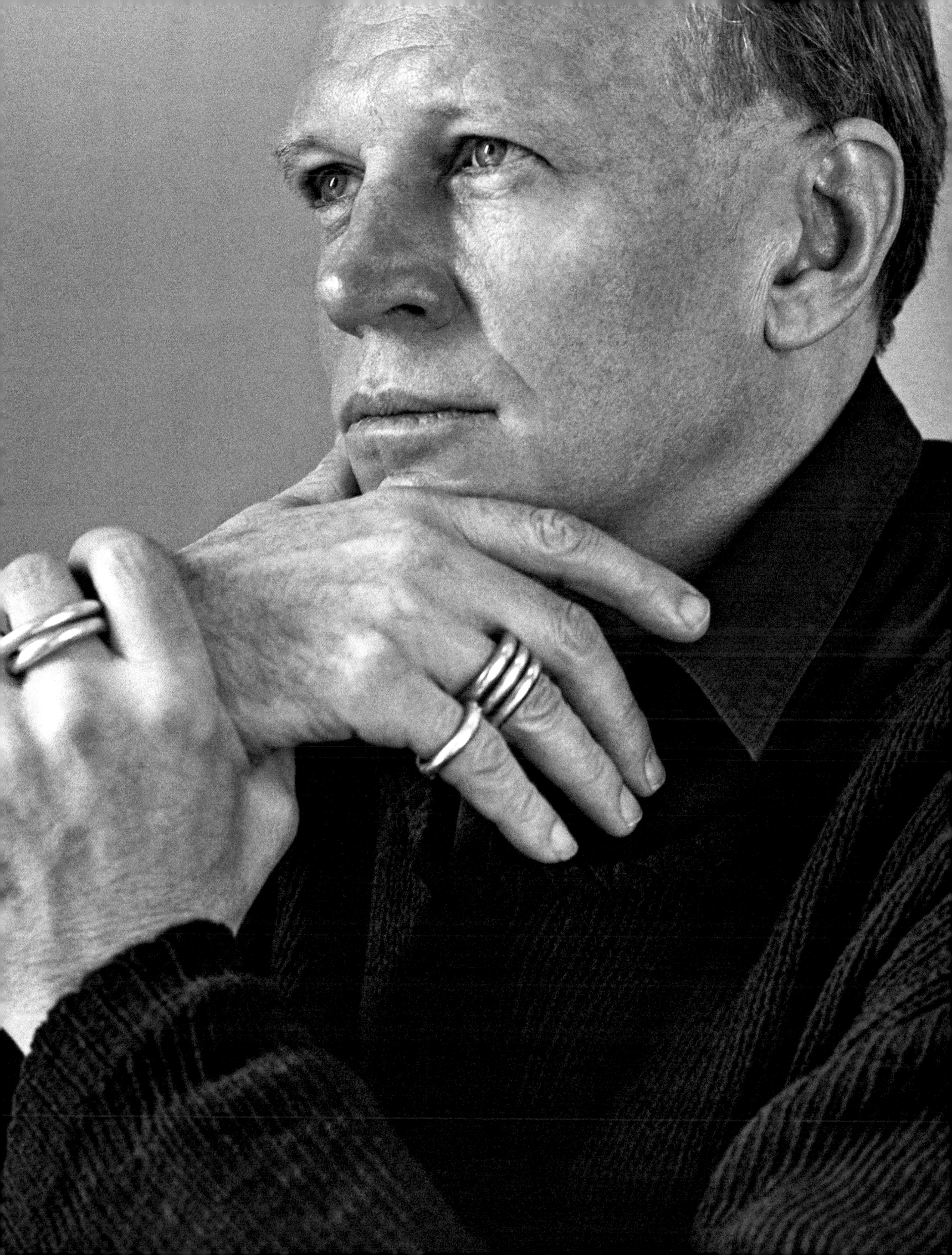

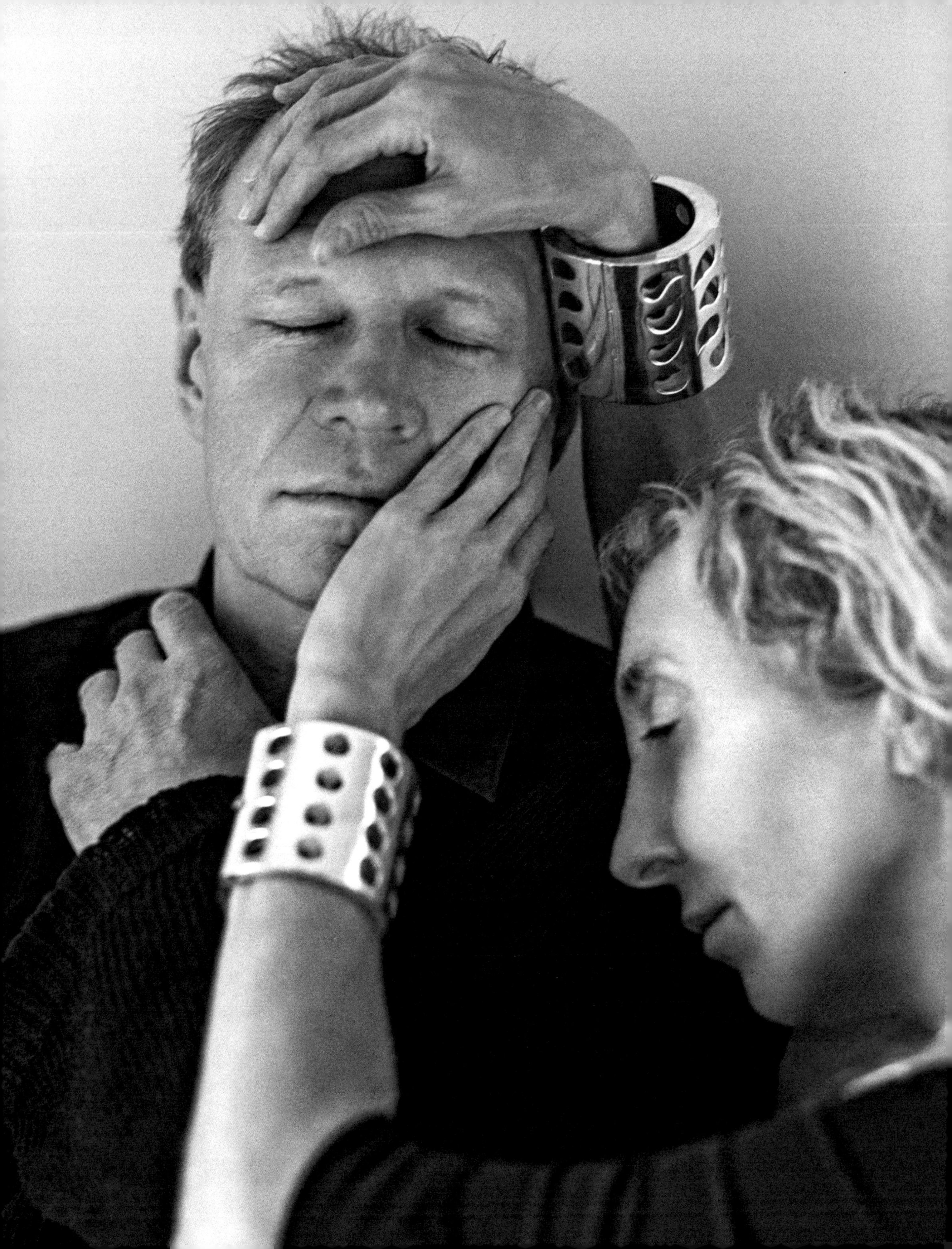

It was another film noir kind of day in Milan. The sun was trying to break through the fast-moving clouds as we searched down a long alleyway for Kris's studio. Of course, there wasn't a number—there wasn't even the name RUHS scratched into the metal of the huge industrial door at the entrance. Kris finally came out front, looming large in his work clothes like a character out of John Steinbeck's play *Of Mice and Men*. We went inside, and he replied in his soft-spoken way as we complimented him on the drawings and sculptures that filled the space, "The light is beautiful in here." On my light meter I was only getting an aperture reading of *f*2.8 at 1/15th. I was reminded of the time I photographed Balthus at his studio in Switzerland, which is built right into the ground. I barely got a reading on my light meter there, too.

As Kris and I walked around the corner to a local boxing club, I asked about my friend Carla Sozzani, his constant companion and the only person I know who understands half of what makes him tick. He agreed that she was the perfect woman to wear his jewelry designs along with her favorite Azzedine Alaïa creations. "Our house in Morocco also has beautiful light," Kris said. "Yes," I laughed, "but only outside on the roof terrace, overlooking the Medina."

It was quite late by the time we got to the boxing club, but I didn't even notice—because I was already busy photographing the fighters in the ring, throwing vicious punches at each other and swearing in Italian, as Kris said in a reassuring way, "Don't worry, you'll love the light."

—BRUCE WEBER, MONTAUK, NY, 2014

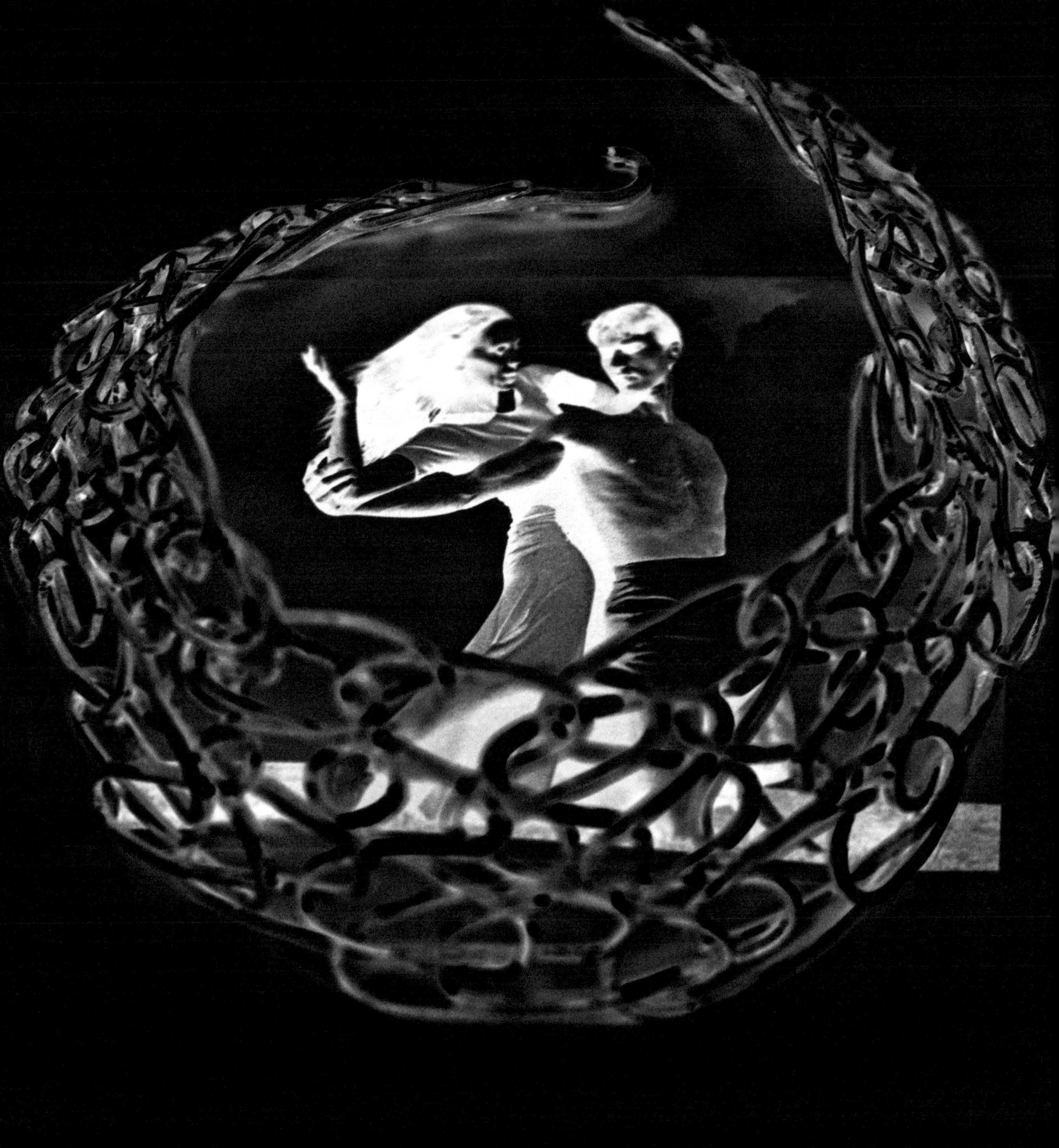

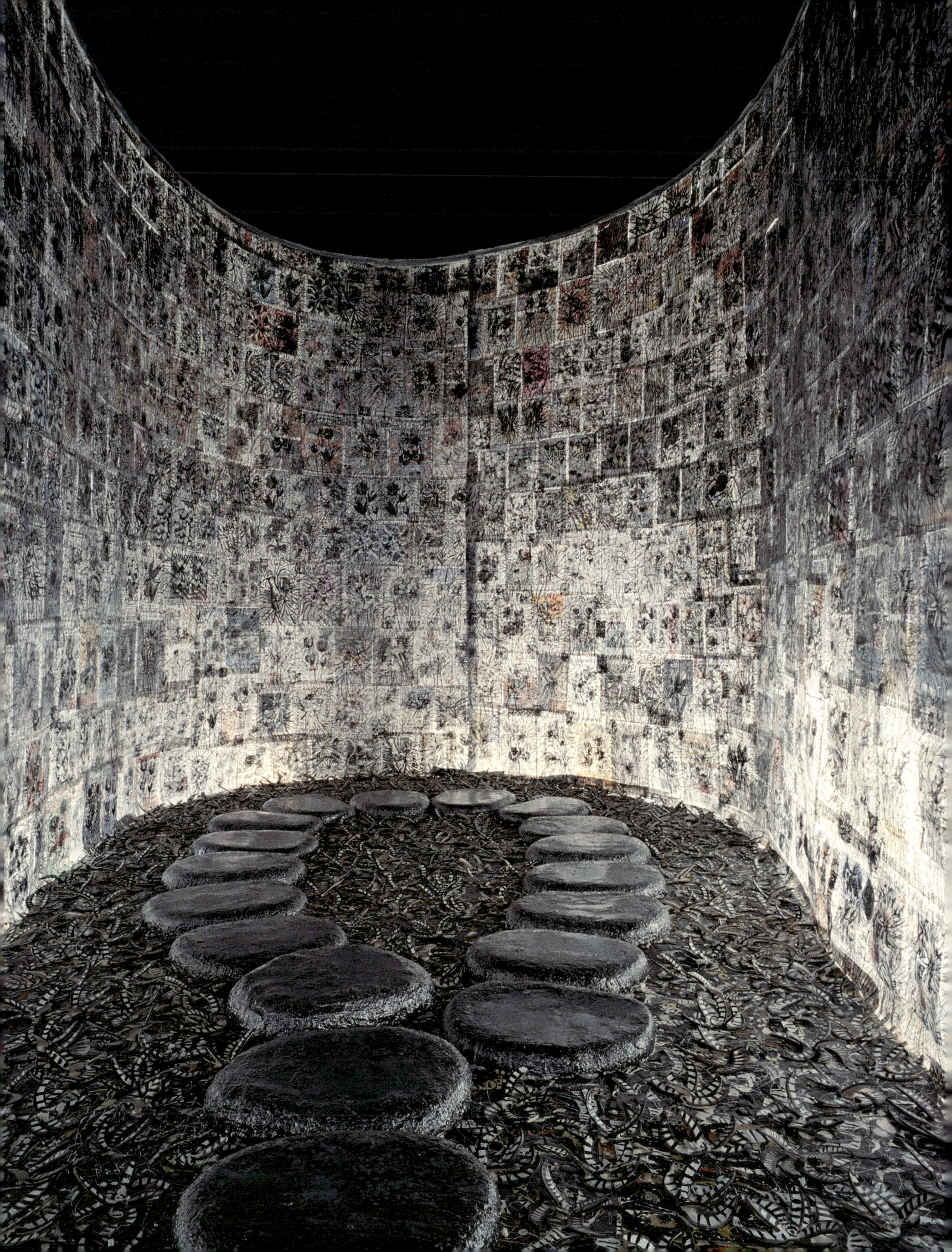

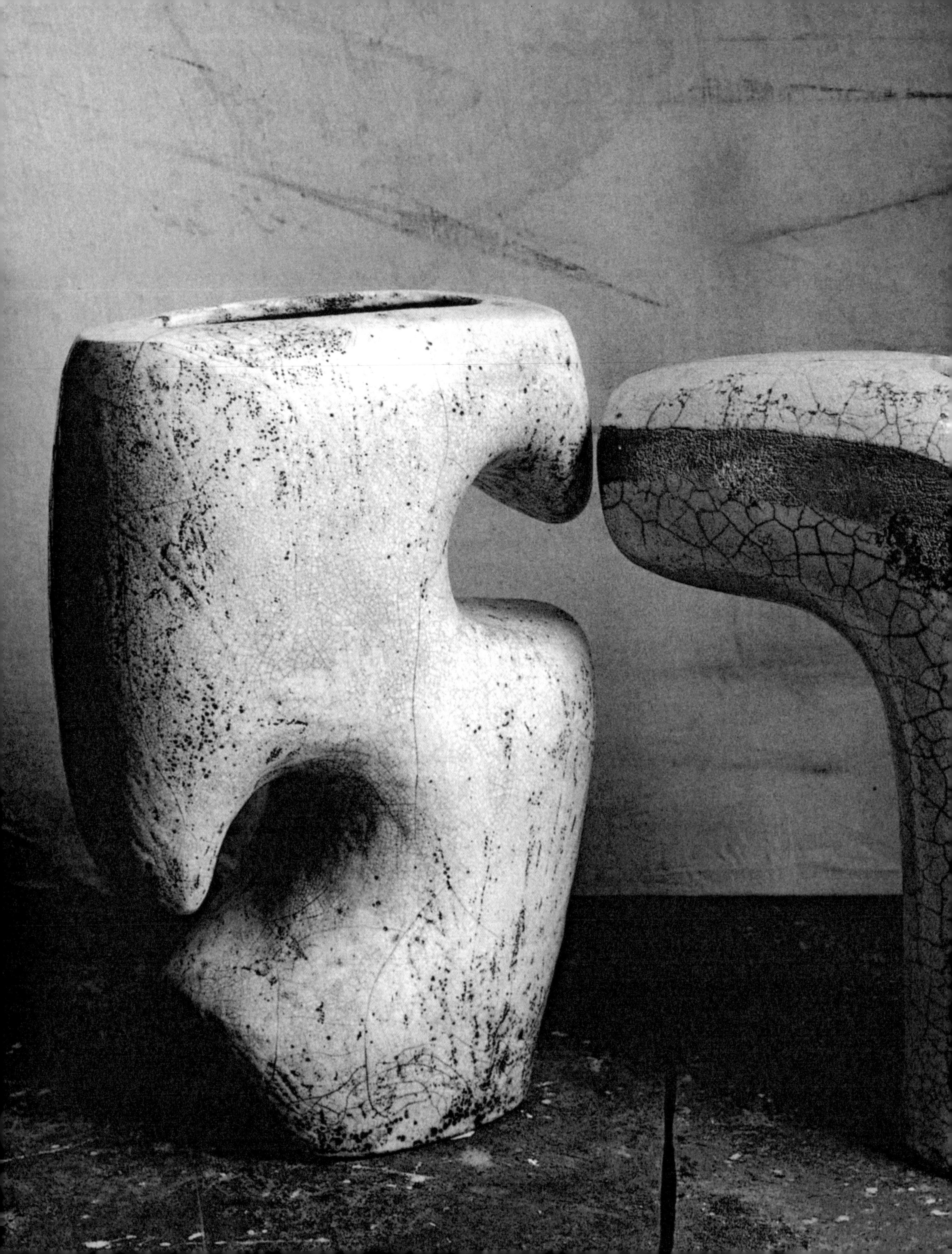

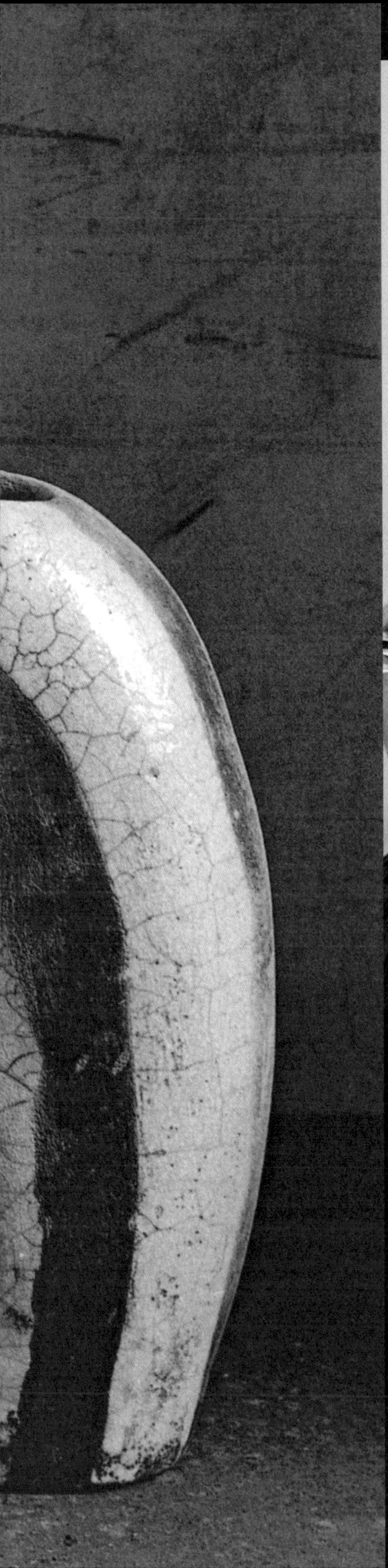
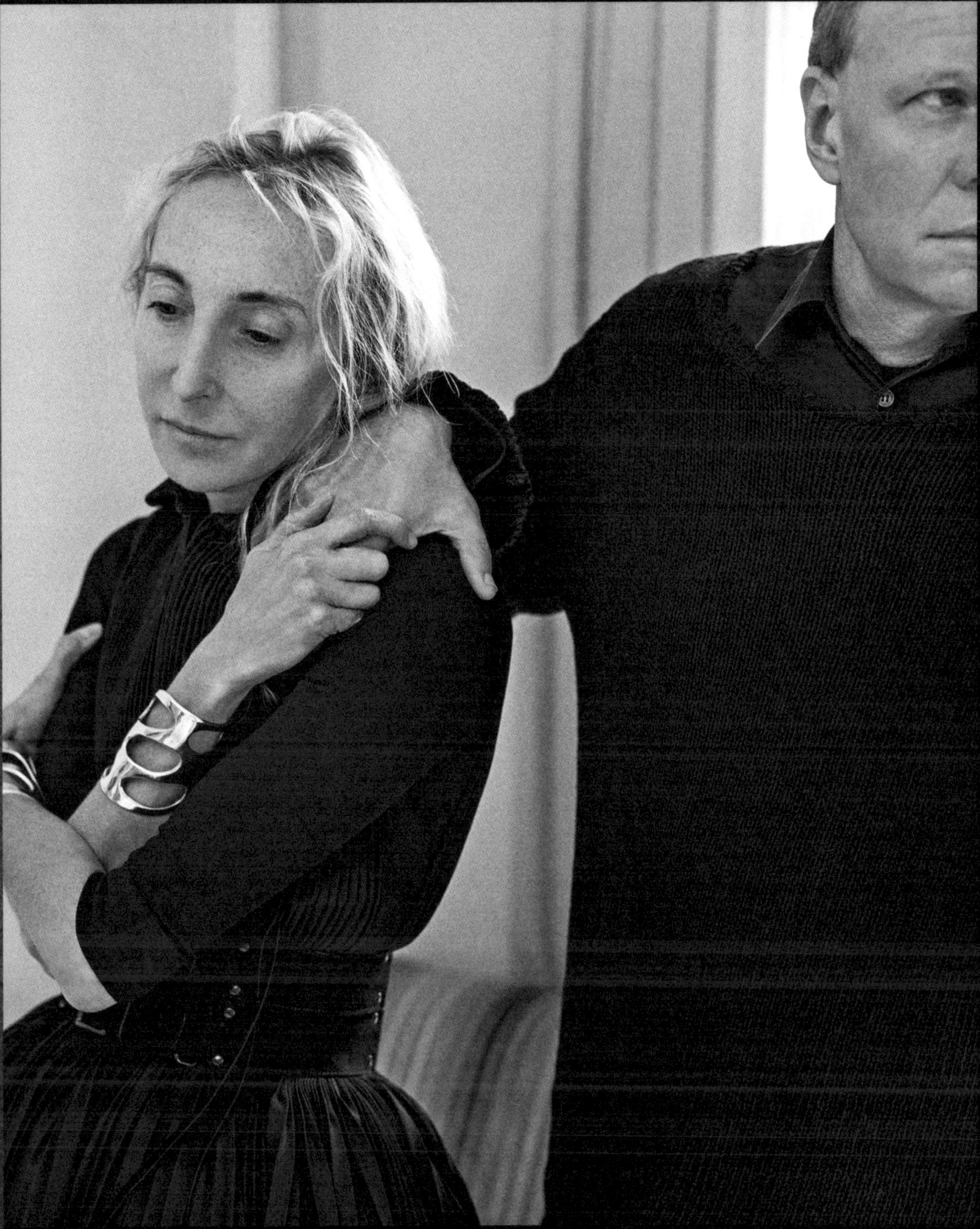

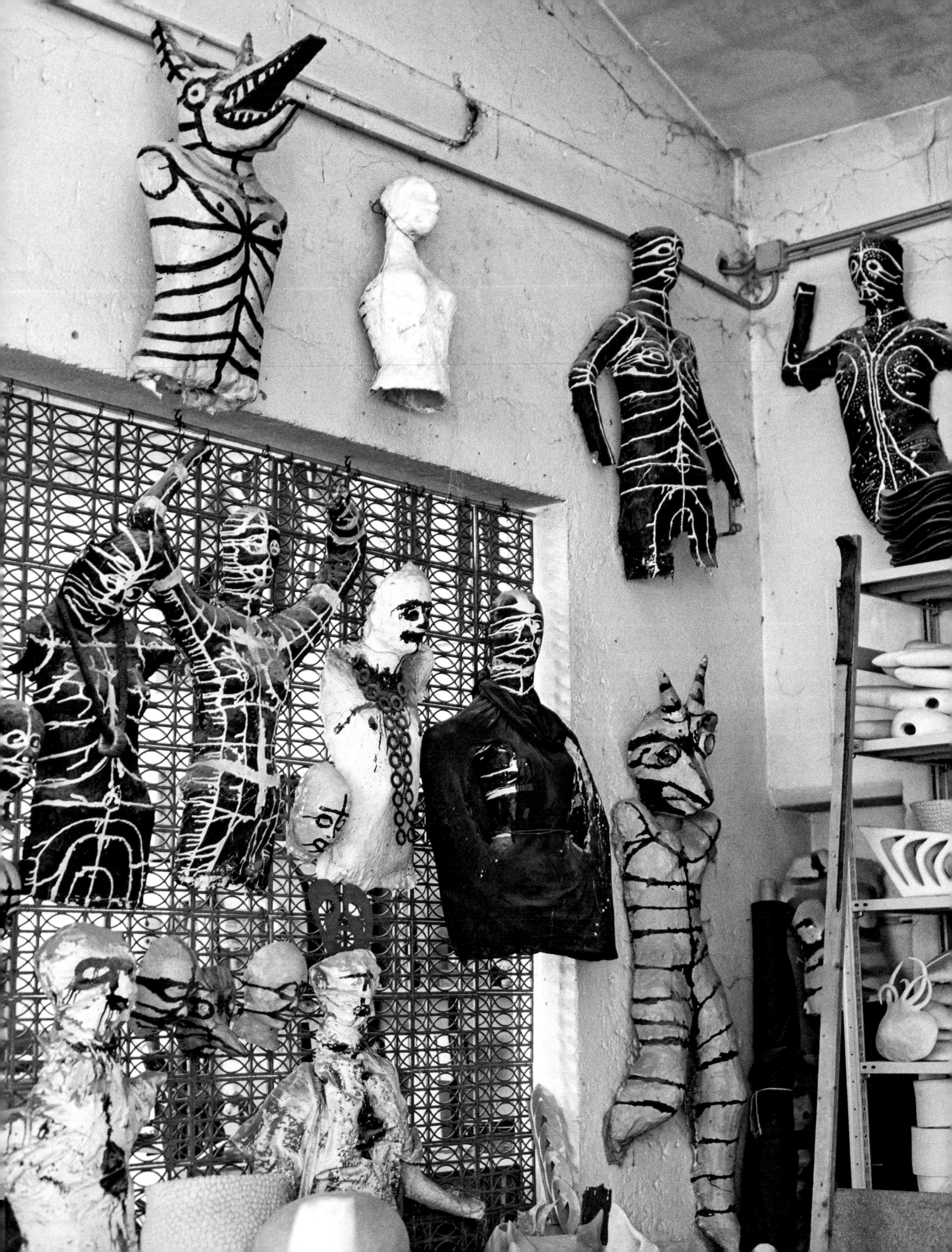

MICHELE OKA DONER Kris, after so many years!

KRIS RUHS A long time, actually.

MOD But it also seems like yesterday we were both young and flagrant. Do you remember visiting my studio?

KR I remember your studio.

MOD You, with your raw materials—all the work you did that had such an "anti-machine" attitude.

KR Anti-technology.

MOD Yes, no industrial revolution for you.

KR No, I have never joined in with that revolution.

MOD How many years ago did you live in New York and have a studio? It must have been the 1980s.

KR I grew up in New York. I think I started leaving in 1989. By the '90s I was absolutely gone.

MOD We're living through one of those big paradigm shifts, you know? The kind when historians will look back and see all the markings of change—the way geologists are able to do when they look at the earth. They can see physical shifts—when things heated up to a certain point or melted. They will do the same thing when they look back at our culture and see those important moments. But this can only be done in hindsight—not so much while we're in it.

The New York you knew is gone, and all that energy has moved to Brooklyn, which of course has become a different thing entirely. It's wonderful what these cycles hold—and 30 years is a cycle.

KR To tell you the truth, I don't really miss New York.

MOD What's interesting is that the artists I knew who bought spaces early did very well when they sold their real estate. They were able to set themselves up in other places and to make some good money for the first time. These beautiful buildings were purchased by people or companies with deep pockets and restored—they have been blasted with water and are clean and you can see the detail of the terra-cotta and the stone.

KR In one way, it's great, no?

MOD You know there's a loss of the broken-window edgy time; I moved in when there were a lot of broken windows. But the air is a lot cleaner and the trucks aren't belching and there are trees. They've been planting them for 20 to 25 years.

KR Yeah, I get back to New York every now and then, and it's surprising. But not having a studio there makes me feel like a tourist, more or less. It's a strange feeling.

MOD If you need to do a tune-up or brushup and need a place to land, the studio is here and you can come by and we'll set you up. It's nice to know there's someone who has files and hammers and all kinds of tools right here in the city. You have a studio in Milan, right?

KR Yes, I live in Milan now.

MOD What took you to Italy?

KR It was a good moment for me to get out of New York. I found the 1980s were a terrible moment there. I needed some change, and Italy is a fantastic place to be. Also—I fell in love with somebody, so it was a love story I guess you could say.

MOD You know it's interesting—after the '80s, the city did accelerate to an extent. Everything did—from the amount of work we were expected to produce to the amount of champagne we drank. Then the '90s came along and made the '80s look quaint.

KR Where has it gone? I don't know if it stopped around that time. Technology has certainly advanced, but I don't think we've learned too many lessons in life from all we've experienced.

MOD Milan to me always seems more of a design city than an art city. Is that accurate?

KR Yeah, at one time it was probably more of an art city. Now that's kind of lost. Milan is pretty much well known for having the design fair every year, but it's also a little bit fashionable here. When I'm in Milan, I'm in my studio more or less. But I've been traveling all over the place—I have a studio up in Morocco that I've been using for years, in Marrakech. I built it a long time ago, before Marrakech became popular in the way it is today. It's a little tricky working there, because the studio is right in the center of the Medina. Lots of people get lost in Morocco. It works or

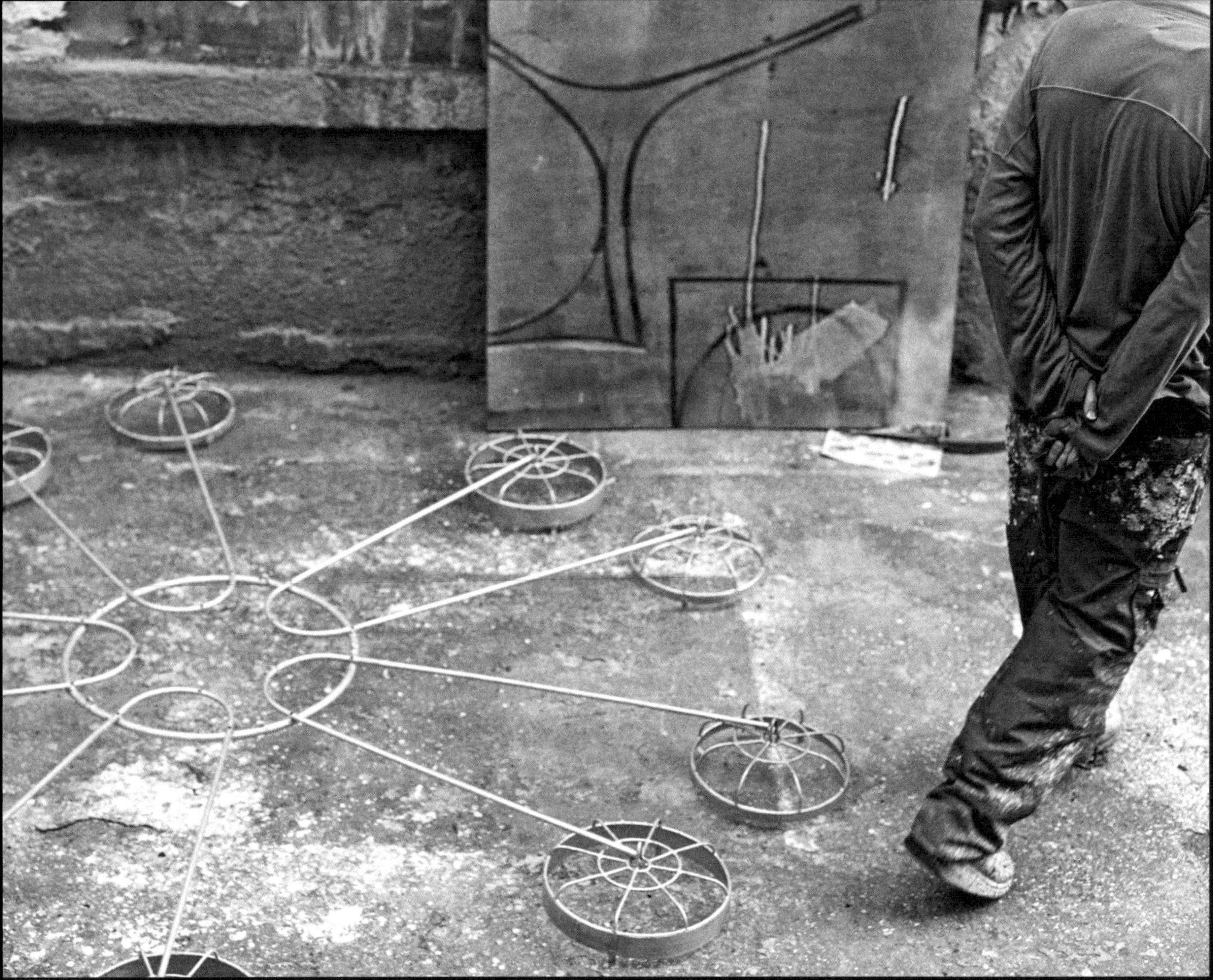

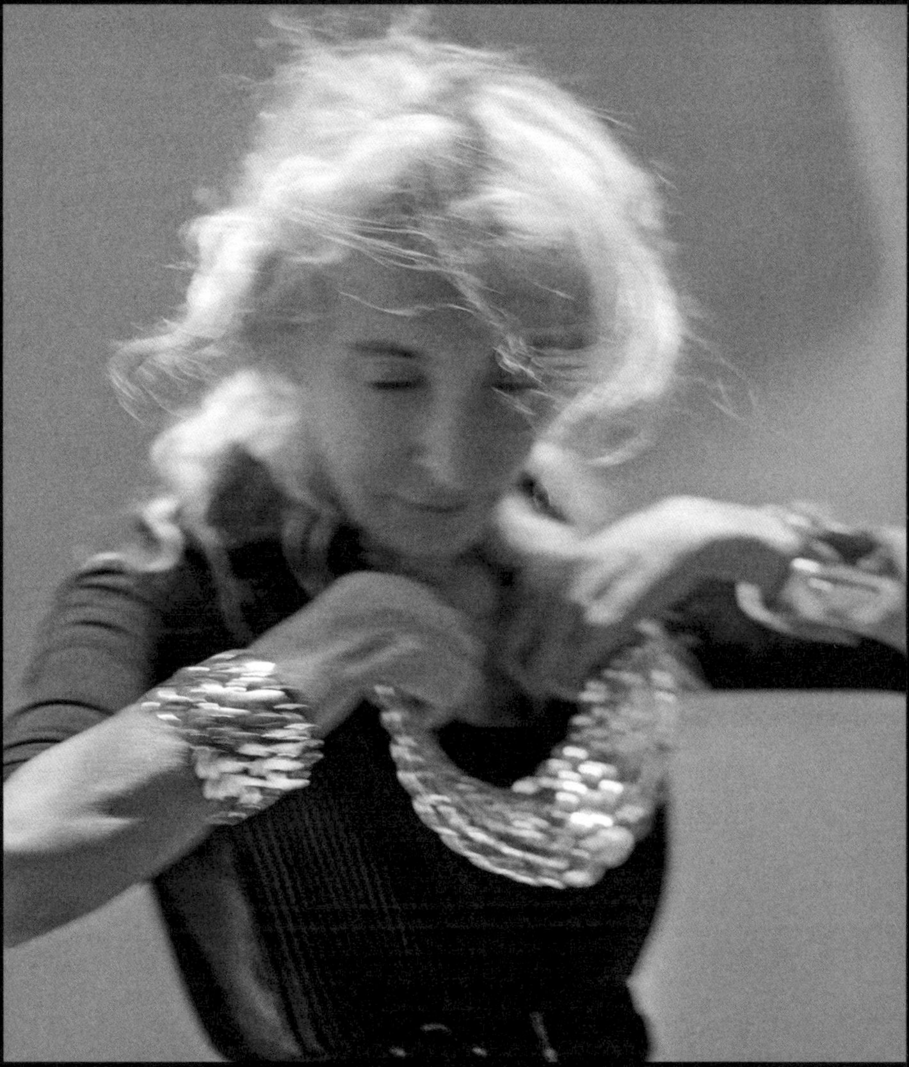

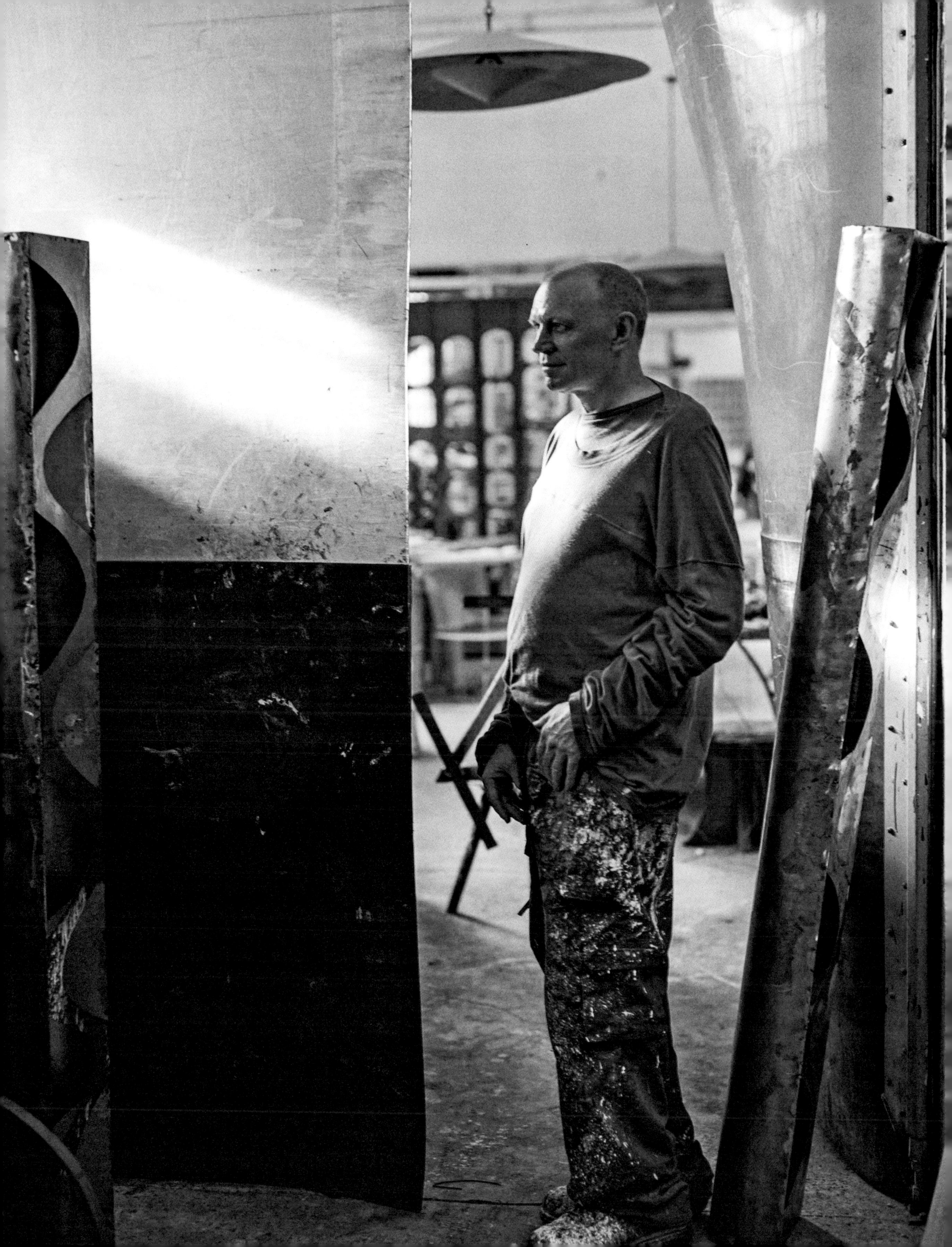

its own time and rhythm. I have friends that have gone there and had disastrous experiences—it looks very alluring. But when you get close, it's not so easy.

MOD What I love about the Medina there—and Morocco in general—is its medieval quality. You still see the ironmongers and the wild creatures. Your work is also very medieval, Kris. You're not a renaissance man, in that sense.

KR There are many things that I connect with in Morocco. The craftsmen are terrific. I hate to say it, but the city has been changing a lot over the last five years. The tourists have definitely changed the environment and atmosphere. It runs the risk of becoming just another place. It's still great, though.

MOD Well, I think we used to romanticize how good it was. I loved the monkeys and the snake charmers. It really is another world.

KR I wish it had stayed just as it was when I first visited.

MOD So what's on your agenda next?

KR I've been doing a lot of work in China now. Shanghai is a nice, crazy city. It's got a little bit of early New York edge to it, because there's a strong international community. There are very interesting areas outside of Shanghai, like Peking. In the countryside, they're doing amazing things in ceramics. There are all these incredible outlets where really interesting things are happening.

MOD I've seen some of the manifestations, and they've published my work in several magazines—clay, glass, everything. They're so interested and interesting! The conversation is about learning, whereas the American conversation is much more about, *How much did you get for it?*

KR Yeah, that American attitude of "Look what I've done..."

MOD ...Which often turns out to be one big bore. And it does take a lot of energy. It's good you've released yourself.

KR I'm also involved with a place called Corso Como here. We started it many years ago—it's got a gallery, restaurant, and bookstore. I've been working on that for the past few years—it gives me an outlet to design many things, work in different media, and collaborate with other artists.

MOD You're such a fertile field, and there are so many aspects of your work, which is unusual in itself. And you've taken it outside the rarified market of the gallery and put it everywhere. I consider that to be the future of art.

KR It has to exist outside of the gallery now, because the gallery has become too removed from what real art is about.

MOD Well, real art has always been and always will be—it just changes form and shape. I think there are many wonderful artists working nowadays in video. The market can't kill art; art will sneak out. It's the aggression of the human spirit. But it's great to see that you've remained so hands-on and earthy even while you're living in a design city that worships the perfection of the machine and is known for its technology. You're still shredding rubber and pounding wood.

KR Milan has got both the good and the bad. It's changed in the years I've been here.

MOD Well, the world is changing and the growth of the Chinese market and their willingness to work is a huge influence on the art and design world. They're the sleeping giant waking up and we're the fat lazy western world. But you're maintaining—you're still a soldier for the cause.

KR I have no choice.

MOD Artists have always been forward thinking—you have to be a warrior because nobody else is going to defend your vision. We can't afford to be anything but what we are. I love the fact that you're such a romantic. It's wonderful you fell in love.

KR Yeah, a little romance is always good, and we've been together for many years.

MOD Yes, and we're lucky. When I lived in Detroit after I finished my years in the University of Michigan, I met a woman who was a painter. She was 25 years older than me, and told me about surviving in the work camps in Poland. She said something I'll never forget, "I wish I had had even crayons to work with." She was hungry to make and couldn't. She survived, and now what she does is create. This is such a simple idea, yet...

KR It's fundamental to our existence, to communicate or express ourselves somehow. We take so much for granted when we think about all the opportunities and the things we have access to. It's amazing.

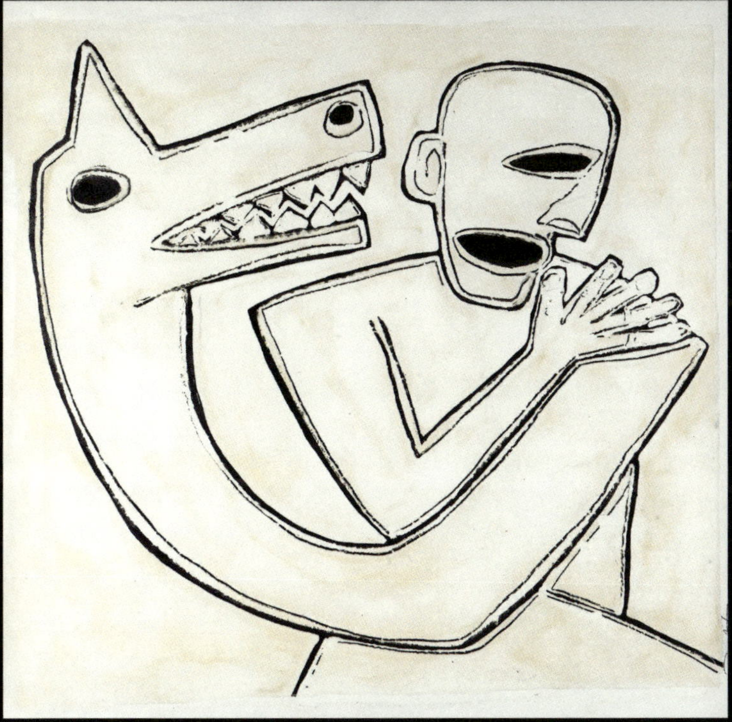

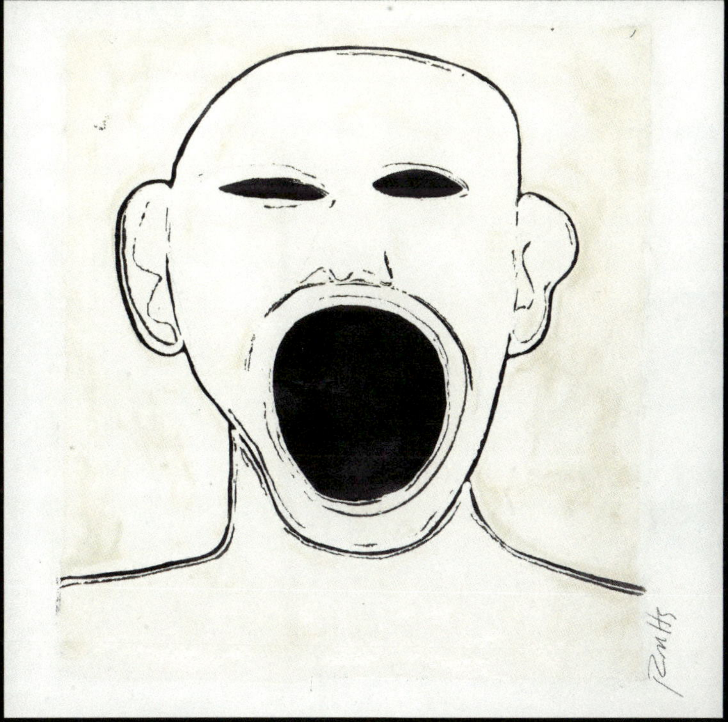

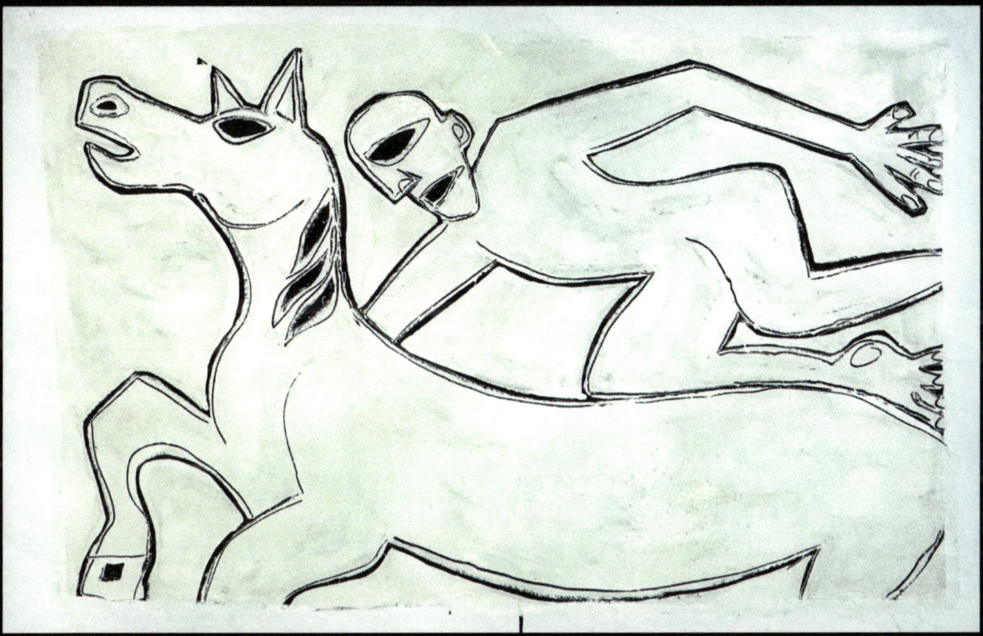

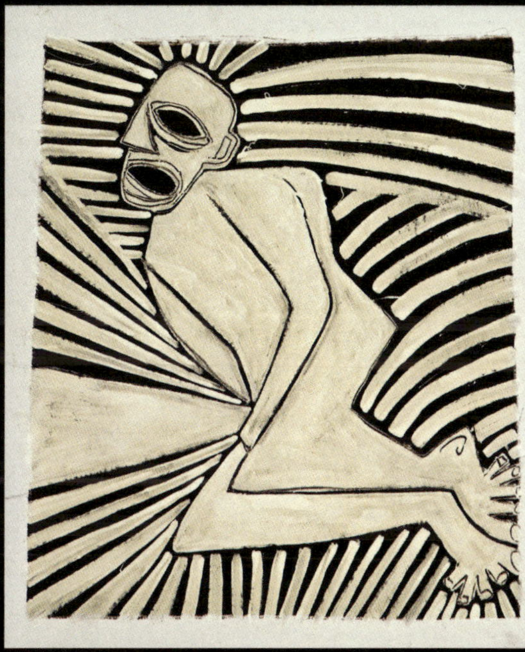

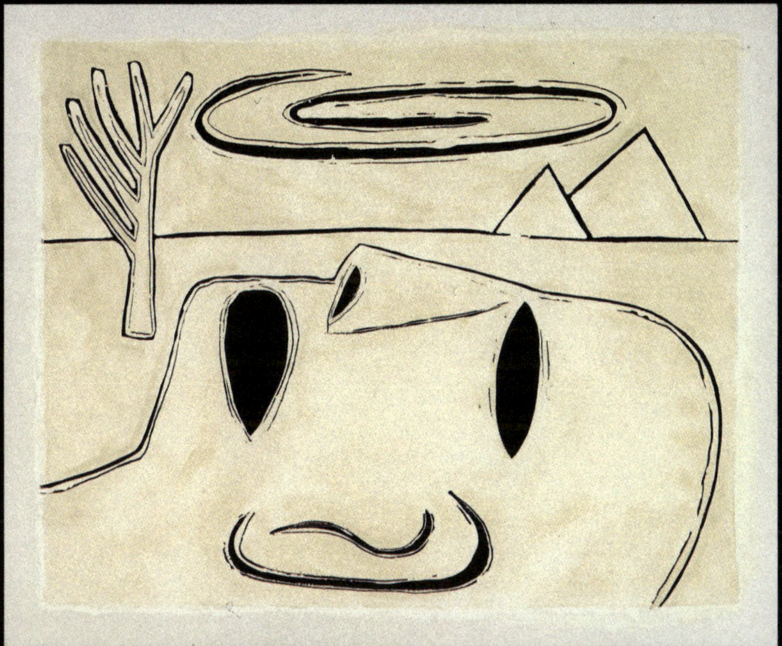

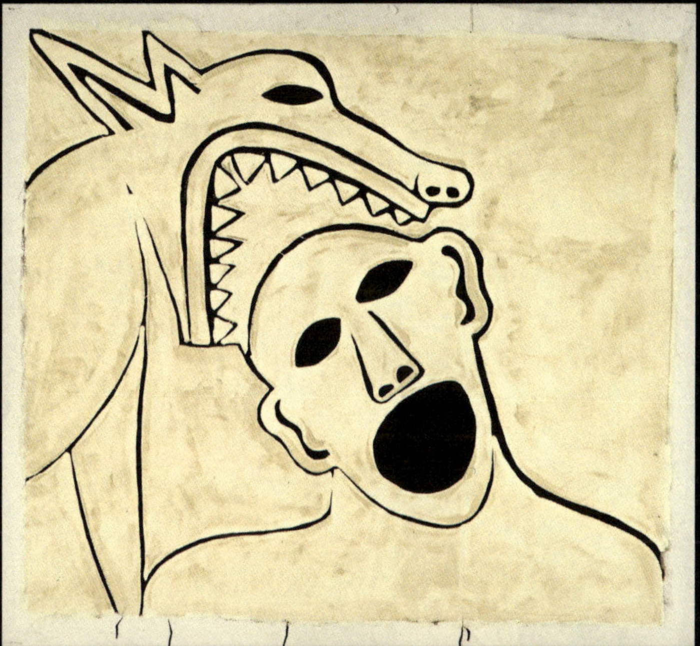

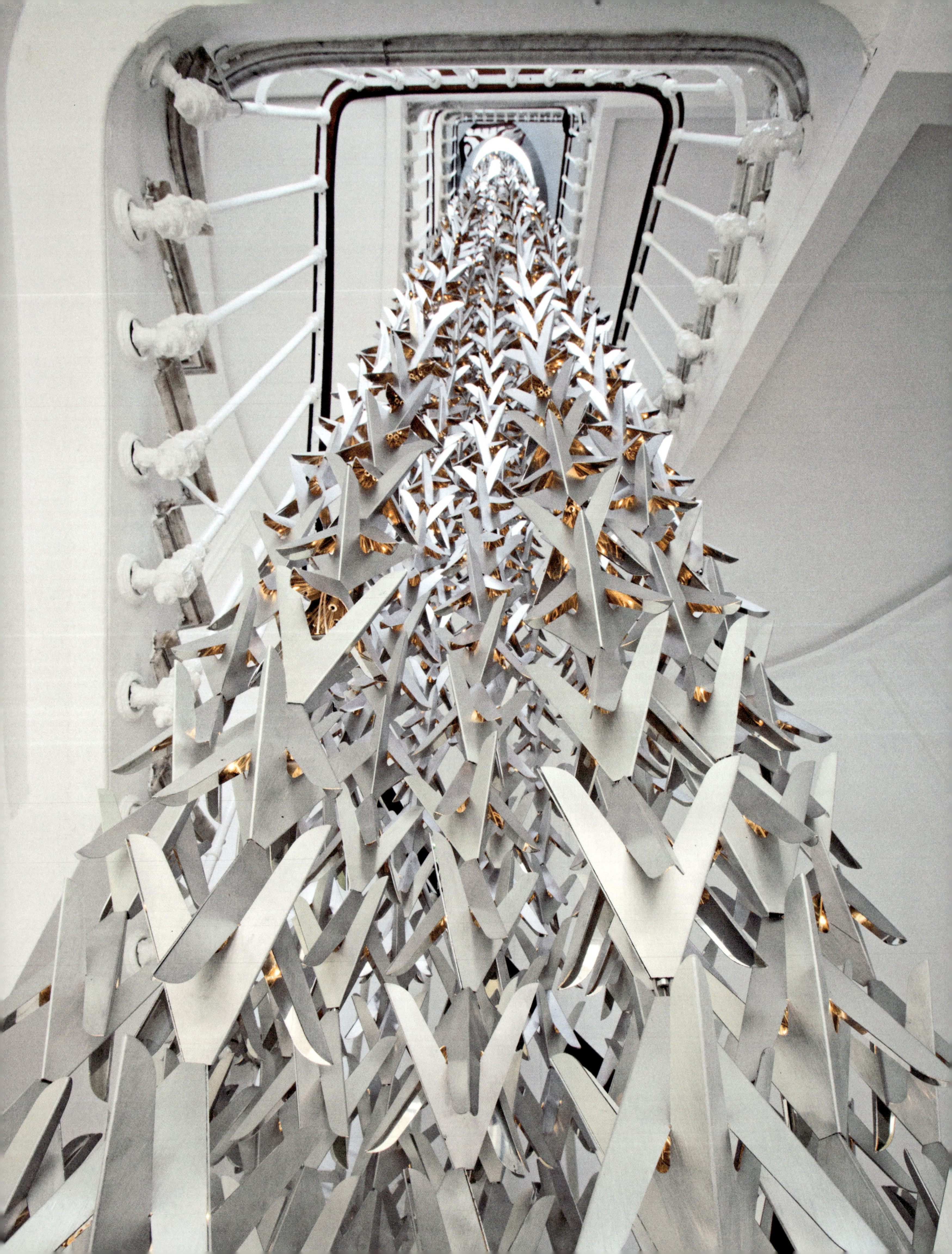

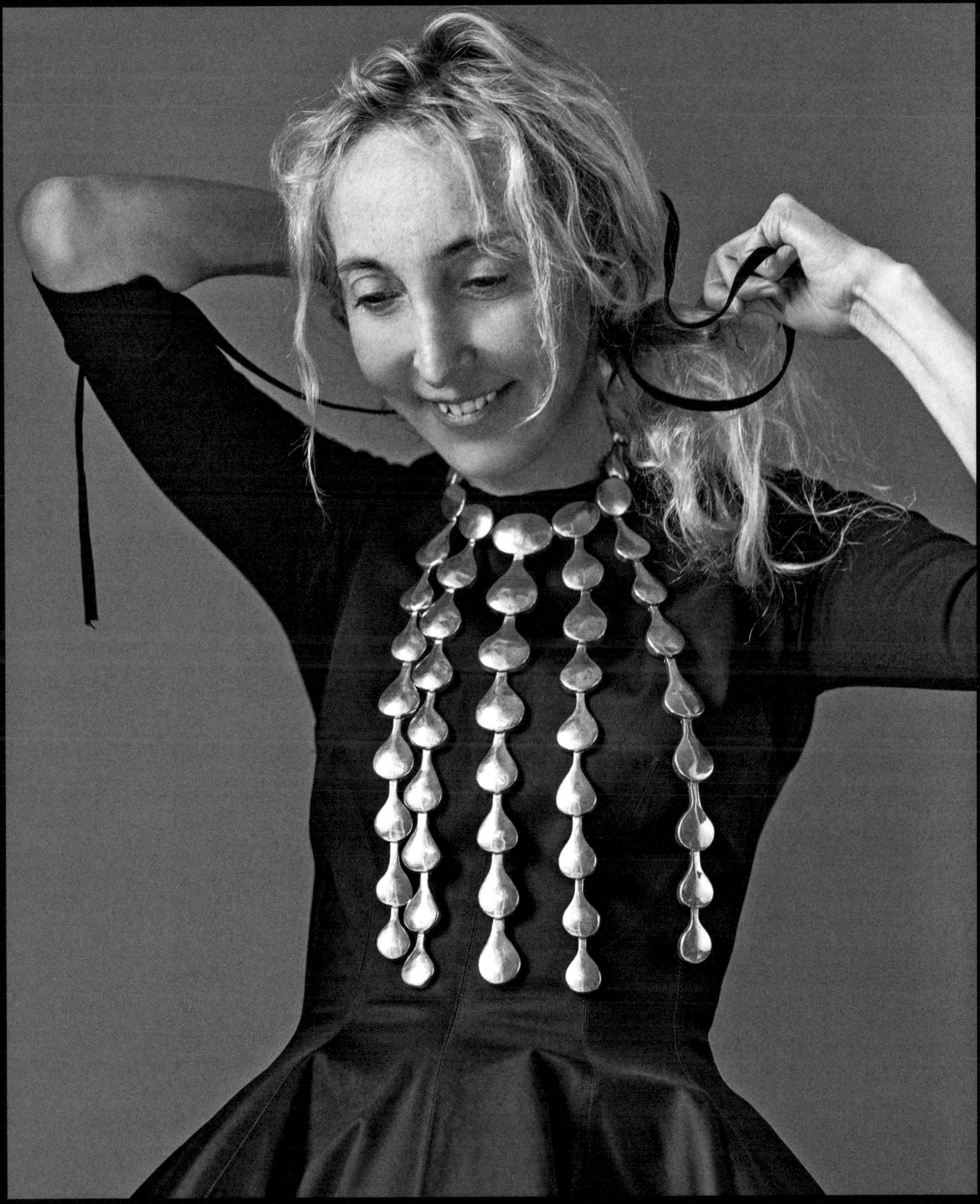

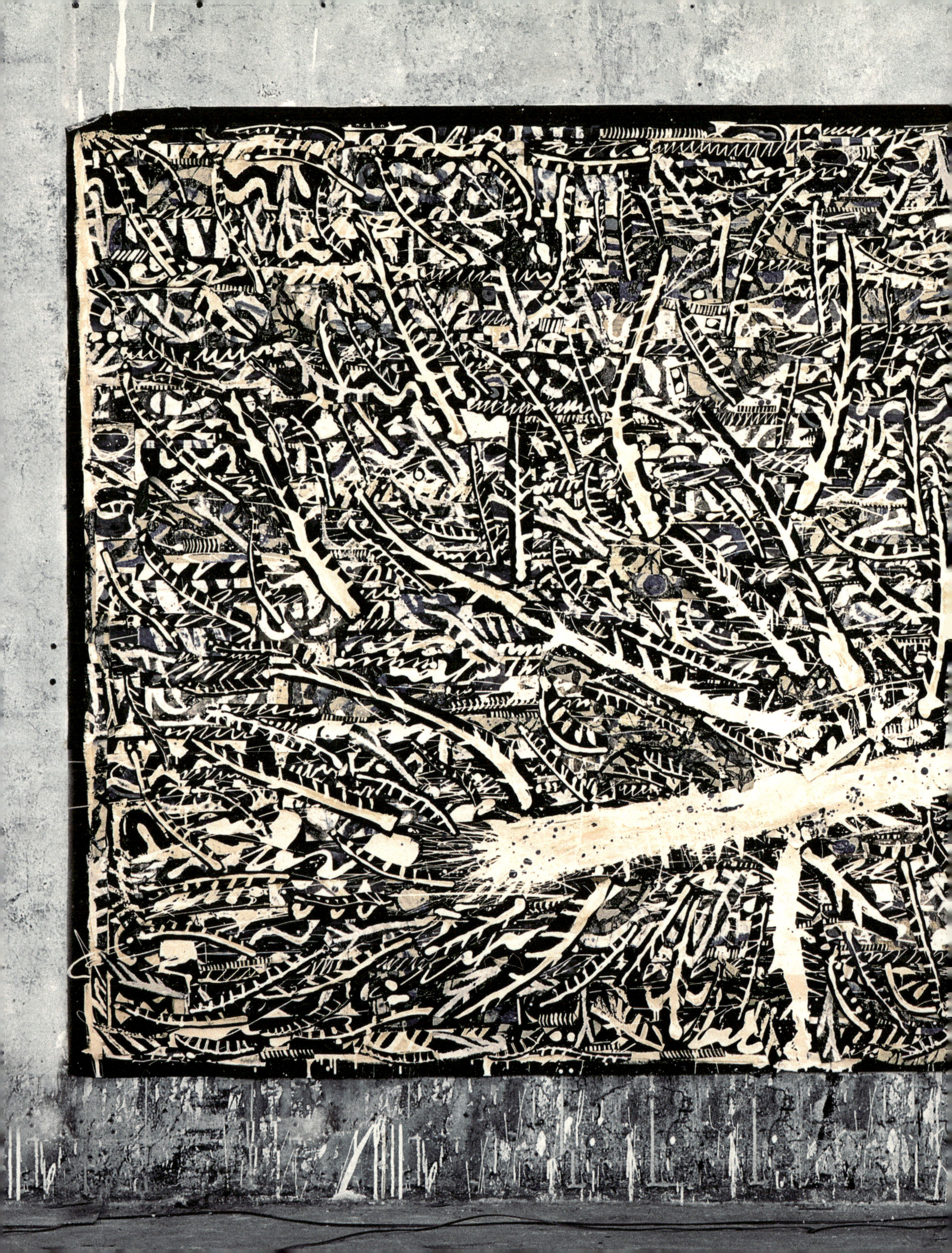

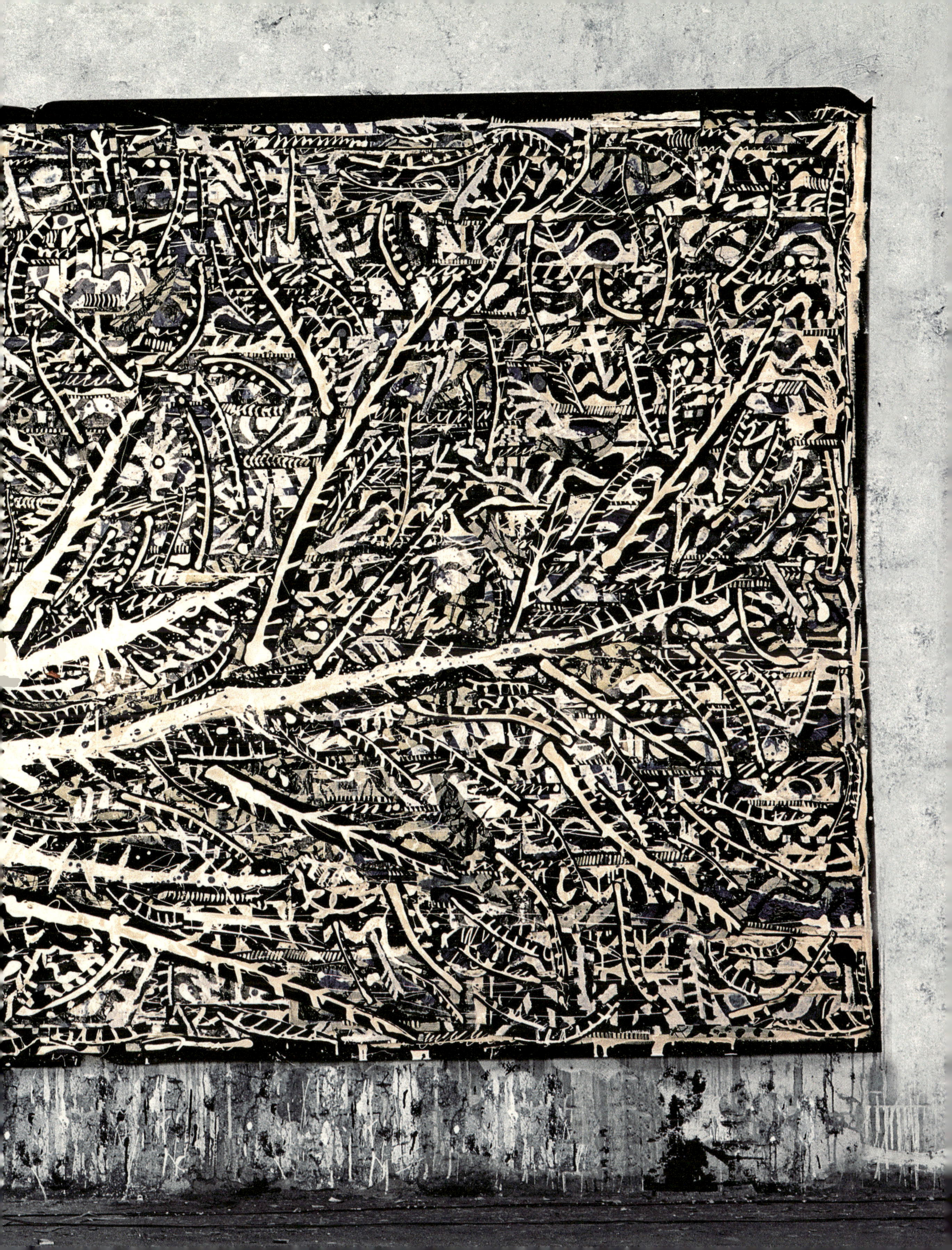

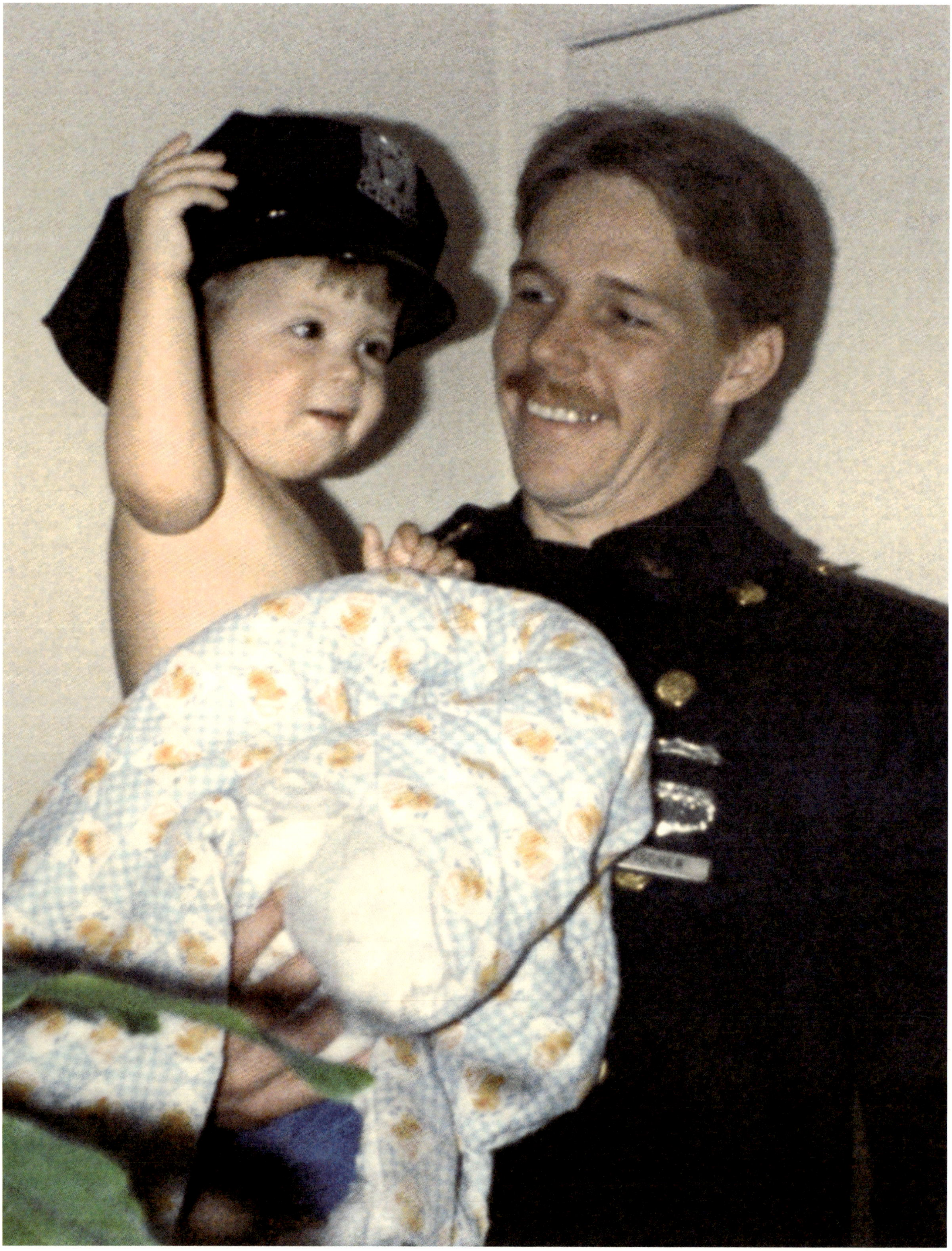

BOYS IN
BLUE

DETECTIVE WILLIAM FISCHER
NEW YORK CITY POLICE DEPARTMENT
EMERGENCY SERVICES UNIT

PHOTOGRAPHS BY
Bruce Weber

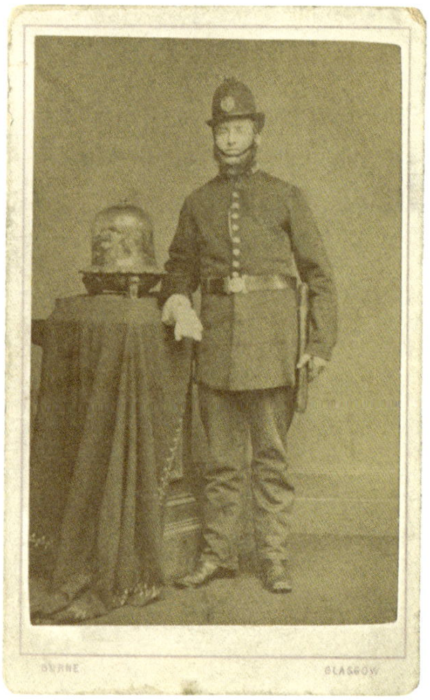

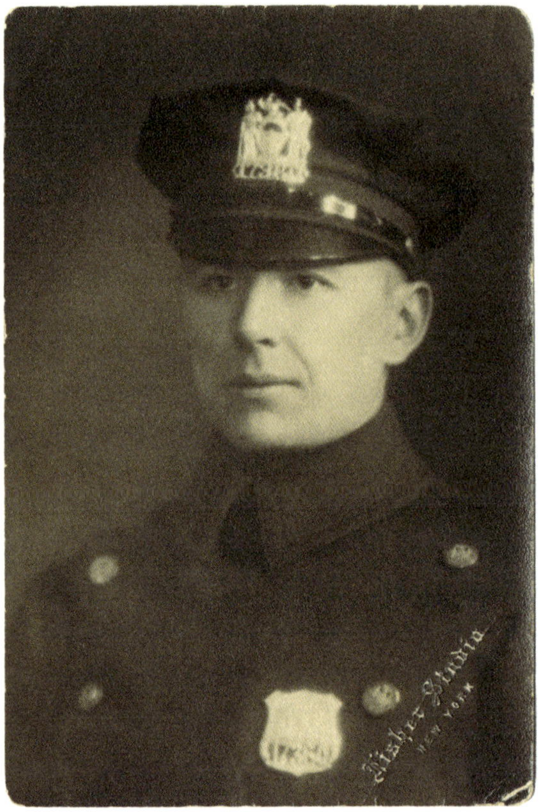

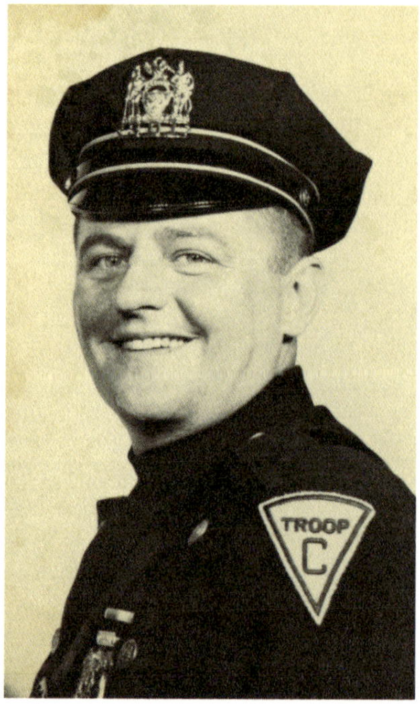

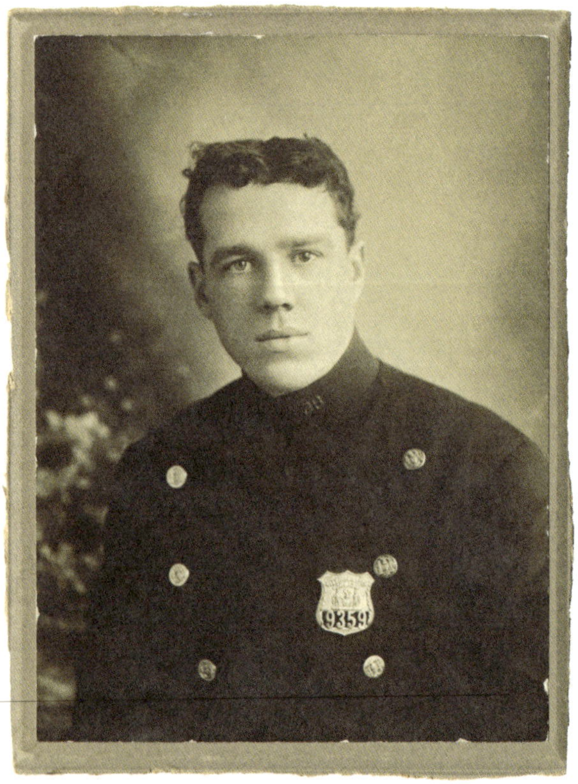

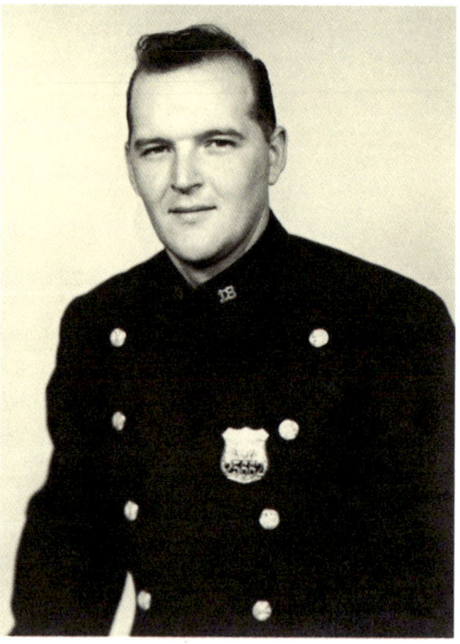

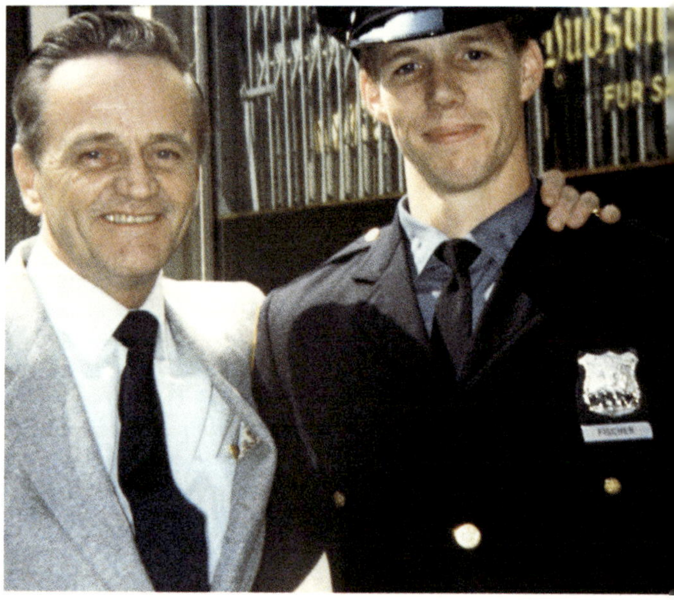

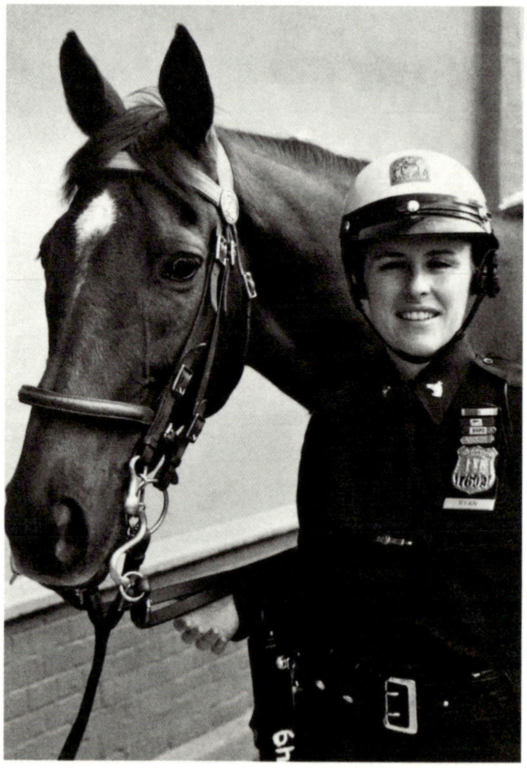

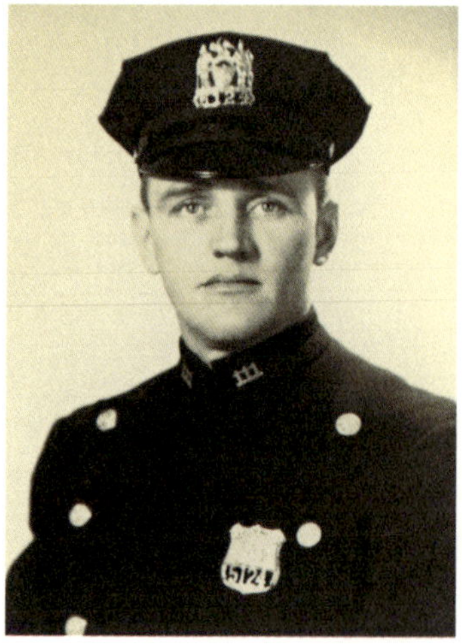

The tradition of police service runs deep in Billy Fischer's family—here, a grouping of some of his many relatives who have been in the NYPD. *Clockwise from top left*: John Laverty, Billy's great-uncle, in a portrait taken in Glasgow in 1910; William C. Ott, Billy's grandfather, 1931; Frederick Fischer Jr., Billy's great-uncle, 1946; Billy with his father, Ronald, at his graduation from the Police Academy in 1985; Ronald Fischer, Billy's father, in his official police portrait, 1954; Patrice Ott, Billy's cousin's wife; Thomas McGrath, Billy's great-uncle, 1913; William Ott, Billy's uncle, 1962 .

Previous spread: Billy and his son Kolin, 1986.

William Fischer lived several lifetimes' worth of trial, tragedy, and triumph during his 24 years of service in the New York City Police Department. After starting out as a beat cop in the notoriously dangerous 113th Precinct in Queens in the mid-1980s, Billy quickly advanced to become part of the elite Emergency Service Unit of the NYPD. This resulted in a career that resembles an incredibly dramatic action film—plane crash rescues, hostage situations, nighttime shootouts, baby deliveries—all culminating in a heartbreaking turn as part of the search-and-rescue efforts at the World Trade Center site after 9/11. He's a recipient of the NYPD's illustrious Medal of Honor, and his time on the force encompasses an almost implausible level of personal commitment and sacrifice. For all his accomplishments, Billy is a modest but prolific storyteller, reflective in his retirement about the meaning and personal consequences of the life he has led. We visited him at his Long Island home, where we met his wife Cynthia, his son Erik—the newest member of the Fischer family to join the NYPD—and his rescue pug, Lola.

I was one of those kids in high school who the teachers *wanted* to leave. When graduation rolled around, they were like, "No, you passed. *Go!*" So I was kind of on my own from the time I was 17 years old. I moved up to Washington Heights to live with my cousin, worked in the garment district, and did odd jobs, a little bit of roofing. I didn't really know what I wanted to do. My whole family was cops—we used to call getting into the department "Irish welfare" (We're all Irish, so I can say that). But being on my own meant I didn't have that structure like the rest of them. I didn't think at first that I was good enough to be a cop. I had to find my own way to the job. But I studied my ass off for the civil service exam and passed. Becoming a cop really saved me. It gave me that purpose, something I could excel at.

From the very beginning, I was what we called a ghetto cop. I worked in East New York and Jamaica, Queens, my whole career. It's not like working in Manhattan, where people want to take their pictures with you. It was basically like—if you got a call, your job was to get the perp into the car before the bottles started being thrown at you. It was very straightforward—you just hoped you'd get your overtime and make it to your pension.

Then there was a plane crash in my precinct—Flight 5050 at LaGuardia Airport. The plane overshot the runway and cracked in half—I think the captain might of had a few pops in him. Myself and another guy got to the scene and started pulling people out of the plane. Afterward the chief asked, "Where do you want to go?" And I'm like, "I want to go home and take a hot shower and change my clothes." He said, "No, you don't understand what I'm saying—you can go to any department you want." I had only about 5 years on the job at that point, but I was able to transfer to the Emergency Service Unit (ESU). It was great for me because I got to do all the crazy shit I did as a kid, only now I got a pat on the back when it went well, instead of getting in trouble for it. I could go climb bridges and rescue kids—was a perfect fit for me.

Once I got into ESU, things unfolded in a very strange way. There were all these different connections to my life that came full circle and started to become part of my career. For example: At about 7 years old, I almost drowned. I came to rest at the bottom of a lake and accepted that I was going to die. Somebody—I don't know who—went down, pulled me to the surface, picked me up over his shoulder, and dropped me down on the beach near my parents. As I was throwing up water, the guy just walked away. We never found out who he was. What's weird is years later, I'm in Emergency Service and take a call: Five kids have fallen through the ice on Baisley Park Pond. None of them can swim, and they have on their winter jackets and backpacks. I happen to be right near where it happened with two other guys. We had exposure suits in the truck and were able to save all five kids. The hospital official said they would only have survived about 5 minutes more. Sometimes I wonder, *Did I get a pass that day when I was a kid in order to be able to do the right thing?*

Here's another strange connection: I got laid off from the loading dock where I was working as a kid. I was young and didn't know what the fuck I wanted to do, but there were openings at a school for handicapped kids where my wife worked at that time. So I took the job, and they put me in a deaf dormitory. I learned to sign there. Then years later, when I became a cop, I had a couple of incidences with the deaf. First I responded to this 4-year-old deaf kid who had blown his hand off with fireworks. I flew with him in the helicopter all the way to Bellevue Hospital, interpreting for him the whole time. They did a little story about it in the newspaper. Then another time, we got a call about a deaf suicide jumper—he was going to kill himself over his girlfriend by jumping off the Lexington School for the Deaf in Jackson Heights. I knew enough sign language to be able to talk this kid out of committing suicide. That one ended up being on the front page of the *New York Post*. Turns out, the fireworks kid I helped was going to that very same school at the same time. His teacher came up to me afterwards and says, "Somebody wants to see you." So I go into her classroom and look around and see this kid standing there with one hand—and I sign, "I remember you." And he turns to his friends and signs, "I told you!" So I go over and hugged him and gave him and his friends all these police hats and T-shirts and shit. I never would have thought when I took that job at the school that my career would come around in that way. It's just bizarre, you know?

In 2000, I got shot during a standoff in Gravesend,

Brooklyn. This wack job, a former corrections officer, ordered his parents to leave the house and told them that he wanted to kill as many cops as he could. The parents reported him to the police, and he shot one of the first two guys who went up to the house in the shoulder. We all regrouped, and I did the entry into his house. The guy had escaped out the back, so we did a secondary search of the backyard. It started to rain like crazy. The guy had bunkered down and was shooting at us from a basement stairwell. My knees were shaking, my heart was going nuts—I took cover but could hear the rounds whistling by the side of my face. In a situation like that, you kind of lose your senses. Everything just shuts off: My hearing—off. Distractions—off. The lightning and rain that was going on at the same time—I didn't even notice it. I just focused on him. When I got shot, I checked myself out—saw I was OK—and then everything engaged with him again. It's a weird process your body goes through in that situation.

After seven minutes of trading fire, myself and another guy—we had to kill him. I grew up Irish Catholic, so that was a big issue I had to deal with. I talked to my priest, and he said, "Listen, to turn the other cheek doesn't mean get your ass kicked and lay there. You have a right to survive." But that was one of those times in my career when I had a moment of clarity, like, *Fuck, I almost died today*. It dawned on me that I wasn't even supposed to be on duty that night—I had done a tour change so I could be at my son's birthday party. I just used that realization as a way of getting through the next job. Some crazy shit would always come up that would distract me, so I'd just gobble up more trauma and put it away. It wasn't until I left the job, got off that speeding train, that it came back around to bite me in the ass.

It's funny—before you get into the police department, they ask you, "Why do you want to be a cop?" Some guys will talk about the pension, job security, the benefits. Others will say they want to help people. It wasn't until I retired that it dawned on me: It *was* really just about helping people. In my time on the force, I met evil people and I met people in need. I actually can say—and I'm not trying to sound like an asshole here—that I have literally saved people's lives. If I didn't do what I did they would have died in that moment. That is something that you can't get paid enough to do—because deep down inside you know you did the right thing.

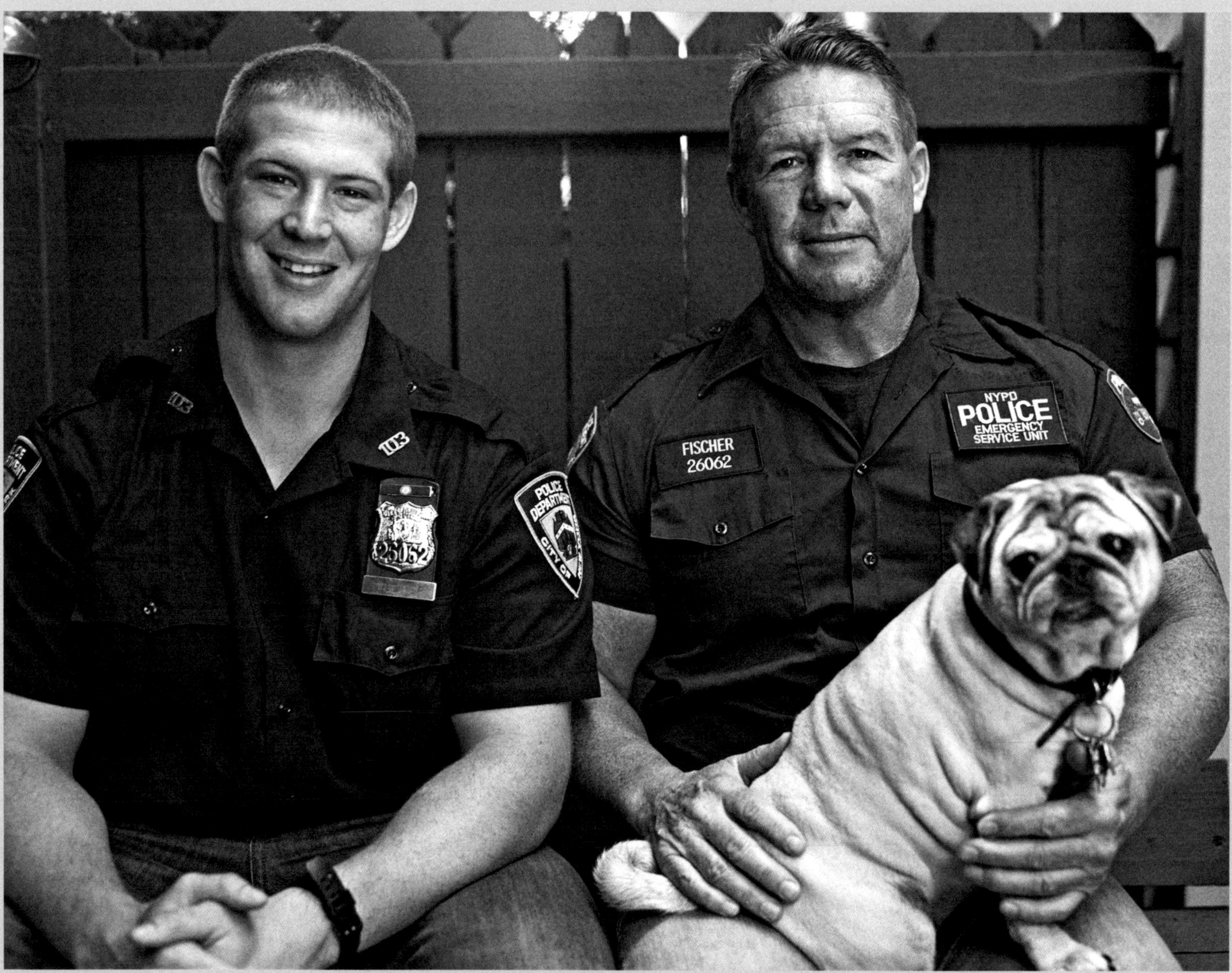

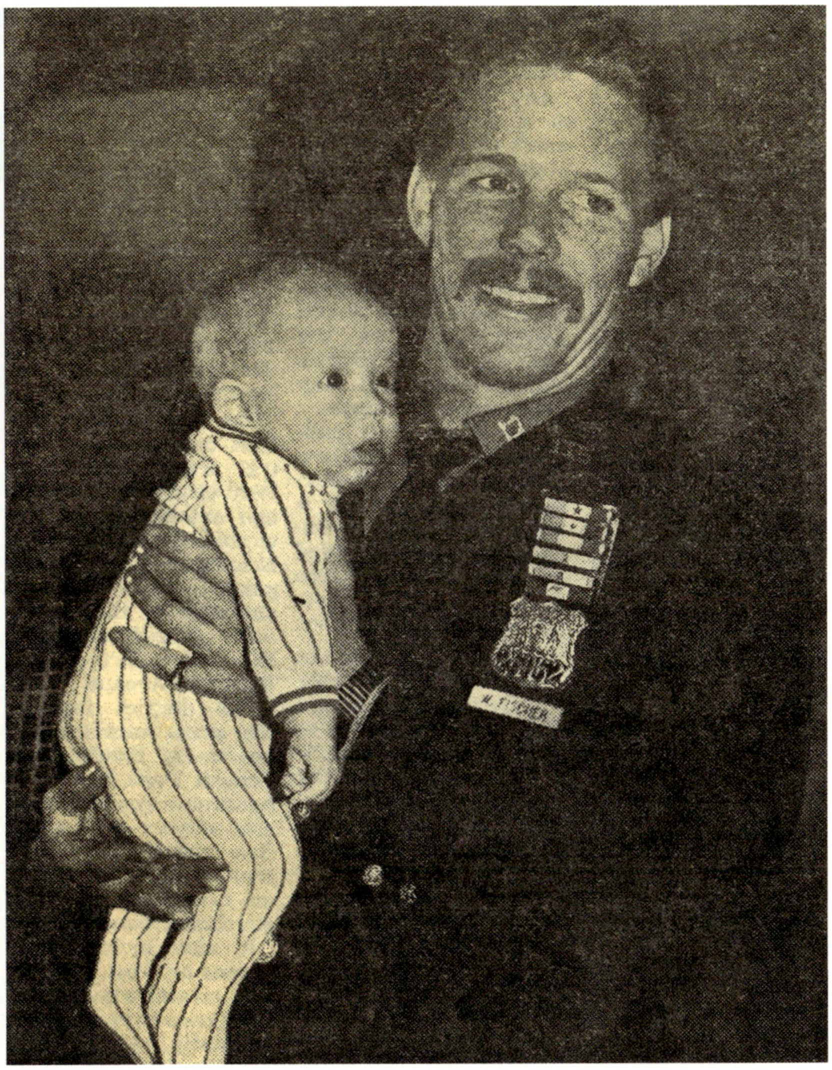

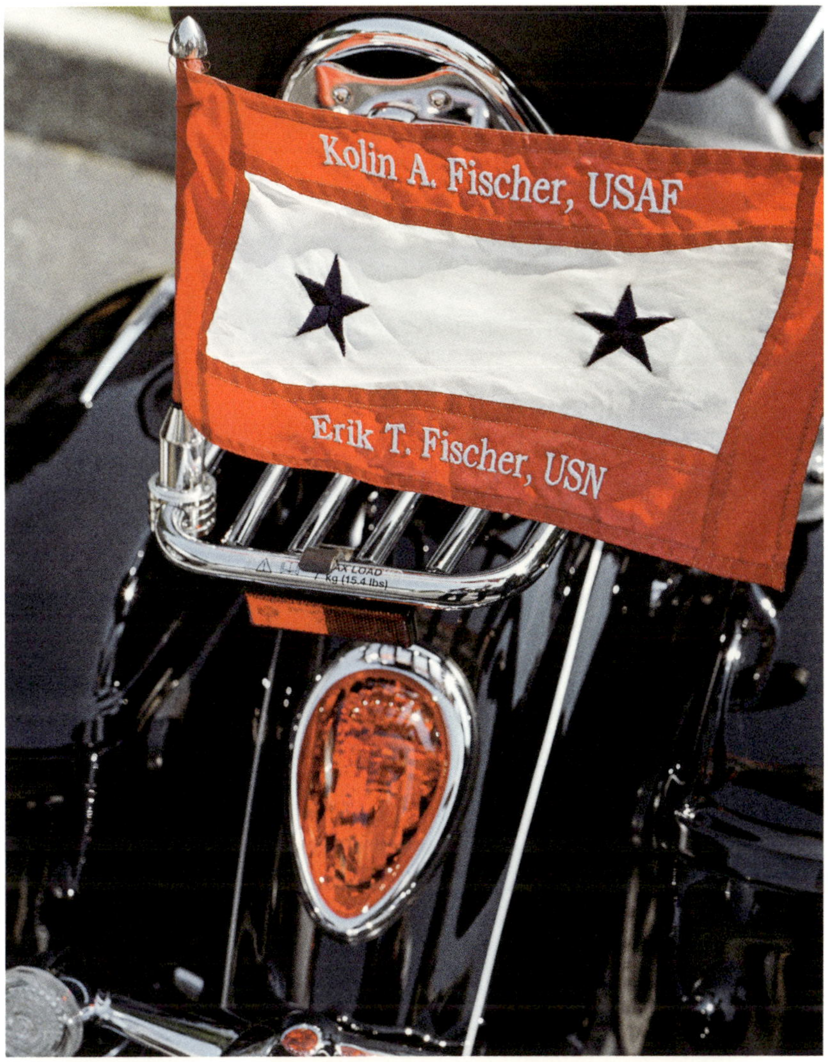

Clockwise from top left: Billy with Erik in his Yankee onesie after rescuing passengers from the USAir crash at LaGuardia Airport; Billy's 2300 cc Triumph Rocket 3 Touring Bike, which he rides as part of the Blue Knights Motorcycle Club; Kolin Fischer, Billy's son, who now is an analyst for the Department of Defense; Billy with his son Kolin, father, Ronald, and grandfather, William; *Opposite*: Billy and Erik in uniform.

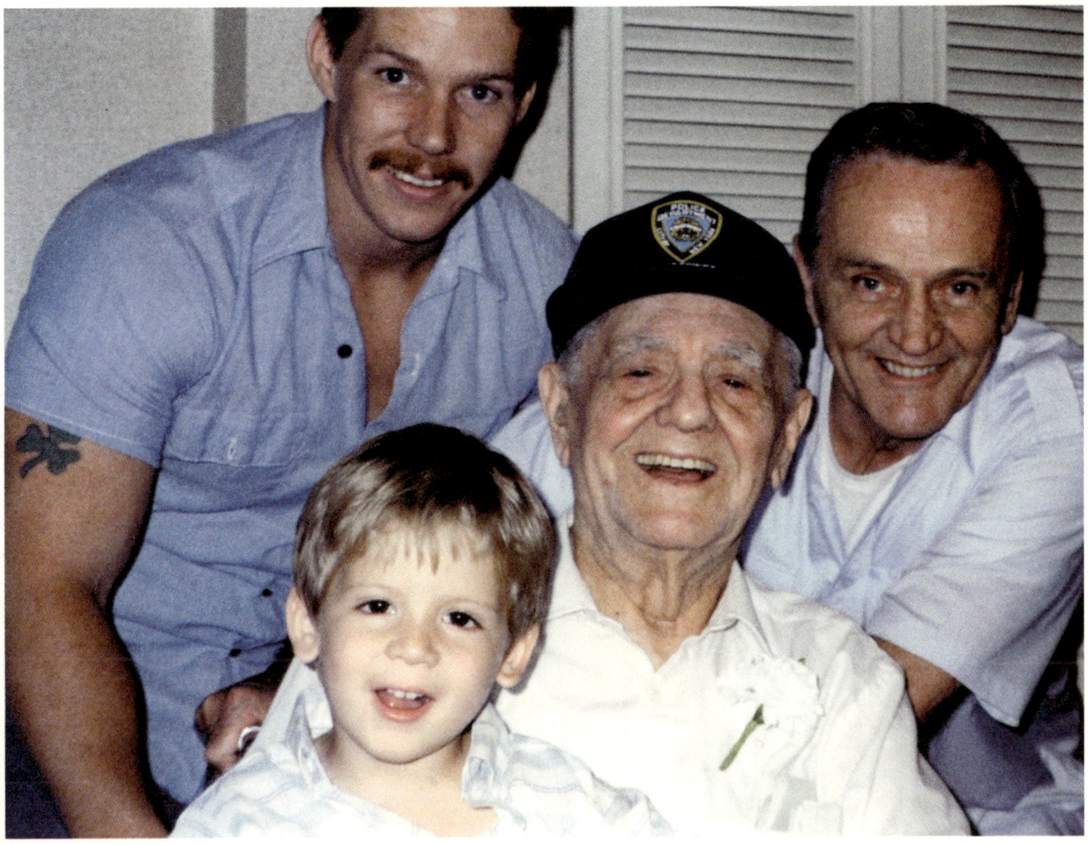

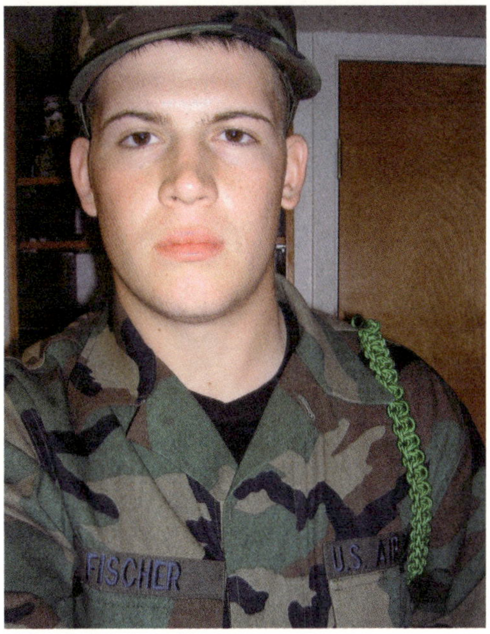

Why Disney's afraid of this monster

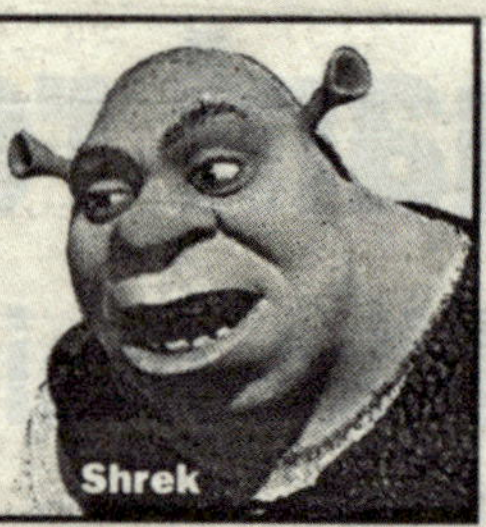

PAGE 47

Why was bus driver's slay victim still on the streets?

PAGE 5

CELEBRATING 200 YEARS

NEW YORK POST

ONLY 50¢

METRO EDITION

WEDNESDAY, MAY 9, 2001 / Partly sunny, 70 / Weather: Page 45 www.nypost.com • 50¢

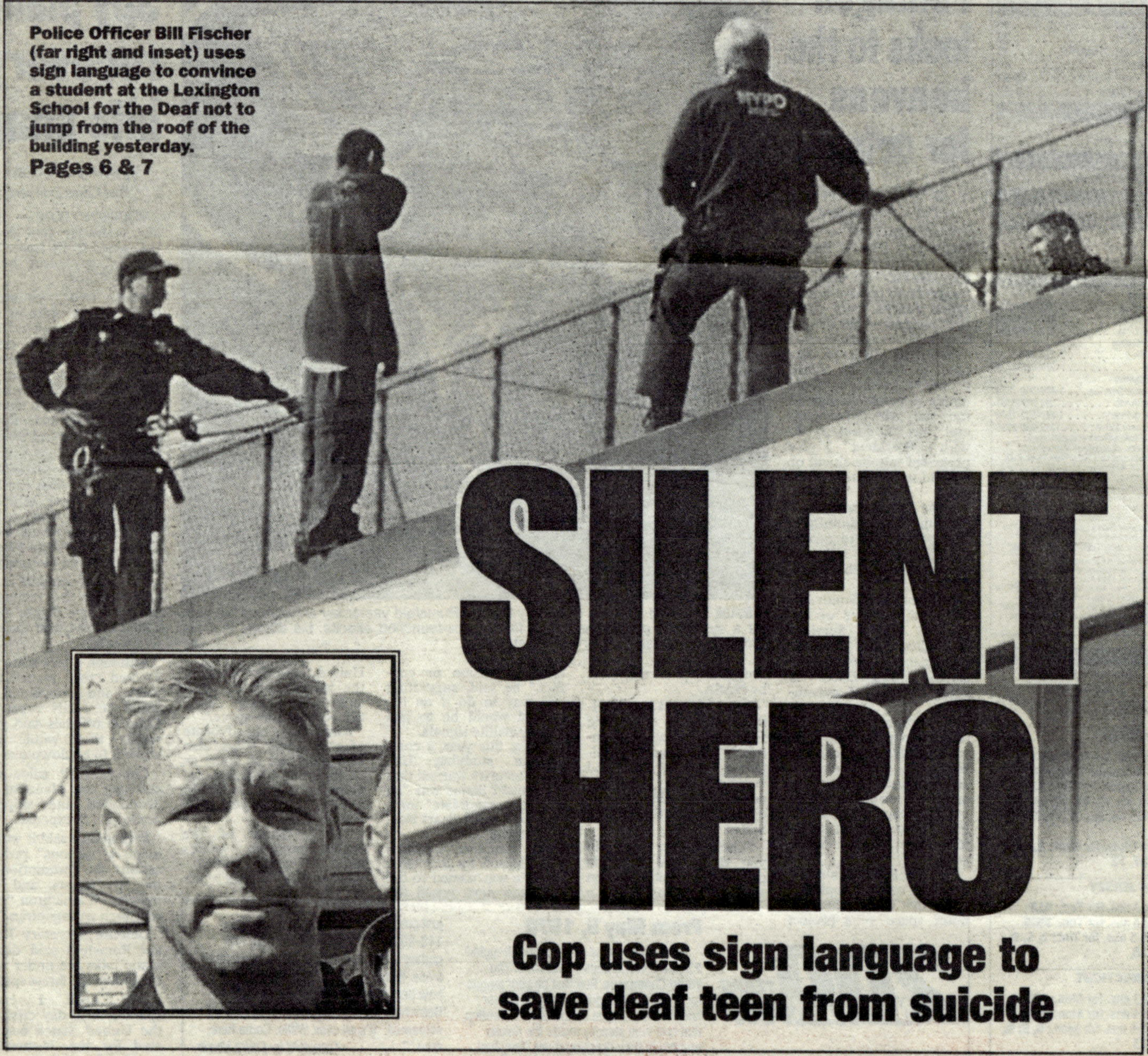

Police Officer Bill Fischer (far right and inset) uses sign language to convince a student at the Lexington School for the Deaf not to jump from the roof of the building yesterday.

Pages 6 & 7

SILENT HERO

Cop uses sign language to save deaf teen from suicide

New York Post: Jim Alcorn

4 STAR ★ ★ ★ ★ FINAL

DAILY NEWS

$1.00 www.nydailynews.com NEW YORK'S HOMETOWN NEWSPAPER Sunday, August 13, 2000

SPECIAL REPORT: DEMOCRATIC CONVENTION

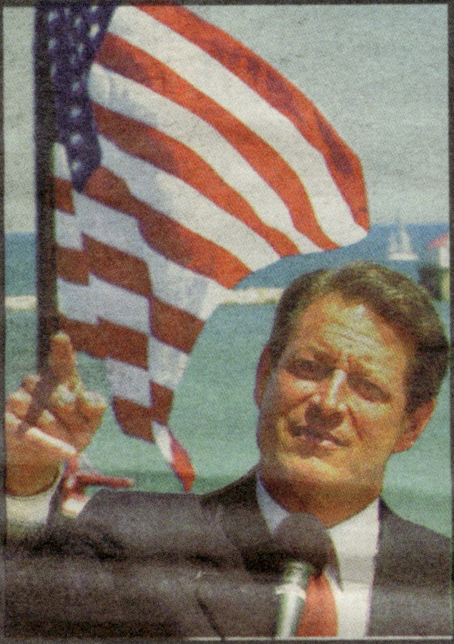

ON HIS OWN

How Al Gore can escape Bill's shadow and beat Bush

Kramer, Nelson in L.A.

★ ★ ★

FULL COVERAGE BEGINS ON PAGE 5

5 COPS SHOT

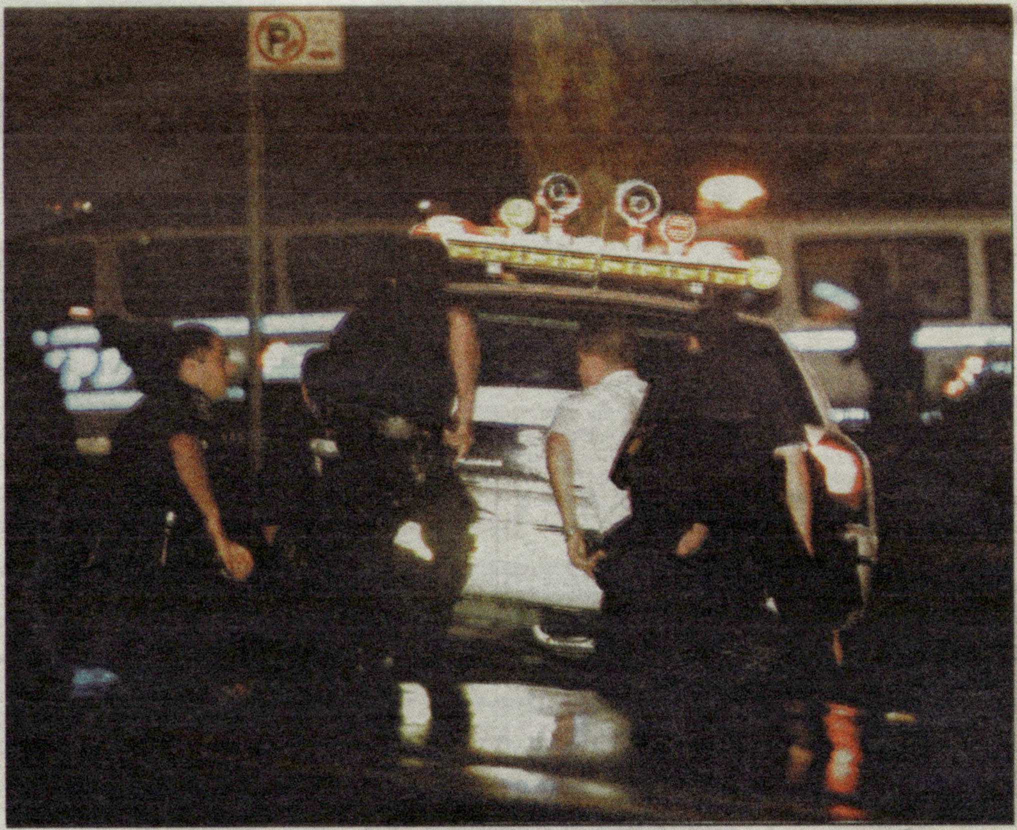

DAVID BURNS

Barrage of bullets ends six-hour standoff in Brooklyn; gunman slain

SEE PAGES 2 & 3

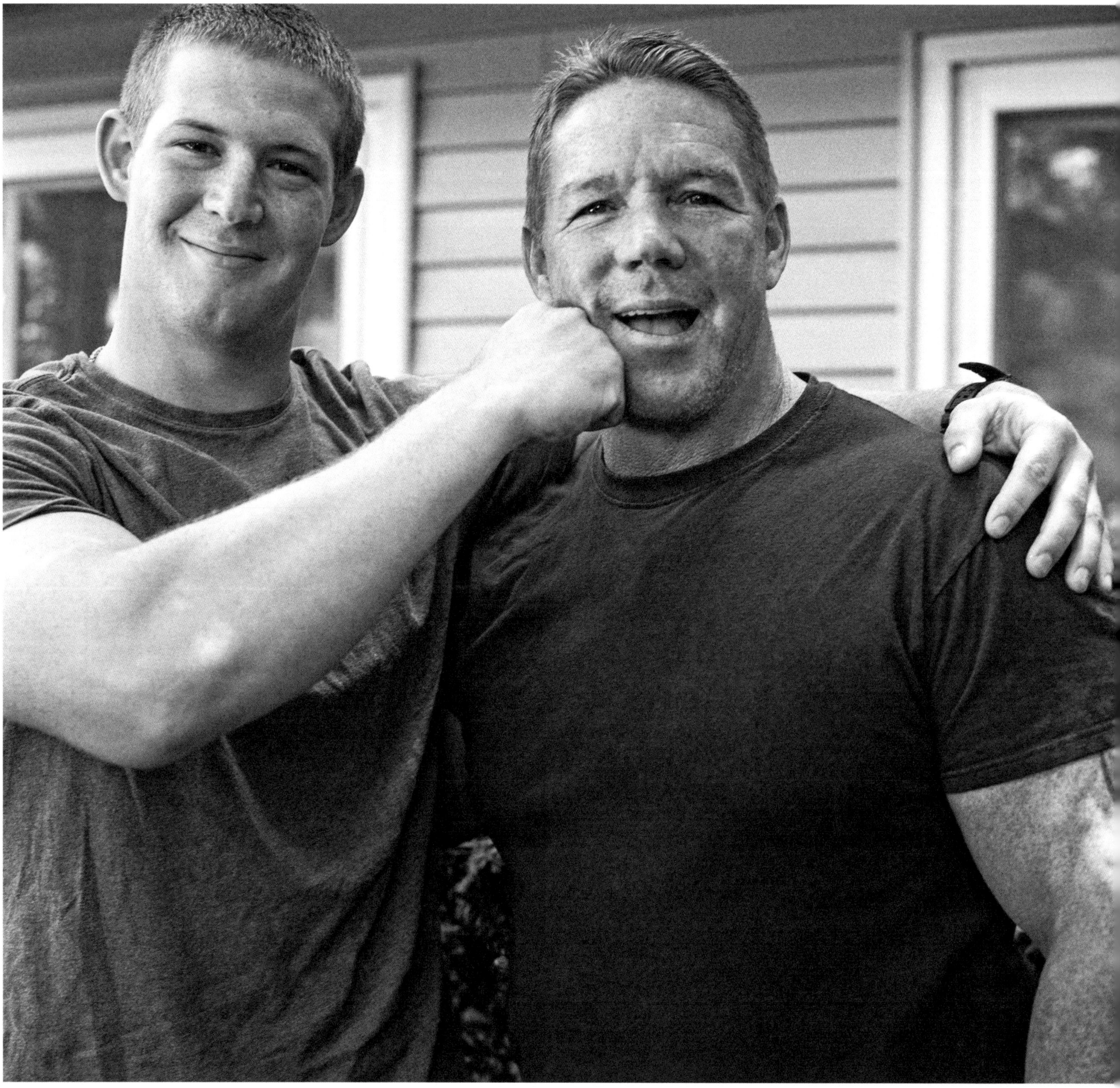

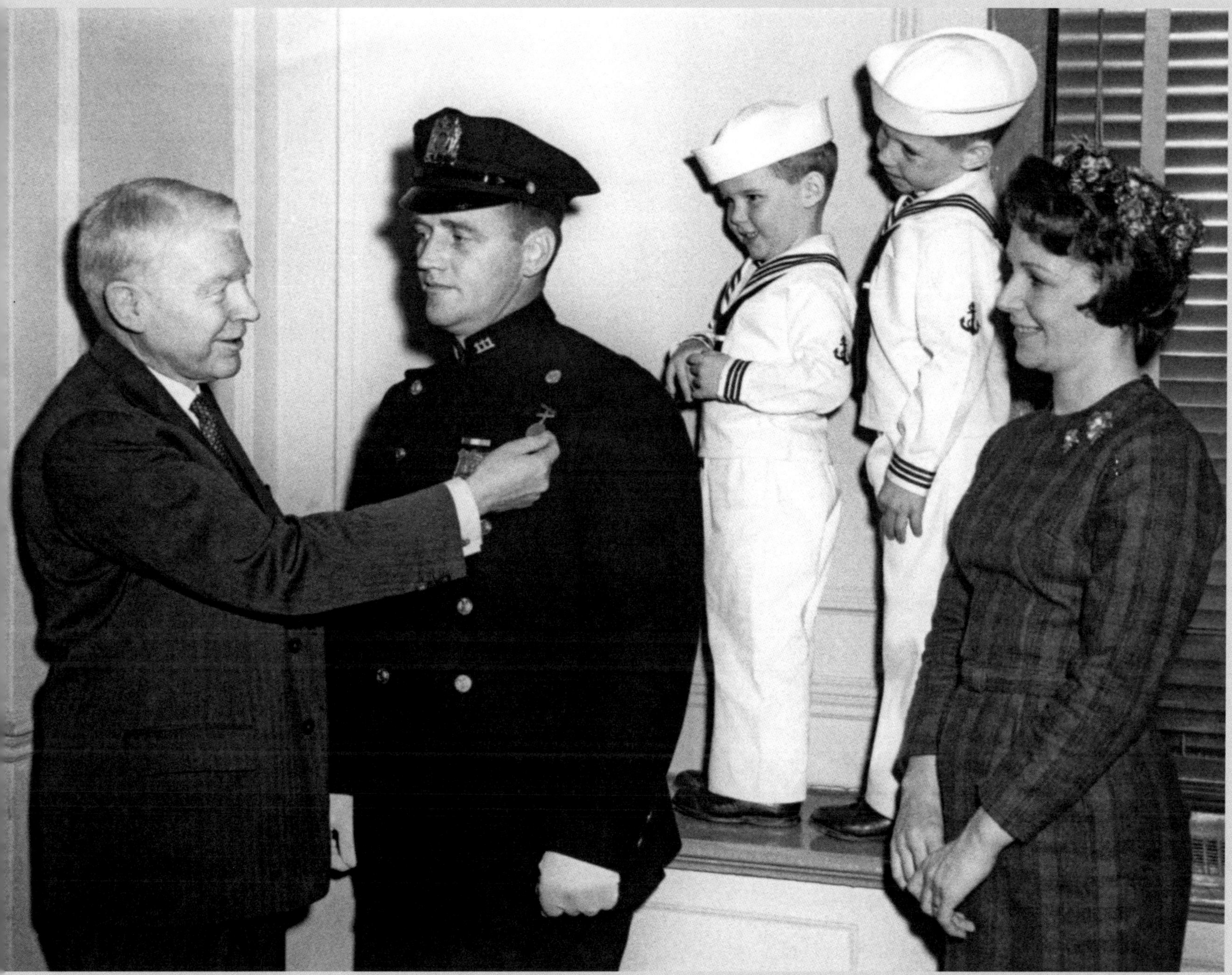

Opposite: Billy with his son Erik, a first-year NYPD rookie. After being stationed in Japan with the Navy for several years, Erik decided to take the entrance exam for the Academy. Upon graduating, Erik was given his father's old badge number: 26062. He's currently stationed at the 103rd Precinct in Jamaica, Queens—the same place where his grandfather worked. *This page*: Billy with his mother and brother at a ceremony at which his father received a Lifesaving Award in 1965.

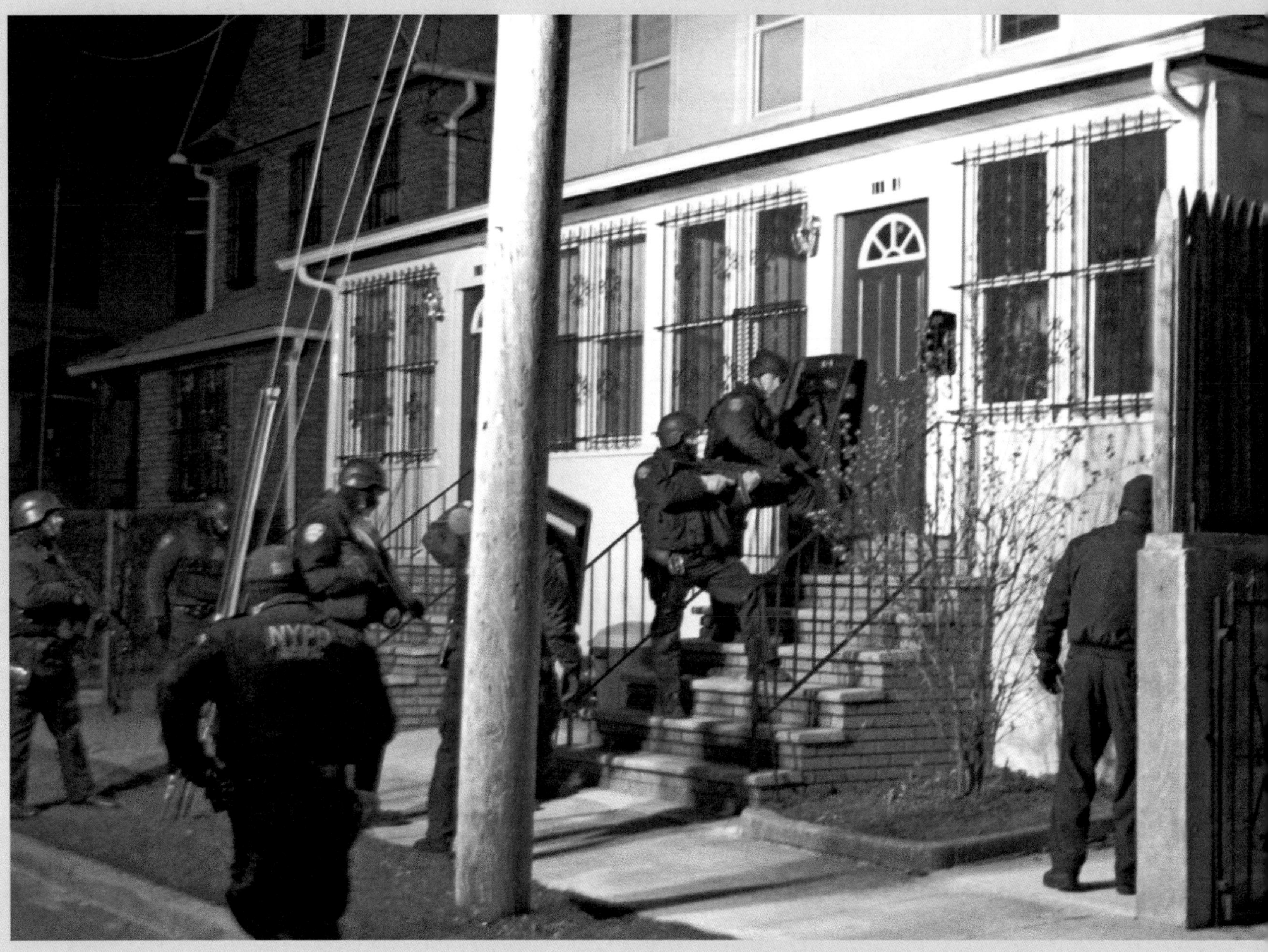

This page: Billy takes the lead during an event that took place on January 10, 2004. The ESU squad responded to a search/manhunt for a little girl named Destiny. Her father had killed her mother's new boyfriend and then kidnapped her. The police thought they might be inside this house. It turns out that they weren't—Destiny was found later that day, and her father was arrested. Billy described his role in a situation like this one: "The shield covers from your face down to your nuts. You have to position it just right, so that when you go through the door, if anyone shoots, the shield takes the impact and the guy behind you can shoot over your shoulder. The guy with the shield is the one who's supposed to get shot at." *Opposite*: Billy's tattoo, based on the photograph from that evening.

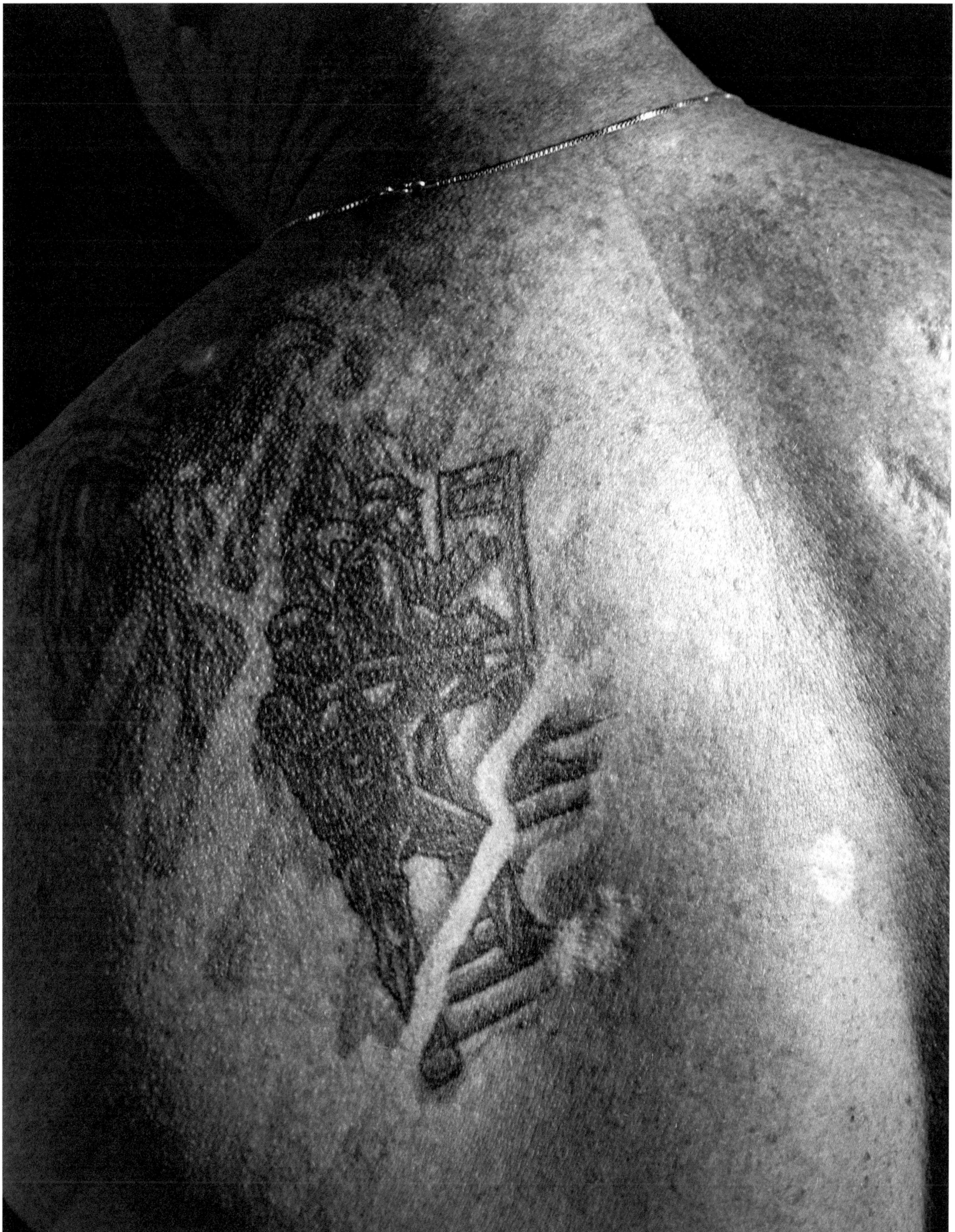

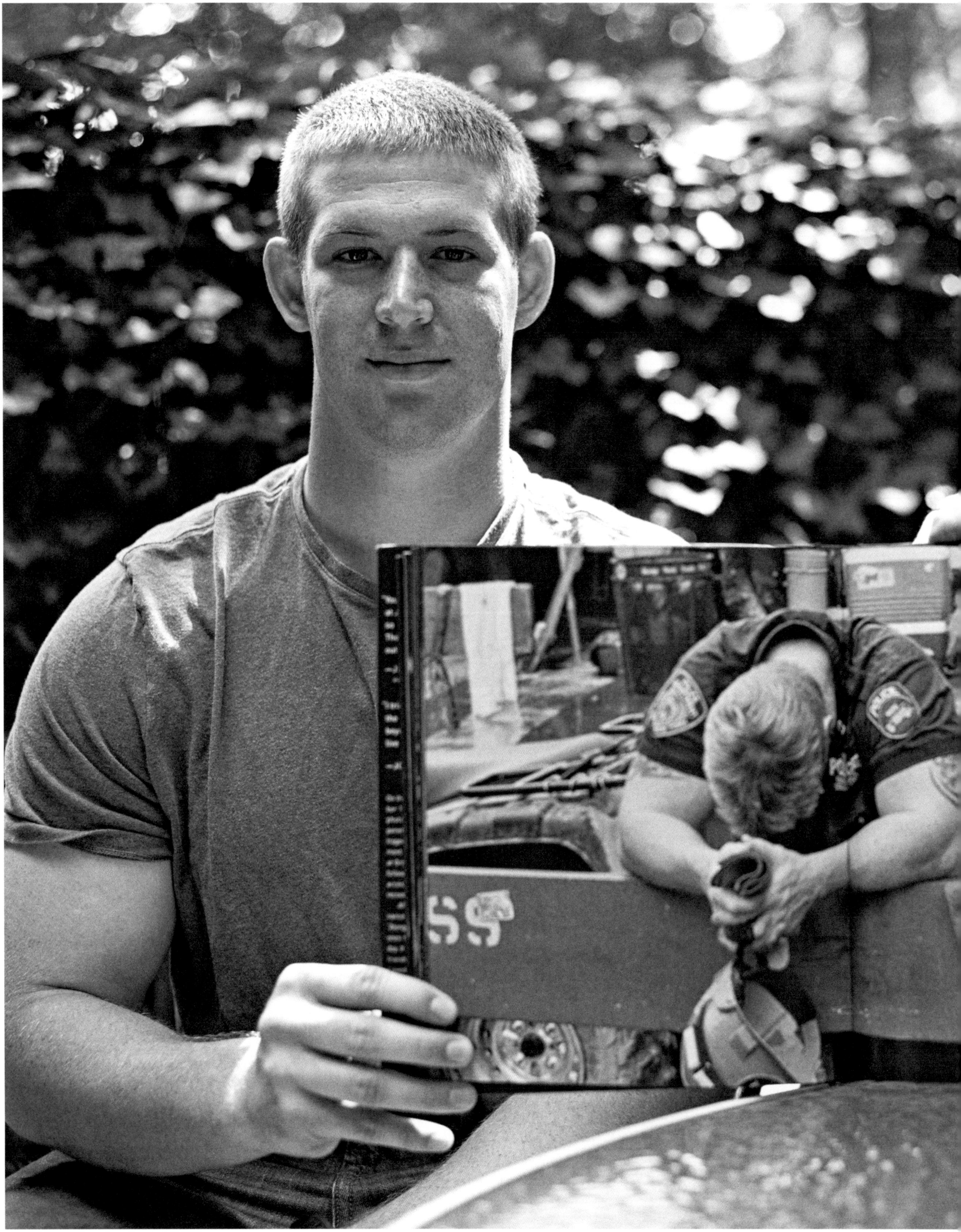

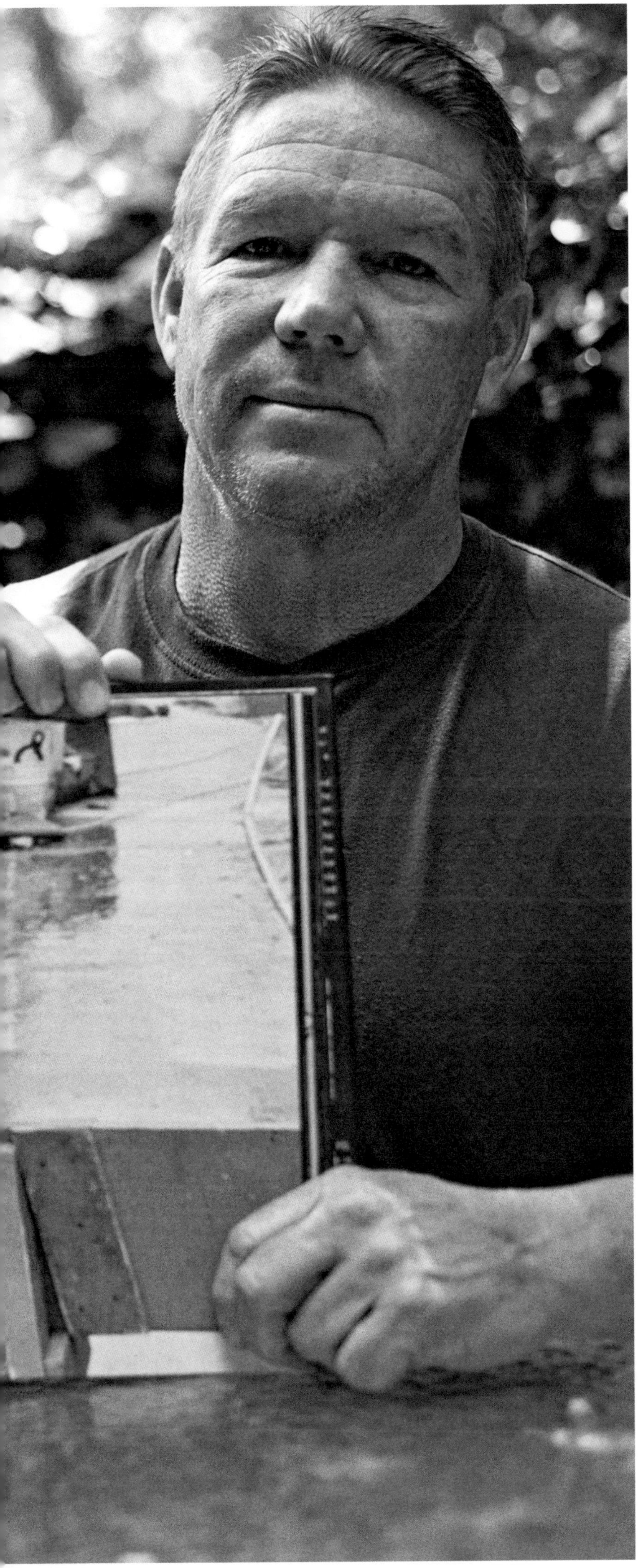

Father and son holding a copy of John Botte's book *Aftermath: Unseen 9/11 Photos by a New York City Cop,* which features the famous photograph of Billy Fischer at a barricade near the World Trade Center site. Billy told us how it happened: "This picture was taken shortly after 9/11. I had been working probably around 12 hours already. About a month and a half later, I'm in a suit, on loan to the Hercules counterterrorism team. John was in one of those two-story coffee shops downtown. He sees me getting out of the car with my partner from above, and even though I have a suit and trench coat on now, he recognizes the top of my head. He comes running down and asks, 'Were you Emergency Service?' And I said, 'Yeah, but I'm kind of on loan to intel for a little bit, you know?' He says, 'I took a picture and I'm pretty sure it's you.' Sure enough, it was my big Irish head."

A first-year NYPD officer, Erik has a demeanor that is sincere and direct. He says, "It's kind of weird hearing these stories and knowing that if these things happened to my father, they could happen to me. So I just move forward—there's only so much I can do to prepare for future experiences and try to make the best decisions I can when something big happens to me. Hopefully I won't experience another 9/11 or be caught in a shoot-out. I pray for that every night—but if it does happen, I want to be prepared."

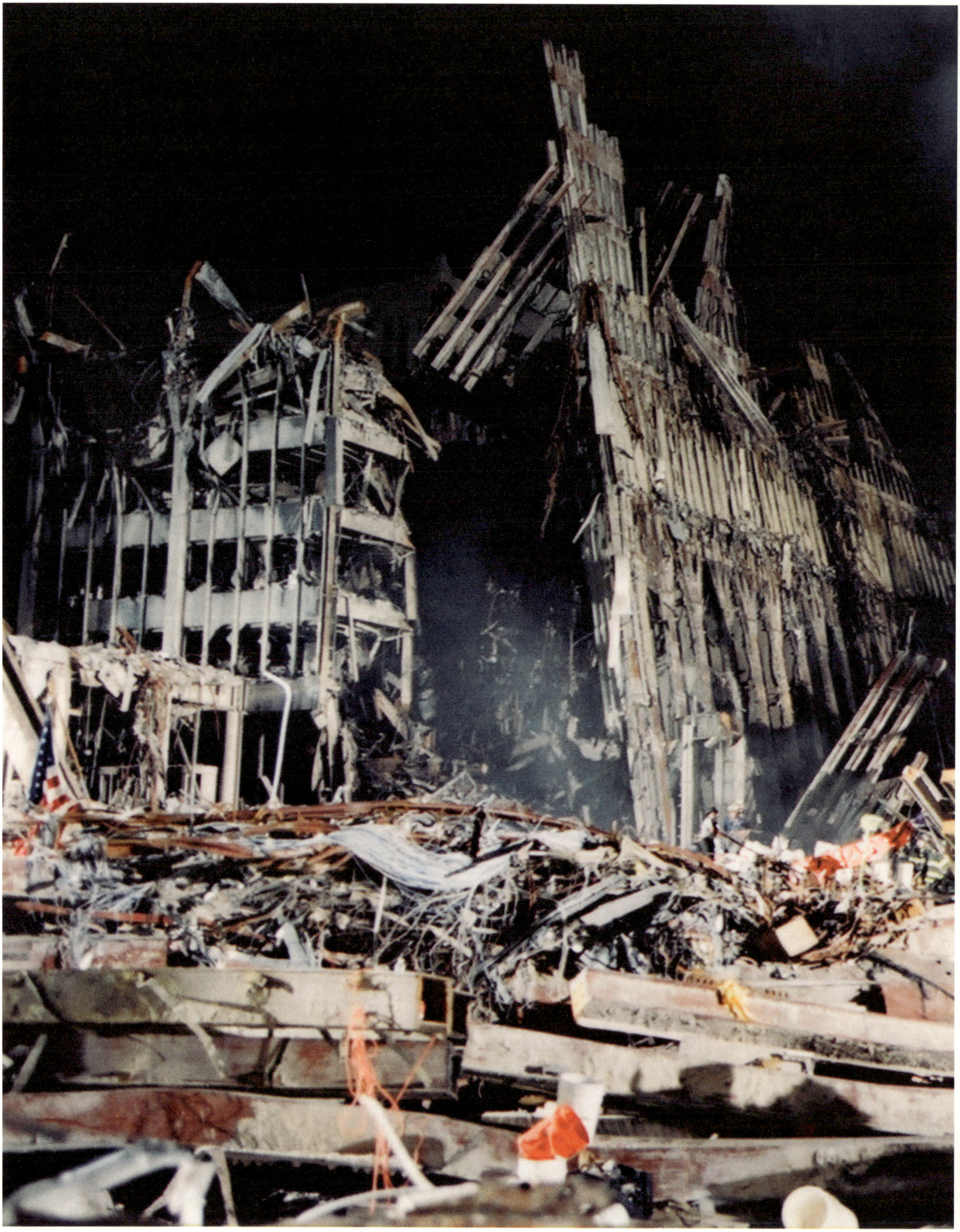

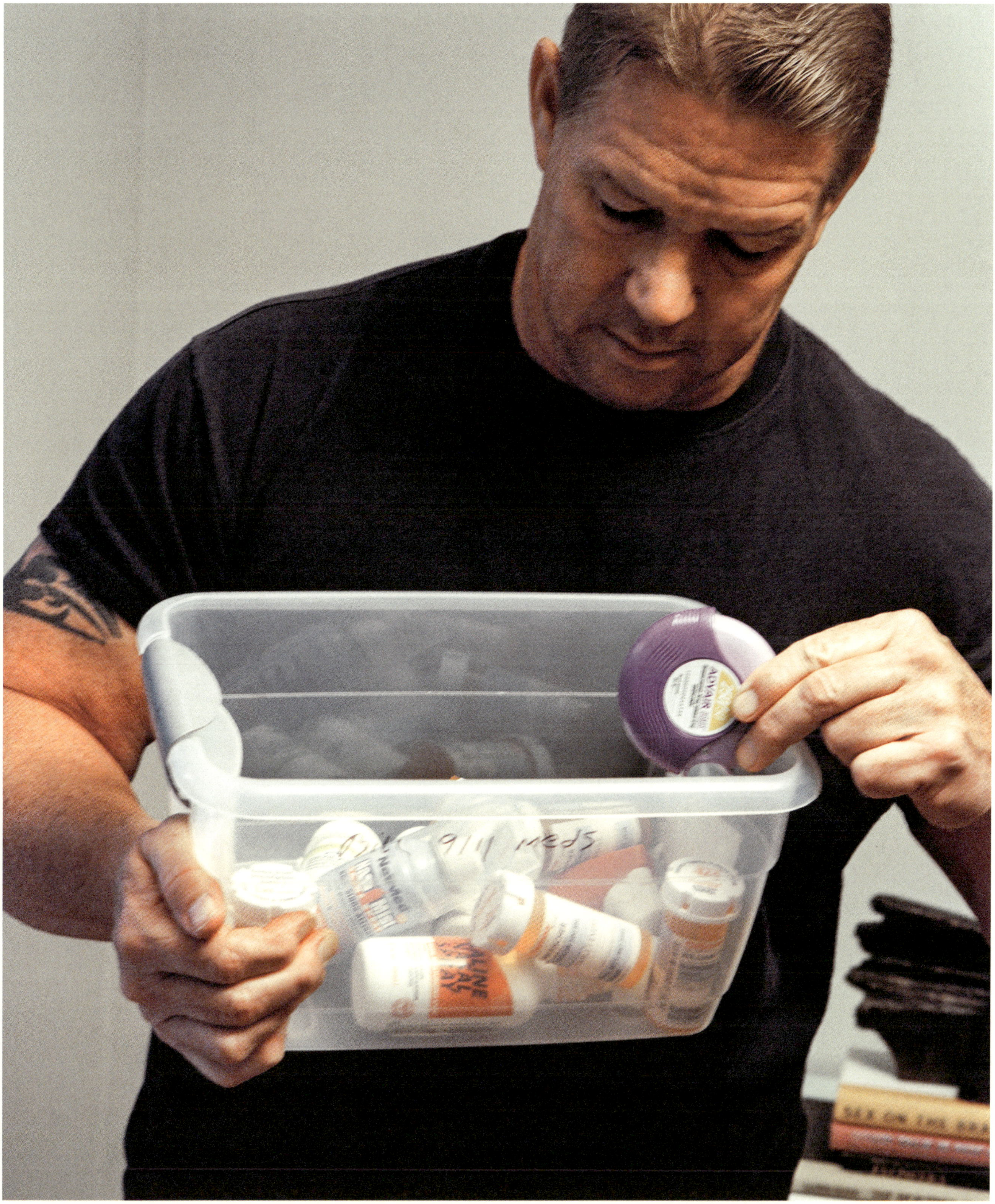

Billy showed us the prescriptions he needs to take daily for 9/11-related conditions—various inhalers and anti-anxiety, migraine, and grieving medications.

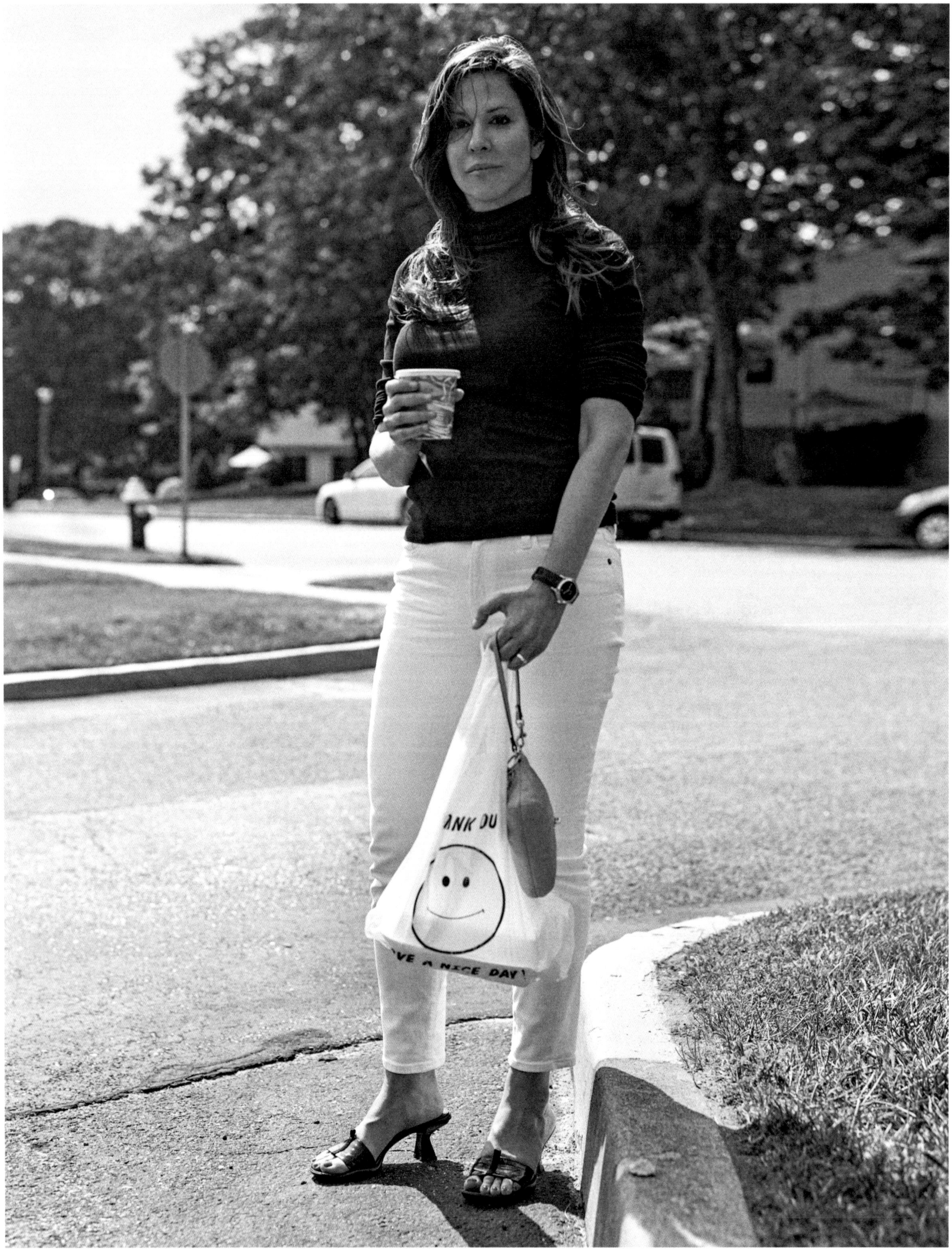

CYNTHIA FISCHER

BILLY'S WIFE

I met Bill in high school. I guess I was attracted to the bad boy. It was the late 1970s. Things were wild and I didn't have any supervision. I started being harassed by these boys. One of them had asked me out and I said no, so they started doing all these terrible things—they put gasoline on my lawn and set it on fire; they spray-painted profanities on my car. When Bill found out about it, he drove up to the whole group and said, "Do you know anybody who likes to play with spray paint?" One of the guys said, "I don't know what you're talking about." So Bill replied, "Let me tell you something. Anything else happens to her, I don't care if it was you, I'm coming back for *you*." And that was the last time I was bothered. From that day on, I was in love. Bill has always been that strong guy in my life.

I grew up in an upper-class Jewish family. You either married a doctor or a lawyer; you did not marry an Irish-Catholic cop. When we decided to get married, my family tried everything to get me to change my mind—they tried to bribe me! But Bill was my protector and there was no going back.

I think as the wife of a cop you do things to protect yourself. Bill would always come home with these incredible stories, but as he was talking I'd be thinking about the laundry list of things I had to do—just kind of blocking out what he was describing as a way of coping with it. In Emergency Service, they have a big truck and they work upstairs and have coffee and meals together. I used to imagine him drinking coffee, safe in the precinct—that worked until Bill started to show up on the news.

I work as a therapist, so I know what post-traumatic stress looks like. Even with all the crazy experiences Bill has been exposed to, he seemed OK until about 2000. After the shoot-out in Brooklyn he got all of this positive media attention. The guys in the police department are like his brothers. But when that community wasn't in place, when his brothers weren't around him, all that disturbing, violent stuff he had experienced caught up with him. I remember saying just before September 11th, 2001, "I'm worried about you." I thought he needed to take a break.

After 9/11, Bill started to sleep with all his supplies nearby: He'd have string, water, a little knife. The trauma of that day definitely impacted our marriage. And I think it affected my kids too—9/11 is definitely part of the reason why both of my boys went into the military. Over time, Bill and I have been able to find ways to make our marriage work. But there's a real price to this way of life.

I worry about Erik, who's now a fresh-faced rookie like Bill used to be. I wonder where Erik will be in 20 years. I know it's a different time—crime is down significantly in New York, the streets aren't the same. But I pray every night that he stays safe. I'm extremely proud of him—I couldn't be more proud—but at the same time I know the cost.

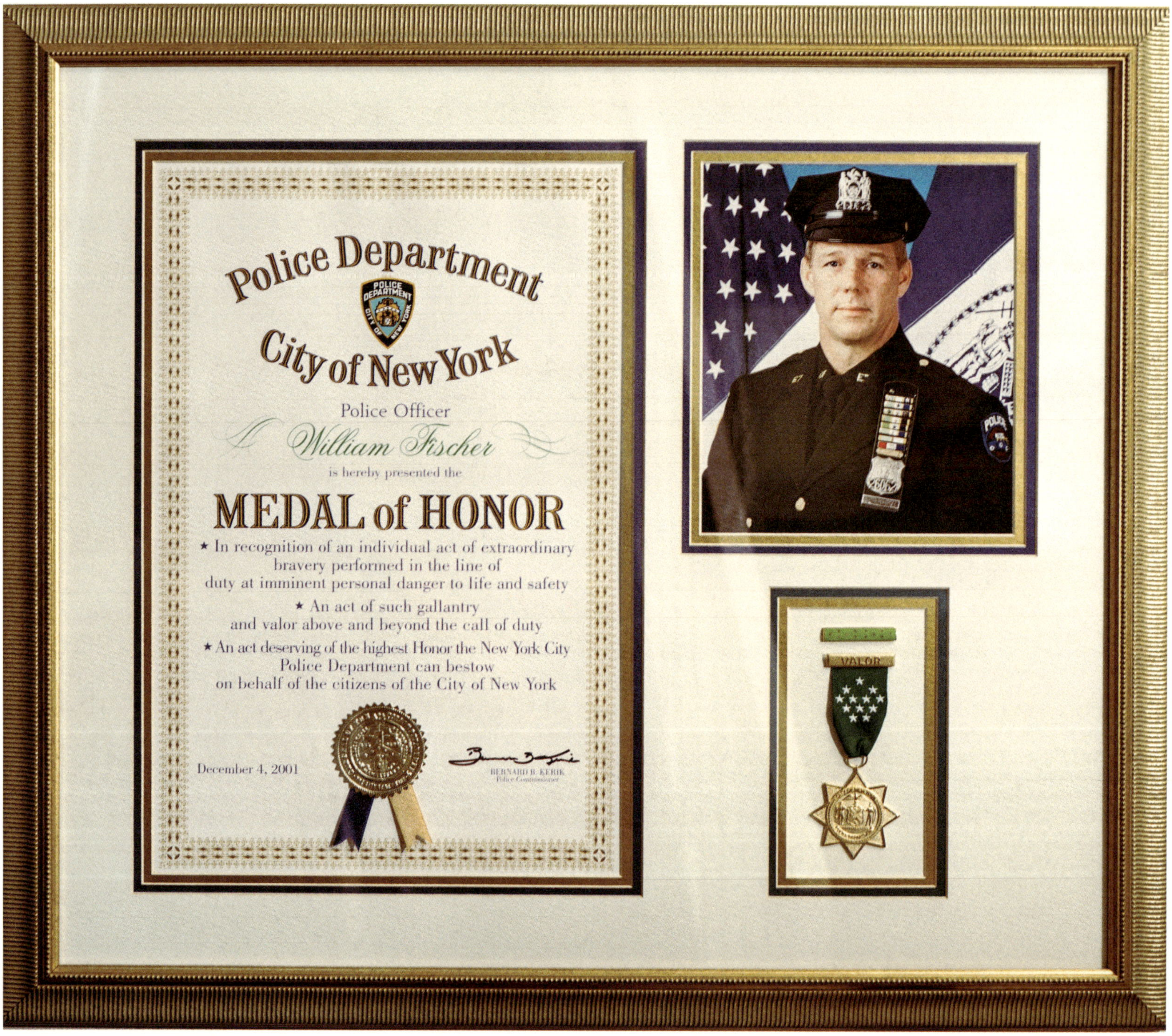

"When people are in trouble, they call the cops. When the cops are in trouble, they call Emergency Service..."

—MARK MULITZ, RETIRED NYPD DETECTIVE

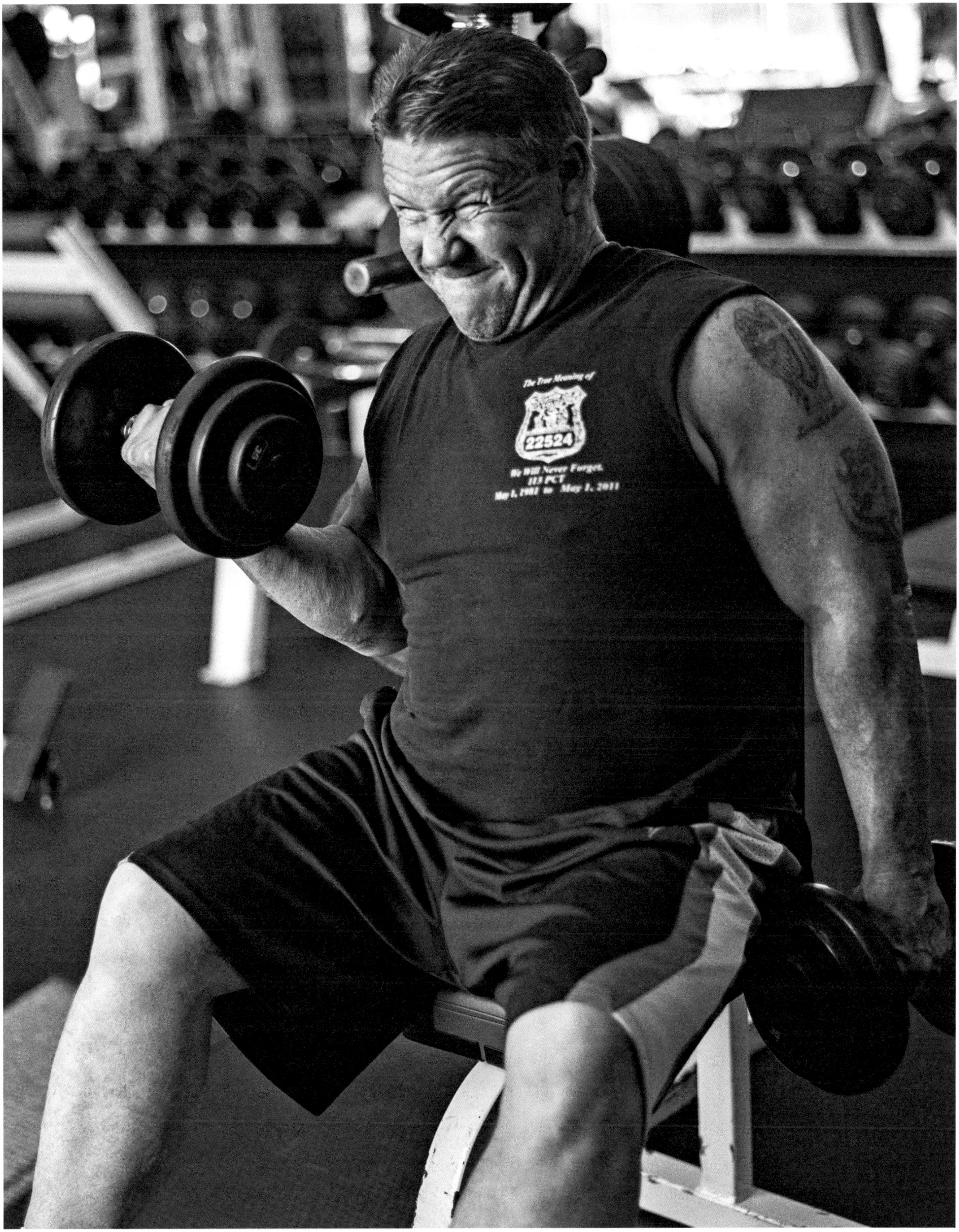
22524

We took Billy and Erik to lunch at the Hollbrook Diner together with John Gigilia and our friend Mark Mulitz, both retired NYPD. It didn't take long for the stories to start flying.

"IT'S LIKE A FISH!"

JOHN You see stuff as a cop that people don't believe. You go from high to low; you deliver a baby and then you're dealing with a D.O.A...

BILLY You remember when we delivered that baby over in Jamaica? This lady was shopping at a baby store when she goes into labor. She was carrying a bag with all these clothes from the store in it, and to be honest, she looked like she couldn't really afford to buy the clothes. We get there and I ask her, "What number kid is this for you?" She goes, "Five." I say, "How long have you been in labor?" She says, "Long enough." I say, "You ready to go?" She says, "Yeah." So she delivered the baby right there. I didn't realize it, but after 4 kids, the 5th is like spitting out a pit. I thought it was going to be this slow process—there'd be the arm, the head. But this was like, "Oh shit!" It had this cord and it looked like it was covered in cheese and I was just like, "What the fuck?" It's like a fish! So the ambulance shows up, and I say to the woman, "Where's the clothes you were going to buy?" She pointed, "Oh, over here." I say, "Quick, we got to mop all this all up." So she's looking at me like this and I say, "Don't worry about it—they're not going to want these clothes back." So I stuff them all in a bag for her and say, "You're good to go." She winks at me as they get her into the ambulance to go to the hospital. The ambulance guy's like, "What's with all the clothes?" And I said, "Just take them with her." The Indian guy who owned the store started just bitching us out, "You can not take!" I said, "No pay! It's emergency!" as the ambulance took off.

"TAKE A PICTURE WITH US"

BILLY You remember that naked guy with the broken camera? We get a call for Rockaway Boulevard, so we pull up to the service road and are like, "What the fuck?" We see this dude, he's like 6'4"—and he has this old, broken-ass camera with the back hanging out. There was nothing in it—just a broken flap with shit hanging out that he was holding by its broken strap. So we pull up to him and say, "Listen guy, just calm down, there's a hospital..." But he just keeps pretending like he's taking pictures of us. He's dancing around, completely naked. His dick's hanging out, bouncing off his legs as he's running. John goes to talk to him and he says, "Look! I can do a propeller spin!" and starts turning it around. Now the traffic is backing up on the Belt Parkway service road—they don't even care about the light. Everybody's out of their cars as we're trying to catch him, honking their horns. He's bobbing, giving us head fakes; dust is flying. It was a show. He keeps saying, "As you can see, officers, I am unarmed. Not a stitch on me." Finally I say, "Listen, come take a picture with us, let's take a picture of you with us." And he's like, "All right." So we end up giving his broken-ass camera to someone else and he comes and poses with us and—boom—we took him down. You don't know when you decide to become a cop that you'll be doing this wacky shit.

JOHN You don't want to have to wrestle a naked guy.

BILLY Yeah, but he wasn't that bad of a guy—he was just a nut. Probably smoked some bad shit that day.

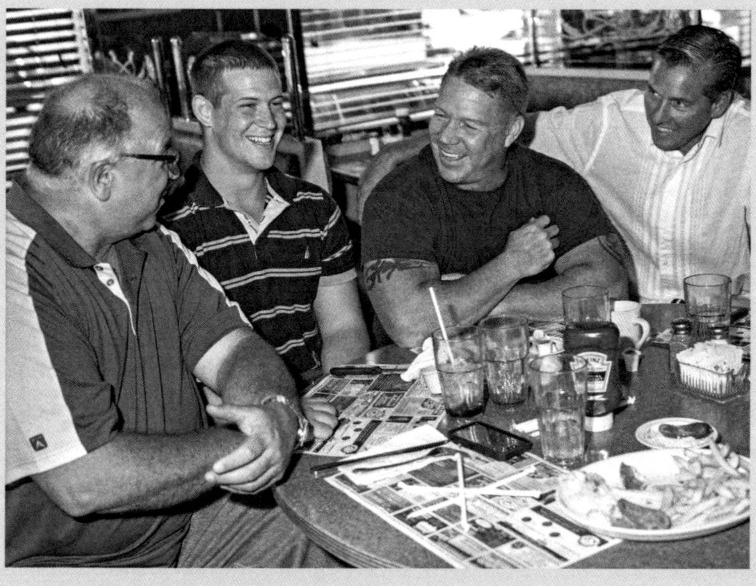

"YOU DON'T BELIEVE ME"

BILLY I've probably told these story so many times, I could get up and go to the bathroom and Erik could finish them.

JOHN How about the EDP (*emotionally disturbed person*) call with the Christ on the wall?

BILLY I don't remember that one.

JOHN We get to the residence and go into this pitch-black room. There's like one 20-volt light bulb in the whole house. So the guy's sitting in the middle of the room, and I ask him, "What's up?" He goes, "I'm possessed." We go, "By who?" and he's like, "The Devil. You don't believe me, do you?" Billy and I look at each other and say, "No." There's a picture of Christ on the wall and he goes, "Satan is Lord. Move!" and the picture rattles. So now chills go down my spine. Billy and

I are looking at each other like, "Do that again." He says, "The devil is the ruler over all of earth" or whatever, like, "Christ is not. Move!" And the picture rattles again. We were like, "We better handcuff this guy before he points at us!" So we go to grab the guy and the Christ picture comes flying off the wall. He had tied fishing string from the picture to his leg so he could move it from where he was sitting. But when that thing came off the wall, I was thinking, "Ah!"

"WORST OF THE WORST"

MARK I worked with a guy named Terry McGee up in the 32nd Precinct in Harlem. He was a good friend—we came on the job together. Terry's one of the toughest cops I've ever met personally, an Irish guy from the Bronx. He had been a paratrooper in the 82nd Airborne. He was one of the most active guys I met—bringing in gun arrests, robberies—all kinds of violent crimes. One time while responding to a family dispute, a guy stabbed Terry in the side of his face. He got some stitches and couldn't wait to get back to work. A couple years later there were all these livery cab robberies going on in the precinct—Terry was following one of them up Eighth Avenue and 145th Street. When they pulled the car over, there was a guy lying on the floor with a .45 caliber handgun who shot Terry in the stomach. In the ambulance on the way to the hospital he pulled the round out of his stomach by himself. It's crazy—I can't even imagine that. Then in the late 1980s Terry was assigned to a homicide squad that they nicknamed WOW: "Worst of the Worst." He was out looking for guys that had committed the worst homicides in the Bronx at the time. It was such a difficult assignment, but that's why they put Terry out there.

After 9/11 happened Terry was assigned to the joint terrorism task force. He had a case that started in New York but took him to Portugal. He had been there a couple of months working the case when he got a day off and decided to go surfing. He ended up flipping up in the air and landing on his head by accident. Just like that, he was paralyzed. People on the beach saw him out there, pulled him to the shore, and got him to this hospital in time. To this day Terry's paralyzed from the neck down. It's just kind of ironic that with all the things that he had been through in the police department, that fluky thing happened on his day off.

There's not a cop out there that doesn't know who Terry is. He's still active in the police department—they never retired him. He's a mentor now, going around to give talks at different precincts. Terry has 5 kids of his own, and he adopted two more—his sister had cancer and passed away, and I think they were her kids. To this day, Terry is the guy out there working and doing tons of overtime just to take care of his kids and try to make things better for the guys on the force. He's pretty amazing.

"YOU PROMISED ME"

JOHN There were a lot of characters in the 113 (*Jamaica precinct*). Lots of good cops.

BILLY John and I got out of the Academy at the same time, so we were rookies together. We took this call one time—a 12-year-old girl had been walking to free lunch in the summertime at her school when this guy comes out of his house and takes her into his basement by knifepoint and rapes her. John and I only had like 6 months or something on the force at that point. The girl reported it, so we ended up going over to the house to ID the guy. John stays with the girl in the car, and I say to him, "When I give you the high sign, tell her to pick her head up and confirm that it's him." I knock on the door and the guy says, "What do you want?" I said, "Look I'm just trying to close this thing out—someone said that someone from here threw a bottle at them last week. I just need to settle this thing. Could you just step outside for a second? I'm late for lunch, I've got to go." The guy says, "Yeah, where's that motherfucker at?"

So he steps outside onto the lawn. The girl picks her head up and screams and we take him down. The girl had to go to the special victims. Her father, who's a security guard, came up to the precinct to talk to the detectives. I introduce myself, tell him what happened. He's this big, strong black guy, and I could see him welling up. I look at his hip and notice his gun. So I grab it and say, "Listen to me—I'm not sure if you're supposed to have this thing or not. I'm not asking—I'm telling you to go home. I got this. That guy is going to do a lot of time." So the father said, "Fine," and left. He was going to go in and kill the guy in his holding cell. I sent him home and we ended up putting the rapist away for 21 years.

Years later—by that time John had gone on to highway and I was part of Emergency Service—I'm driving along and suddenly realize that I'm close by that girl's address. I see some kids playing outside, pull up, and ask, "Hey what's going on guys? Does someone named Renee live here?" One of the kids says, "That's my mom." "Tell her an old friend of hers is here, Bill Fischer." She came running out of the house crying and she started hugging me, "I never forgot you guys. You guys promised me you were going to put him away and you did." Turns out she had gone into the theater, performed on Broadway. I never saw her again, but it was so cool to see we were like, connected, even after all that time.

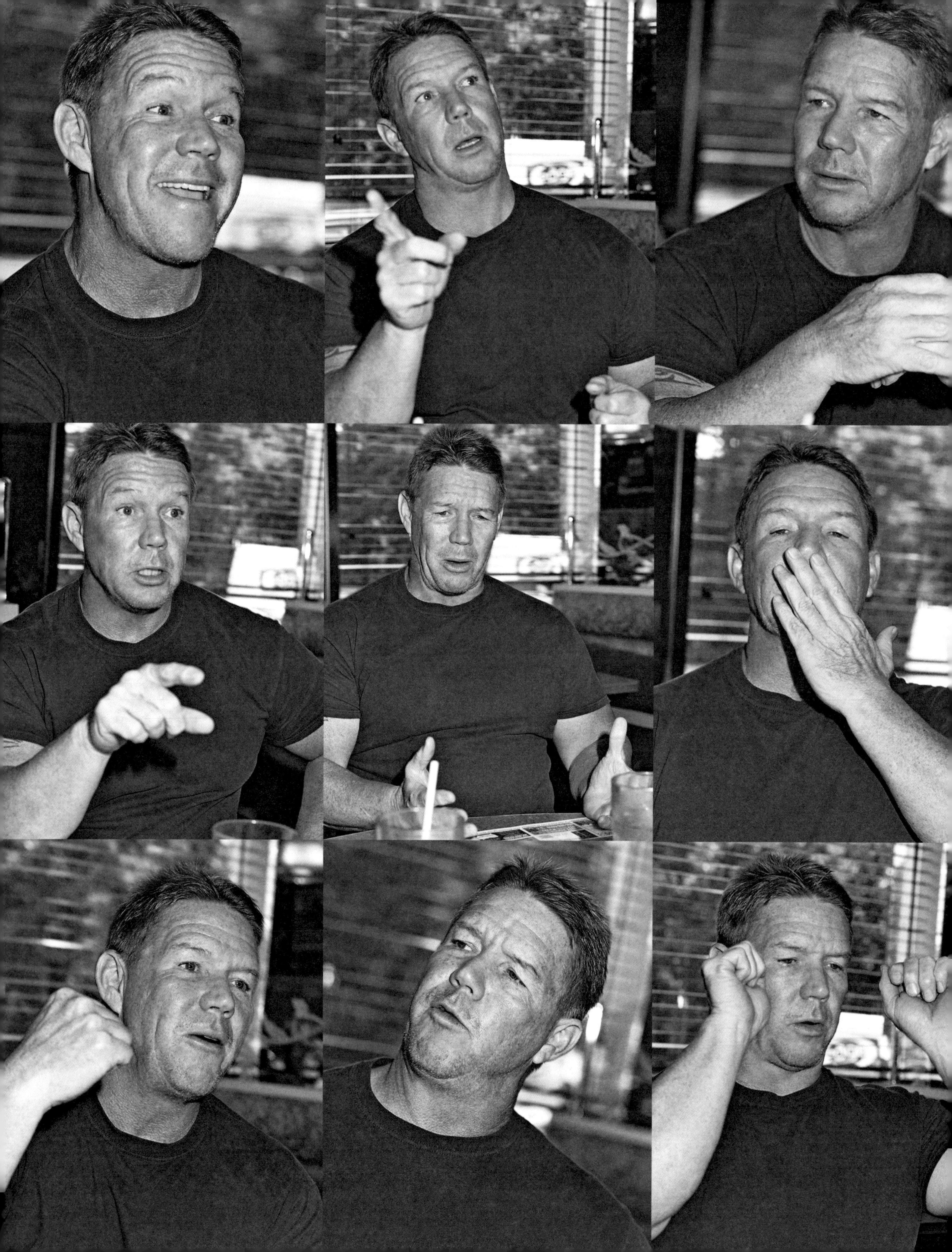

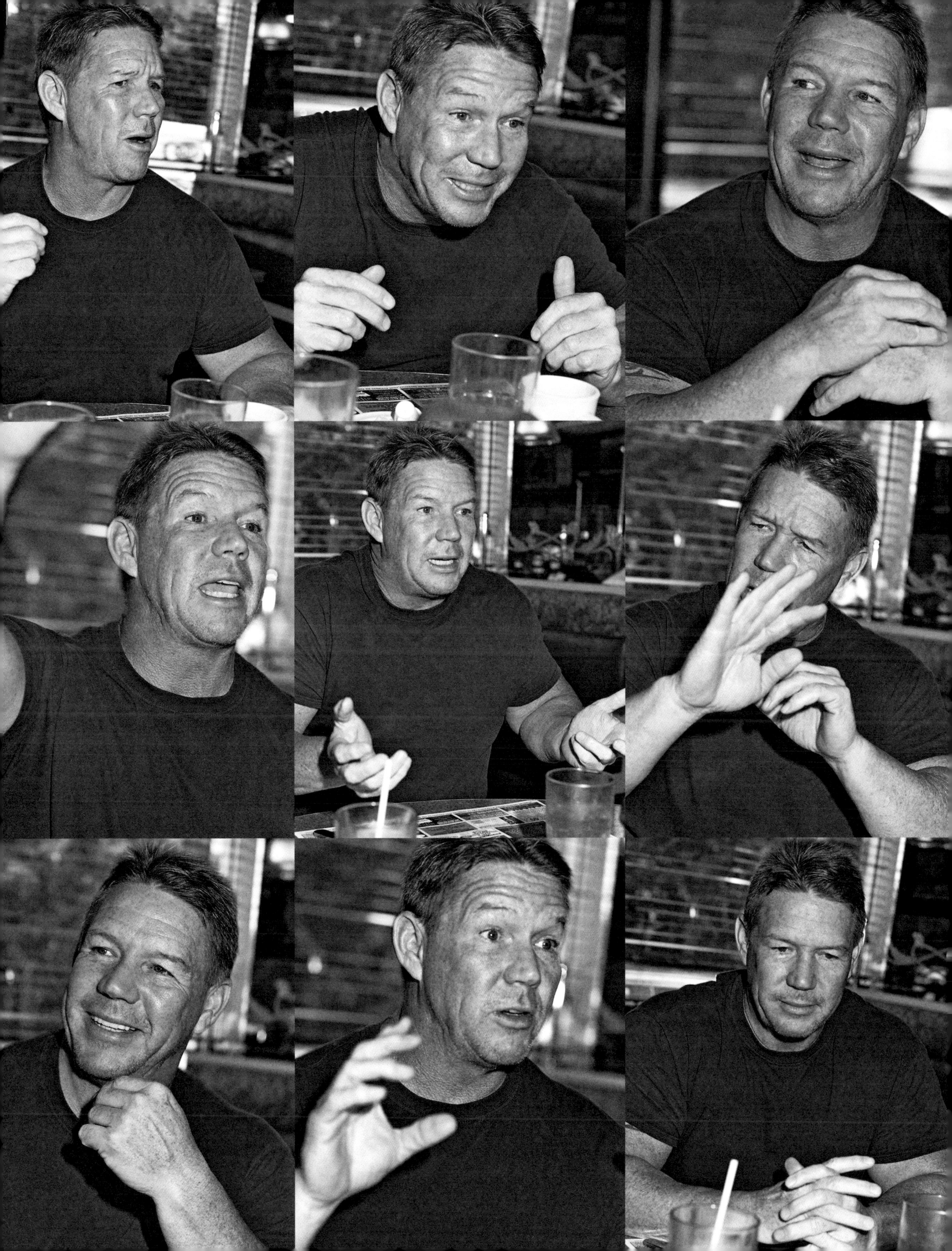

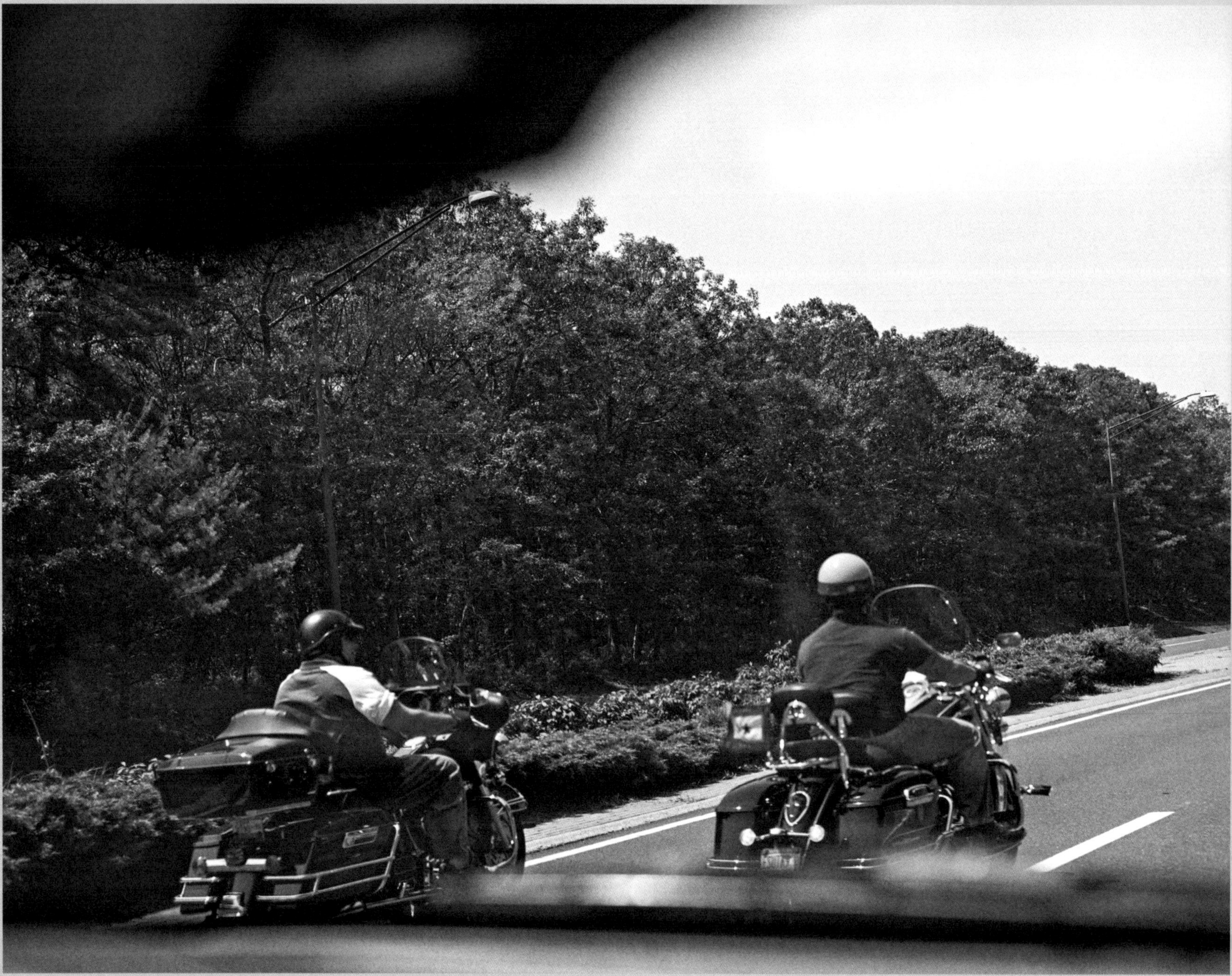

"When my son joined the force, I told him, 'Listen, always be honest and treat people fair. Don't bring prejudice onto the job. Do these things and you'll be able to put your head on the pillow every night and sleep fine. The way you treat people is the way you're going to get treated back.' That's the absolute truth. I'm not talking out of my ass, I'm talking out of experience. Don't rush into anything—if shit's going to happen, it's going to come to you. In the beginning it's hard because you're like a new racehorse, you just want to go. The fact is, anything that's going to happen to you is just going to present itself. So, I say, keep an even pace, and learn how to deal with it. Each experience you have, you become a better cop in the way you handle things, and each new experience helps you with the next one."

—DETECTIVE BILLY FISCHER, NYPD

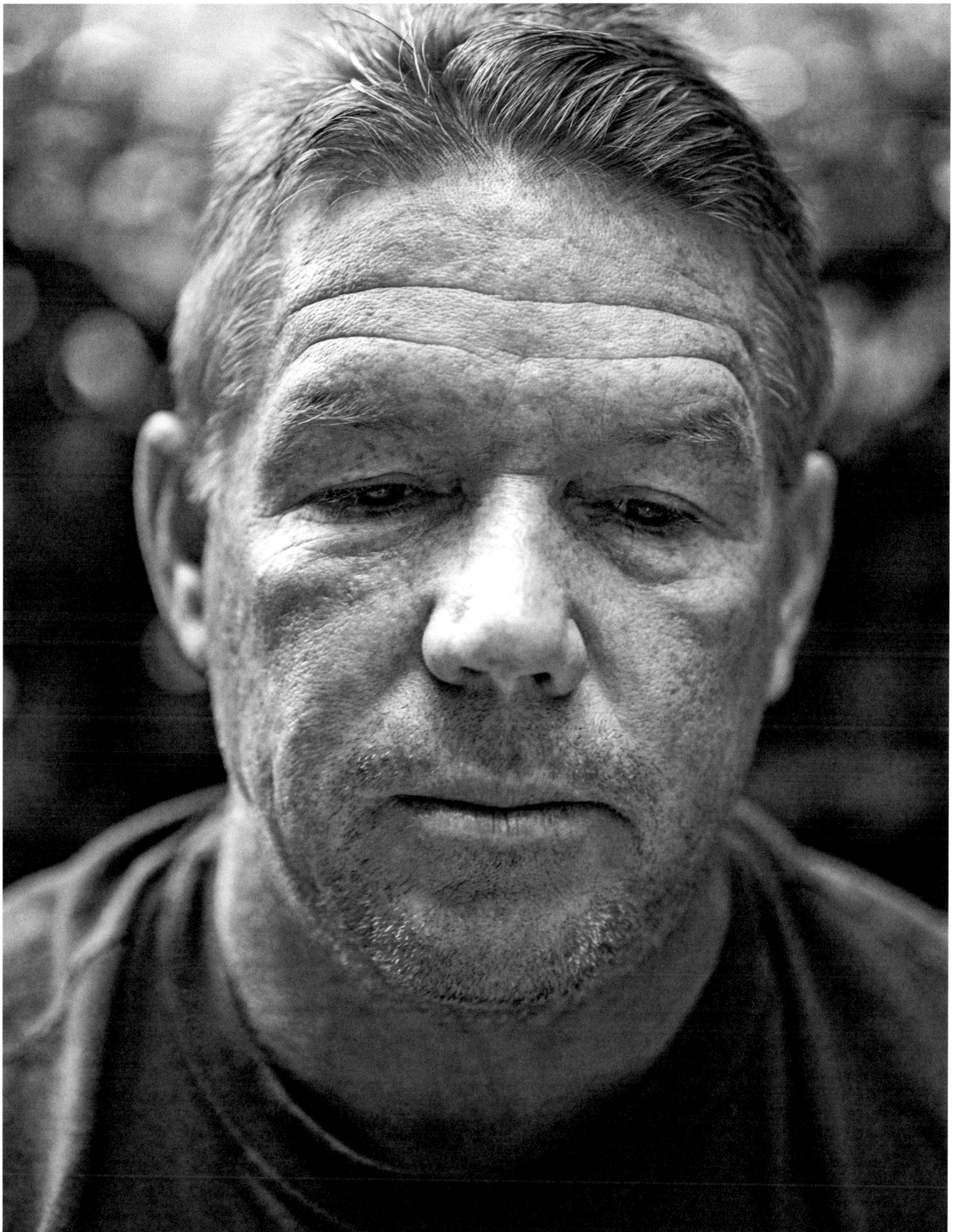

DARIA
HALPRIN
AND
MARK
FRECHETTE
IN
ZABRISKIE
POINT
BY
BRUCE
DAVIDSON

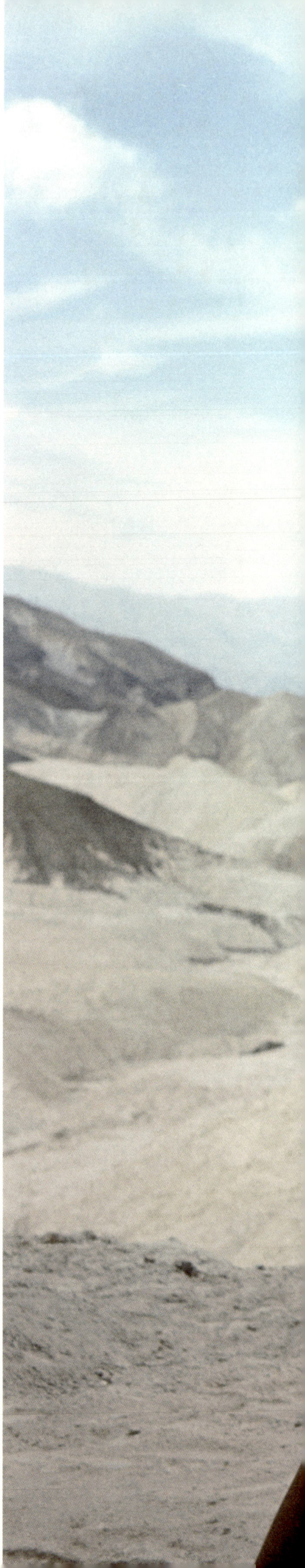

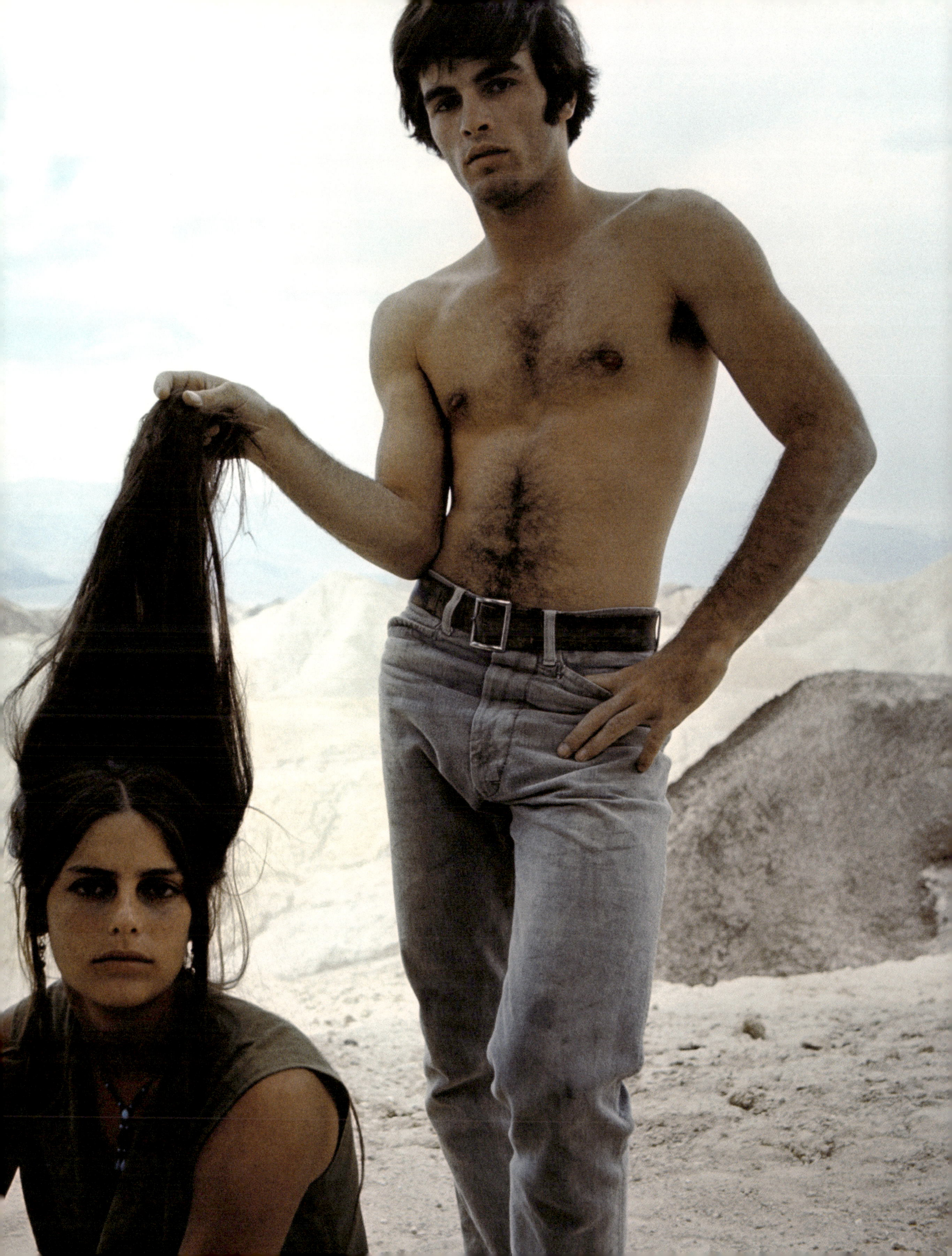

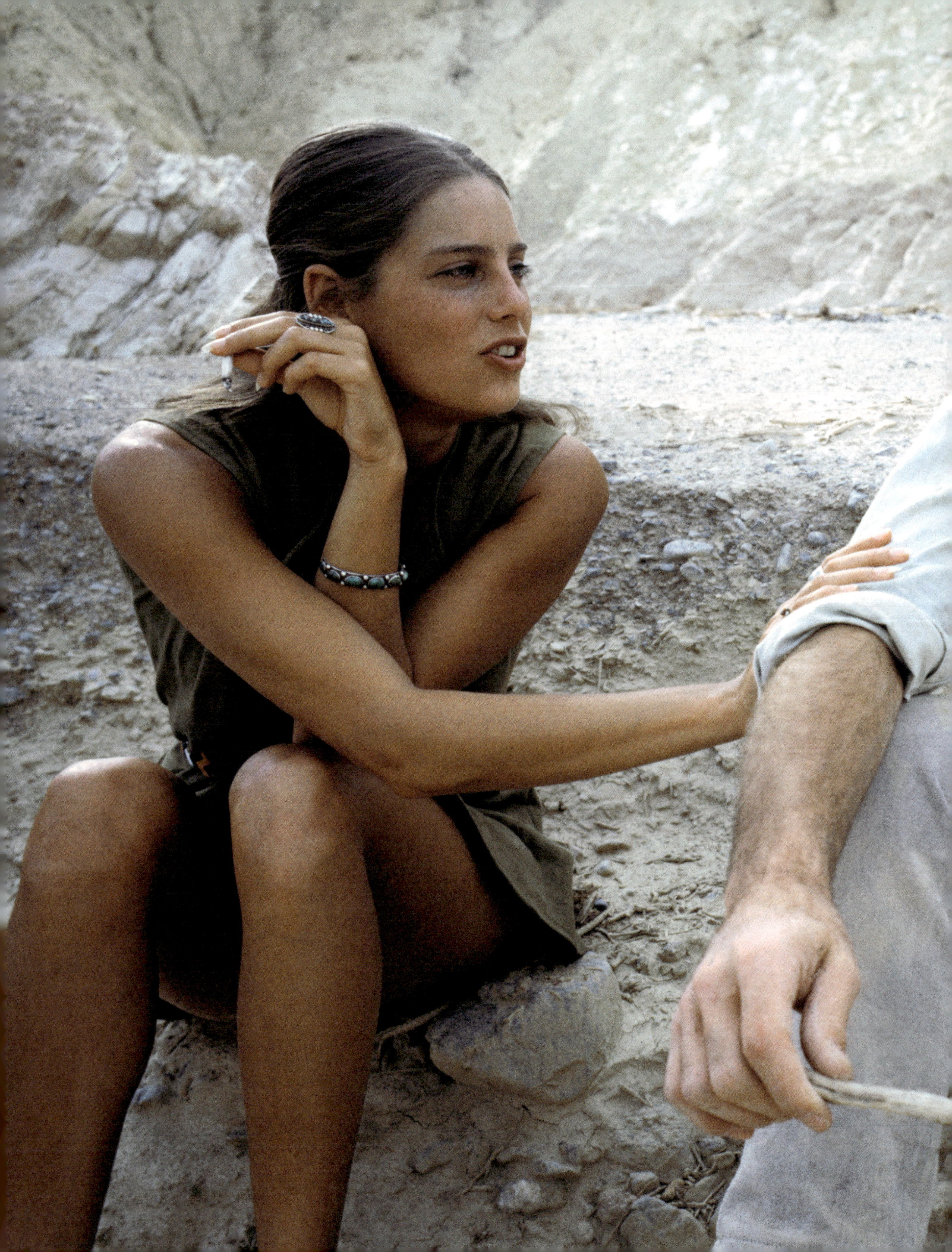

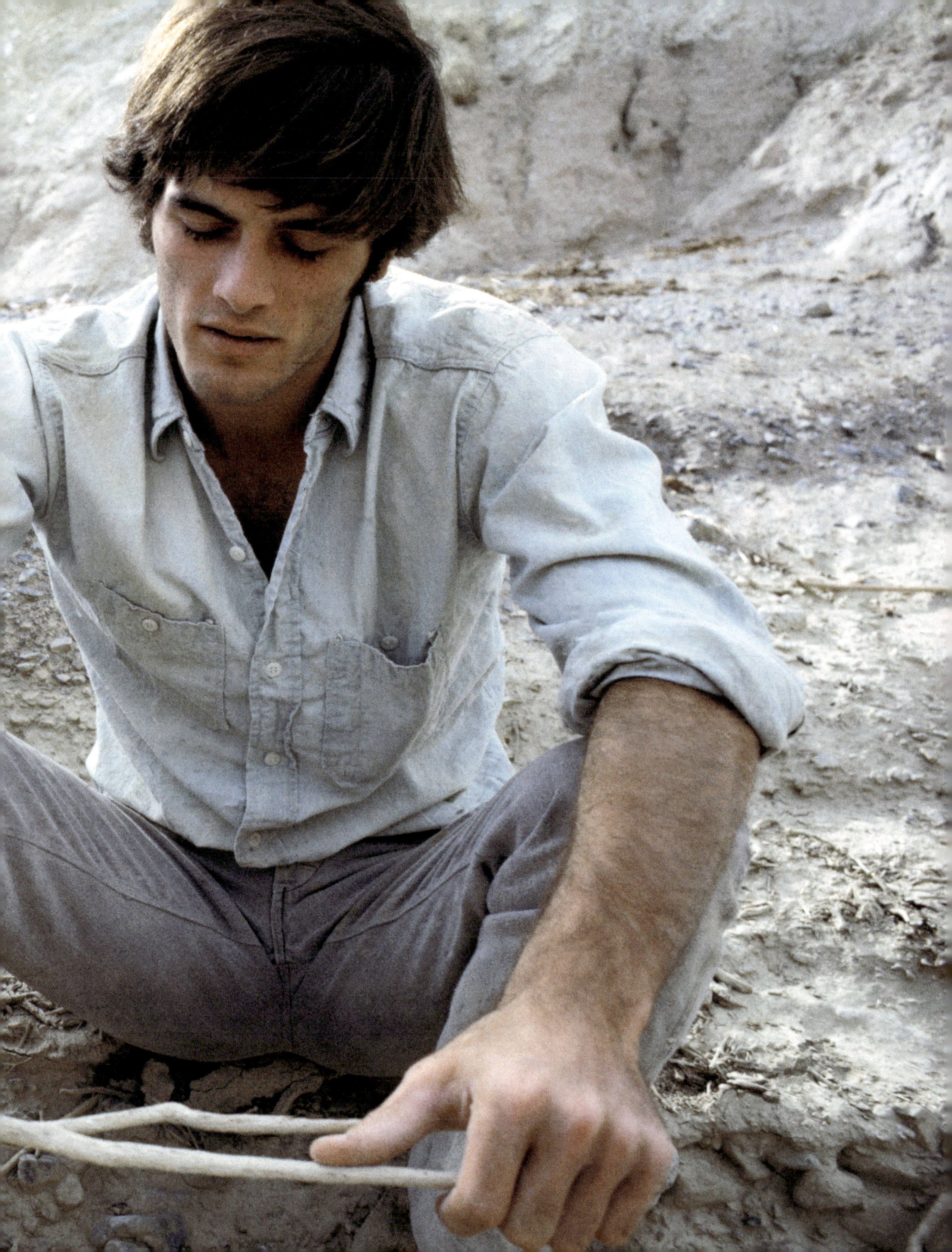

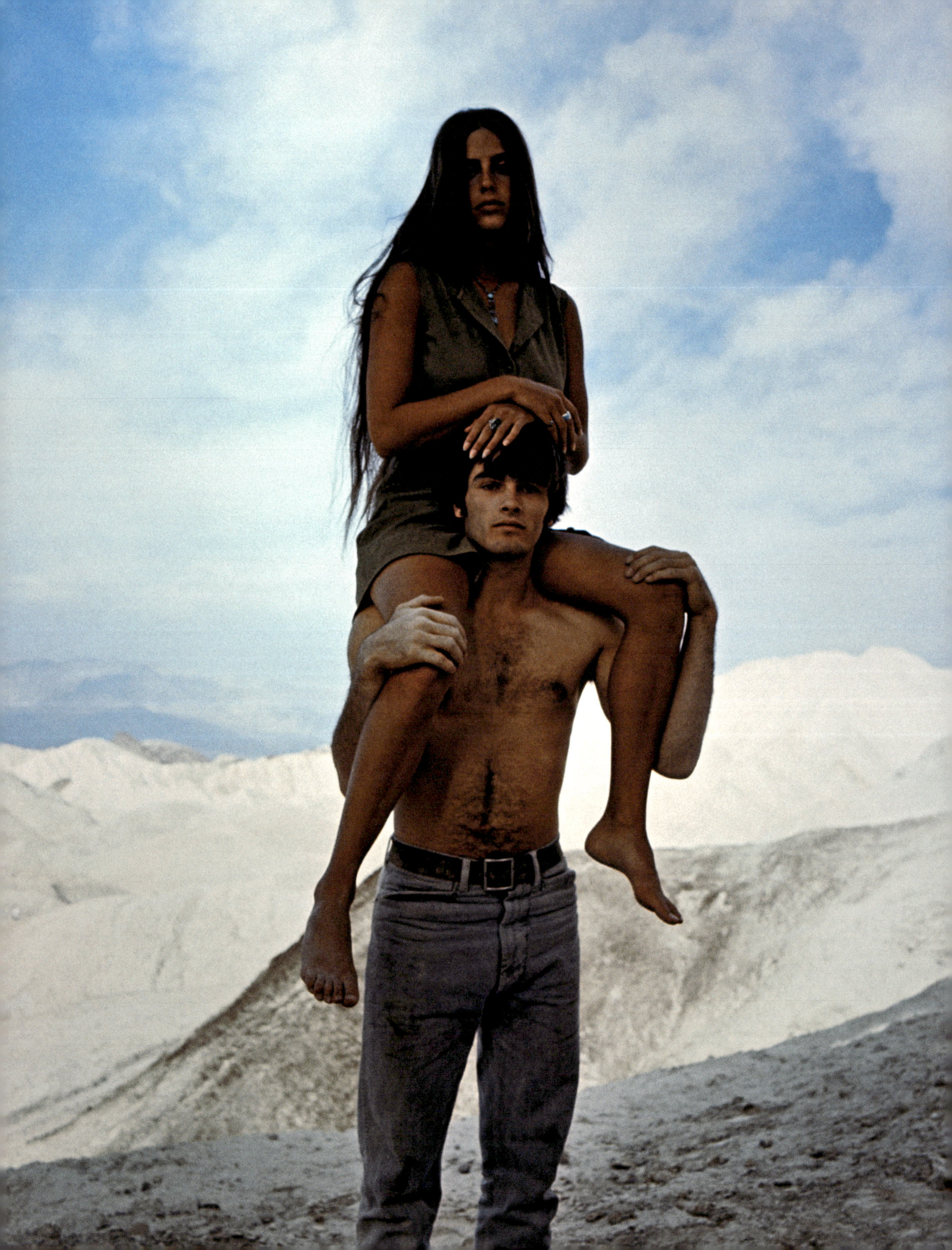

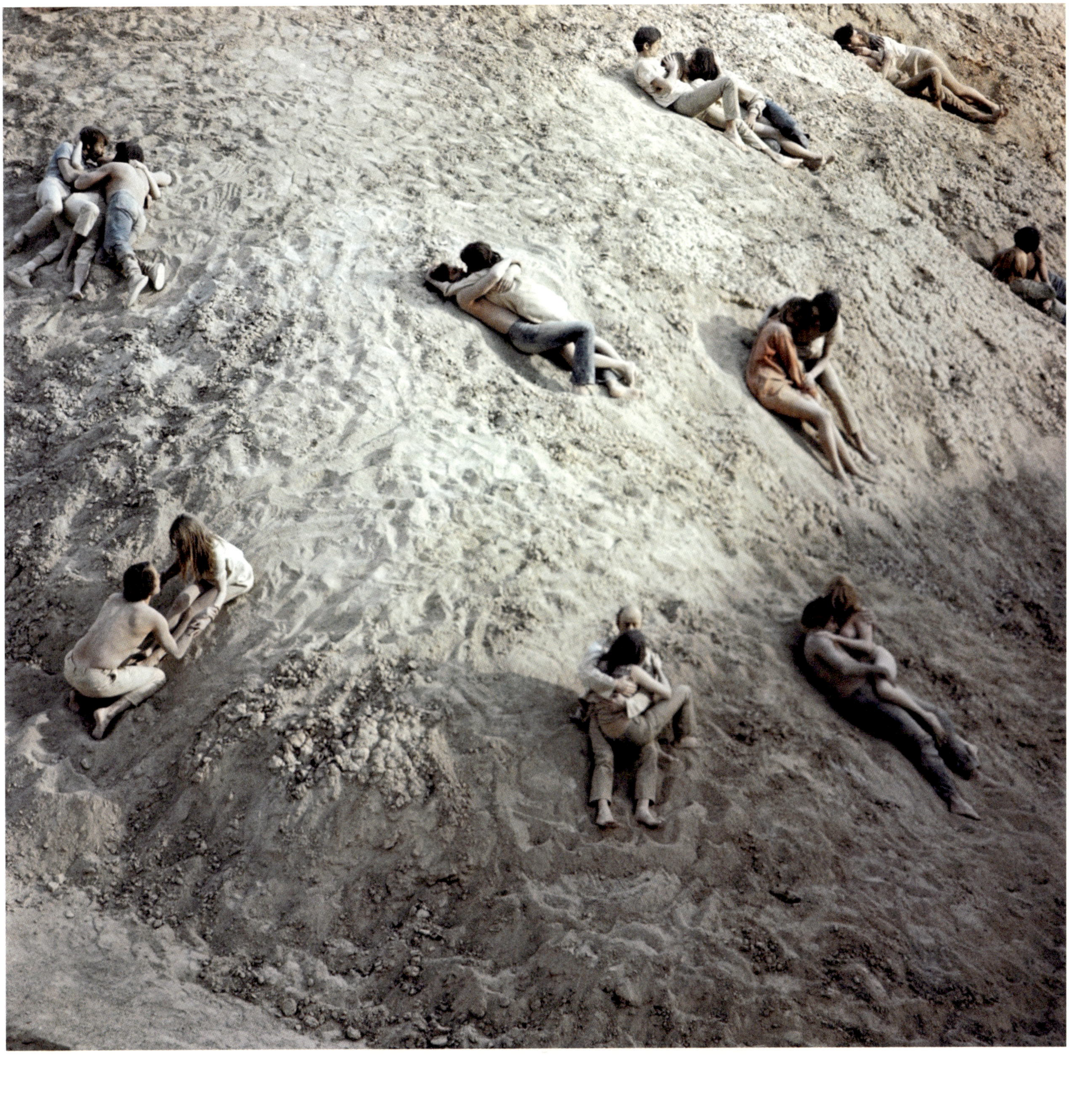

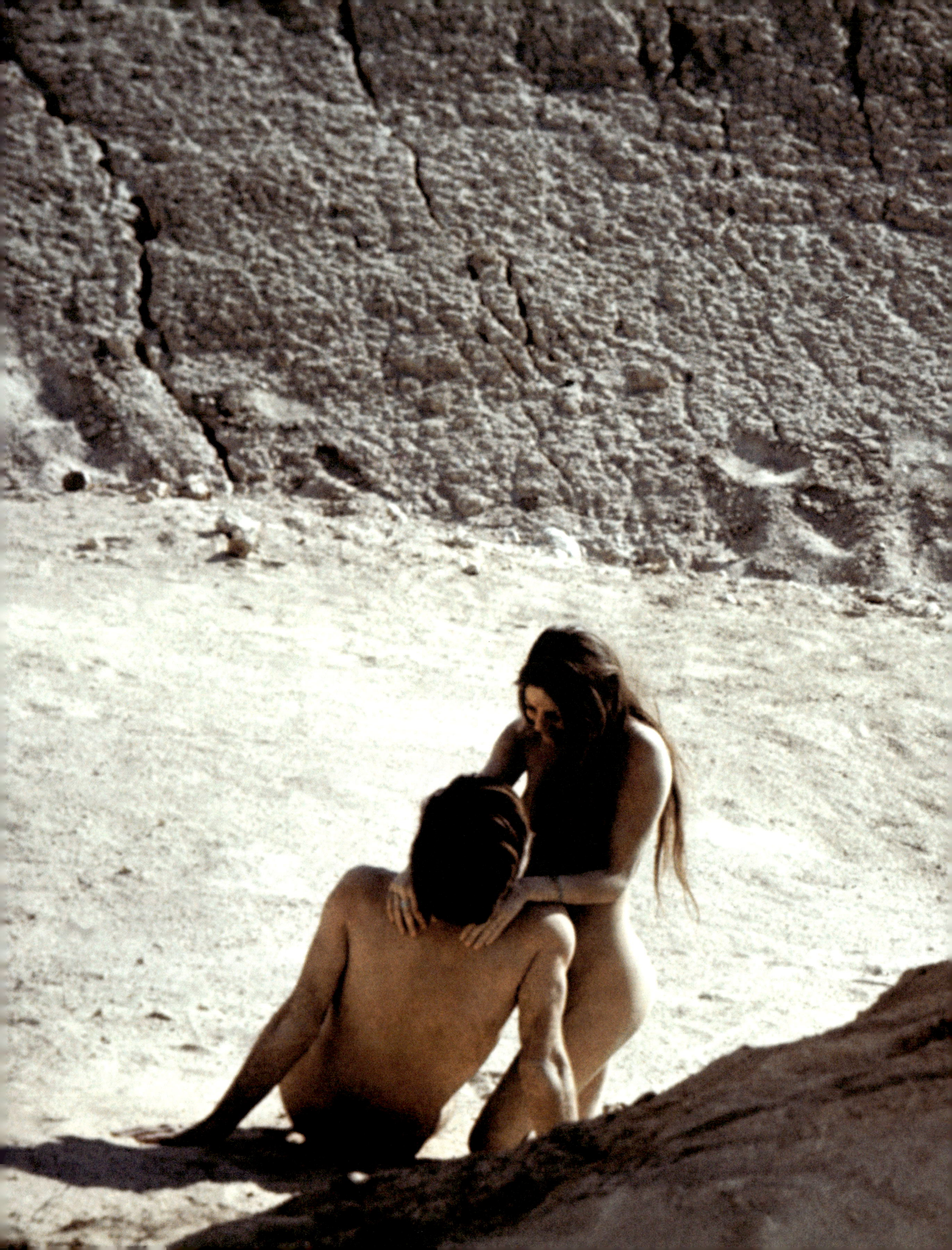

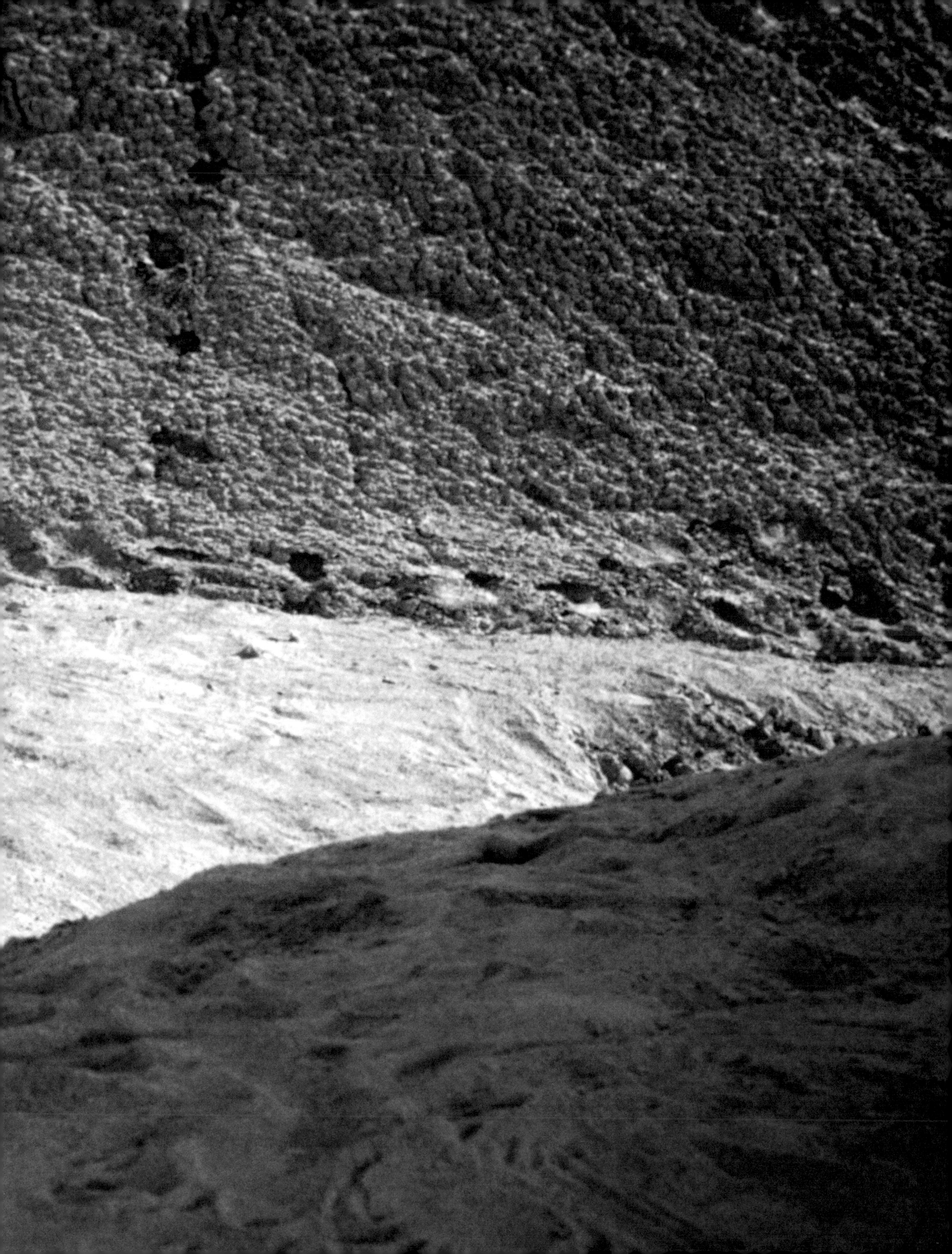

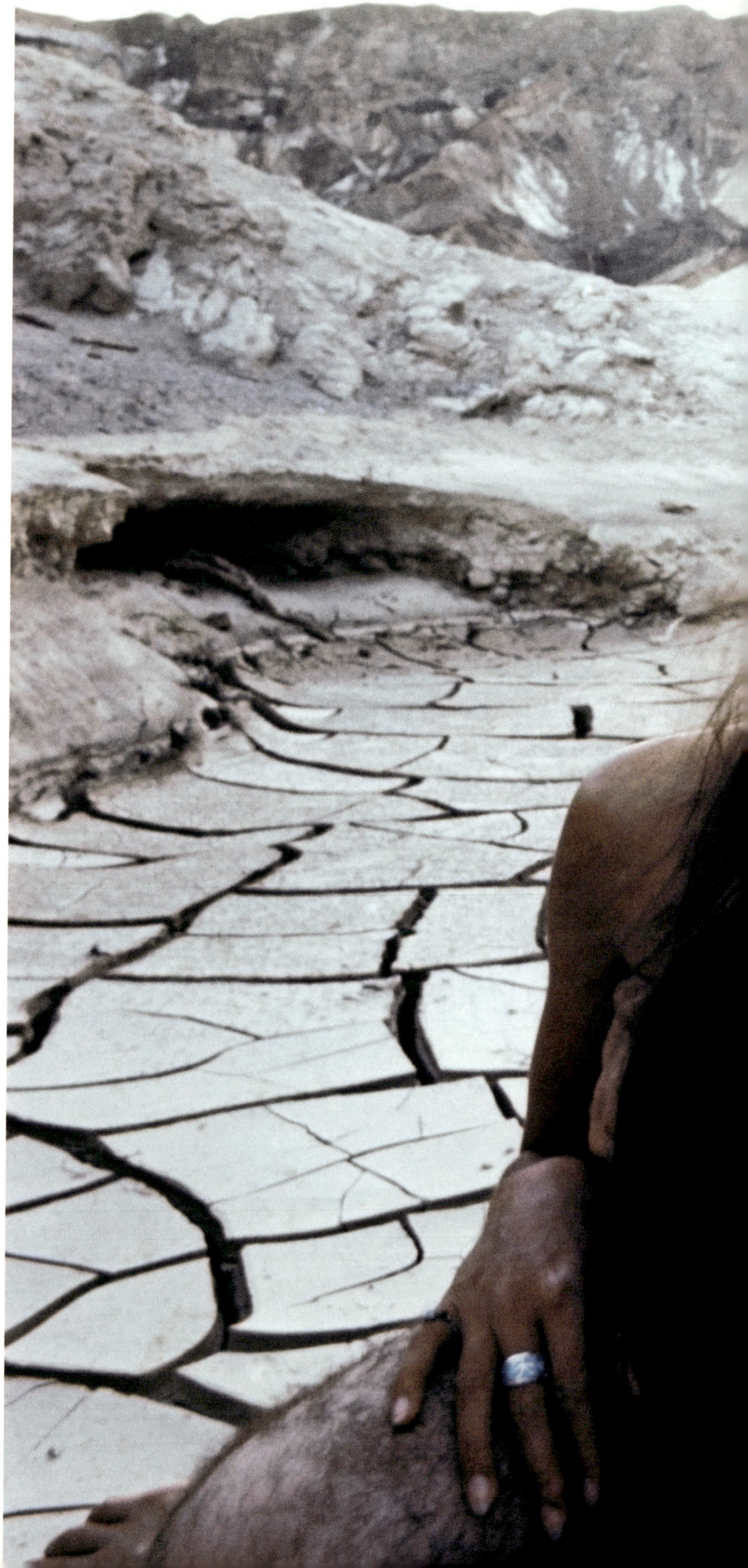

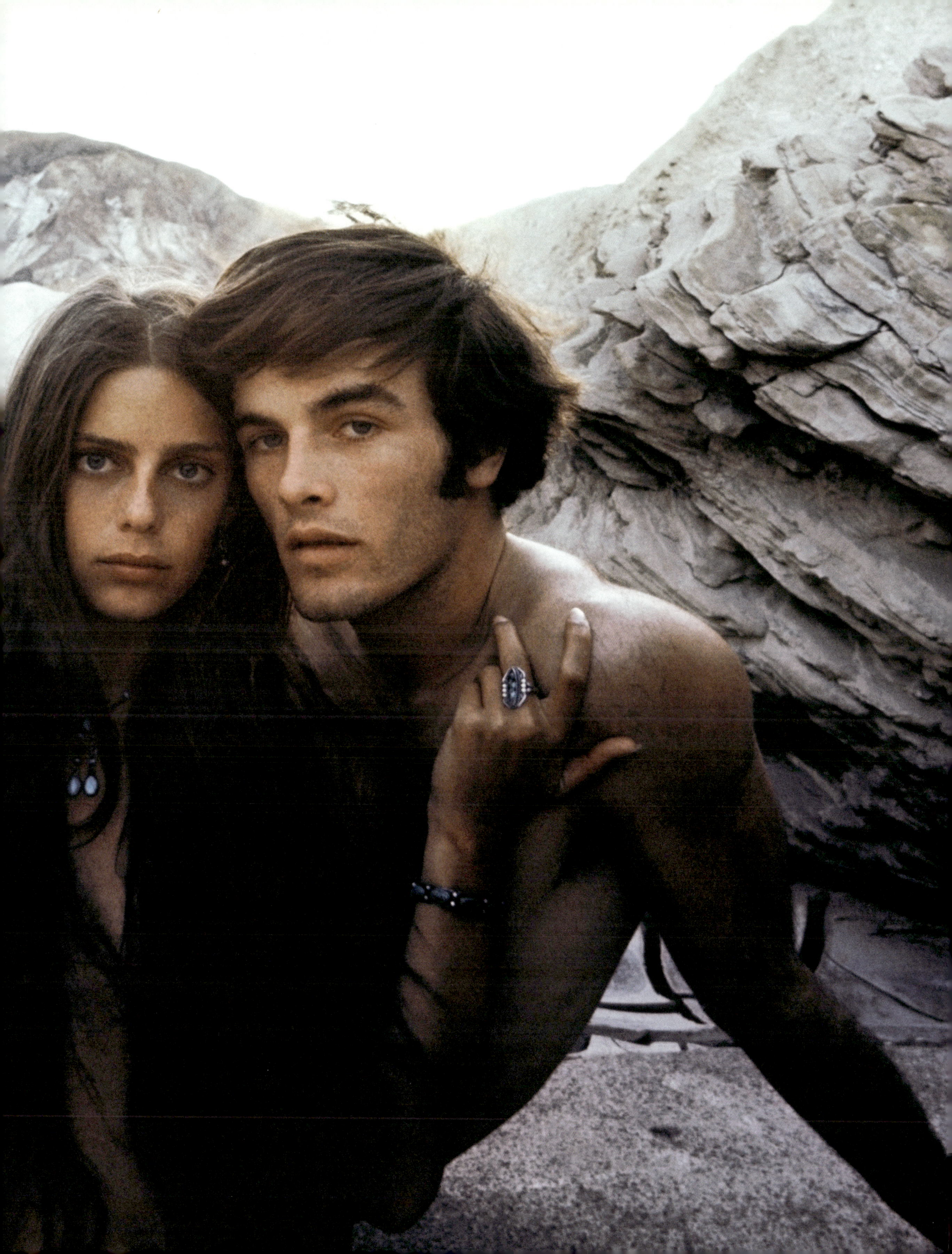

The last thing you expected to see on the April 6, 1970, episode of The Dick Cavett Show *was this eclectic group of guests: Mel Brooks, Rex Reed, and the two young stars from the film* Zabriskie Point*—Mark Frechette and Daria Halprin. Mark had already demonstrated his combustible temperament in a previous television appearance, when a political debate turned into a fistfight with one of the other panelists, a Yale University graduate. As Mark recounted that story to Mr. Cavett, Daria looked on serenely in a pale blue dress. You could tell how shy she felt as a "stranger in a strange land."*

Mr. Cavett asked Mark how the director, Michelangelo Antonioni, had found him for Zabriskie Point. *Mark said, "I was standing at a bus stop when I got into an argument with a man leaning out of a window three stories above me. Antonioni saw me and said, 'I want him for my film.'" Mel Brooks asked Mark, "Did you win the argument?" Mark wore a tight smile as Mel continued, "It's hard to have a fight with a guy three stories up." The tension grew—Mark kept mumbling one-word answers to Mr. Cavett's questions; Rex Reed kept asking, "What is it like to work with Antonioni?" Daria remained silent throughout. To break the mood, Mel Brooks finally yelled out, "Talk, Daria, talk!"*

Now 44 years later, Daria Halprin reflects on the extraordinary experience of making the film that changed the course of her lfie.

BRUCE WEBER Daria, you've been a mystery to me for so many years, so it's an honor to finally be talking to you. I've done some research—I know your father Lawrence was an environmental designer, and your mother Anna was a dance pioneer in the art scene of San Francisco. Then when you were six, you appeared in a ballet that your mother created called *Daughters of the Voice.* Aside from that, I don't know much. Where do you live now?

DARIA HALPRIN I live in Marin County. The Tamalpa Institute where I practice is in San Rafael.

BW It's so beautiful there. I was wondering if performing in your mother's dance company as a child helped you when you went to work on *Zabriskie Point.*

DH Actually the reason that I was found for the film was through my involvement with dance. I did not respond to a call, the call responded to me—it came and grabbed me by the arm and took me along for the ride. I had been part of a documentary called *Revolution* that explored the avant-garde art scene in the San Francisco Bay area. Sam Shepard was out there at that time and worked on the screenplay. Allen Ginsburg, Bob Graham, and the whole San Francisco Committee were involved. I think Antonioni must have seen *Revolution.* He met with an agent named Anne Brebner who helped him to reach me—she knew I was a student at U.C. Berkeley. They actually called me in the art department. I still have no idea how they managed to track me down there. I just remember the phone ringing in the art studio—somebody answered, then came over and said, "Hey, Daria, Antonioni is on the phone for you." I laughed, and said, "Yeah, right."

BW You must have thought it was a prank!

DH I did, because in my spare time I used to watch all the Antonioni and Bergman films at the Berkeley Cinema. The girl said, "No, he's on the phone, I'm telling you!" And that's how the whole great adventure started.

BW It's interesting to me that you are now doing all this work about emotional health and movement and physicality with your teaching at the Tamalpa Institute. I always felt that Antonioni's films were about the absence of emotion—and yet the desire to find a human connection. Working with him must have been a big transition for you.

DH My encounter with Antonioni actually caused me to reject my path as an actor. After working with him, I felt the actor's life was too dangerous and ungrounded for me. *Zabriskie Point* gave me a completely different orientation and helped me to find a new way of realizing my destiny. It helped me to see that my passion, talent, and skills were best expressed through a different kind of performance. I had a baby, which made me feel like I needed to reconstruct my life and return to my roots. So in 1975, I started teaching expressive arts therapy. It was once said, "The greatest art is born out of necessity." Now I'm devoted to practicing that idea. It has been transformative for me and the people that I've had the great fortune to work with. I wrote a book about this journey called *The Expressive Body in Life, Art, and Therapy.* Through my research, I have come to realize how healing creativity can be for people.

BW I just recently read of your connection to Dennis Hopper.

DH Yes, Dennis and I were married for a while. We had a daughter, Ruthanna, who is a writer in Los Angeles. Dennis was terrific, but he was really a madman back then. Nobody could live with him, and it was particularly difficult for those of us who he loved the most. Yet Dennis was very influential in my development as an artist—being with him led me to some very interesting new paths.

BW I remember thinking when I saw *Zabriskie Point* that it felt like you and Mark were on a journey to find yourselves, even more than just acting in a film.

DH That's very true. I think our journey was an allegory—both for Antonioni's film and for himself as a director. Many people found him very difficult because of what they perceived to be a lack of feeling and empathy. But that was not what I personally experienced with him—I felt a great deal of warmth and sentiment and care. I may have been one of the lucky few, but he was very kind to me. Mark had a very different relationship with him.

BW What was Mark like as a person? Did he have the same kind of art background that you did?

DH Not at all. He was a street kid with a lot of raw talent, but he didn't have a chance to cultivate it. Mark was very challenged. He was filled with angst, a rebel who never really found the right outlet. If you've looked into his short history, you know he met a very tragic end.

BW It's true. In light of everything that happened to him afterwards, it's ironic to me that in *Zabriskie Point*, Mark has that one line in the meeting with all of the young revolutionaries: "I'm willing to die, but not of boredom." His character in the film is so impulsive and expresses such turmoil—it's almost like he's a reflection of what Mark experienced in real life. After the film, I read he was involved in a bank robbery in Boston, and that one of his accomplices was killed by the police. It turns out that Mark's gun wasn't even loaded. Then he died under mysterious circumstances in the gym of the prison where he was serving his sentence.

His story is just incredibly sad. But in spite of all this, Daria, so many young people watched *Zabriskie Point* and looked at these pictures you did with Bruce Davidson and saw in you and Mark examples of how we wanted to break free, even if we didn't know how to express it. Antonioni's film turned you both into romantic rebels and role models for us.

DH I think that was very much in the bloodstream of our generation. I'm aware that because of the film, Mark and I became symbolic motifs for people in that way. Maybe that's partly because I hadn't had much formal training in making the transition between being a nonverbal dancer and working with a script as an actor. Through that process there were a lot of risks taken—some things lost and others gained. As we're talking, I am very aware of the connection between the past and my present work.

BW Did you ever reach out to Mark after he went to prison?

DH Briefly, but it was complicated. We had really lost touch and gone in very different directions. I was also processing challenges with Dennis at the time. It was all too much.

BW You always seemed to pick these kinds of men like Dennis and Mark who really needed a mother figure.

DH (*Laughing*) I think that my husband of the past 30-some-odd years would appreciate if I respond to that in a very specific way. I've always gravitated toward dynamic, talented, big-presence kind of men. I think that over time, I have learned to find the balance between that kind of energy and the spirit symbolized by someone like Bruce Davidson, who is really just kind and decent. I grew up around so many artists that for me, being a creative person always meant you had to be a little crazy. With Bruce, that wasn't the case at all. He was such a talented artist, and yet so genuine and humble. I remember he wore these khaki shorts—the opposite of ostentatious. Working with him was an entirely new experience for me. When I visited New York after *Zabriskie Point*, Bruce would invite me over to visit with his wife and kids. I remember they were all so solid, which was something I didn't have a lot of in my life at that time. To this day, I have a series of photographs that Bruce took of me hanging in the hallway of our home.

BW You were so lucky to have that experience with Bruce. He really captured the relationship between you and Mark.

DH You're absolutely right. It was as if he connected with the emotion behind Antonioni's abstraction. The last time I saw Antonioni was really extraordinary. The Pacific Film Archives hosted a retrospective program for his 80th year—they showed all of his films. Because he'd had a stroke and couldn't speak, I was asked to get up on the stage and talk on his behalf. So I stood up there, trying my best to introduce *Zabriskie Point*, and as I looked out into the audience, I saw my daughter sitting right next to him. I think at that time she must have been 17 years old. It was such a profound moment for me, connecting the old path with my new life, having it all come full circle with him. We all have our destiny waiting for us—and as I get older, I appreciate those kinds of connections all the more.

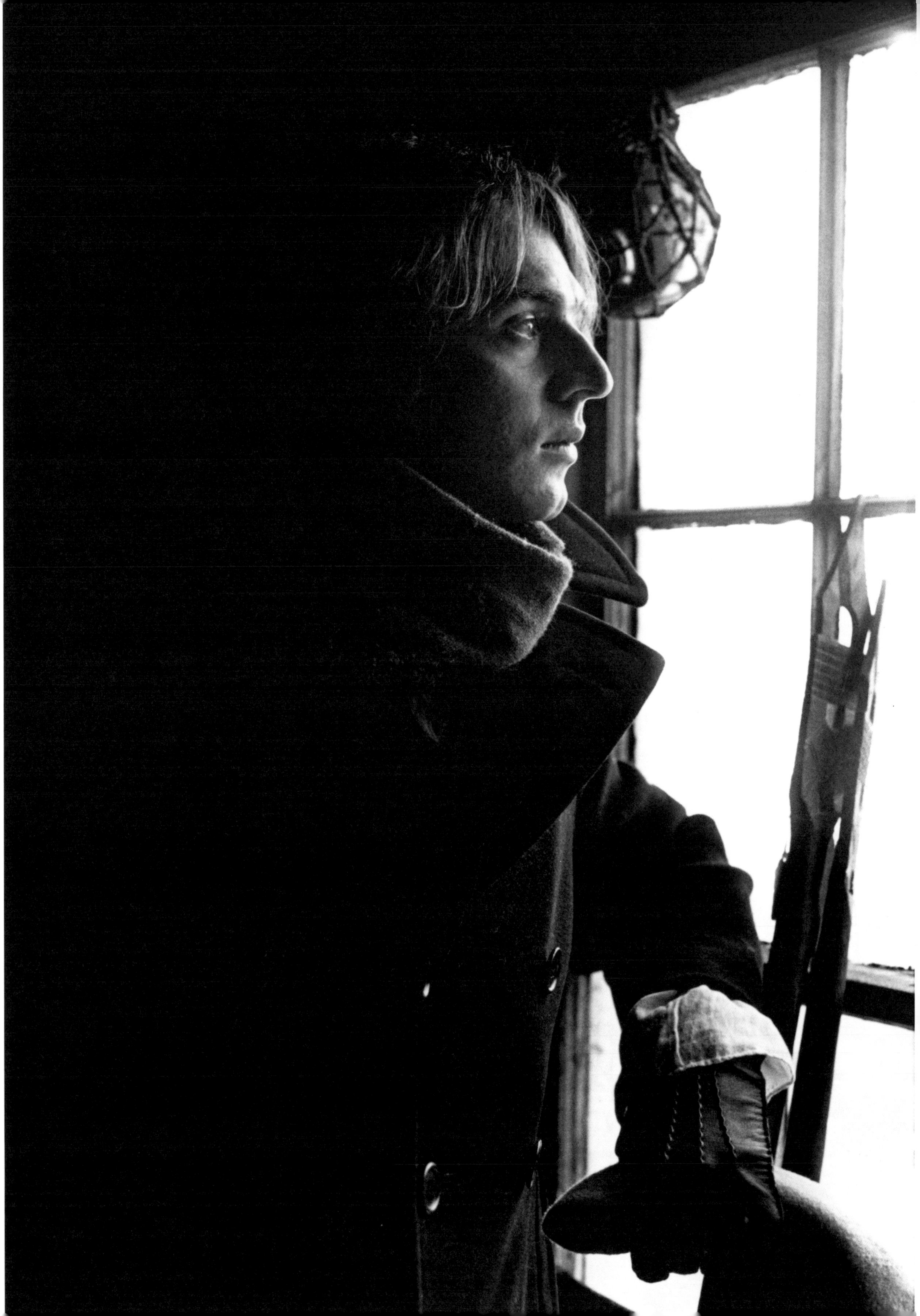

He's no good
but we don't love them
because they're good
do we.
So why do we love them?
Because they're beautiful?
Because they're stupid.
What's stupid about being
beautiful?
Beauty has brains of its own.
Let's face it
to be beautiful and loved
is about the smartest thing
you can be.

I support the striking coal miners
But will the striking coal miners
support me.

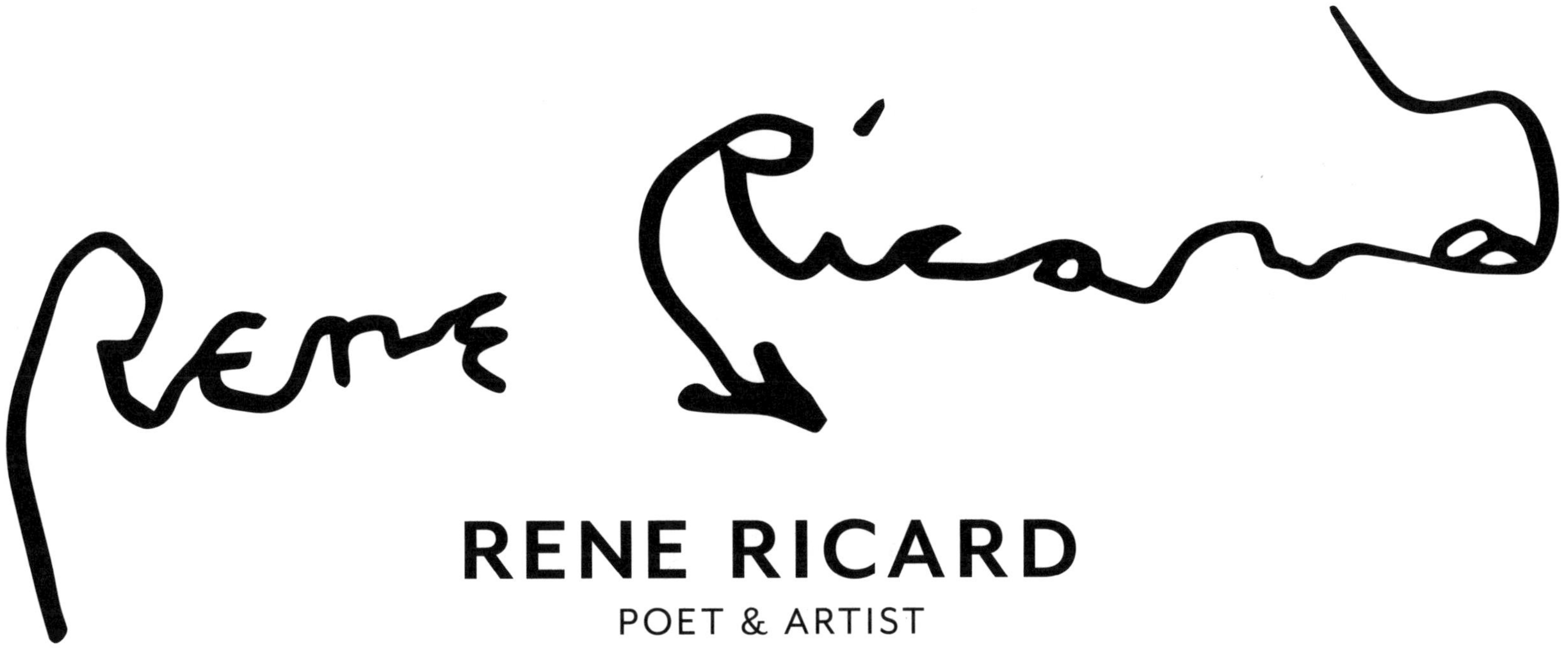

RENE RICARD

POET & ARTIST

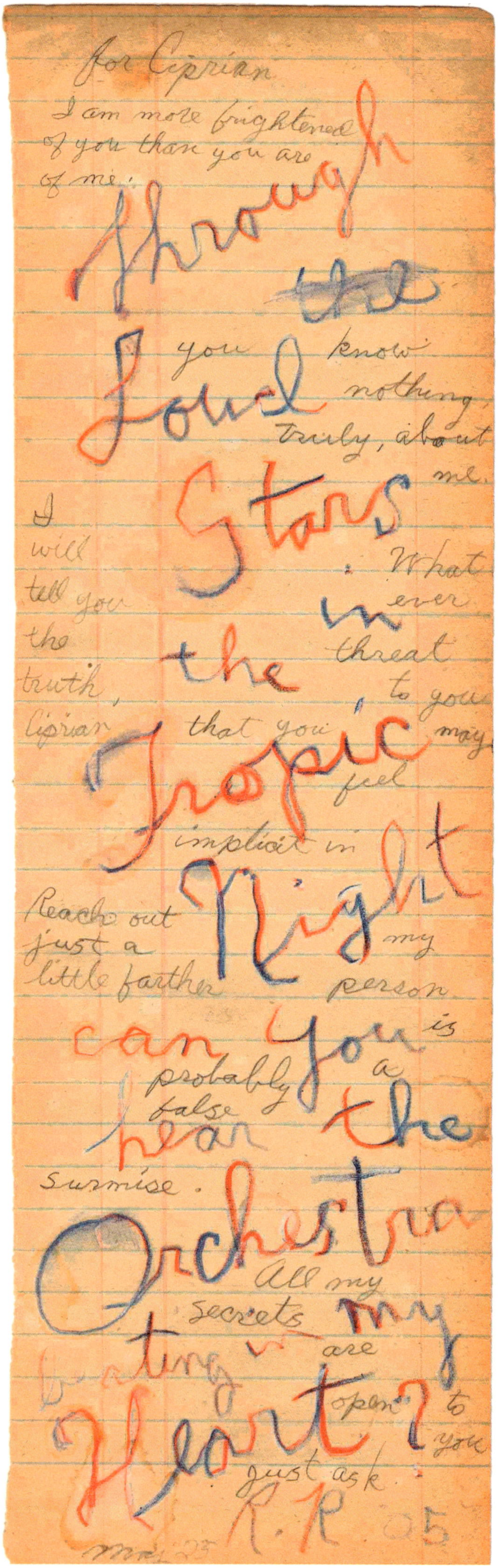

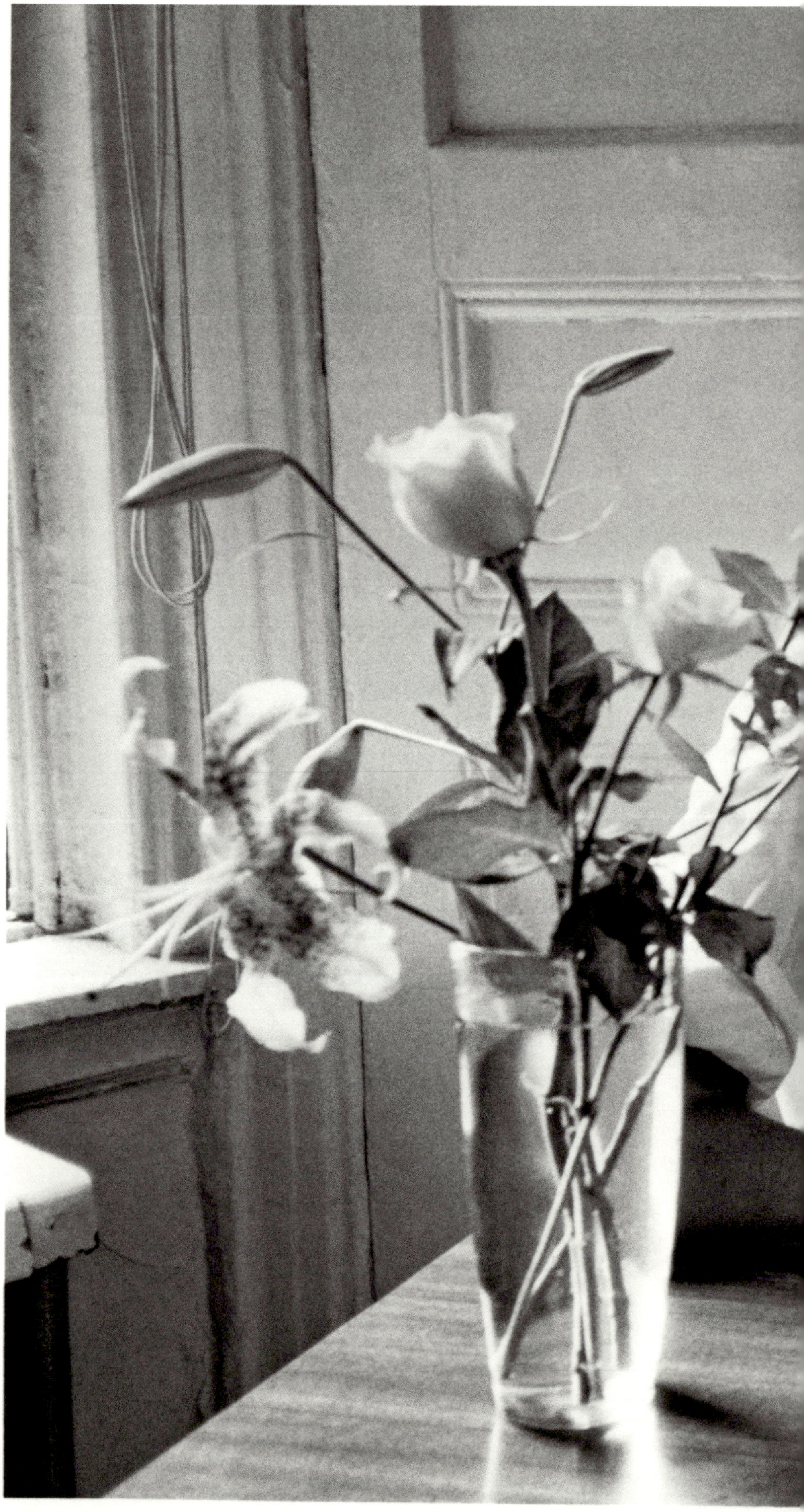

Rene Ricard visiting from acr

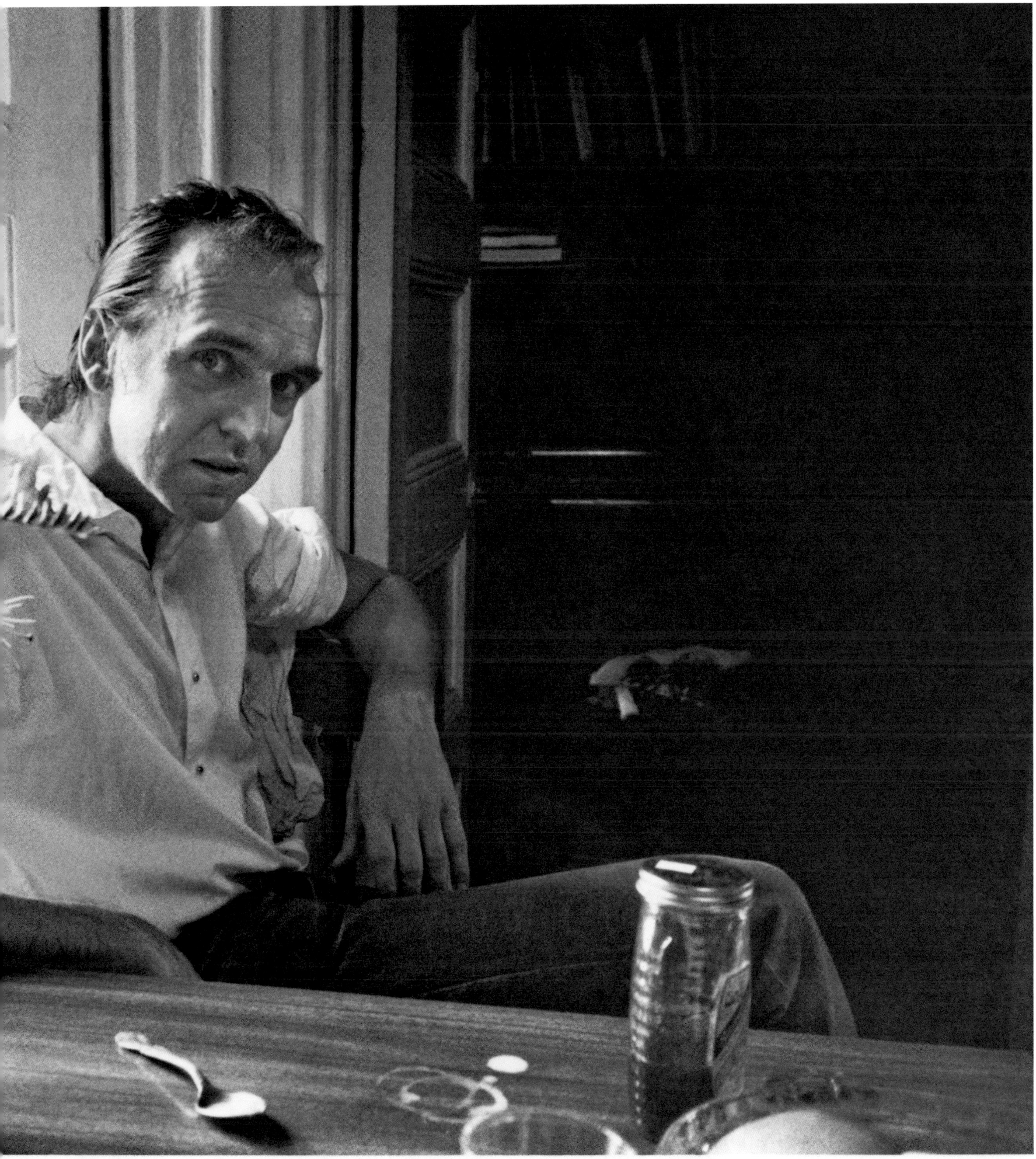

…the hall, my kitchen July 29, 1986. Allen Ginsberg

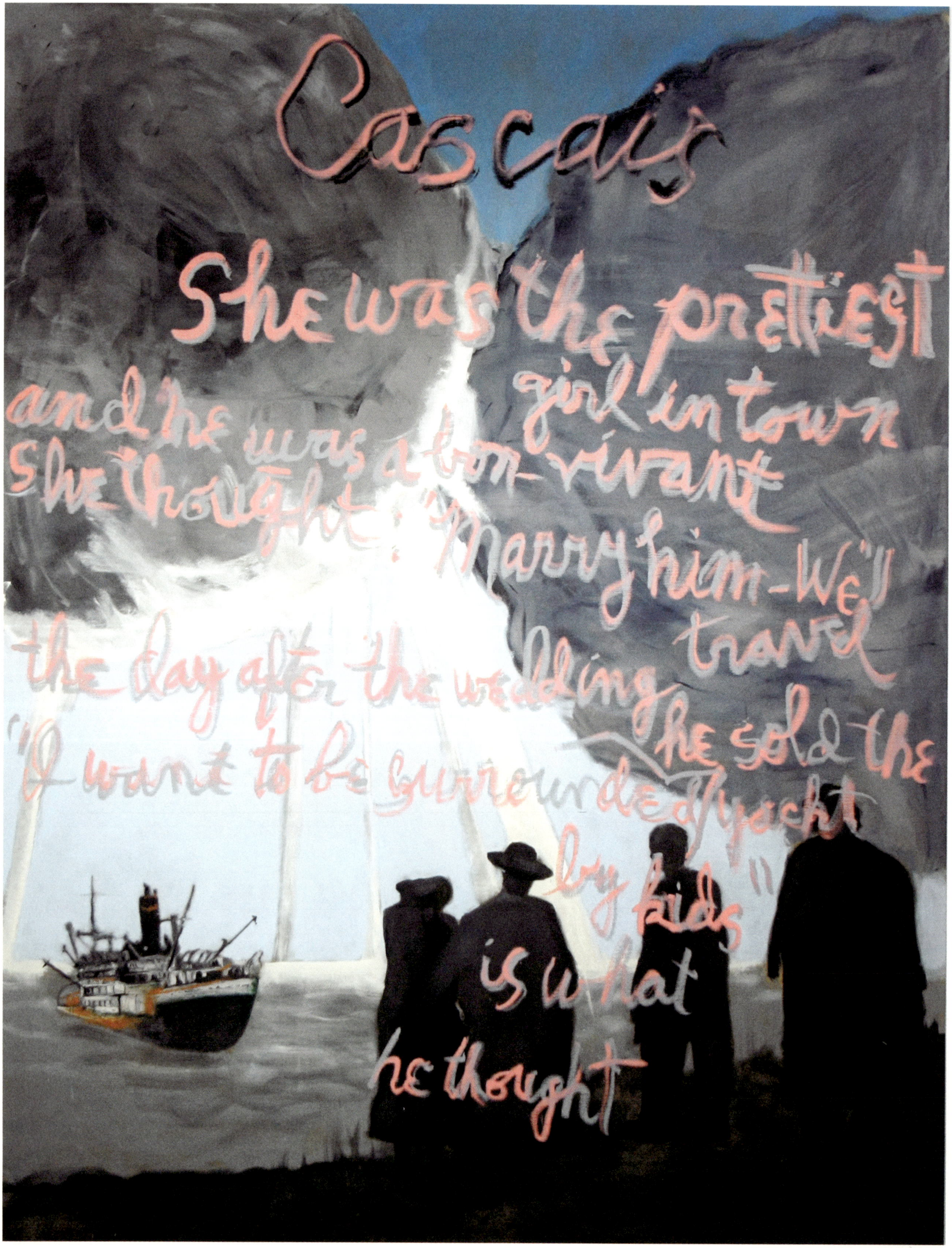
Cascais
She was the prettiest
girl in town
and he was a bon-vivant
She thought: "Marry him - We'll
travel
the day after the wedding
he sold the
yacht
"I want to be surrounded
by kids"
is what
he thought

VITO SCHNABEL

CURATOR

Rene was a fixture in my family from an early age. He was particularly close with my sister and mother—he lived at my mom's house on and off for years. Rene was just this character who I loved being around and began to understand more as I grew up. We became quite close once I graduated from high school and started studying art with him—we would meet four times a week and spend about five hours together at the Met or MoMA or the Frick. Sometimes we would drive down to Washington, DC, or go to the Yale Art Museum. Rene had this ability to contextualize artworks, particularly from a historical perspective. That's how I learned all about the Italian Renaissance right up through Dutch painting. Even if he was talking about a work from the 1980s, Rene could explain the history of the piece through some little story he remembered.

Rene was one of the last of his era. He inserted himself into the middle of a couple of Warhol films where he thought it was important to be. He championed Jean-Michel Basquiat from the very beginning, writing a legendary essay about him titled "The Radiant Child." Whether he was critiquing Brice Marden or Francesco Clemente or my father, Rene was arguably one of the best art writers in the world at that time. It put him into a unique category—artists respected him and his work when he started painting.

His first art was writing, but in the last 15 years of his life, all of Rene's poetry came through in the form of his secretive paintings. He could paint a really good picture—he had a magical eye and a magical touch. We did a couple of shows together—whether in New York or Los Angeles or London, they were always an adventure. Though he would put together all the ideas and sketches for the paintings, you were never quite sure if he was going to get them done on time. But Rene never once let me down, ever. For all the hysteria and the madness that went along with working with Rene, it was a very fruitful relationship, an experience I'll never forget.

We did good things together; we did bad things together. We got into fights; we laughed. I would always bump into him on the streets of New York at the weirdest times; he might ask me for 20 bucks. Then occasionally I'd be out, and see him from across the street—and before I could even talk to him he would ask, "Do you need some dough to get home?" He was very sensitive and kind in that way.

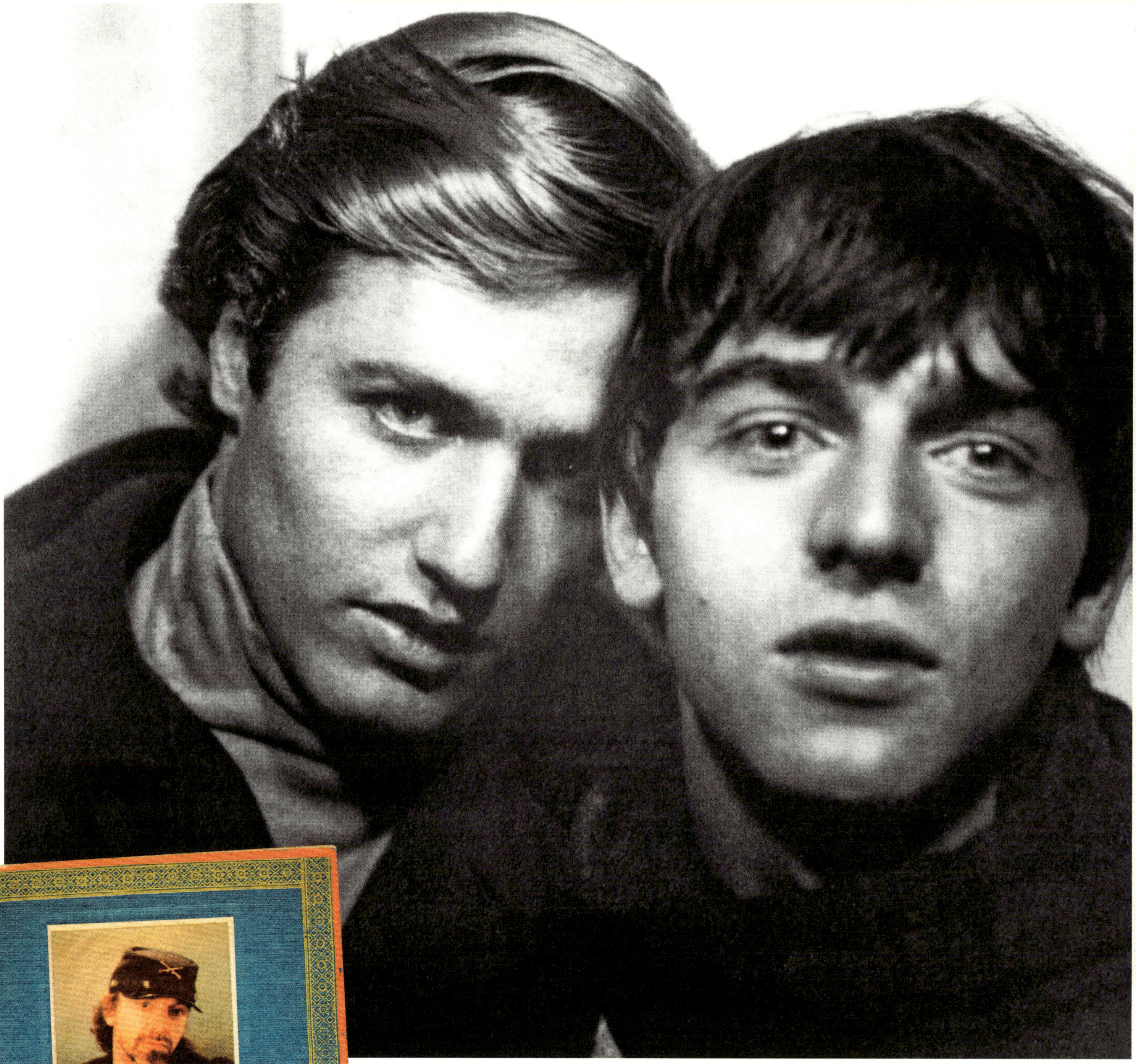

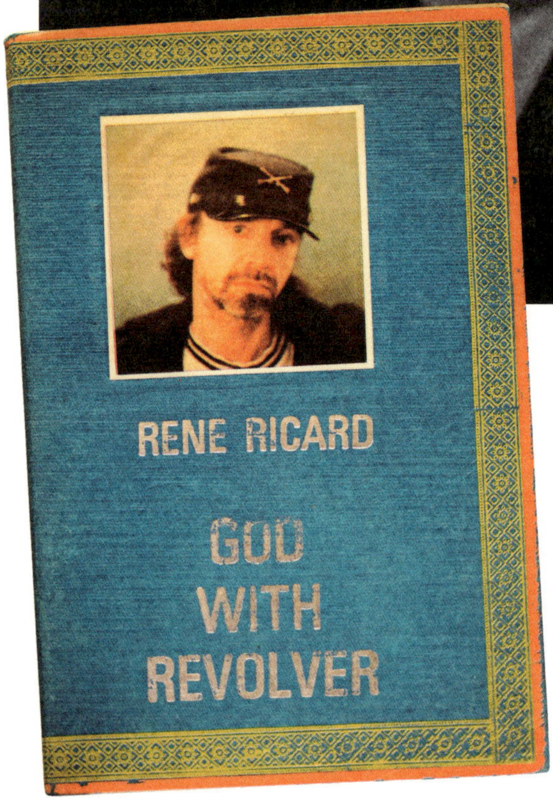

Drapes in this room:
Avocado, Harvest Gold, and Pumpkin.
Someone designed this print
Someone manufactured it
And these people, of all things, bought them.
Now try to convince me that there isn't a
Conspiracy of ugliness.

—Rene Ricard

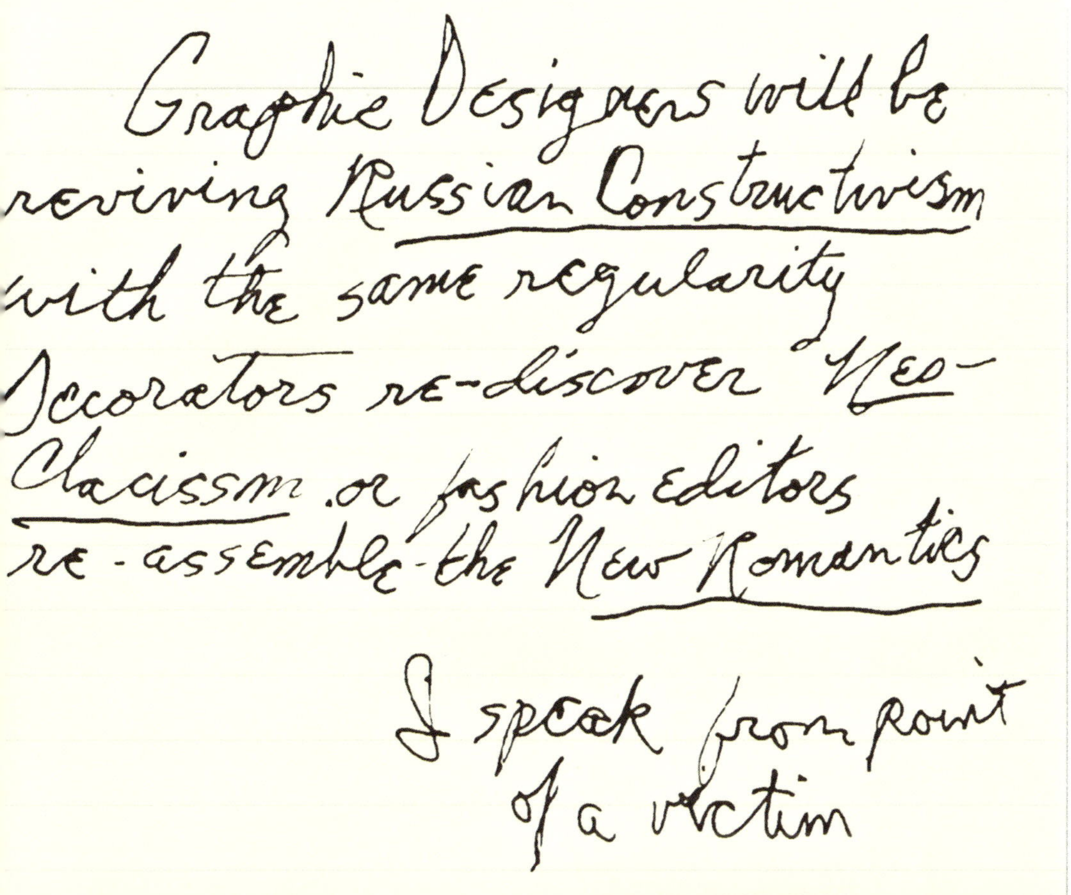
Graphic Designers will be reviving Russian Constructivism with the same regularity Decorators re-discover Neo-Clacissm or fashion editors re-assemble the New Romantics

I speak from point of a victim

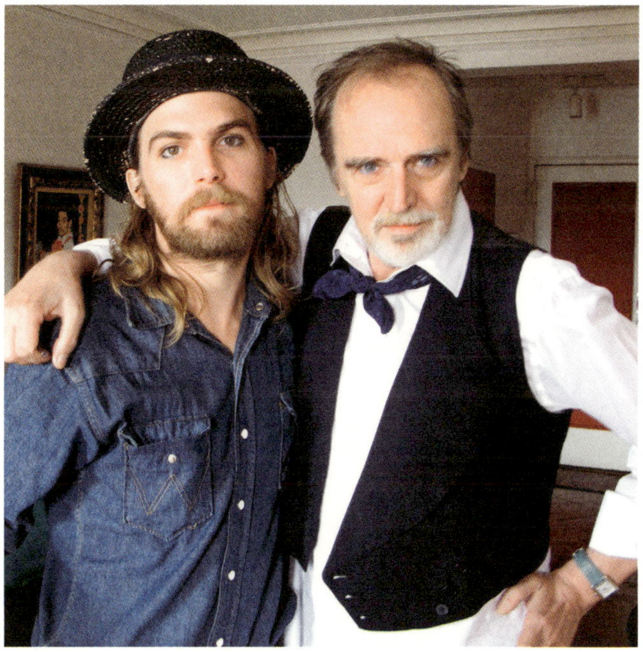

This page: Rene with the artist Dash Snow, 2009; *Opposite*: Rene with the poet, photographer and filmmaker Gerard Malanga in a photobooth, 1966.

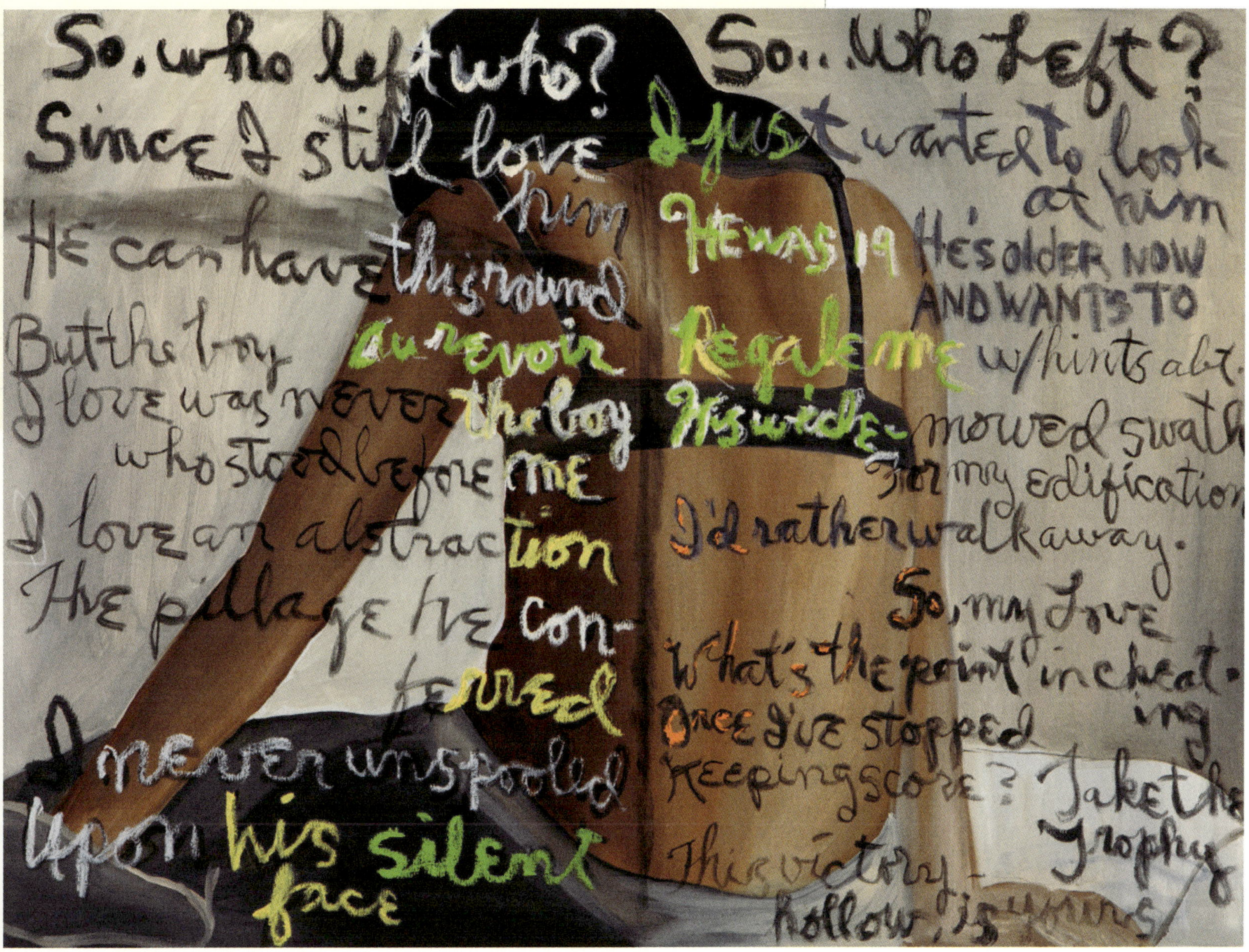

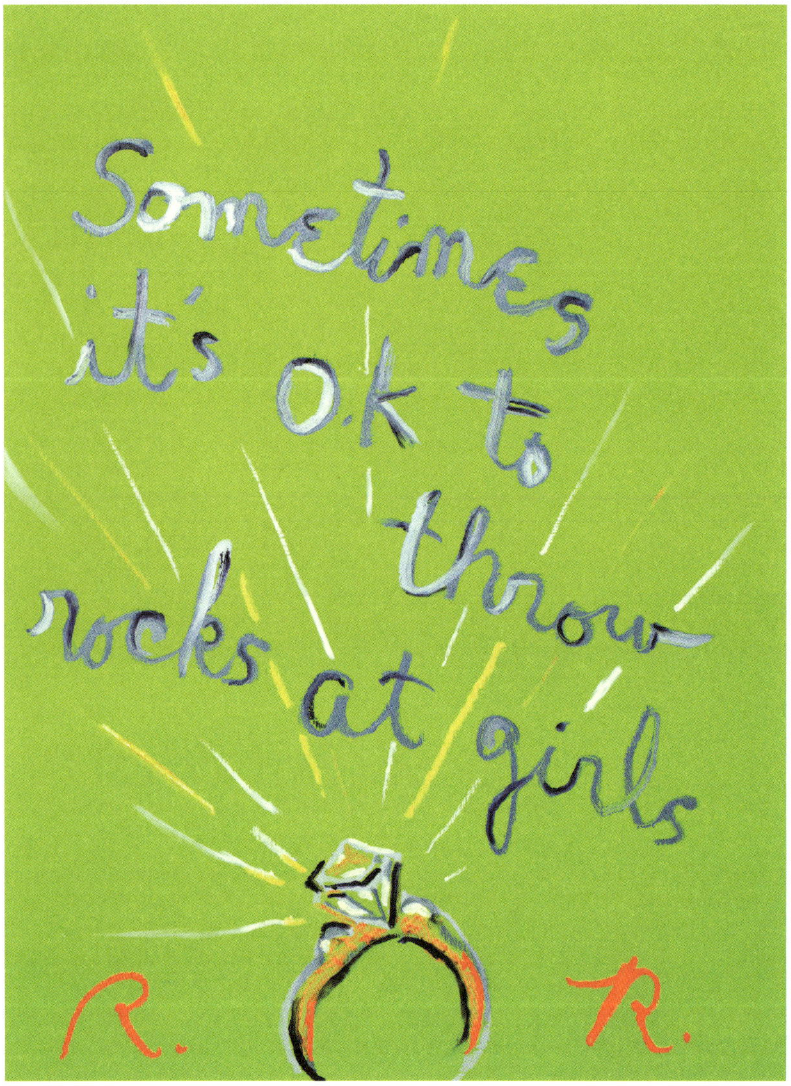

ALICE NOTLEY

I was black in Sweden
And Blonde in California
I was an American in Paris
And a Millionaire in a backward nation
I was everything and its opposite
Sex and the cigarette after sex
I was a punk in Jail
The only woman in a ten mile radius
I was the Oasis in their desert
The cream in their coffee
The highest jumper where they jump
And did they ever.

—Rene Ricard

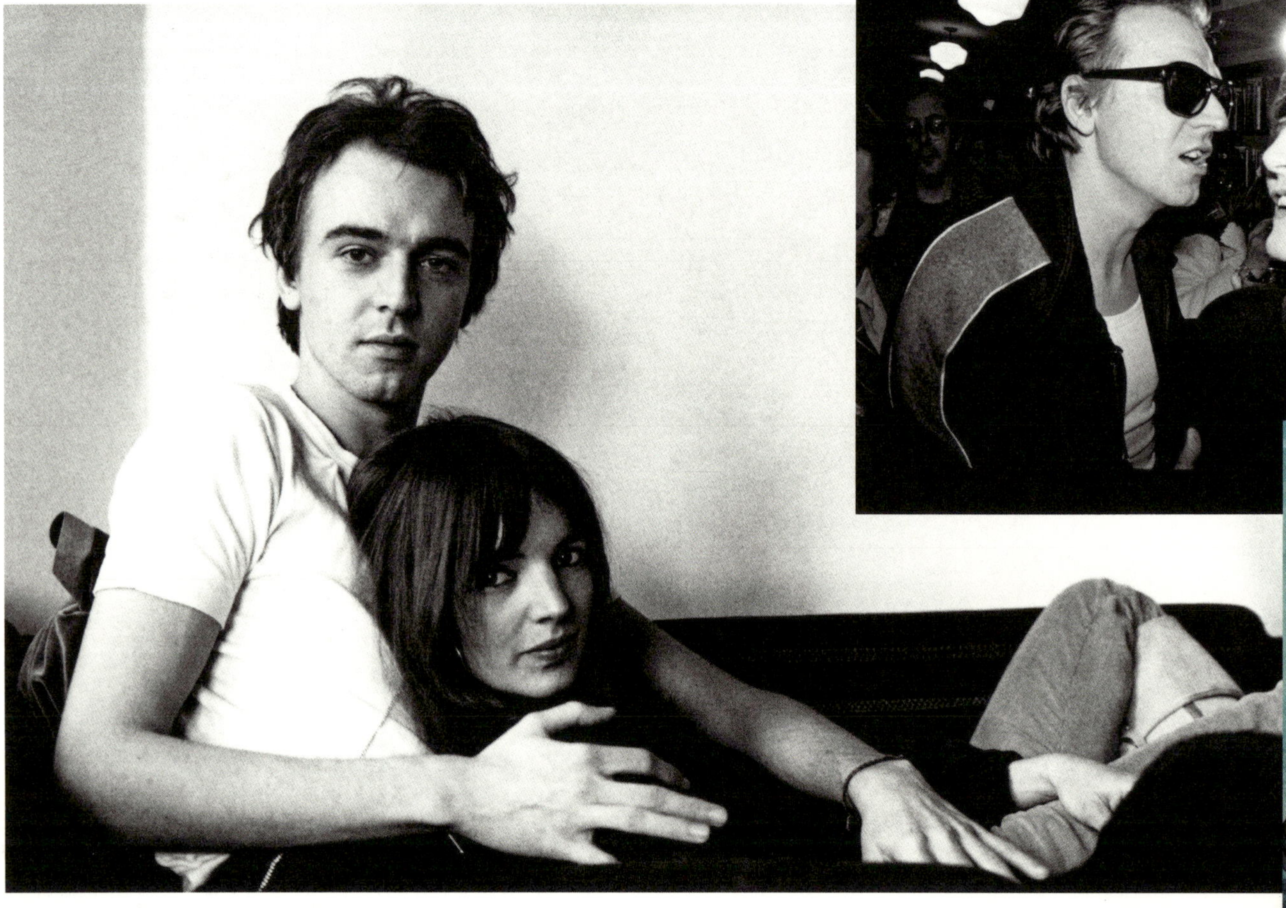

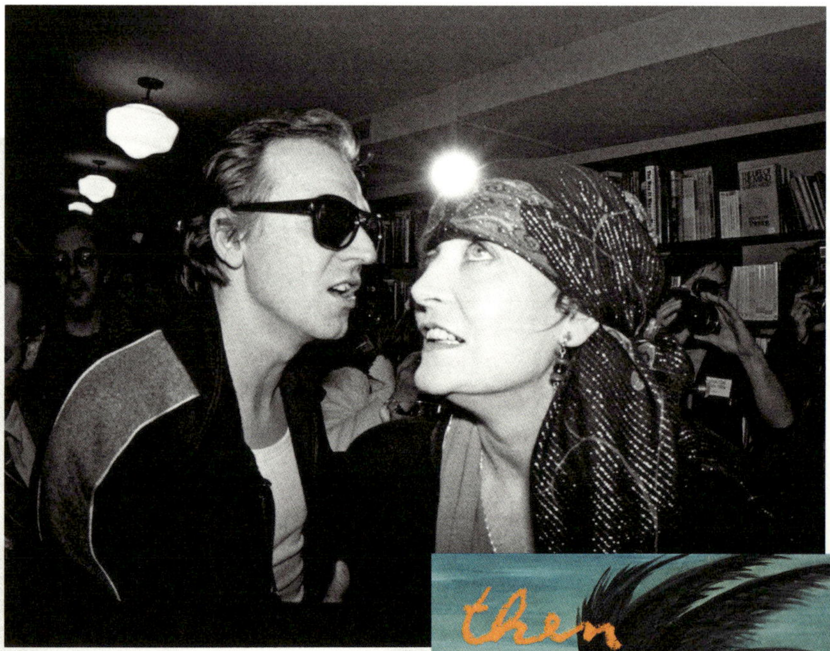

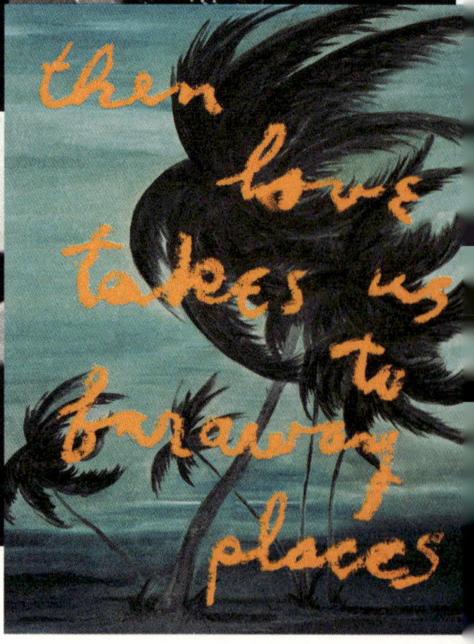

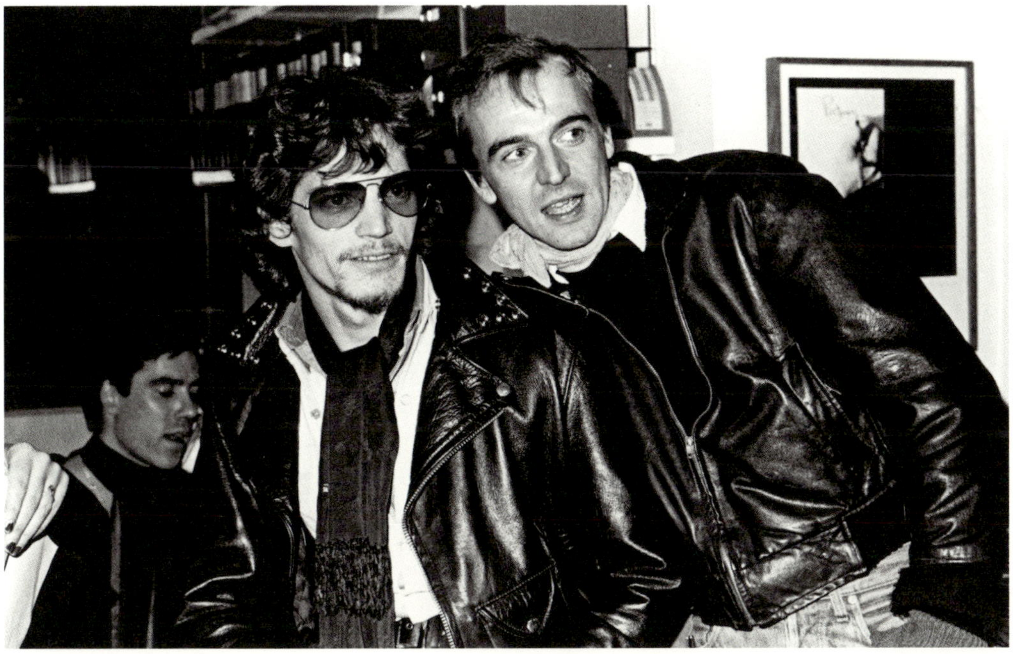

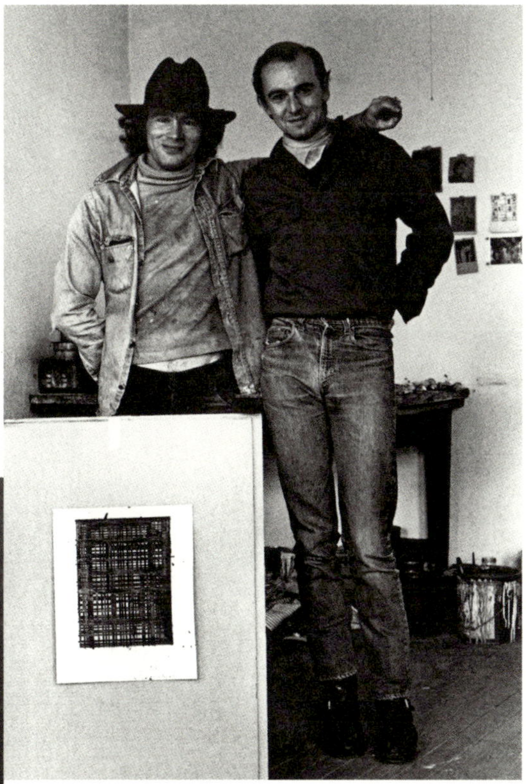

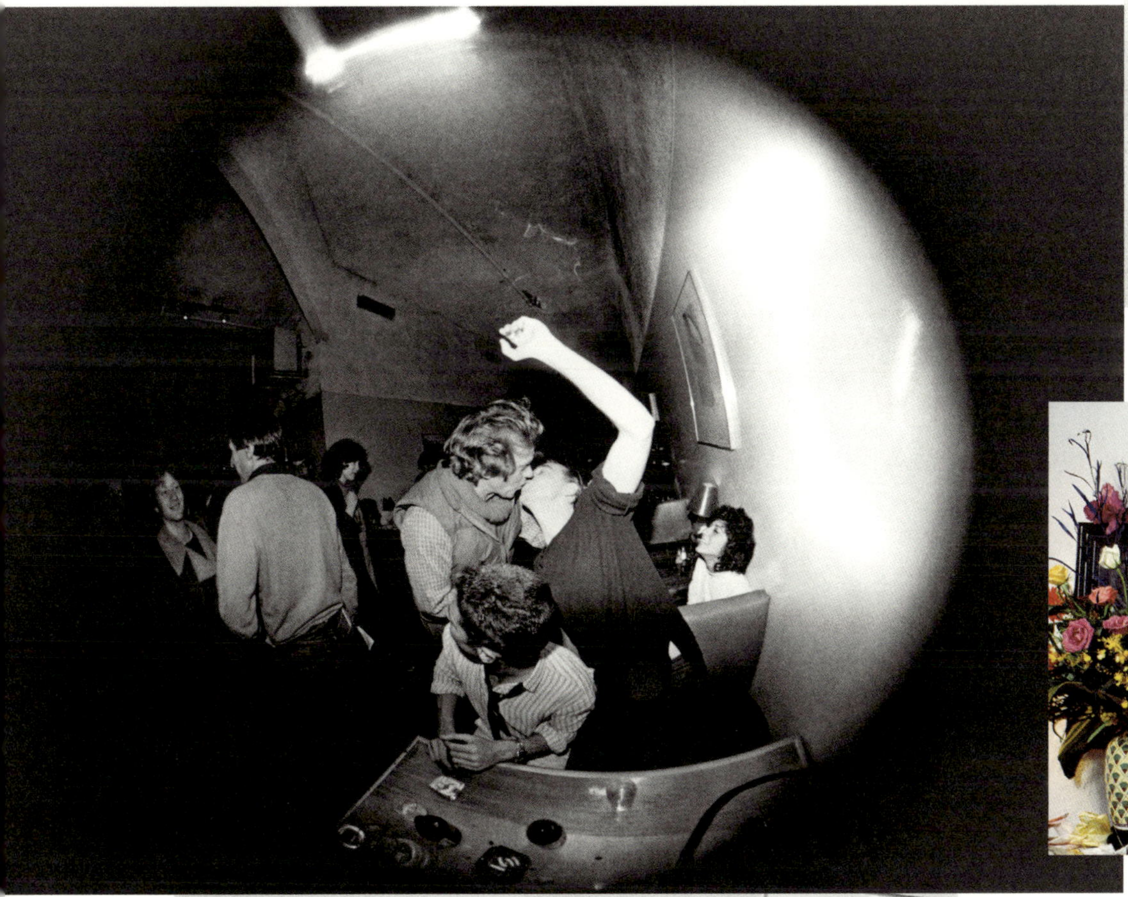

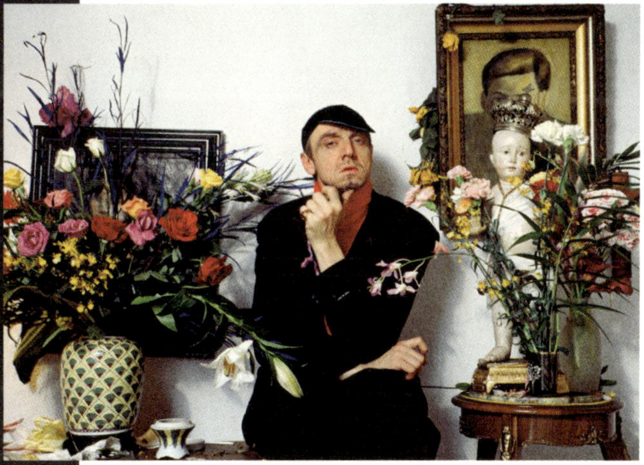

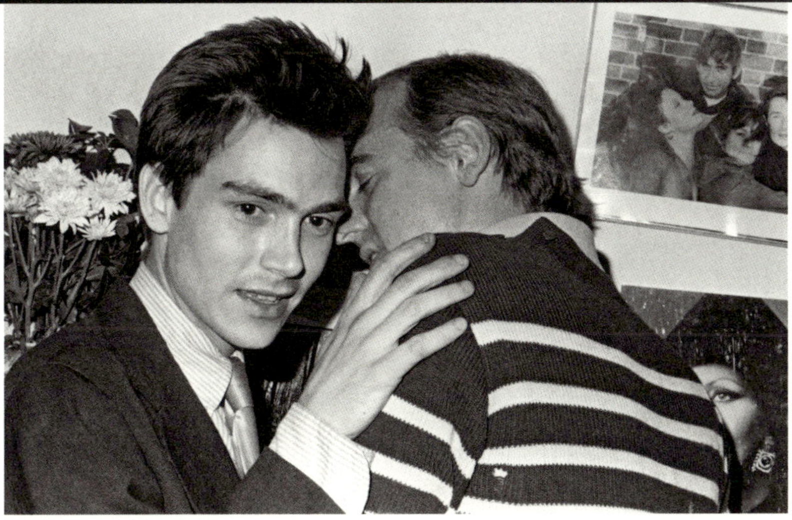

This page—clockwise from top left: Rene and Robert Mapplethorpe at Holly Solomon Gallery, 1977; Rene with Brice Marden in his studio, 1976; Rita Barros's portrait of Rene at the Chelsea Hotel, 1989; Rene and Duncan Hannah at Robert Mapplethorpe's gallery opening, 1977; Rene and Louie Waldon at Lower Manhattan Ocean Club, 1978; *Opposite page—left*: Rene and Delia Biddle in London, 1972; *Right*: Rene and Maxine de la Falaise at the Books & Company Party to celebrate William Burroughs, 1978. *All photographs on this spread by Gerard Malanga except where indicated*.

FRANCESCO CLEMENTE

ARTIST

Supplication

O poetry, visit this house often,
imbue my life with success,
leave me not alone,
give me a wife and home.

Take this curse off
of early death and drugs,
make me a friend among peers,
lend me love, and timeliness.

Return me to the men who teach
and above all, cure the
hurts of wanting the impossible
through this suspended vacuum.

—JOHN WIENERS

Rene Ricard admired the poetry of John Wieners, but he would have disagreed with every word of John's "Supplication." Rene did not pray for poetry to visit his house. Poetry was his house. And since poetry was his house, Rene was never truly homeless, even when, for a period, he slept on the F train.

Rene didn't consider drugs a curse; he made drugs into a friend. And Rene had the ability to befriend and to gently dismiss someone in the breath of a single sentence.

Rene didn't pray to be spared the hurts of wanting the impossible; he knew how fortunate he was to be wounded, because only if you are wounded will you search for healing, and for poetry.

Rilke said: "Beauty is but the beginning of terror." Rene chose to live in that suspended vacuum, where beauty comes to life in the face of darkness. And beauty did come to life, not only in Rene's poetry, but in his conversation about art and flowers and jewelry.

Thirty five years ago Rene climbed on a chair, at four in the morning, at One University Place, and sang. The aria was the one Tosca sings before her death, *Vissi d'Arte, Vissi d'Amore....* "I lived of art alone, I lived of love alone, I never hurt a living soul." These could have been his parting words when he slipped out of life, quickly and quietly, and almost unseen, as he always managed to do when he left a party. When Rene left a party, it was almost as if he had the ability to gather with him his wit, his brilliance, the very memory of himself like so many pieces of clothing and leave no trace.

Poets are liars, because language itself is a lie. This reluctance of Rene to leave any trace betrays his awareness of this, and the terror Rene inspired sometimes was not due to the fact that he told the truth, but to the fact that, through his sense of poetry, and through his sense of humor, and through his sense of the absurdity and cruelty of life, he knew how to expose the lie of the truth.

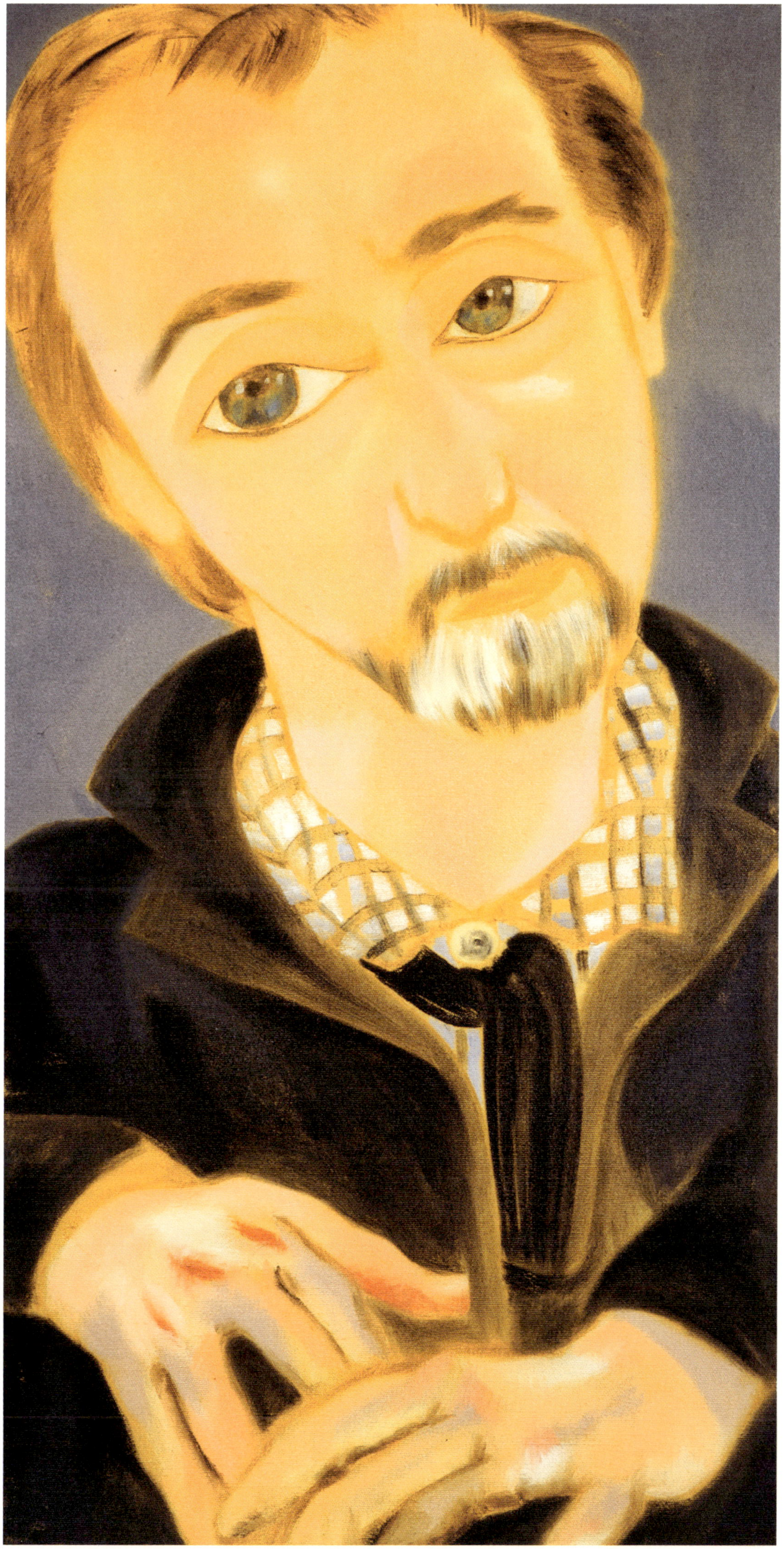

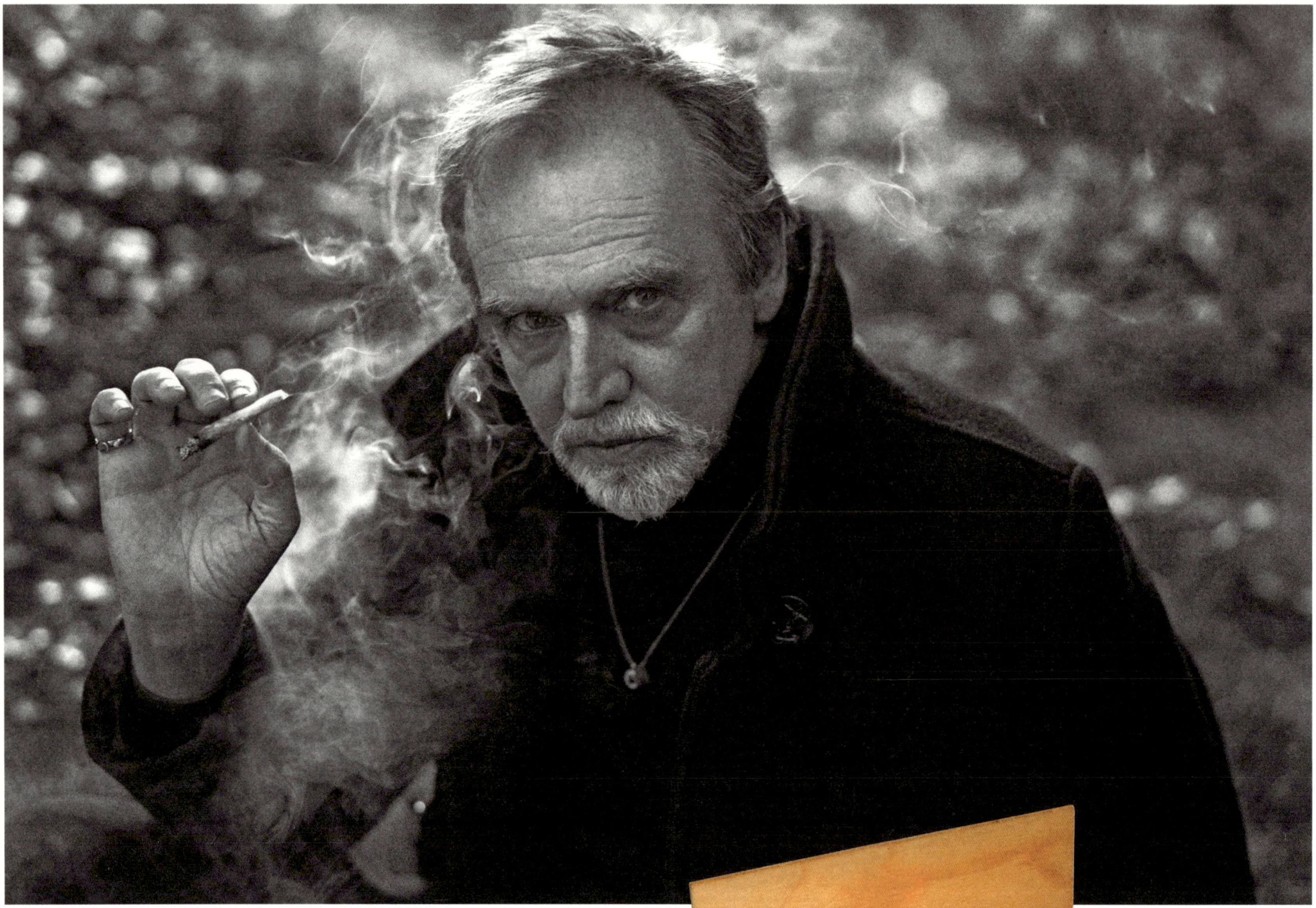

This page—top: Rene in New York City, 2008 by Matt Jones; *Bottom*: Two views of a rarely seen work from the collection of Francesco and Alba Clemente. The inscription on outside of the small wooden box reads, “This Box Contains the Heart of Rene Ricard.” When open, its contents are revealed: an spent lighter and a single boa feather.

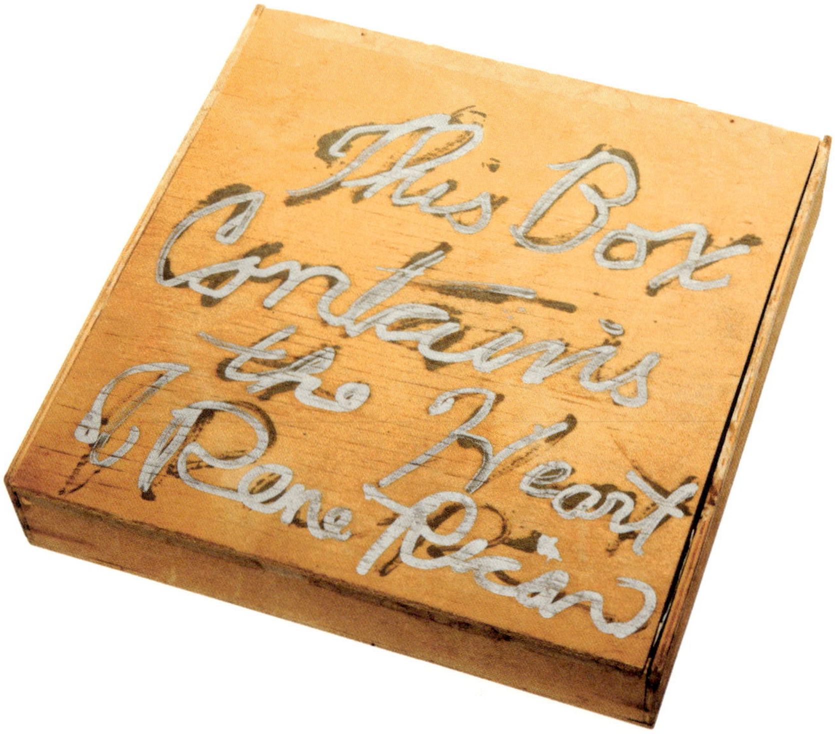

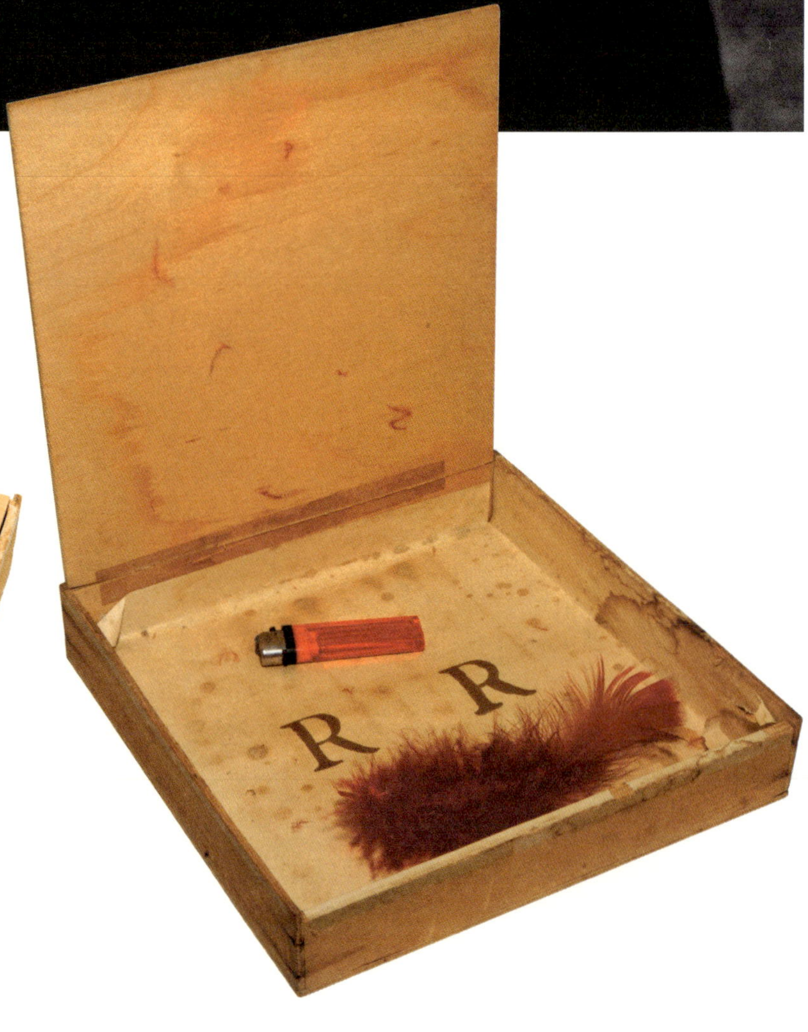

RAYMOND FOYE

PUBLISHER

Growing up in Lowell, Massachusetts, I often took the train to Boston to visit the Grolier in Harvard Square, a bookshop devoted entirely to poetry. A handful of cafés and publishing collectives promoted poetry readings, and the scene was dominated by the gothic shadow of John Wieners, already possessed by drugs and madness. In those days Rene was a devotee of John Wieners. He also used to buy heroin from John, which Wieners sold under the counter at Filene's department store where he briefly worked in the mid-1960s.

The poetry community in Boston was small, but Rene was already famous for his wild beauty, blinding intelligence, and fearsome wit. He dropped out of school after completing eighth grade and embarked on an independent study program that largely involved seducing Harvard boys. When I visited Provincetown for the first time, he was also famous there. Even when there were only 15 or 20 people who knew who he was, he was famous. There was an aura that surrounded him from the start.

I met Rene Ricard at Allen Ginsberg's apartment during one of my first visits to New York in 1978. I was 21; he was 31. I gave him my address and the next day he woke me up banging on my basement window that faced the street. He had a plan: He'd agreed to write an essay for Pace Gallery and wanted to collect the $10,000 advance. We went up to West 57th Street and waited for the gallery to open. A check was written with a letter to the bank manager and a few minutes later Rene had $10,000 in cash. We immediately went to the Russian Tea Room for blinis, caviar, and vodka. The bill was $900. From there we visited the Charivari boutique, where he bought $900 worth of Jean Paul Gaultier underwear. The day went on in this manner, and early the next morning I dropped him at the men's homeless shelter on the Bowery—penniless.

Several days later I ran into him and inquired about the underwear, which for some reason was the thing that really impressed me. It had been stolen. He'd washed it and placed it out to dry on a park bench and when he woke up it was gone.

I realized I had met one of the extraordinary figures I'd always read about: Villon, Poe, Nerval. Here was the classic poète maudit who lived by a crazy economy that involved throwing something away as soon as one possessed it. Yet throughout the day he repaid loans, treated his poorer friends lavishly, and in general lived like the ruined aristocrat that he was—an esoteric French count fallen on hard times.

It is difficult to describe the fierceness of the man from this distance.

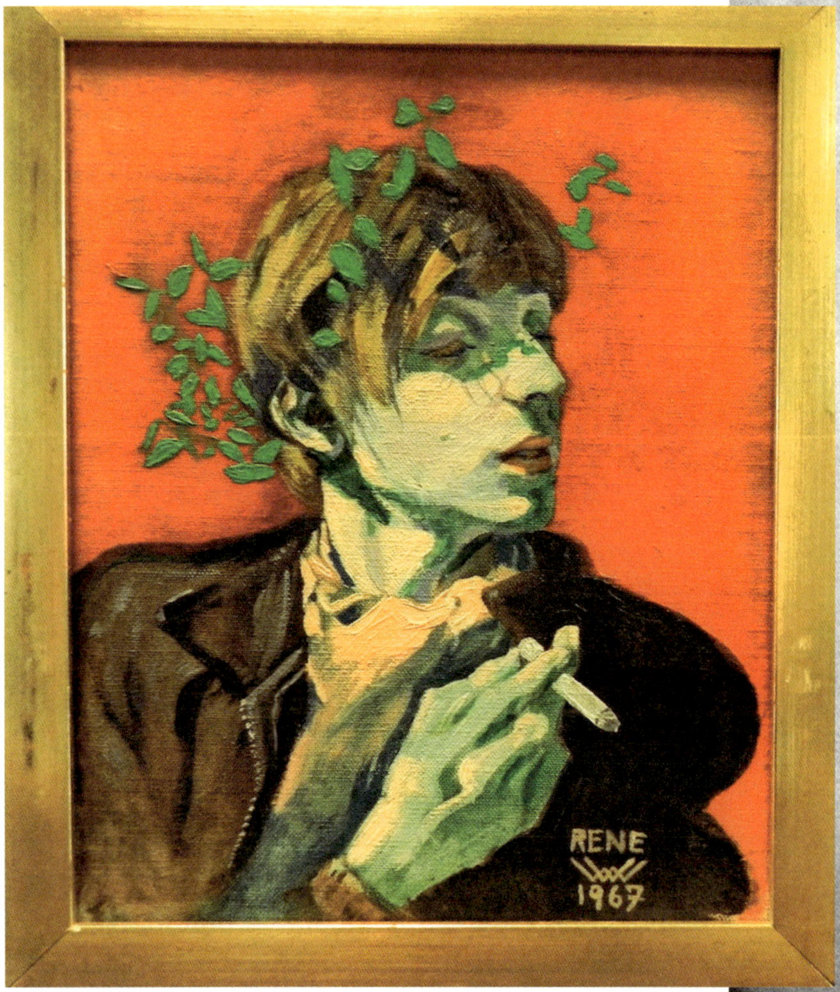

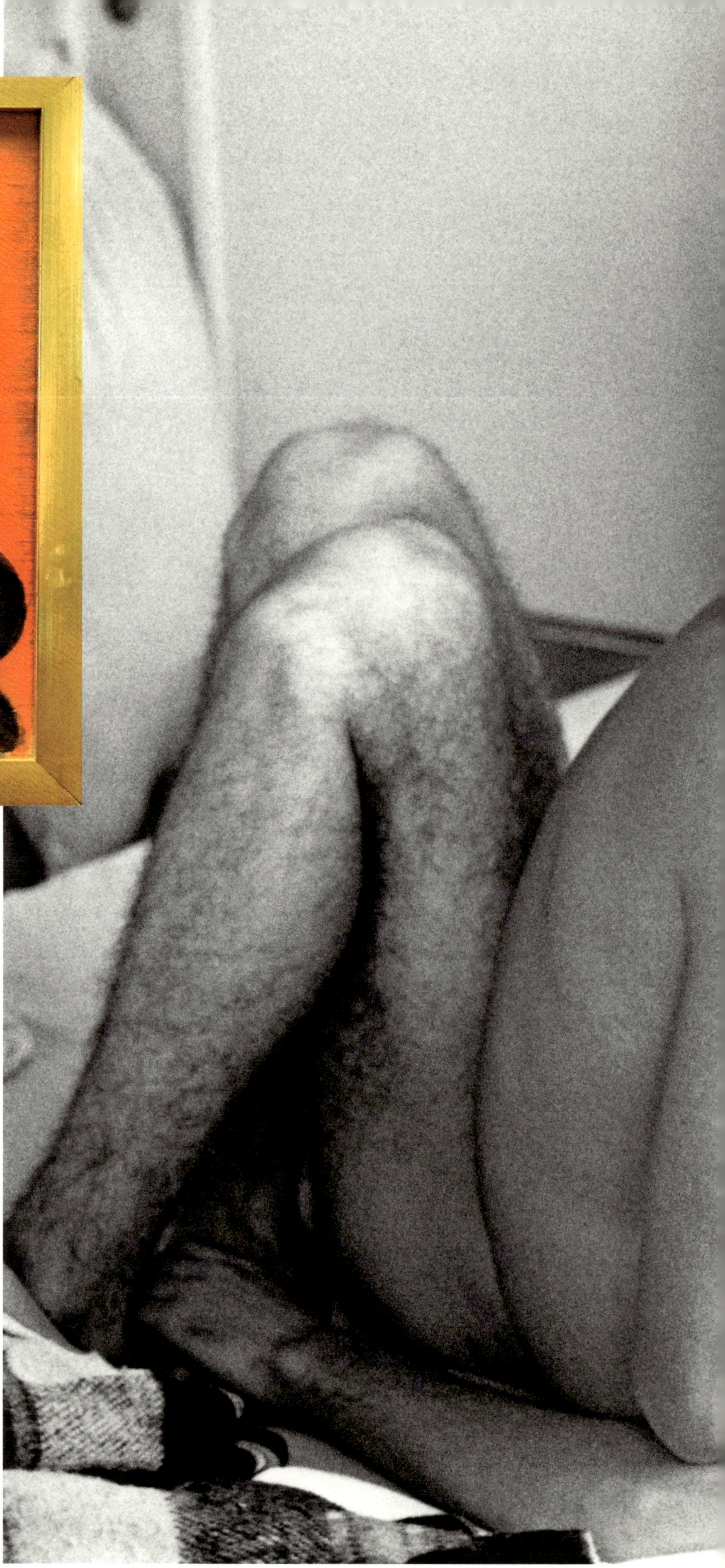

SUDDENLY all suspicion
        and doubt vanishes
Who cares where he is or who
he's with.   Let the winding
paths of youth take him
to those loud low places
the caves and their cavemen.
let those solemn energetic
amusements distract his
easily distracted mind.
A minute of him is a summer
in the resorts where he
offers me his youth in
all its glory one night a
                                week
after fighting the guerilla warfare
                                of fun.

—Rene Ricard

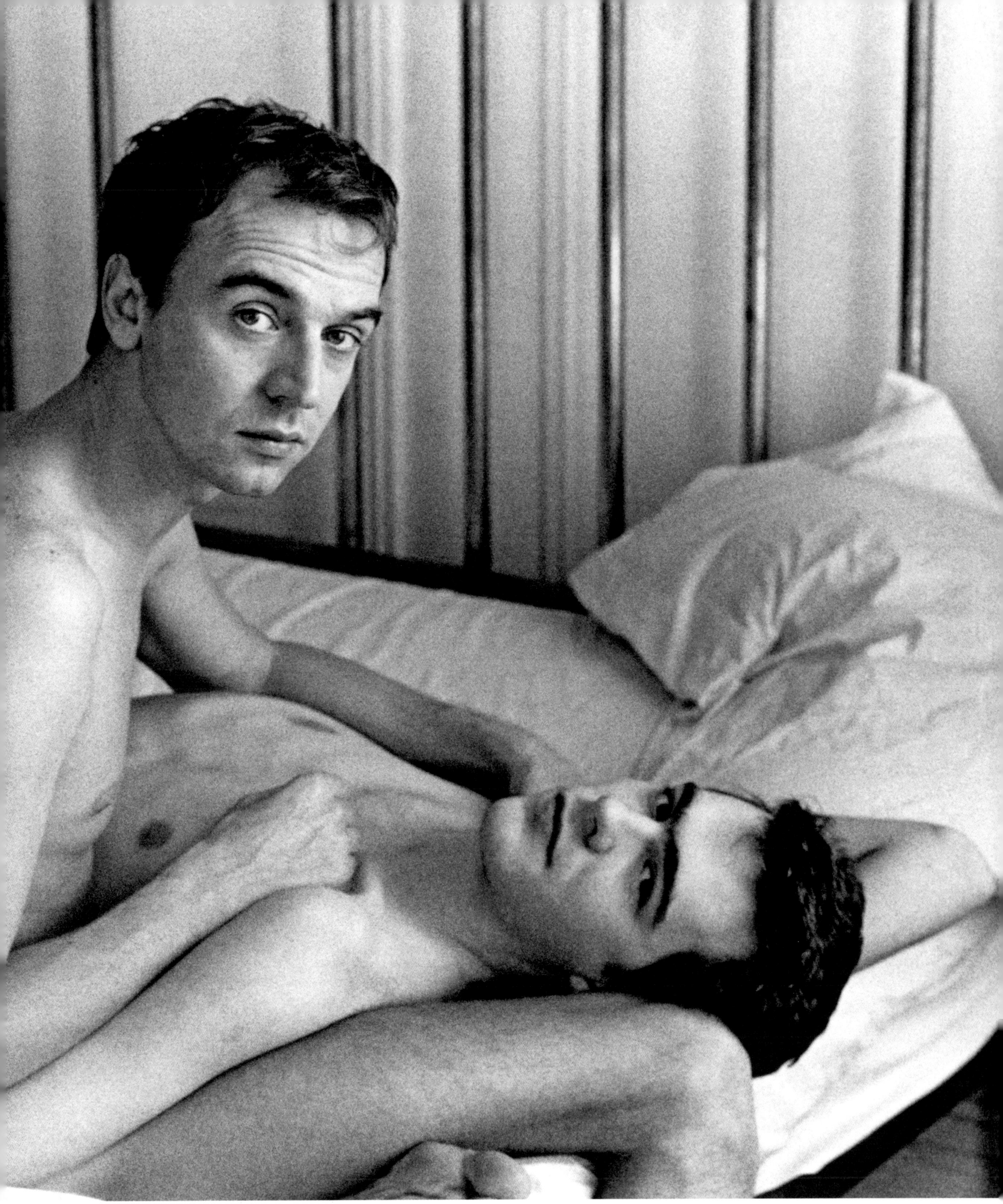

Rene with poet Steven Hall, New York City, 1976
Photo by Gerard Malagna

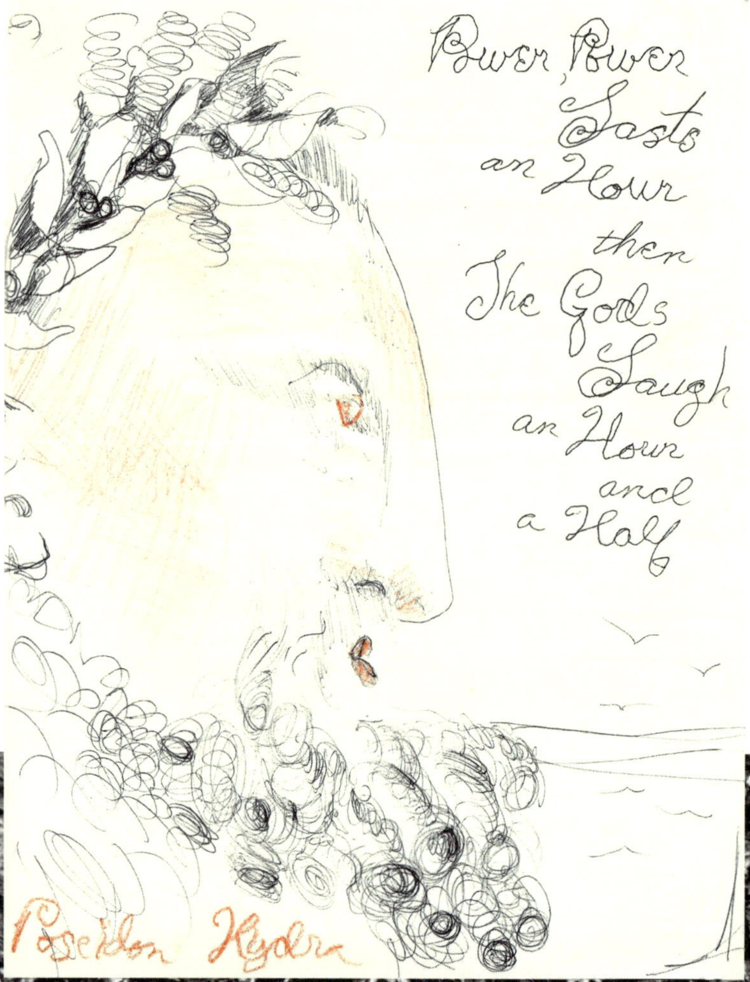

AND then I tried to put myself at
a distance from the subject, but the
distance was just another
angle on the same subject and
it was always the same subject, you.

—*Rene Ricard*

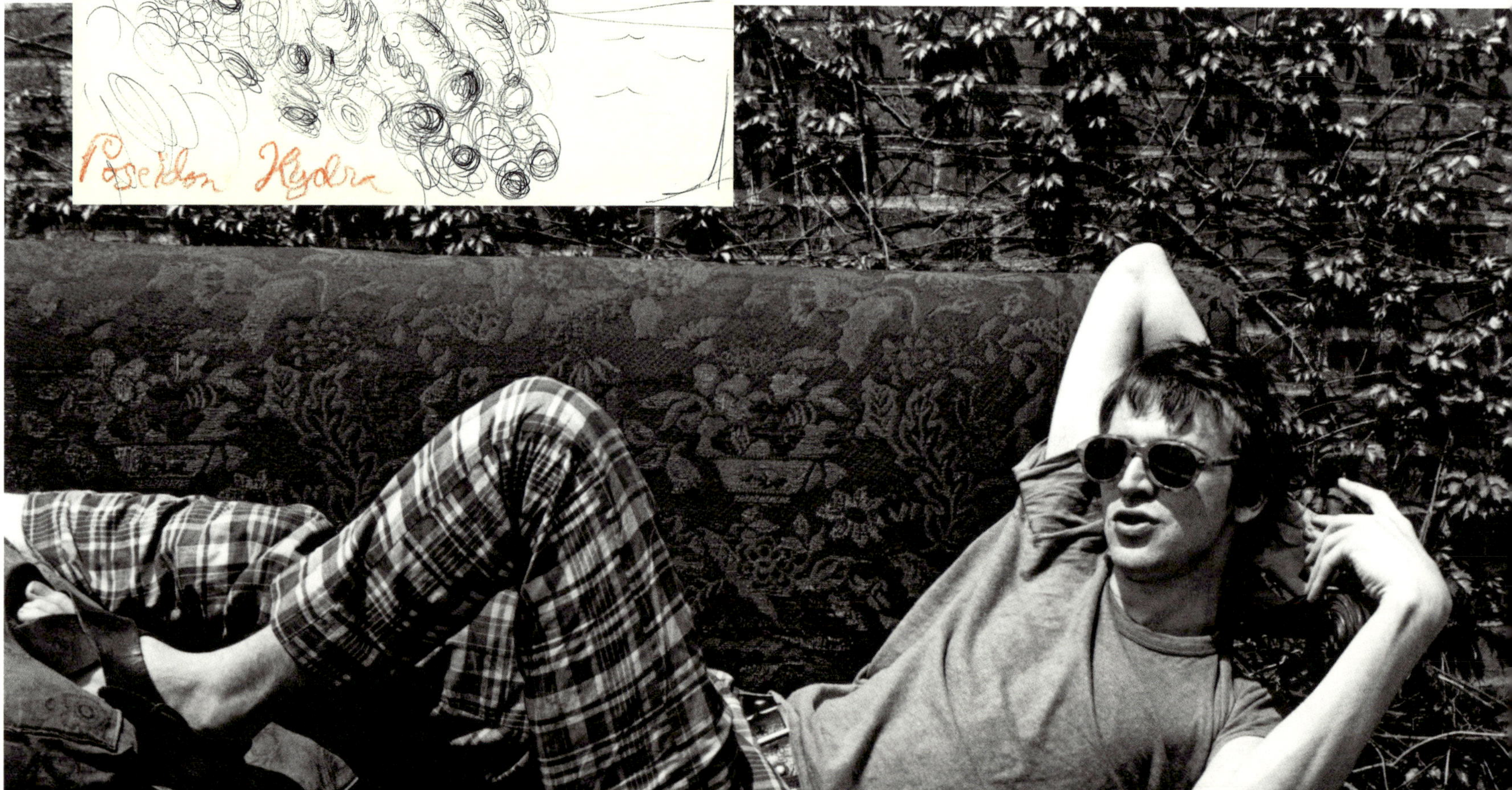

Rene in Boston, Massachusetts, 1970
Photo by Gerard Malagna

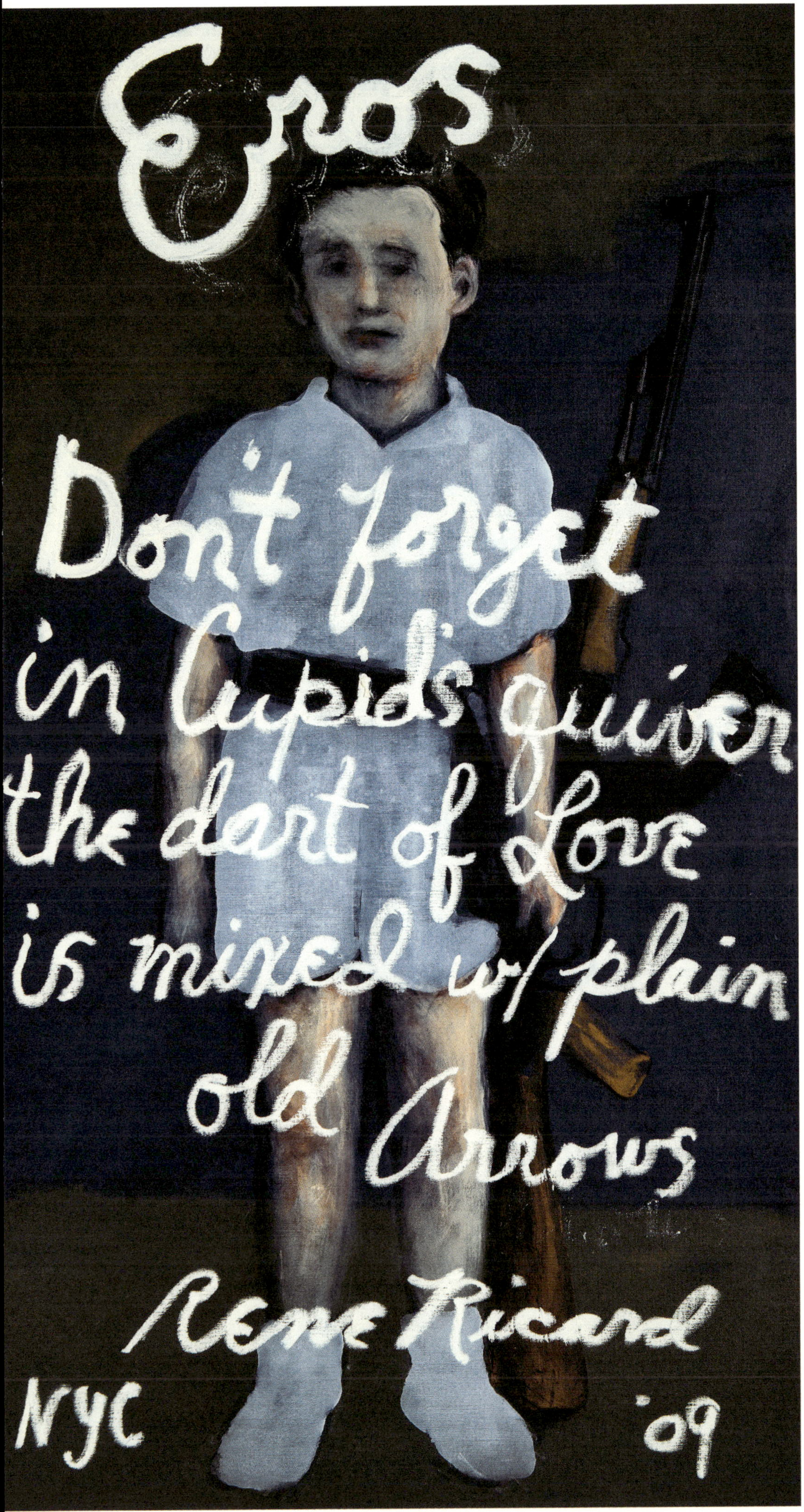

ALBA CLEMENTE

THEATRICAL DESIGNER

N.Y.C. 1980—One University Place
The first minute we met, he sang
beautifully the main aria from *La Tosca.*
I was amused!

Rome, September 1986
We walked around the Eternal City
from church to church.
He knew so much about art history!
I was impressed!

That same night I ended up swimming
in the Bernini Fountain in Piazza Navona.
He stepped in the water to help me out!
It was raining!

N.Y.C. 1990
He spent three days in our garden
on MacDougal Street
planting lilies of the valley with the help
of a scary looking, ex-convict friend!
I was worried!

N.Y.C. 2014— Beth Israel
He was at his best!
Enjoying the love
from so many friends at his bed side!
Wearing his favorite jewels
and curious to know
what was going on in town!

His grand exit from life
had the most elegant timing ever!
Like a great STAR..... as he was!!!!!!

Rene Ricard
(1946–2014)

PLATES

SLIPCASE, COVER, INTRODUCTION

[slipcase] *Diver looking into an undersea cave, near Sardinia, Italy c. 1976,* by Flip Schulke [cover] *Boys swimming in Weeki Wachee Springs, FL, 1969* by Flip Schulke [Front inside cover - p. 1] *US Virgin Islands* by Flip Schulke [p. 2-3] *US Virgin Islands* by Flip Schulke [p. 4-5] *"Christ of the Abyss," John Pennekamp Coral Reef State Park, near Key Largo, FL 1977* by Flip Schulke

WHAT AMERICA LOOKED LIKE TO ME

[p. 6] *Susan Trimble at the farmer's market, Harbor Springs, MI, 2014* by Poppy de Villeneuve [p. 8-9] *View of Lake Michigan from "The Tunnel of Trees," Route 119, Harbor Springs, MI, 2014* by Poppy de Villeneuve [p. 10-11] *Poppy and Daisy de Villeneuve at Windsor Castle, 1984* by Jan de Villeneuve [p. 12] *Poppy in her riding kit, West Sussex, 1986* by Jan de Villeneuve [p. 13, top] *The Griswold and Sedar kids on "Jimmy's Rock," Harbor Springs, MI, 1956* by photographer unknown [p. 13 center] *Flossie Griswold on the beach, Harbor Springs, MI, 1981* by photographer unknown [p. 13 bottom] *The Griswolds on the beach, Harbor Springs, MI, 1965* by photographer unknown [p. 14 top left] *Tom Griswold with his catch, Harbor Springs, MI, 1966* by photographer unknown [p. 14 bottom left] *Jan Griswold, Harbor Springs, MI, 1967* by photographer unknown [p. 14 right] *Poppy de Villeneuve, Alyssa Griswold, Daisy de Villeneuve and Sarah Griswold, Harbor Springs, MI, 1987* by photographer unknown [p. 15 top] *Daisy and Poppy De Villeneuve with Alyssa and Sarah Griswold, Harbor Springs, MI, 1986* by photographer unknown [p. 15 bottom] *Lake Michigan, 1972* by photographer unknown [p. 16-17] *Peter and Joe Crittenden at the farmer's market, Harbor Springs, MI, 2014* by Poppy de Villeneuve [p. 18] *Daisy and Poppy de Villeneuve aboard the QE2, Southampton, England, 1985* by Jan de Villeneuve [p. 19] *Drew Dunkel and Cade Trudeau, Harbor Springs, MI, 2014* by Poppy de Villeneuve [p. 20-21] *Tom Graham at home, Harbor Springs, MI, 2014* by Poppy de Villeneuve [p. 22] *Beatrice Lapham with her dog Mosey, Harbor Springs, MI, 2014* by Poppy de Villeneuve [p. 23] *Jordan Breighner and Katherine Brines, Harbor Springs, MI,* 2014 by Poppy de Villeneuve [p. 24] *Flossie Griswold, Jim Ward, Jim Griswold and Tom Griswold having a headstand contest, Harbor Springs, MI, 1965* by photographer unknown [p. 25] *Turkey's Café, Harbor Springs, MI, 2014* by Poppy de Villeneuve [p. 26] *Caylin Bonser and Rachel Howse at Howse's Fudge Shop, Harbor Springs, MI, 2014* by Poppy de Villeneuve [p. 27, top & bottom] *Howse's Fudge Shop, Harbor Springs, MI, 2014* by Poppy de Villeneuve

A DOG THAT ROARS LIKE A LION

[p. 28-29] *Aslan, Chesapeake, Virginia, 2014* by Bruce Weber [p. 30] *The Mastiff's Winner Trophies and Ribbons, Chesapeake, Virginia, 2014* by Bruce Weber [p. 31] *Susan Ochsenbein's Home, Chesapeake, Virginia, 2014* by Bruce Weber [p. 32] Mastiff Magazine-Collection of Susan Ochsenbein [p. 33] Mastiff Magazine. Collection of Susan Ochsenbein [p. 34] *Cuddles, Chesapeake, Virginia, 2014* by Bruce Weber [p. 35] *Susan and Eshita, Chesapeake, Virginia, 2014* by Bruce Weber [p. 36] *Susan and Teddy, Chesapeake, Virginia, 2014* by Bruce Weber [p. 38] *Aslan, Chesapeake, Virginia, 2014* by Bruce Weber [p. 39] *Trooper, Shinra and Eshita, Chesapeake, Virginia, 2014* by Bruce Weber [p. 40] *Zeus, Los Angeles, California, 2014* by Bruce Weber [p. 41] *Seer, Los Angeles, California, 2014* by Bruce Weber [p. 42 top left] *Tibetan Mastiff and its Handler, Lhasa, Tibet, China* by photographer unknown [p. 42 top right] *Gazer, Chesapeake, Virginia, 2014* by Bruce Weber [p. 42 center left] *Aslan, Chesapeake, Virginia, 2014* by Bruce Weber [p. 42 bottom left] *Tapestry in Susan Ochsenbein's Home, Chesapeake, Virginia, 2014* by Bruce Weber [p. 42 bottom right] *Janoo Winning Best Bred By Exhibitor and Award of Excellence at Eukanuba Dog Show 2011, Orlando, Florida, 2011* by Perry Phillips [p. 43 top] *Cairn with Prayer Flags atop a Hillock next to Tso Moriri, Tso Moriri, Ladakh, India* by Alex Treadway [p. 43 bottom left] *Huxley, Icebreaker King of the Pecos, London, England, 2014* by Bruce Weber [p. 43 bottom right] *Susan and Khumba Chesapeake, Virginia, 2014* by Bruce Weber [p. 44] *Shinra, Chesapeake, Virginia, 2014* by Bruce Weber [p. 45] *Jaan and Aslan, with the Puppy Eshita, Chesapeake, Virginia, 2014* by Bruce Weber [p. 46-47] *Mastiff Carving in Susan Ochsenbein's Home, Chesapeake, Virginia, 2014* by Bruce Weber

NO SNOWFLAKE EVER FALLS IN THE WRONG PLACE

[p. 48] *Ekapuwe and Peter Matthiessen, New Guinea, 1961* by Jan Broekhuijse [p. 50 top] *Women running around Peter Matthiessen, New Guinea, 1961* by Jan Broekhuijse [p. 50 bottom] *Peter Matthiessen, Ekali, Wali, Robert Gardner, and Karl Heider waiting to film during the Harvard-Peabody expedition, New Guinea, 1961* by Jan Broekhuijse [p. 51 top left] *Peter Matthiessen on Bathurst Inlet in Canada's Nunavut Territory, 1980* by photographer unknown [p. 51 top right] *Peter Matthiessen and Hans Teensma in Oglala, SD, 1979* by Hans Teensma [p. 51 bottom] *Peter Matthiessen in the Arctic Wildlife Refuge, 2002* by Subhankar Banerjee [p. 53 top left] *Peter Matthiessen in Sagaponack, NY, c. 1960* by photographer unknown [p. 53 top right] *Peter Matthiessen in Sagaponack, NY, 1995* by Jill Krementz [p. 53 bottom] *George Plimpton & Peter Matthiessen in Sagaponack, NY, 1973* by Jill Krementz [p. 54] *The Great Auk, short-winged member of the Alcidae Family, c.1900* by artist unknown [p. 57] *Porters, sherpas and Peter Matthiessen in Ringmo, Nepal, 1973* by George Schaller [p. 58-59] *Peter Matthiessen with the sherpas Tukhten, Jang-bu, Gyaltsen, and Dawa in Saldang Pass, Nepal, 1973* by George Schaller [p. 60-61] *Peter Matthiessen bathing in the Cheyenne River near Edgemont, SD, 1979* by Hans Teensma

DAYS IN OJAI

[p. 62-63] *Boys on horses, 1930* Thacher School Archive/Photographer unknown [p. 64] *Lacrosse game, 1967* Thacher School Archive/Photographer unknown [p. 65] *Poster detail from Thacher Archive, Ojai, CA, 2014* by John Scott [p. 66 top] *Sherman Thacher with his horse, c. 1890* Thacher School Archive/Photographer unknown [p. 66 center] *Main Building, 1895* Thacher School Archive/Photographer unknown [p. 66 bottom] *Gymkhana, 1920* Thacher School Archive/Photographer unknown [p. 67] *Thacher Gymkhana Parade, Ojai, CA, 2014* by Lisa Eisner [p. 68-69] *Thacher Class of 1935* Thacher School Archive/ Photographer unknown [p. 70 top] *Student dorm, 1902* Thacher School Archive/ Photographer unknown [p. 70 bottom] *Becky Cornwell in her dorm, Ojai, CA, 2010* by Lisa Eisner [p. 71] *Thanksgiving dinner, 1952* Thacher School Archive/Photographer unknown [p. 72-73] *Sack race on horseback, 1920* Thacher School Archive/Photographer unknown [p. 74-75] *Katherine Halsey, Thacher Horse Program Instructor, Ojai, CA, 2014* by John Scott [p. 76] *Jordan Perry practicing for Thacher Gymkhana, Ojai, CA, 2014* by Lisa Eisner [p. 77] *Maximilian Damon practicing for Thacher Gymkhana, Ojai, CA, 2014* by Lisa Eisner [p. 78 top] *Isabelle Doubleday at Thacher Gymkhana, Ojai, CA, 2014* by Lisa Eisner [p. 78 bottom] *Tobi Oyinlola & Jackson Carroll during riding practice, Ojai, CA, 2014* by Lisa Eisner [p. 79 top left] *Horse Camp Director Rene Duykaerts, Ojai, CA, 2014* by John Scott [p. 79 top right] *Wade Warren grooming his horse, Ojai, CA, 2010* by Lisa Eisner [p. 79 bottom] *Competitors taking a break during Thacher Gymkhana, Ojai, CA, 2010* by Lisa Eisner [p. 80-81] *Peter Ammon and friends during Thacher Gymkhana, Ojai, CA, 2014* by Lisa Eisner [p. 82 top left] *Thacher Art Studio, 1967* Thacher School Archive/Photographer unknown p. 82 top right] *Musical Intructor Michael Ehrardt teaching a classical bass lesson, c. 1960* Thacher School Archive/ Photographer unknown [p. 82 bottom right] *Jack Huyler with students, c. 1950s* Thacher School Archive/Photographer unknown [p. 82 bottom left] *Avery Hellman in her dowm room, 2010* by Lisa Eisner [p. 82 center left] *Students playing chess in the parlor, 1893* Thacher School Archive/Photographer unknown[p. 83] *Momo Lewis, Ojai, CA, 2014* by John Scott [p. 84] *Alex's dorm, Ojai, CA, 2010* by Lisa Eisner [p. 85] *Thacher horse program offices, Ojai, CA, 2014* by Lisa Eisner [p. 86 top] *Thacher Roughhouse, 1906* Thacher School Archive/ Photographer unknown [p. 86 bottom right] *Thacher Outdoor Program Director Brian Pidduck with students, Ojai, CA, 2014* by Lisa Eisner [p. 86 bottom right] *Soccer game, 1967* Thacher School Archive/Photographer unknown [p. 87 top left] *Basketball game, 1970s* Thacher School Archive/Photographer unknown [p. 87 top right] *New Roughhouse construction, 1970* Thacher School Archive/Photographer unknown; [p. 87 center, right] *Riders visiting soccer practice, Ojai, CA, 2010* by Lisa Eisner [p. 87 bottom right] *Swimming in the reservoir* Thacher School Archive/Photographer unknown [p. 87 bottom left] *Girl's basketball game, 1985* Thacher School Archive/Photographer unknown [p. 87 center left] *Boy's lacrosse team victory, 1989* Thacher School Archive/Photographer unknown [p. 88-89] *Hayden Howard on a Thacher camping trip to Montaña de Oro State Park, 2014* by Dana Vancisin [p. 90-91] *Thacher yearbooks, Ojai, CA, 2014* by John Scott

OUR FRIEND IN ROME

[p. 92-93] *The Guild Theater, Squirrel Hill, Pittsburgh, PA, c. 1960s* by photographer unknown [p. 95] *Monica Vitti and Michelangelo Antonioni in Via Veneto, Rome* by Paolo di Paolo [p. 96-97] *Pier Paolo Pasolini at the "Monte dei Cocci" in Rome* by Paolo di Paolo [p. 98] *From the "Impossible Encounters" series, Vittorio De Sica and Monica Vitti* by Paolo di Paolo [p. 100] *Via Veneto, Rome* by Paolo di Paolo [p. 101] *Luchino Visconti during a play rehearsal* by Paolo di Paolo [p. 102-103] *Anna Magnani at her oceanside villa in San Felice Circeo* by Paolo di Paolo [p. 104-105] At the Caroglio resort, Naples by Paolo di Paolo [p. 106] *Marcello Mastroianni on the set of "Hello Rudy,"* by Paolo di Paolo [p. 107] *On the Tiber, Rome* by Paolo di Paolo [p. 108] *Orgosolo, Sardinia* by Paolo di Paolo [p. 109] *Giulietta Masina and Federico Fellini* by Paolo di Paolo [p. 110-111] *Simone Signoret and Yves Montand on their honeymoon, Rome* by Paolo di Paolo [p. 112-113] *Sophia Loren on the set of "Pane; Amore, e..."* by Paolo di Paolo [p. 114] *Pier Paolo Pasolini at the "Monte dei Cocci" in Rome* by Paolo di Paolo [p. 115] *Pier Paolo Pasolini* by Paolo di Paolo [p. 117-117] *Marriage in Abruzzo* by Paolo di Paolo

IT WAS A LOVE STORY I GUESS YOU COULD SAY

[p. 118-119] *Kris Ruhs's Studio, Milan, Italy, 2011* by Bruce Weber [p. 121] *Kris Ruhs, London, England, 2009* by Bruce Weber [p. 122] *Kris Ruhs and Carla Sozzani, London, England, 2009* by Bruce Weber [p. 124] *Kris Ruhs's Jewelry, London, England, 2009* by Bruce Weber [p. 125] *Environmental Installation, 2007* by Kris Ruhs [p. 126] *Raku Vases, 2001* by Kris Ruhs [p. 127] *Kris Ruhs and Carla Sozzani, London, England, 2009* by Bruce Weber [p. 128] *Kris Ruhs's Studio, Milan, Italy, 2011* by Bruce Weber [p. 130 top] *Kris Ruhs in his Studio, Milan, Italy, 2011* by Bruce Weber [p. 130 bottom] *Carla Sozzani in Kris Ruhs's Jewelry, London, England, 2009* by Bruce Weber [p. 131] *Kris Ruhs in his Studio, Milan, Italy, 2011* by Bruce Weber [p. 133 top left] *Untitled, 2000* (Oil on paper) by Kris Ruhs [p. 133 top right] *Untitled, 2000* (Oil on paper) by Kris Ruhs [p. 133 middle left] *Untitled, 2000* (Oil on paper by Kris Ruhs [p. 133 middle right] *Untitled, 2000* (Oil on paper) by Kris Ruhs [p. 133 bottom left] *Untitled, 2000* (Oil on paper) by Kris Ruhs [p. 133 bottom right] *Untitled, 2000* (Oil on paper) by Kris Ruhs [p. 134] *Falling Stars, 2013* (Installation) by Kris Ruhs [p. 135] *Carla Sozzani in Kris Ruhs's Jewelry, London, England, 2009* by Bruce Weber [p. 136-137] *Untitled, 2002* (Oil on Paper) by Kris Ruhs

BOYS IN BLUE

[p. 138] *Billy and Kolin Fischer* by photographer unknown [p. 140 top left] *John Laverty, Glasgow, 1910* by photographer unknown [p. 140 top center] *William Ott, 1931* by photographer unknown [p. 140 top right] *Frederick Fischer Jr.,* 1946 by photographer unknown [p. 140 center right] *Billy and Ronald Fischer at Billy's graduation from the Police Academy, 1985* by photographer unknown [p. 140 bottom right] *Ronald Fischer, 1954* by photographer unknown [p. 140 bottom left] *Patrice Ott* by photographer unknown [p. 140 center left] *Thomas McGrath, 1913* by photographer unknown [p. 140 center] *William Ott, 1962* by photographer unknown [p. 142] *Erik and Billy Fischer with Lola, Holbrook, NY, 2014* by Bruce Weber [p. 143 top left] *Billy and Erik Fischer in a newspaper clipping from the* New York Post by photographer unknown [p. 143 top right] *Billy Fischer's Triumph Touring Bike, Holbrook, NY* by Bruce Weber [p. 143 bottom right] *Kolin Fischer* by photographer unknown [p. 143 bottom, left] *Billy, Kolin, Ronald, and William Fischer* by photographer unknown [p. 144] New York Post cover, May 9th, 2001 [p. 145] Daily News cover, August 13, 2000 [p. 146] *Erik and Billy Fischer, Holbrook, NY 2014* by Bruce Weber [p. 147] *Ronald Fischer receiving the Lifesaving Award, 1965* by photographer unknown [p. 148] *ECU in action, 2004* by photographer unknown [p. 149] *Billy Fischer's tattoo, Holbrook, NY, 2014* by Bruce Weber [p. 150-151] *Erik and Billy Fischer with John Botte's book* Aftermath, *Holbrook, NY, 2014* by Bruce Weber [p. 152] *World Trade Center site* by photographer unknown [p. 153] *Billy Fischer with his medications, Holbrook, NY 2014* by Bruce Weber [p. 154] *Cynthia Fischer, Holbrook, NY 2014* by Bruce Weber [p. 156] *Billy Fischer's Medal of Honor, Holbrook, NY, 2014* by Bruce Weber [p. 157] *Billy Fischer at Eastern Athletic Club, Blue Point, NY, 2014* by Bruce Weber [p. 158] *John Giglia, Erik Fischer, Billy Fischer and Mark Mulitz at the Holbrook Diner, Holbrook, NY, 2014* by Bruce Weber [p. 160-161] *Billy Fischer telling stories at the Holbrook Diner, Holbrook, NY, 2014* by Bruce Weber [p. 162] *John Giglia and Billy Fischer on their motorcycles, Holbrook, NY, 2014* by Bruce Weber [p. 163] *Billy Fischer, Holbrook, NY, 2014* by Bruce Weber

DARIA HALPRIN AND MARK FRECHETTE

[p. 164-165] *Mark Frechette and Daria Halprin during the filming of Michelangelo Antonioni's* Zabriskie Point, *1968* by Bruce Davidson [p. 166-167] *Mark Frechette and Daria Halprin during the filming of Michelangelo Antonioni's* Zabriskie Point, *1968* by Bruce Davidson [p. 168] *Mark Frechette and Daria Halprin during the filming of Michelangelo Antonioni's* Zabriskie Point, *1968* by Bruce Davidson [p. 169] *Filming of Michelangelo Antonioni's* Zabriskie Point, *1968* by Bruce Davidson [p. 170-171] *Mark Frechette and Daria Halprin during the filming of Michelangelo Antonioni's* Zabriskie Point, *1968* by Bruce Davidson [p. 172-173] *Mark Frechette and Daria Halprin during the filming of Michelangelo Antonioni's* Zabriskie Point, *1968* by Bruce Davidson

RENE RICARD

[p. 176] *Rene Ricard in New Bedford, Massachusetts, 1970* by Gerard Malanga [p. 178] Excerpt from the notebooks of Rene Ricard [p. 179] *Rene Ricard visiting from across the hall, my kitchen, July 29, 1986* by Allen Ginsberg [p. 180] *Untitled: "Cascais," 2011* (Oil, chalk on canvas) by Rene Ricard [p. 182] *Rene Ricard and Gerard Malanga in a photobooth, 1966* by Gerard Malanga [p. 183 top left] Excerpt from the notebooks of Rene Ricard [p. 183 top, right] *Rene Ricard and Dash Snow at the Chelsea Hotel, New York City, 2009* by Rita Barros [p. 183 bottom] *Untitled* by Rene Ricard [p. 184 top right] *Untitled "Sometimes it's ok..." 2012* (oil on linen) by Rene Ricard [p. 184 bottom left] *Rene Ricard and Delia Biddle in London, 1972* by Gerard Malanga [p. 184 center right] *Rene Ricard with Maxine de la Falaise at the Books & Co. party to celebrate William, New York City, 1978* by Gerard Malanga [p. 184 bottom right] *Then Love Takes Us, 2010* (archival print, ed. 100) by Rene Ricard [p. 185 top left] *Rene Ricard and Robert Mapplethorpe at Holly Solomon Gallery, New York City, 1977* by Gerard Malanga [p. 185 top right] *Rene Ricard with Brice Marden in his studio, New York City, 1976* by Gerard Malanga [p. 185 center left] *Rene Ricard and Louie Waldon at Lower Manhattan Ocean Club, New York City, 1978* by Gerard Malanga [p. 185 center right] *Rene Ricard at the Chelsea Hotel, New York City, 1989* by Rita Barros [p. 185 bottom] *Rene Ricard and Duncan Hannah at Robert Mapplethorpe's gallery opening, New York City, 1977* by Gerard Malanga [p. 187] *Rene Ricard, 2006* (oil on canvas) by Francesco Clemente [p. 188 top] *Rene Ricard, New York City, 2008* by Matt Jones [p. 188 bottom] *Untitled (Sculpture)* by Rene Ricard; Photograph by Chris Domurat [p. 190] *Self-Portrait, 1967* (oil on canvas) by Rene Ricard [p. 191] *Rene Ricard with poet Steven Hall, New York City, 1976* by Gerard Malanga [p. 192 top] Excerpt from the notebooks of Rene Ricard [p. 192 bottom] *Rene Ricard, Boston, Massachusetts, 1970* by Gerard Malanga [p. 193] *Eros, 2008-2009* (acrylic, oil, charcoal, conte crayon) by Rene Ricard

ENDPAPERS

[p. 196-197] *James Dean just before his fatal car crash, 1955* by photographer unknown [p. 199] *Billie Holiday, Golden Beach, FL, 2014* by Bruce Weber [back inside cover] *Ticonderoga, #100, Miami-Nassau Race, 1954* by Stanley Rosenfeld

CREDITS

[Slipcase, cover, front inside cover, p. 1-5] Copyright © Flip Schulke

[p. 6, 8-9, 16-17, 19-23, 25-27] Copyright © Poppy de Villeneuve [p. 10-15, 18, 24] Courtesy of the Collection of Jan de Villeneuve

[p. 28-31, 34-36, 38-41, 42 top right, center left, bottom left; 43 bottom left, bottom right; 44-47, 118-119, 121, 122, 124, 127, 128, 130, 131, 135, 142, 143 top right; 146, 149, 150-151, 153, 154, 156-158, 160-163, 199] Copyright © Bruce Weber

[p. 32-33, 42 bottom right] Courtesy of the collection of Susan Ochsenbein [p. 42 top left] Copyright © National Geographic Society [p. 43 top] Copyright © Alex Treadway/ National Geographic Society

[p. 48] Photograph by Jan Broekhuijse © President and Fellows of Harvard College, Peabody Museum of Archaeology and Ethnology, Harvard University, PM# 2006.15.1.30.21 (digital file# 155710164) [p. 50 top] Photograph by Jan Broekhuijse © President and Fellows of Harvard College, Peabody Museum of Archaeology and Ethnology, Harvard University, PM# 2006.15.1.15.28 (digital file# 98600011) [p. 5 bottom] Photograph by Jan Broekhuijse © President and Fellows of Harvard College, Peabody Museum of Archaeology and Ethnology, Harvard University, PM# 2006.15.1.39-19 (digital file# 150160203) [p. 51 top left; 53 top right] Courtesy of Maria Matthiessen collection [p. 51 top right; 60-61] Copyright © Hans Teensma [p. 51 bottom] Copyright © Subhankar Banerjee [p. 53 top right, bottom] Copyright © Jill Krementz [p. 54] Copyright © Hulton Archive / Getty Images [p. 55] "The Outlying Rocks", from WILDLIFE IN AMERICA by Peter Matthiessen, copyright © 1959 by Peter Matthiessen, revised and renewed © 1987 by Peter Matthiessen. Used by permission of Viking, a division of Penguin Group (USA) LLC. UK rights secured. Reprinted by permission of Donadio & Olson, Inc. [p. 56] "Westward" from THE SNOW LEOPARD by Peter Matthiessen, copyright © 1978 by Peter Matthiessen. Used by permission of Viking, a division of Penguin Group (USA) LLC. UK rights secured. Reprinted by permission of Donadio & Olson, Inc. [p. 57-59] Copyright © George Schaller

[p. 62-64, 66, 68-69, 70 top, 71, 72-73, 82 top, center, bottom-right; 86 top, bottom-left; 87 top, center-left, bottom] Courtesy of The Thacher School Archive [p. 65, 74-75, 79 top left; 83, 90-91] Copyright © John Scott [p. 67, 70 bottom, 76-78, 79 top right, bottom; 80-81, 82 bottom left; 84-85, 86 bottom left; 87 center right] Copyright © Lisa Eisner

[p. 92-93] Courtesy of Pittsburgh City Photographer Collection, 1901-2002, AIS.1971.05, Archives Service Center, University of Pittsburgh [p.95-117] Copyright © Paolo di Paolo. Reprinted by permission

[p. 125, 126, 133, 134, 137] Courtesy of Kris Ruhs Studio

[p. 176, 182 top; 184 bottom left; 184 top right; 185 top left; 185 top right; 185 middle left; 185 bottom left; 191, 192 bottom] Copyright © Gerard Malanga [p. 177, 184] Poems from *Rene Ricard: 1979–1980* by Rene Ricard. Copyright © Rene Ricard 1979. Reprinted by permission of the Estate of Rene Ricard, Raymond Foye, Administrator [p. 178, 183, 192 top] Notebook pages courtesy of the Estate of Rene Ricard. Raymond Foye, Administrator [p. 179] Photograph Copyright © The Allen Ginsberg Estate 2014 [p. 180, 184, 183] Paintings courtesy of Vito Schnabel [p. 182, 192] Poems from *God With Revolver* by Rene Ricard. Copyright © Rene Ricard 1989. Reprinted by permission of the Estate of Rene Ricard. Raymond Foye, Administrator [p. 183 top right; 185 middle right] Photographs copyright © Rita Barros [p. 183 bottom, 190] Painting Courtesy of the Estate of Rene Ricard. Raymond Foye, Administrator [p. 184 bottom right] Painting courtesy of Exhibition A [p. 186] Poem from *Selected Poems: 1958–1984* by John Wieners, Edited by Raymond Foye. Reprinted by permission of David R. Godine, Publisher, Inc. Copyright ©1986 by John Wieners, Edited by Raymond Foye [p. 187] Painting courtesy of Francesco Clemente [p.188 top] Photograph copyright © Matt Jones. [p. 188 bottom] Sculpture courtesy of Francesco and Alba Clemente

[p. 196-197] Copyright © Bettman / Corbis

[p. 200] "This Nearly Was Mine" Copyright © 1949 by Richard Rodgers & Oscar Hammerstein II. Copyright renewed by Williamson Music (ASCAP), an Imagem Company, owner of publication and allied rights throughout the world. International Copyright Secured. All Rights Reserved. Used by Permission.

[Back inside cover] Copyright © Mystic Seaport, Rosenfeld Collection

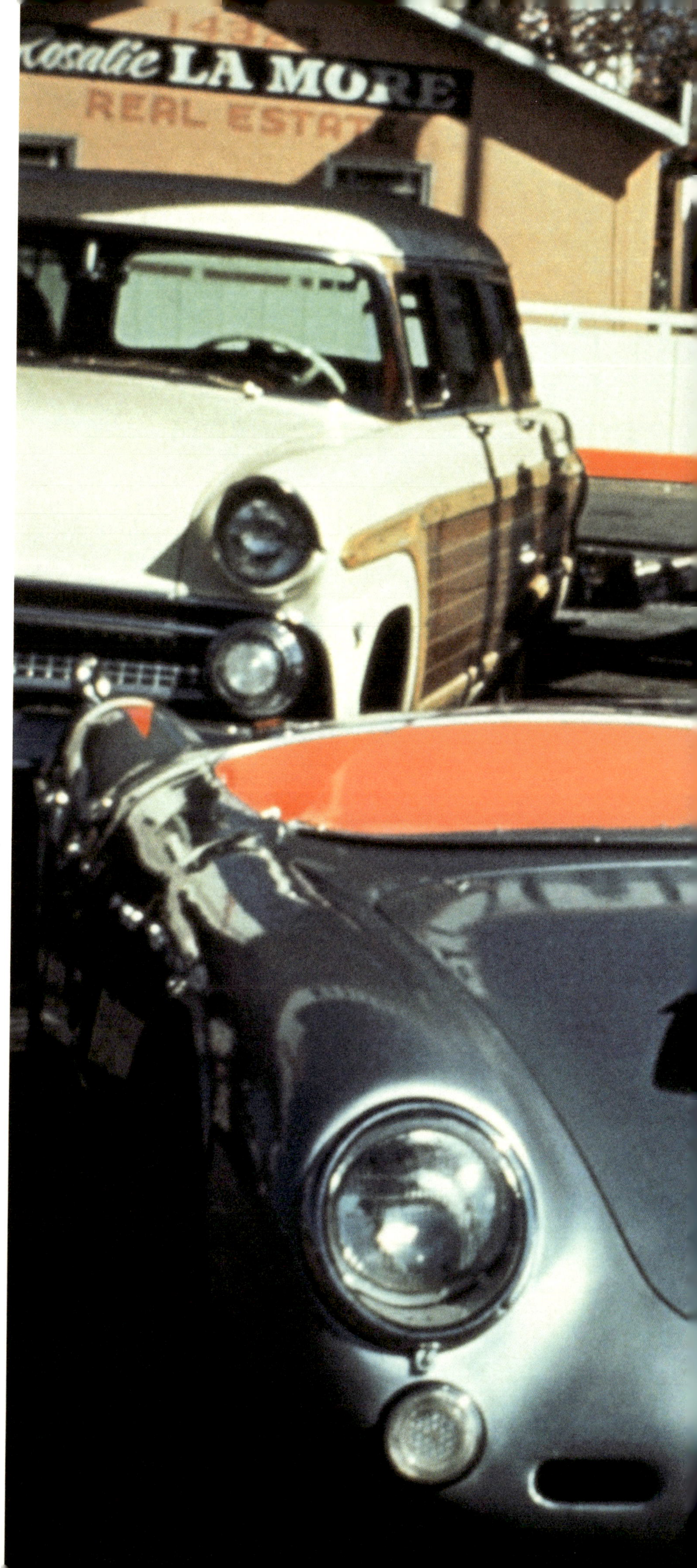

James Dean
WITH HIS SILVER
PORSCHE SPYDER 550
HE NAMED
"Little Bastard"
JUST HOURS BEFORE
HIS FATAL CRASH

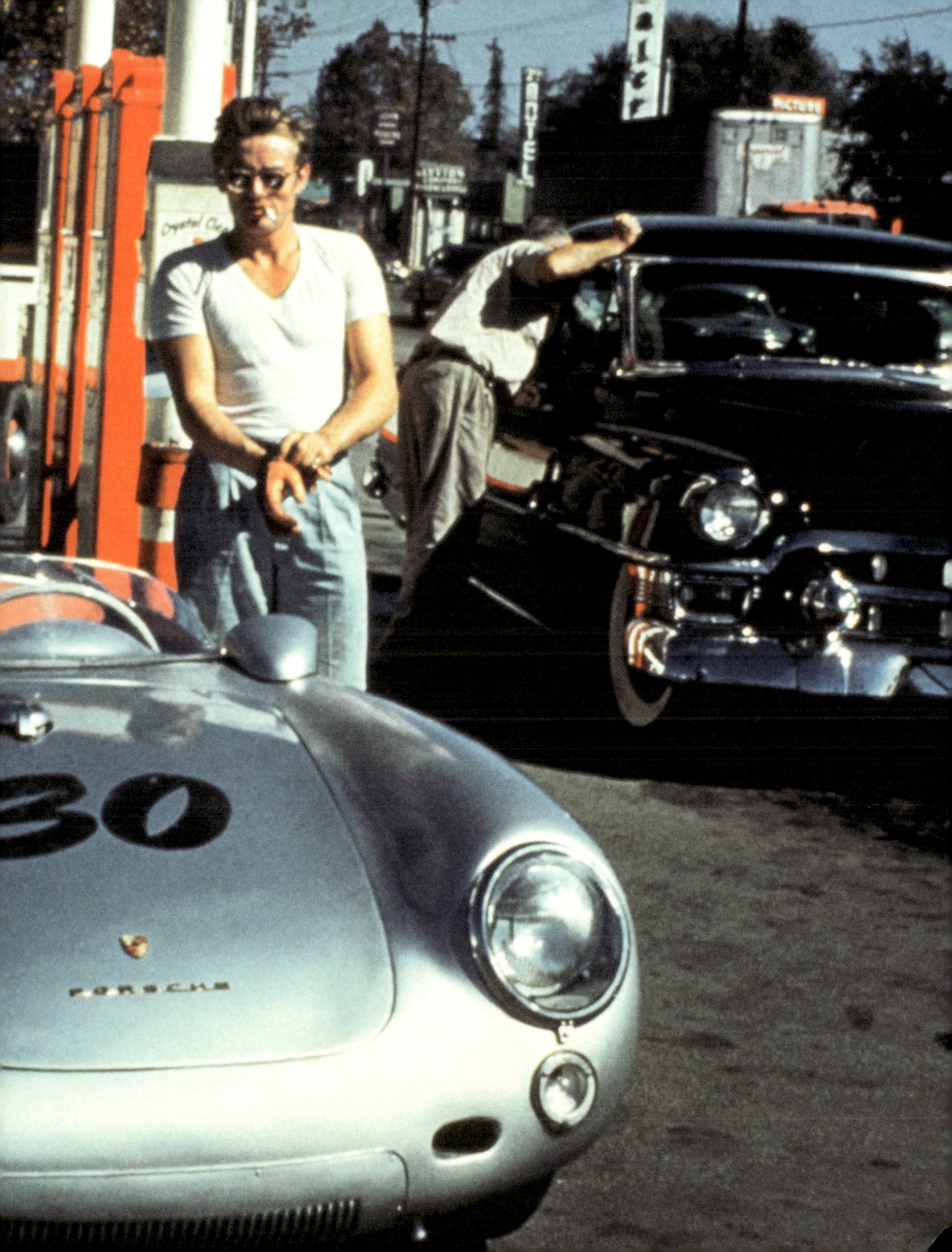
MOTEL
30
PORSCHE

EDITORS

BRUCE WEBER · NAN BUSH · NATHANIEL KILCER
MATTHEW RICHARDS · SKYLAR PITTMAN · KELLY FAGAN

ART DIRECTOR
NATHANIEL KILCER

CONTRIBUTORS
POPPY DE VILLENEUVE · LISA EISNER · JOHN SCOTT

ACKNOWLEDGEMENTS

Hendrik teNeues · Vicki Dwight, Michael Amoruso & Chelsea Photographic Services

Flip Schulke · Susan Ochsenbein · Peter Matthiessen · Maria Matthiessen · Paolo di Paolo · Bruce Davidson · Daria Halprin Michael Mulligan, The Students, & Teachers of The Thacher School · Kris Ruhs · Carla Sozzani · Michele Oka Doner · Rene Ricard William, Cynthia, Kolin & Erik Fischer

Gary Truman · Mark Mulitz · John Giglia · Rebecca Peterson · Chris Land · Bonnie Laforge · Silvia di Paolo · Jan & Daisy de Villeneuve John & Debra Griswold · Raymond Foye · Francesco & Alba Clemente · Vito Schnabel · Gerard Malanga · Rita Barros · Matt Jones Ricardo Kugelmas · Peter Hale · Madeline Sparer · Chelsea Burgess · Caterina Amato · Francesca Spiller · James Procek · Hans Teensma Jeffrey Cardenas · Doug Kuntz · Jill Krementz · Michael Schulman & Magnum Photos

Joseph DiGiovanna · Chris Domurat · Jeff Tautrim · Sean Jackson · Jonnie Chambers · Ryan Brinkmann · Hillery Estes · Jeanine Morick Jeannette Shaheen · Eva Lindemann · Gwen Walberg · Dawn Tomassone · Jonathan Bernstein · Dawn Boller · Elizabeth Murphy Luke Adler · Suze & Julio Mazzei · Richard Amaro · Angel Orozco · Christine Agro · Reynaldo Herrera · Boris & Virginy McNertney Natalia Ortega · Owen Devalk · Victorine Lamothe · Alwine Krebber · Sandra Klimt

David Hutchings · Paul Jasmin · Sam Shahid · Betty Eng · Dimitri Levas · Allan Mindel · Francis Grill · Franca Sozzani · Anna Wintour Graydon Carter · Helmut Lang · Edward Pavlick · Victor Alfaro · Pablo Alfaro · Derek & Sophie Craighead · Wolfgang & Gelila Puck Tom Kartsotis & The Shinola Family · Jason Binn & Family · Ingrid Sischy · Sandy Brant · *Always* Elizabeth Taylor

Dr. Ibraheem · Paul Martino · Dr. Lannie & Behna Gardner · Dr. Patrick Dalton · Carrie Hunt & Noe, Jasper & Beau Dewitt Jeremy, Kathy, Oscar & Lucia Dewitt · Ron, Nancy, Jamie & Meghan Bush · Dennis Lennox · Clayton & Holly Shui · Tommy Marengo Deguinaldo Da Costa · Cece Mota · Michele Porto · Soledad Villanueva · Fernanda Yanzaguan · Robin Coppola · Paulo Da Cruz Javier & Maria Cuevas · Fabiola Arredondo · Dr. Tom Sessa · Dr. Wayne Winnick · Pat & Tom Downing · Barbara & Ernie Tompsett Tommy Lee · Dr. Stuart Froum · Dr. Mike Farber · Dr. Wendy Bressler · Dr. Steve Withrow & Colorado State University Animal Cancer Center

Billie Holiday · Little River · Dream Catcher · Kodiak · Tao · Hud · Elvis · Hope · Jazz

ALL-AMERICAN XIV—AFFAIRS OF THE HEART

PUBLISHED BY TENEUES PUBLISHING GROUP [www.teneues.com]

EDITORIAL COORDINATION VICTORINE LAMOTHE, TENEUES PUBLISHING COMPANY **PRODUCTION COORDINATION** ALWINE KREBBER, TENEUES VERLAG **COLOR SEPARATIONS** ORT MEDIENVERBUND

teNeues Media Am Selder 37
47906 Kempen, Germany
Phone: +49-(0)2152-916-0
Fax: +49-(0)2152-916-111
e-mail: books@teneues.de

Press department: Andrea Rehn
Phone: +49-(0)2152-916-202
e-mail: arehn@teneues.de

teNeues Digital Media GmbH
Kohlfurter Straße 41–43
10999 Berlin, Germany
Phone: +49-(0)30-7007765-0

teNeues Publishing Company
7 West 18th Street
New York, NY 10011, USA
Phone: +1-212-627-9090
Fax: +1-212-627-9511

teNeues Publishing UK Ltd.
21 Marlowe Court, Lymer Avenue
London SE19 1LP, UK
Phone: +44-(0)20-8670-7522
Fax: +44-(0)20-8670-7523

teNeues France S.A.R.L.
39, rue des Billets, 18250 Henrichemont, France
Phone: +33-(0)2-4826-9348

ISBN 978-3-8327-9859-8
Library of Congress Control Number: 2014943590

While we strive for utmost precision in every detail, we cannot be held responsible for any inaccuracies, nor for any subsequent loss or damage arising.

Bibliographic information published by the Deutsche Nationalbibliothek. The Deutsche Nationalbibliothek lists this publication in the Deutsche Nationalbibliografie; detailed bibliographic data are available in the Internet at http://dnb.d-nb.de.

Printed in Belgium.

teNeues Publishing Group
Kempen
Berlin
London
Munich
New York
Paris

teNeues

MIX
From responsible sources
FSC® C014767

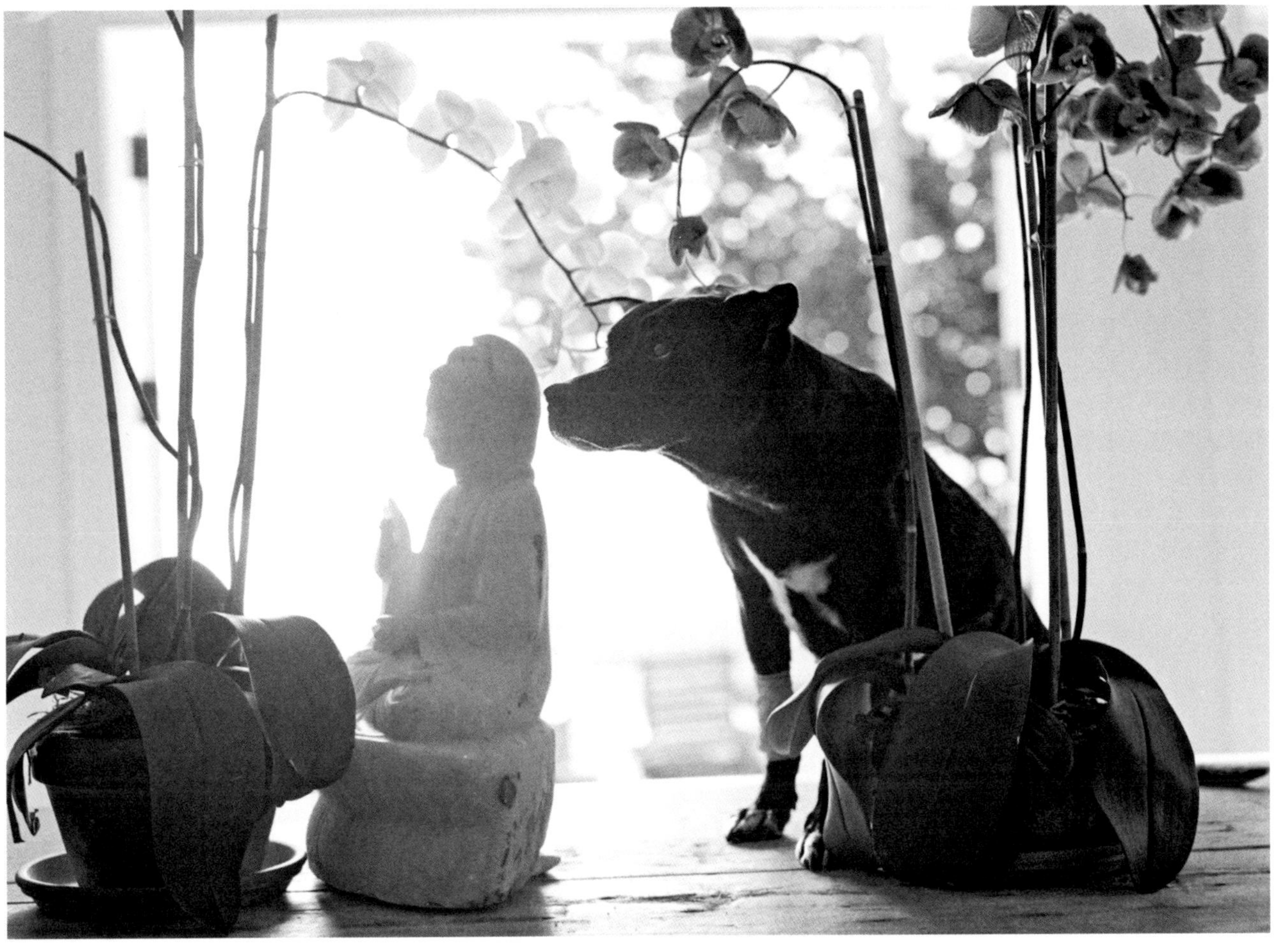

DEDICATION

HONORING BILLIE HOLIDAY

A beloved dog is like the house you grew up in: comfortable, complex, and in its own way an island in paradise. I can't describe why Billie Holiday—a black lab-pit bull mix—came into our lives 10 years ago on that rainy night during the Miami Film Festival. She was tied up to a pole with an extension cord—and wore a ribbon the colors of the French flag in a perfect bow around her neck. Little did I know that this dog was to become our shadow. Friends always said she was meant for us, and that we had the "luck of the Irish" by finding each other in this world.

She was tough, bold, and heartbreaking, just like the jazz singer. We considered calling her Ella, Sarah, or Lena after the "incredible Ella Fitzgerald," "the sassy Sarah Vaughan," or the "one and only Lena Horne." All were contenders for the name of this precious female pup—but it was Nan who thought of Billie Holiday, which ended up hitting just the right note.

Billie and my camera were fast friends. I first photographed her on our porch in the Adirondacks, standing on top of a record player with a vinyl copy of *Billie Holiday Sings* nearby. She went on to appear in magazines all over the world and found herself—not that she was surprised—with a ton of fans. In our home where she grew up, framed photographs of Billie line the mantel above the fireplace, together with pictures of our family.

I can honestly say Billie loved babies, and disliked small white dogs with a passion. But she fell in love with her five golden retriever brothers, always with an alpha-dog attitude. As romantic as any Billy Straythorn song, she was all about tough love—you had to earn it.

Now that the sun shines brightly on the grass, one searches for her lost shadow behind us—yet when the sky at sunset turns pink, in those few lasting moments of flickering blue light, there she is—sending her blessings to all who loved her.

—BRUCE & NAN, MONTAUK, NY, 2014

This Nearly Was Mine

AS SUNG BY FRANK SINATRA

One dream in my heart, one love to be living for
One love to be living for, this nearly was mine
One girl for my dream, one partner in paradise
This promise of paradise, this nearly was mine

Close to my heart she came, only to fly away
Only to fly as day flies from moonlight
Now, now I'm alone, still dreaming of paradise
Still saying that paradise once nearly was mine

So clear and deep are my fancies
Of things I wish were true
I'll keep remembering evenings
I wish I'd spent with you

I'll keep remembering kisses
From lips I'll never own
And all the lovely adventures
That we have never known

Now, now I'm alone
Still dreaming of paradise
Still saying that paradise
Once nearly was mine

WRITTEN BY ROGERS & HAMMERSTEIN